CRITIQUE & BETRAYAL

CRITIQUE & BETRAYAL

Essays from the
Radical Philosophy Archive
VOLUME 1

EDITED BY
AUSTIN GROSS
MATT HARE
MARIE LOUISE KROGH

Published in 2020 by
Radical Philosophy Archive
www.radicalphilosophyarchive.com

ISBN 978-1-9162292-0-4 (pbk)
ISBN 978-1-9162292-1-1 (ebook)

The electronic version of this work is licensed under
a Creative Commons Attribution-NonCommercial-
NoDerivatives 4.0 International License (CC-BYNC-ND).
For more information, please visit creativecommons.org.

The right of the contributors to be identified as authors
of this work has been asserted by them in accordance
with the Copyright, Designs and Patents Act, 1988

Designed and typeset in Calluna by illuminati, Grosmont
Cover design by Lucy Morton at illuminati
Printed by Short Run Press Ltd (Exeter)

A catalogue record for this book
is available from the British Library

Contents

INTRODUCTION

The time of critique
AUSTIN GROSS, MATT HARE & MARIE LOUISE KROGH   3

KANTIAN RIPPLES

1 Spontaneous generation: The fantasy of the birth
   of concepts in Kant's *Critique of Pure Reason*
   STELLA SANDFORD   19

2 Hegelian phenomenology and the critique of reason
   and society
   PETER OSBORNE   45

3 The vertigo of philosophy:
   Deleuze and the problem of immanence
   CHRISTIAN KERSLAKE   71

DISOWNED ENLIGHTENMENTS

4 Feminism and the Enlightenment
   PAULINE JOHNSON   103

5 Will the real Kant please stand up:
   The challenge of Enlightenment racism
   to the study of the history of philosophy
   ROBERT BERNASCONI   129

6 Exchange on Hegel's racism
   JOSEPH McCARNEY & ROBERT BERNASCONI   151

7 The philosopher's fear of alterity: Levinas, Europe
   and humanities 'without Sacred History'
   ANDREW MCGETTIGAN   166

INTERLUDE

8 *Peter Rabbit* and the *Grundrisse*
   ROSA AND CHARLEY PARKIN   193

BETRAYALS

9 Oedipus as figure
   PHILIPPE LACOUE-LABARTHE   199

10 Generations of feminism
   LYNNE SEGAL   223

11 Name of the father, 'one' of the mother:
   From Beauvoir to Lacan
   FRANÇOISE COLLIN
   INTRODUCED BY PENELOPE DEUTSCHER   247

12 Black Socrates? Questioning the philosophical tradition
   SIMON CRITCHLEY   269

CRITIQUE IN THE EXPANDED FIELD

13 Marx's Eurocentrism:
   Postcolonial studies and Marx scholarship
   KOLJA LINDNER   295

14 Who needs postcoloniality? A reply to Lindner
   HARRY HAROOTUNIAN   324

15 Race, real estate and real abstraction
   BRENNA BHANDAR & ALBERTO TOSCANO   340

16 Anti-castism and misplaced nativism:
   Mapping caste as an aspect of race
   MEENA DHANDA   362

   SOURCES   387
   IMAGE CREDITS   388
   INDEX   389

 **ESSAYS FROM THE
RADICAL PHILOSOPHY ARCHIVE**

SERIES EDITOR Peter Osborne

This new series of books from the archive of the first 200 issues of the British journal *Radical Philosophy* (1972–2016) offers thematic selections of articles on topics that continue to innervate theoretical and political debates on the Left.

VOLUME 1 *Critique & Betrayal*
  ed. Austin Gross, Matt Hare & Marie Louise Krogh
VOLUME 2 *Philosophy & Nations*
  ed. Austin Gross, Matt Hare & Marie Louise Krogh
  FORTHCOMING
VOLUME 3 *Societies of Assessment*
  ed. Austin Gross, Matt Hare & Marie Louise Krogh
VOLUME 4 *Philosophies of War*
  ed. Mark Neocleous

www.radicalphilosophyarchive.com

Previous anthologies from *Radical Philosophy*

Spheres of Action: Art and Politics (2013)
  ed. Éric Alliez & Peter Osborne
Philosophies of Race and Ethnicity (2002)
  ed. Peter Osborne & Stella Sandford
A Critical Sense: Interviews with Intellectuals (1996)
  ed. Peter Osborne
Socialism, Feminism and Philosophy: A Radical Philosophy Reader (1990)
  ed. Peter Osborne & Sean Sayers
Radical Philosophy Reader (1985)
  ed. Roy Edgley & Richard Osborne

5 MINUTES
5 MINUTI
5 PERC

INTRODUCTION

The time of critique

AUSTIN GROSS, MATT HARE &
MARIE LOUISE KROGH

'Our age', wrote Immanuel Kant in 1781, 'is the genuine age of critique, to which everything must submit.'[1] This note, from the first edition of the *Critique of Pure Reason*, does not so much announce the critical age as crystallize it. Kant's consciousness of the modernity of critique implies, as a corollary, the relegation of the 'dogmatic' to the past. The first *Critique* was an epoch-making book, defining the reception of the Enlightenment, such that the critical age would become the age of the *Critiques*. In his famous 1843 letter to Arnold Ruge, Karl Marx borrows the Kantian costume, reactivating the battlefield metaphors in which Kant had shrouded his announcement of the critical project. 'Anarchy' and 'confusion' reign among the social reformers of the 1840s as to what future they are fighting for, precisely because they attempt 'dogmatically to prefigure the future'.[2] The hubris of the reformers, analogous to that of dogmatic metaphysicians in Kant's version, is to have made claims on the future. But instead of undertaking a critique of our own faculties – to delimit the extent of our right to speak about the future – Marx proposes to 'find the new world ... through the critique of the old'.[3] The critical project is thus reactivated by Marx within the context of a political movement. The task of critique consequently takes a more militant shade as a weapon in the war between classes:

> If the designing of the future ... is not our affair, then we realize all the more clearly what we have to accomplish in the present – I am speaking of the *ruthless critique of everything existing*, ruthless in two senses: The criticism must not be afraid of its own conclusions, nor of conflict with the powers that be.[4]

The knot between critique and the present becomes more densely wound. In Marx's letter, critique is not only 'what we have to accomplish at present', but also a critique of the present.

The essays gathered in this volume – from the archive of the British journal *Radical Philosophy* – speak to, or from within, the assumption that thinking has to measure itself against its time and that this task, in some sense or another, implies a critical gesture. The temporality of critique to be found in this collection is, however, consistently more complicated than it was for Kant. Although critique is still something to be undertaken 'at present', Kant's age is long gone. Written over a period which spans 40 years, from 1975 to 2015, these essays are from *a* critical age, no longer *the* critical age. And if critique is still a task for our times, it is also indisputably something that has been handed down to us. The handing-down of critique poses the problem of how it is to be taken up, that is, not only the reflective assessment of the relation between the present and a critical tradition, but also and just as importantly the question of how critique must be transformed in order to be enacted in a new present. In the quarrel between those for whom fidelity means cryogenic preservation and those for whom it signifies transformation, each party will cast the other as a traitor.

In the reception history of critical philosophy, one of the recurring motifs that exemplifies this problem most clearly is that of metacritique. Almost as old as the Kantian *Critiques* themselves, the term was first introduced in the late eighteenth century by Johann Georg Hamann and Johann Gottfried Herder, to name the exhibition of conditions and dependencies of reason which stood beyond the domain of transcendental philosophy. In Herder's book-length *Metacritique of the Critique of Pure Reason*

(1799) and Hamann's shorter 'Metacritique on the Purism of Reason' (written in 1784 but only published in 1800), it was specifically used to address Kant's disavowal of language as a medium of reason and the consequent neglect of the historicity of the institution of language in reason's self-critique. But the conditions that metacritique points to are not always linguistic. Take Stella Sandford's article on metaphors of biological generation in the *Critique of Pure Reason*, which opens this collection. Language and metaphor certainly constitute one of the fields into which her reading displaces the *Critique*. But another aspect of this reading is the dimension of what Sandford calls 'fantasy',[5] and in particular a fantasy with regard to sexual difference, which structures Kant's efforts to keep matter under form's control. The very purism and self-sufficiency of reason (to undertake its own critique, but also to see itself as giving birth to pure concepts by parthenogenesis) is seen as grounded in such a fantasy.

Critical social theory, historical materialism, and even G.W.F. Hegel's *Phenomenology of Spirit* could also be situated as forms of metacritique, a proposal which Garbis Kortian ventured in his 1979 *Metacritique*, a book whose power was precisely to read the whole lineage of critical theory through Hamann and Herder's term. Hegelian phenomenology is, however, a particularly paradoxical case, as is discussed in Peter Osborne's contribution on Gillian Rose's *Hegel Contra Sociology*. Hegel does not denounce the self-sufficiency of reason or of philosophy, but only the self-sufficiency of the standpoint of 'knowledge' (or 'cognition' as *Erkenntnis* is often translated) defined in a technical sense by the separation of the knowing subject and the known object. The Hegelian metacritique of epistemology attempts to show that it is only within the field of absolute knowing – or only within an encyclopedic development from logic to the philosophy of spirit – that epistemological problems can be resolved, and not in any sense from the point of view of epistemology itself. The common point between Hegelian and Hamannian metacritiques is the 'critique of the self-sufficiency of epistemology', but it is one they make for disparate reasons. In Hamann's case, metacritique undermines the self-sufficiency of philosophy itself, while in Hegel's it simply marginalizes epistemology within philosophy. Marxist metacritique and that of critical social theory are, by contrast, more akin to Hamann's original sense of metacritique. They construct political, historical, social and economic domains beyond philosophy's own purview, by which philosophical production can be seen to be conditioned. Yet critique in this sense extends beyond the boundaries of what can be glossed as 'metacritique', insofar as it is not primarily (or only) concerned with situating philosophy. Rather, the way in which the critique of political economy resituates philosophy as a social practice is of a piece with the broader displacement it performs on politics. In this sense, we can also ask what is to come of it. In the post-War period, thinkers like Hannah Arendt attempted to rehabilitate the register of the political against what they saw as a single tendency towards its liquidation by bureaucratization, capitalist economism, technological development and Marxism itself, in its Soviet form. We might understand Arendt's writings as a critique not only of totalitarianism but equally of the critique of political economy. At that time, it was possible to confuse the Marxist critique of the pretensions of law and culture with the real annihilation of politics undertaken by the enemies of the social revolution. But to rehabilitate the political as an antidote to modern bureaucracy was a project doomed for reasons that, precisely, dialectical materialism could have indicated: namely, that under the circumstances, the philosophical-political forms to which appeal was made could only represent a deceptive universality. Political economy and its critique remain actual because they outline the conditions under which the political can viably be reaffirmed. The idea that either politics or philosophy might constitute autonomous fields becomes questionable or indeed objectionable once they are situated in an expanded field of contestation.

This is of course not the same as saying that the inheritance of the critique of political economy articulated by Marx's *Capital* has remained without problematizations, even from within Marxist registers. To a large extent, the history of Marxism (from the early twentieth century onwards) has been precisely the history of various disputes over how to actualize an emancipatory critique of capitalism, with anti-imperialist and feminist movements as privileged sites for interventions. This is reflected in this collection by a number of essays that further expand the field of critique by confronting philosophy and political economy with work in critical geography and critical race theory. Brenna Bhandar and Alberto Toscano engage in the continuous and often fraught work of reassessing the categories of political economy, by thinking through the 'articulation of race, property and capitalist abstraction'.[6] From this perspective, processes of racialization do not appear as something to be accounted for *in addition* to the critique of political economy, via some theoretical supplement, but as a differential inscribed within the very category of 'property' itself. In this sense, Bhandar and Toscano's essay exemplifies one inroad for moving beyond a stark divide in the recent history of critique, intimately bound to the dual heritage of Enlightenment as a site for both universalist emancipatory ideals and a profound Eurocentrism. In the aftermath not only of the academic popularization of postcolonial studies but just as importantly of anti-colonial liberation struggles themselves, one of the most contested theoretical fields has been that marked by the conjunction of questions concerning global economy with those concerning the Eurocentrism of Marx's writings.

The tendency to frame all such questions through an opposition between Marxism, on the one hand, and postcolonial literary studies on the other, tends to sacrifice the complexity of theoretical objects for the sake of academic polemic. This is one of the points made in Kolja Lindner's contribution here. Drawing on postcolonial critiques produced since the publication of Edward Said's *Orientalism* (1978), Lindner attempts a rapprochement of the two on the basis of a fourfold differentiation within the concept of Eurocentrism: in the form of white supremacist ethnocentrism; in the construction of non-European 'others' as distorted mirror images of Western European self-conceptions of political subjecthood; in (avowed or unavowed) commitments to developmentalist teleologies on the model of 'first Europe – then elsewhere'; and in the simple but less than benign obliviousness to cultures and histories other than those which might merit the name 'Western'.[7] On this basis, Lindner performs the largely Marxological work of weighing where Marx's writings fall, at various points of his theoretical development, along such a spectrum of overlapping and interacting Eurocentric tendencies. For Marx as for Kant, the history of their modes of critiques interweaves with those of the critical reception of their textual productions.

This brings us back to subtler questions of the politics of reading, as forefronted by the influential reformulations of critique initiated by Paul Ricœur in the second half of the twentieth century. In the introduction to his 1965 *Freud and Philosophy*, Ricœur baptized Marx – along with Friedrich Nietzsche and Sigmund Freud – as one of the three 'masters of suspicion', and coined the label 'hermeneutics of suspicion', to which Sandford's piece also makes allusion.[8] What is a hermeneutics of suspicion? Ricœur neatly distinguishes the sort of doubt at stake here from Cartesian doubt. Rather than doubting the existence of objects, hermeneutics of suspicion doubt consciousness itself, going so far as to suppose consciousness to be 'false'. But the hermeneutics of suspicion does not stop here, and this is why it is not simply a radicalized scepticism. Instead, it supposes that there is something thinking, something rational, to which consciousness has no access, and goes on to pose 'the question as to what thought, reason, and even faith still signify' beyond what consciousness believes it knows of them. The suspicious 'art of *interpreting*' attempts to decipher this reason beyond consciousness.[9]

Of course, since its coinage, the hermeneutics of suspicion has not always been understood in these strict terms. The phrase itself is often taken to refer to radicalized scepticism, or to a suspicious political 'unmasking' (another term emphasized by Ricœur) of strategies concealed beyond falsely neutral discourse. It was perhaps more in these senses that suspicion was taken up as an imperative by theorists in many disciplines, and under a variety of different guises, including, that of parody. It also became the object, in turn, of several critiques, which often present themselves as critiques of critique itself, no longer in a metacritical sense, but as denunciations of the vanity, futility, or illusions of over-clever critical discourse – as seen here in 'Peter Rabbit and the *Grundrisse*', a piece from *Radical Philosophy*'s more irreverent early days.

One of the most important problematizations of the hermeneutics of suspicion, from the field of queer theory, was Eve Kosofsky Sedgwick's essay, 'Paranoid Reading, Reparative Reading', which rewrote 'suspicion' as 'paranoia'.[10] Drawing on Kleinian psychopathology, Kosofsky Sedgwick defined paranoid reading in terms of the splitting of good and bad objects. To take a case from our anthology: what would one make of an attempt to save Kant or Hegel from their racist comments by emphasizing that the rest of their philosophy does not presuppose such comments, which can charitably be excised? Conversely, what if the engagement with their racism is simply a denunciation, demanding their ejection from classrooms and research? To split an ambivalent object always means saving some good (if only ourselves, the critical judges) and ejecting the bad. When we are concerned with constructing a Kant who can speak to certain current mainstream, narrowly 'philosophical' concerns, we are, in fact, censoring and burying another Kant who is not irrelevant so much as unbearable. Precisely this Kant, the racist and misogynist Kant, is in certain ways more relevant to contemporary concerns than the one constructed by generously separating good from bad.

The way Robert Bernasconi approaches Kant and Hegel's racism is the precise opposite of a paranoid reading. Kosofsky Sedgwick's own reference to Kleinian 'reparation' provides a suggestion precisely along these lines: to orient thinking towards ambivalence rather than trying to eliminate it. To put it another way, it is precisely the 'coexistence'[11] of the good and bad Kant that is most relevant. The most interesting questions to ask about Kant are not whether his cosmopolitanism can be affirmed without his white supremacist views, but rather what his cosmopolitanism *does* to his racism: whether it intensifies it and how it transforms it, and, finally, whether there would be any way of rethinking cosmopolitanism in order to exclude or undermine racism. All of these questions are not simply questions about Kant, of course, because what is at stake is the theoretical schema underpinning a liberal international order. These questions are precisely oriented by the ambivalence that haunts the re-actualization of Kant.

They are also questions about distance. This is thematized by Andrew McGettigan's essay in the collection, which concludes by questioning the extent to which the capacity for an ambivalent reading such as Bernasconi's relies on a certain 'privilege of latecomers'.[12] For McGettigan, the very focus on methodological questions as to what is and is not extractable from a thinker distracts from the devastating consistency found between the racism of a philosopher like Emmanuel Levinas and the core tenets of not only his philosophy but also the ideal of European culture in which it is rooted. A consistency then, not only within the thinker's work, but also with our own time. Different consequences are to be drawn from what Fred Moten – in an extended elaboration on McGettigan's essay – calls 'a sustained, practically originary distortion'[13] in Levinas's writings. For this figure of consistency as critique, the act of insisting on reading a body of thought as a whole, of refusing to treat certain detestable comments as 'minor' or 'irrelevant', is extended into a challenge to the reader to represent themselves as implicated in this consistency, and consequently into a challenge to the kind of separation implied in reading or exegesis itself.

Such concerns with the politics of reading connect with what Kosofsky Sedgwick called paranoid reading's 'faith in exposure'. Drawing on another important objection raised against critique, in the 1980s, by Peter Sloterdijk, Kosofsky Sedgwick pointed out that the kind of unmasking that the hermeneutics of suspicion can produce seems hopelessly irrelevant to 'enlightened false consciousness', consciousness that already knows it is false and learns nothing from the unmasking.[14] How does an objection like this one square with the kind of critical work gathered in this volume? Even when they are occupied with unmasking, the critical endeavour of these essays is not to denounce 'falsehood' pure and simple, but to lay out the language, fantasy, political economy or strategy at work beneath the surface.

It would have come as a surprise to philosophers from other centuries that one day critique would be theorized under the name of 'hermeneutics'. If this is not surprising to us, it is because of another significant fork in critique's history: from Hegel onwards, critique implied historicization. But the construction of the concept of history bifurcated over the course of the nineteenth century. On the one hand, with Marx's historical materialism, historical metacritique meant an opening of philosophy onto social struggles and the relations of production; on the other hand, Wilhelm Dilthey and after him Martin Heidegger would construct historicity in hermeneutical terms. Transmission and the interpretation of cultural inheritance appeared as crucial conditions for thought. Since philosophy is conditioned by its reception of a tradition that it cannot fully master, the hermeneutical construction of history falls, in a way, within the lineage of metacritique.

This new construction of historicity became an important tool for hermeneutics itself: by taking stock of the ways in which our reception of traditions is determined, focused or distorted, we are able explicitly to work against tendencies that cover up or, more interestingly, neutralize the contents being handed down. If tradition itself tends to neutralize and betray what it conveys, a critical reception, which does violence to tradition, is the only way to retrieve its contents. Critique, in short, became an organon of tradition.

What this means for the task of critique depends on the way in which tradition's neutralizing tendency is constructed. One can, for example, construct the problem in terms of the way the original experience behind a specific piece of terminology, or a specific argument, gets lost. This interpretation is what gives rise to the metaphorics of 'sedimentation' and critical 'reactivation' that Simon Critchley's piece here seeks to problematize. Such phenomenological hermeneutics is not, however, chiefly concerned with what was supposedly given in that original experience, but rather with the determinate attitude towards it which allowed it to be given. The function of such a critique is to reveal the partiality of the inherited concept. A classic case is Heidegger's suggestion that the original experience from which the concepts of form and matter were drawn was the experience of crafting and producing. His point is not that there is some rich content given when we produce an object, and that we philosophers need to get back in touch with that experience, but rather that to produce something involves a specific attitude that leaves its mark on the concepts generalized from such cases. The progressive decontextualization of concepts from the experiences with which they were once tied concerns Heidegger primarily because it loses the trace of their partiality, allowing generalization to reign.

There is another, more political way of constructing such a tendency. Some concepts can only be properly understood as interventions in a political context. As a result, the progressive reception that distances them from this context and detaches them as self-sufficient concepts can be seen as a neutralization. The work of the historian of political thought would be to return to each of the contexts in which a political concept was reformulated to see the way in which its formulation could be construed as an intervention in that context, rather than simply a theory. Someone trying to retrieve these interventions (against their neutralization) must not only struggle against the transformation of interventions into theories, but also against their valorization as a canon of texts by recognized authorities. The inheritance of a political movement cannot easily be identified with the texts it produced or the authors who were remembered from it. Nowhere in this collection are these tensions more visible than in Lynne Segal's reflections on the disjunction between the Women's Liberation Movement in the 1970s and the later generation of 1990s academic feminists. Observing that two then-contemporary collections of feminist theory offered 'their readers a full index of *names* ... but no index of *topics*' – which is to say that they organized the field in terms of authors rather than struggles or demands – Segal notes that:

> However you cross-reference it, just a few aspects of women's actual resistance 'around the world' seem to have gone missing. Almost no effort is made in these texts to refer back to the activities and goals of Women's Liberation, only an attempt to contrast theoretical positions as ideal types. The reason is, of course, that this is an easy way to *teach* feminism as an academic topic. But you cannot translate the time of theory and its fashions into political history without absurd caricature.[15]

We should avoid reducing these comments to the shopworn dramaturgy of a good political concrete being papered over by a bad theoretical abstract. Rather, this is a point at which the risk of academicization may take the form of a philosophical recuperation of political movements' discourses. In fact, even the presentation of their thought as a series of critiques (the critique of patriarchy or the critique of heteronormativity, for example) can be one way of transforming them into neutralized philosophical contents. The struggle against neutralization, having rallied itself under the banner of critique, undergoes a surprising reversal of fidelities: it becomes a worry about the neutralizing effect of interpreting past struggles.

Notes
1. Immanuel Kant, *Critique of Pure Reason*, trans. Paul Guyer and Allen W. Wood, Cambridge University Press, Cambridge, 2009, p. 100, trans. modified; Immanuel Kant, *Kritik der reinen Vernunft*, Felix Meiner Verlag, Hamburg, 1956, p. 7.
2. 'For a Ruthless Criticism of Everything Existing', in Robert C. Tucker, ed., *The Marx–Engels Reader*, 2nd edn, Norton, New York, 1978, p. 13.
3. Ibid., trans. modified; Karl Marx and Friedrich Engels, *Briefwechsel bis April 1846*, MEGA, Dritte Abteilung, *Briefwechsel*, Band 1, p. 54.
4. Ibid., trans. modified; Marx and Engels, *Briefwechsel*, p. 55.
5. Below, p. 40.
6. Below, p. 340.
7. Below, p. 297.
8. A more literal translation of the book's French title would be *On Interpretation: An Essay on Freud*. See Paul Ricœur, *Freud and Philosophy*, Yale University Press, New Haven, 1970, pp. 30–35.
9. Ibid., p. 33.
10. 'Paranoid Reading, Reparative Reading' in Eve Kosofsky Sedgwick, *Touching Feeling*, Duke University Press, Durham and London, 2003, p. 124.
11. Below, p. 139.
12. Below, p. 185.
13. Fred Moten, *The Universal Machine*, Duke University Press, Durham and London, 2018, p. 5.
14. See Peter Sloterdijk, *Critique of Cynical Reason*, trans. Michael Eldred, University of Minnesota Press, Minneapolis, 1988.
15. Below, pp. 227–8.

KANTIAN RIPPLES

1 Spontaneous generation: The fantasy of the birth of concepts in Kant's *Critique of Pure Reason*

STELLA SANDFORD

In the second edition of the *Critique of Pure Reason*, at the end of the transcendental deduction of the categories, Kant distinguishes the doctrine of transcendental idealism from competing theories of knowledge – or, more specifically, theories of the relation between concepts and experience – by characterizing them in terms of various theories of biological generation. Transcendental idealism, he writes there, is 'a system of the epigenesis of pure reason', while empiricism is akin to *generatio aequivoca* (what we now call 'spontaneous generation'). If there is a 'middle way' between these – Cartesian innatism, perhaps – it is 'a kind of preformation-system of pure reason'.[1]

Attempts to explain the enigmatic idea of an 'epigenesis of pure reason' have tended to seek illumination from what is known of Kant's theoretical commitments in and contributions to the natural sciences – specifically, theories of generation and embryological development – from which the metaphor is drawn. No one pretends that this is straightforward, not least because Kant's position (especially during the period of the two editions of the *Critique of Pure Reason*) is difficult to pin down, and commentators have come to very different conclusions. Further, it is not simply a question of determining where Kant stood in relation to the competing theories in order to read that position back into the metaphor in the *Critique of Pure Reason*. For aspects of Kant's philosophy were influential in biological theory itself. In particular, Kant's explication and defence of the necessity of the regulative idea of purposiveness in the study of natural organisms in the 'Critique of Teleological Judgment' chimed with, and was further taken up in, some of the most important work in biology in Germany at that time.[2] Connected with this, remarks in the Transcendental Dialectic in the *Critique of Pure Reason* show how Kant understood the essential regulative function of the ideas of pure reason in the field of natural history, concerning, specifically, the classification of nature, including classifications of 'race'. Indeed, Kant's own theory of race – a bio-geographical anthropology of human diversity – is both based on and suggests further developments in the theory of human generation.[3]

The Kant literature has recently become increasingly interested in his contributions to the natural, social and human sciences (particularly geography and anthropology) and their possible relations to the canonical philosophical works. Discussions of the metaphor of epigenesis in relation to eighteenth-century German biology are part of this trend and as such are intrinsically interesting. Furthermore, there is no other way into the metaphor of epigenesis than via these theories of biological generation, for they supply the frame of reference within which the metaphor works. However, the limitation of this approach is that it explains precisely nothing about transcendental idealism that we did not already know. Treating the biological theories, including Kant's own contributions to those theories, as a neutral basis for explanation, commentators who take this approach attempt to produce some accommodation between the biological theory of epigenesis and the doctrine of transcendental idealism, to lay out the terms of an analogy between them, but they do not ask, further, what the ground of the affinity between them might be. In a sense, these are interpretations of the metaphor devoid of all *suspicion*. But there is something very suspicious about the metaphor of epigenesis in the *Critique of Pure Reason*, not least its exceedingly ill-fitting relation to the doctrine of transcendental idealism. These are also interpretations devoid of all *criticism*, both of the biological theories at issue and of Kant's philosophy.

In what follows I will locate the metaphor, as one must, within the field of eighteenth-century theories of generation, but also view it textually, in the context of the larger set of metaphors of generation, birth and biological ancestry in the *Critique of Pure Reason*. For although this is the only reference to epigenesis in the *Critique of Pure Reason*, other biological metaphors and metaphors of generation permeate the book, most particularly and perhaps most unexpectedly where the characterization of the pure concepts of the understanding – 'the ancestral concepts [*Stammbegriffe*] that comprise the pure cognition'[14] – are concerned. Following this textual lead, I will suggest a suspicious, critical interpretation of the meaning of the metaphor of epigenesis, one which goes significantly beyond the idea that it corresponds to the biological theory. Pulling together some of Kant's scattered references to and various uses of theories of biological generation, I propose a feminist interpretation of the generative metaphorics of Kant's presentation of the spontaneous production of the pure concepts by the understanding, arguing that the dominant generative model for the production or origin of the categories is in fact not epigenesis but *parthenogenesis*, the only generative model that could have secured the epistemic status and legitimacy – the *a priori* purity – of the categories in the *Critique of Pure Reason* for Kant. Finally, I will show how this generative model – both required by and *destructive of* the 'purism'[15] of the *Critique of Pure Reason* – is part of the gendered imaginary subtending Kant's transcendental idealism, in which the biological metaphor simultaneously attempts to deny and yet cannot fail to reveal the empirical stain on the purity of the *a priori* concepts.

Preformationism vs epigenesis

For Kant, the chief aim of transcendental philosophy, and hence of its outline in the *Critique of Pure Reason*, is that 'absolutely no concepts must enter into it that contain anything empirical, or that the *a priori* cognition be entirely pure'. Pure *a priori* cognitions are 'not those that occur independently of this or that experience, but rather those that occur *absolutely* independently of all experience'.⁶ The ground of such cognitions are the pure concepts of the understanding, and part of the task of transcendental critique is to exhibit these concepts in their necessity. But this means: to demonstrate their necessity *for experience*, their objective reality, or their validity for empirical objects of cognition. This is the central problem: the *necessary* relation between the pure *a priori* concepts, which are absolutely independent of experience, and experience itself. The solution famously lies in thinking this necessity 'transcendentally'.

Kant specifies the originality of transcendental critique by contrasting it with John Locke's 'physiology of the human understanding'. Locke's 'physiological derivation' of general concepts, Kant says, concerns a question of fact ('the explanation of the possession of a pure cognition'⁷) whereas the transcendental deduction of the categories is a question of right, of the *legitimacy* of the postulation of the categories as not only subjectively necessary but also objectively valid and objectively real. But how is it, Kant asks, that there can be a necessary agreement between experience and the concepts of its objects? This can be thought, he says, in only two ways:

> either the experience makes these concepts possible or these concepts make the experience possible. The first is not the case with the categories (nor with pure sensible intuition); for they are *a priori* concepts, hence independent of experience (the assertion of an empirical origin would be a sort of *generatio aequivoca*).⁸

By *generatio aequivoca*, or 'equivocal generation', Kant means what we now call 'spontaneous generation', the generation of living things from something essentially different, for example the spontaneous generation of worms from a compost heap. Having rejected this possibility, associated here with Locke's physiological empiricism,

> only the second way remains (as it were a system of the epigenesis of pure reason): namely that the categories contain the grounds of the possibility of all experience in general from the side of

the understanding. If someone still wanted to propose a middle way between the only two, already named ways, namely that the categories were neither self-thought *a priori* first principles of our cognition nor drawn from experience, but were rather subjective predispositions for thinking, implanted in us along with our existence by our author in such a way that their use would agree exactly with the laws of nature along which experience runs (a kind of preformation-system of pure reason), then ... this would be decisive against the supposed middle way: that in such a case the categories would lack the necessity that is essential to their concept. For, e.g., the concept of cause, which asserts the necessity of a consequent under a presupposed condition, would be false if it rested only on a subjective necessity, arbitrarily implanted in us, of combining certain empirical representations according to such a rule of relation.[9]

The metaphorical association of the transcendental ideality of the categories with epigenesis is, on the face of it, rather odd. As the contrast with Locke's empirical epistemology was meant to show, the categories cannot be explained naturalistically because they are legislative with regard to nature. Thus the biological metaphors, and most particularly the employment of the idea of epigenesis to explain something of the specificity of the status of the categories, seems to offer us a paradox: they appeal – albeit metaphorically – to a theory of natural generation to explain the status of the categories in the context of an argument that the categories cannot be explained in natural terms. So what is the metaphor meant to do? Can the idea of epigenesis help explain the specificity of transcendental idealism? What, if anything, does it illuminate concerning the status or the function of the categories or of their 'products'?

Although the metaphor of epigenesis and the related metaphors of generation in the *Critique of Pure Reason* evoke more of the context of the scientific debates concerning theories of generation than simply the alternatives of preformationism and epigenesis, a brief account of these two different theories and Kant's attempts to mediate between them is nevertheless a good place to start in attempting to answer these questions. According to the earliest versions of preformationism, all of the embryos that will develop into the generations of adult organisms 'pre-exist' either in the female egg (the 'ovist' theory of preformation) or the male spermatozoon (the 'animaculist' or 'vermist' variants of the theory).[10] Preformationist theories hold that in biological reproduction a pre-existent embryo is somehow provoked into development, where 'development' means the growth or enlargement of pre-existent parts, not the generation by the parents of a new organism. Perhaps the best-known exponent of preformationsm is Nicolas Malebranche, who first formulated the idea in 1674 that all embryos had existed since the beginning of the world, created by God, all contained or encased one within the other, awaiting their appointed time. This is the theory of individual preformationism, or *emboîtement*, what Phillip Sloan calls the 'strong preformationist' or 'pre-existence' theory.[11]

By Kant's time the most prominent preformationists (notably Albrecht von Haller) did not endorse individual preformation, but a version of the theory according to which preformed *germs* contain all the essential parts of the foetus. In Haller's words, from 1758:

> It appears very probable to me that the essential parts of the fetus exist formed at all times; not, it is true, in the way that they appear in the adult animal: they are arranged in such a way that certain prepared causes ... form in the end an animal which is very different from the embryo, and yet in which there is no part that did not exist essentially in the embryo. It is thus that I explain development.[12]

Preformationism was motivated, in great part, by the inadequacy – or indeed absence – of any plausible contemporary mechanical explanation for the complex phenomena of life and organic organization. It was also, of course, theologically motivated. These considerations, it seems, were more important than whether the preformed embryo or germ was located in either the ovum or the spermatozoon, although in fact *ovist* preformationism was the dominant version.[13] The force of the sexual-political context of these preformationist debates was such that both versions – ovist and spermist – tended to be interpreted in terms of the privileged, active role of the male, either in providing the crucial spark that provoked the passive ovum into development (in ovism) or in providing the active animacule itself (animaculiam).[14]

The epigenic view, on the other hand, according to which each embryo was a newly generated organism – the *production* of something genuinely new that had not existed before – was generally based on the presumption of the bi-parental contribution to generation, the mixing of male and female generative fluids or semen. The early mechanistic epigenist theories of Descartes, Maupertuis and Buffon foundered on their inability to offer plausible accounts of how the organism was produced, how the organization of the embryo and its parts developed from previously unorganized material. But a later generation of epigenists – including, notably, Hans Blumenbach – influenced by Kant's account of the regulative principle of purposiveness in the understanding of organisms, 'embraced a teleological view of embryological development, based on a presupposed original state of organization in the generative material'.[15] These theories do not attempt to explain the origin of organization; rather, they presuppose it. With recourse to avowedly mysterious forces (on the Newtonian model) they then attempt to explain the mechanism of the expression of this organization in the generation, growth and maintenance of the organism. For example, Blumenbach – converted to epigenesis after an earlier adherence to Hallerian preformationism – postulated a 'formative drive' (*Bildungstrieb*) to explain this:

> in the previously unformed generative matter of the organised body, after it attained its maturation and arrived at the place of its destiny [namely, the womb], a particular, lifelong active drive is stirred up to initially shape its definite form, then to preserve it for a lifetime, and if it by chance becomes mutilated, to reestablish it if possible.[16]

Kant's relation to the preformation–epigenesis debate was complex.[17] In an early work, 'The Only Possible Argument in Support of a Demonstration of the Existence of God' (1763), Kant proclaims the rule (never abjured) that in seeking the causes of any particular effects we should first of all regard those effects as the necessary results of general laws, presuming the unity of nature, before 'suppos[ing] the existence of new and diverse operative causes'. This is the case even when 'a very precise symmetry seems to require the postulation of a specifically instituted and artificially devised arrangement', as with the delicate beauty of each individual snowflake.[18] But where we find 'products' of nature in which are manifested 'great art and a contingent combination of factors which has been made by free choice in accordance with certain intentions', such as we find in the constitution of plants and animals, this constitution 'cannot be explained by appeal to the universal and necessary laws of nature'. For Kant, 'it would be absurd to regard the initial generation of a plant or animal as a mechanical effect incidentally arising from the universal laws of nature.' Thus two possible explanations for their generation present themselves:

> Is each individual member of the plant- and animal-kingdoms directly formed by God, and thus of supernatural origin, with only propagation, that is to say, only the periodic transmission for the purposes of development, being entrusted to a natural law? Or do some individual members of the plant- and animal-kingdoms, although immediately formed by God and thus of divine origin, possess the capacity, which we cannot understand, actually to generate their own kind in accordance with a regular law of nature, and not merely to unfold them?[19]

These alternatives are versions of individual preformationism and epigenesis. Kant sees problems with both views, and in 'The Only Possible Argument' remains agnostic as to which of the two positions should prevail; the issue cannot be decided on either metaphysical or empirical grounds. Kant rejects the specific *mechanistic* epigenist theories of Maupertuis and Buffon, which postulate explanatory elements that 'are either as incomprehensible as the thing itself [that they purport to explain], or they are entirely arbitrary inventions'; but the alternative – the postulation of a supernatural origin – is 'just as arbitrary': 'Has anyone ever offered a mechanical explanation of the capacity of yeast to generate its kind? And yet one does not appeal for that reason to a supernatural ground.'[20]

However, in an essay from 1775, revised and expanded in 1777, 'Of the Different Human Races', Kant draws on the germ theory of preformation to explain the establishment of what he sees as the different human 'races', adding to this, as Phillip Sloan has pointed out, a conception of 'natural predispositions' (*Naturanlagen*).[21] From the one human species, the development of the different human 'races' is explained in this way:

> various germs [*Keime*] and natural predispositions [*natürliche Anlagen*] had to lie ready in him to be on occasion either unfolded or restrained, so that he would become suited to his place in the world and over the course of the generations would appear to be as it were native and to be made for that place.[22]

The possibilities for the development of different characteristics are, Kant says, 'preformed' (*vorgebildet*),[23] but the spur to the development of these possibilities is environmental and may be absent. Kant uses the same preformationist terminology in the first edition of the *Critique of Pure Reason* in 1781 (though the passage remains in the second edition, too) in relation to the pure concepts of the understanding. The analytic of concepts, he writes, is not an analysis of the content of concepts, but

> the much less frequently attempted analysis of the faculty of the understanding itself, in order to research the possibility of a priori concepts by seeking them only in the understanding as their birthplace [*Geburtsorte*] and analysing its pure use in general; for this is the proper business of a transcendental philosophy; the rest is the logical treatment of concepts in philosophy in general. We will therefore pursue the concepts to their first seeds and predispositions [*Keimen und Anlagen*] in the human understanding, where they lie ready, until with the opportunity of experience they are finally developed [*entwickelt*] and exhibited in their clarity by the very same understanding, liberated from the empirical conditions attaching to them.[24]

Here it is clear that it is the categories themselves that are to be understood as 'preformed', but whether this is a literal claim about their biological origin, as Sloan claims,[25] is debatable; the metaphorical use of the idea of 'birthplace' in the first sentence suggests rather that it is part of an extended metaphor.

'Generic preformation'

A few years later, in his review of Herder's *Ideas for the Philosophy of History of Humanity*, 1784/5, Kant staked out a definite – and original – position on the preformationism–epigenesis debate. In his discussion of epigenesis Herder had proposed a 'genetic force' (*genetische Kraft*) to explain adaption to environmental circumstances. To the extent that this offers an alternative to strict preformationism, spontaneous generation and purely mechanistic epigenesis, Kant was prepared to accept it, with conditions. Herder assumes, Kant says,

> a principle of life, which appropriately modifies *itself* internally in accordance with differences of the external circumstances; with this the reviewer fully concurs, only with this reservation, that if the cause organising itself *from within* were limited by its nature only perhaps to a certain number and degree of differences in the formation of a creature (so that after the institution of which it were not further free to form yet another type under altered circumstances), then one could call this natural vocation of the forming nature also 'germs' or 'original predispositions', without thereby regarding the former as primordially implanted machines and buds that unfold themselves only when occasioned (as in the system of evolution [i.e. preformation]), but merely as limitations, not further explicable, of a self-forming faculty [*eines sich selbst bildenden Vermögens*], which latter we can just as little explain or make comprehensible.[26]

Distancing himself from individual preformationism, Kant seems to suggest, as John Zammito says, that epigenesis itself implies the weaker form of germ preformation: 'at the origin there had to be some inexplicable (transcendent) endowment, and with it, in [Kant's view], some determinate restriction in species variation.'[27]

It was a couple of years after this (in 1787) that Kant introduced the idea of epigenesis as an analogy for the explanation of the relation between the categories and experience in the revised, second edition of the *Critique of Pure Reason*, at the same time explicitly rejecting the use of the idea of preformation for the same purposes. But it is later, in the 'Critique of Teleological Judgment' (1790), that we find Kant's longest discussions of the theories of preformation and epigenesis in the statement of what seems to be his mature position in the debate. And here Kant distinguishes between other aspects of the various theories of generation in a way that helps us to understand the associated field of reference of the epigenesis metaphor in the *Critique of Pure Reason*. In section 80, 'On the Necessary Subordination of the Principle of Mechanism to the Teleological Principle in Explaining a Thing [Considered] as a Natural Purpose', Kant distinguishes, in a footnote, between '*generatio aequivoca*, which is the production of an organized being by the mechanics of crude, unorganized matter', and *generatio univoca*, the production of an organized being from another organized being. As we have seen, the former, *generatio aequivoca*, refers to the idea of spontaneous generation. The latter, *generatio univoca*, may be either *generatio univoca homonyma* – 'where the product shares even the organization of what produced it' (for example, where parents of one species produce offspring of the same species) or *generatio univoca heteronyma*, where the product is an organized being that is different in kind from the organized being that produced it, 'as when, e.g. certain aquatic animals developed gradually into marsh animals and from these, after several generations, into land animals'. In Kant's view the idea of *generatio aequivoca* is absurd. The idea of *generatio univoca heteronyma* is 'not absurd ... not inconsistent a priori, in the judgment of mere reason' but '[e]xperience however does not show an example of it',[28] only examples of *generatio univoca homonyma*: the generation of the same from the same.

A few pages later two more sets of distinctions are introduced. Assuming, as for Kant we must, the teleological principle for natural products, the purposive form somehow generated in the 'cause' of the products of nature can be understood, according to Kant, in terms of either occasionalism or pre-established harmony. The issue here is the explanation for the relationship – or the 'conjoining' – of the teleological principle and the mechanistic process in the generation of organisms. Accordingly occasionalism is rejected because if we assume that 'the supreme cause of the world would, in conformity with an idea and on the occasion of every copulation, directly give the mingling matter its organic structure ... all nature in this production is lost entirely'.[29] We are thus left with the theory of pre-established harmony as a frame for both preformationism and epigenesis. Within this theory, Kant says, we can distinguish between preformationism and epigenesis in terms of another distinction, taken from chemistry – between 'educt' and 'product'. This distinction is explained in the *Lectures on Metaphysics*, in 1793: an *educt* is the result of pre-existent matter ('what was previously there') receiving a new form, whereas a material *product* is something that 'was not previously there at all'.[30] Applying this distinction to the issue of biological generation:

> any organic being generated by another of its kind is considered by this theory [pre-established harmony] to be either the *educt* or the *product* of that other being. The system that considers the generated beings as mere educts is called the system of *individual preformation*, or the *theory of evolution*. The system that considers them as products is called the system of *epigenesis*.[31]

Thus we have the theory of pre-established harmony, according to which 'the supreme cause would have imparted to the initial products of its wisdom only the predisposition [*Anlage*] by means of which an organic being produces another of its kind and the species perpetuates itself',[32] and the two possible 'ways' – both examples of *generatio univoca* – in which it can proceed, individual preformation and epigenesis. Kant now claims that epigenesis is to be preferred on both empirical and rational grounds. Even without the empirical grounds, reason, he says, would from the start be greatly in favor of the kind of explanation [it offers]. For in considering those things whose origin can be conceived only in terms of a causality of purposes, this theory, at least as far as propagation is concerned, regards nature as itself producing [*als selbst hervorbringend*] them rather than as merely developing [*entwickelnd*] them; and so it minimizes appeal to the supernatural, [and] after the first beginning leaves everything to nature.[33]

But epigenesis, which Kant here associates with Blumenbach, must also involve an appeal to a principle of original organization, Blumenbach's *Bildungstrieb* being 'the ability of the matter in an organized body to [take on] this organization'. Thus, in fact, he says, the system of epigenesis might actually be called 'the system of *generic preformation* [*generischen Präformation*], since the productive power of the generating beings, and therefore the form of the species, was still preformed *virtualiter* in the intrinsic purposive predispositions [*Anlagen*] imparted to the stock'.[34] This is a version of epigenesis with strong preformationist elements, or even a preformationist basis. Together, the preformationist basis and the epigenic process are, perhaps, the two elements in the 'conjoining' of the teleological principle and mechanism necessary to the understanding of natural products.

It is worth noting that Kant's idea of 'generic preformation' concerns the generation of organisms within the limits of species variation (species themselves, for Kant, being fixed). As concerns the diversity of the different 'races' of the human species, Kant advocates a stronger preformationist element – with seeds or germs as well as natural predispositions. No doubt part of the explanation for the apparent discrepancy between Kant's appeal to preformationism (with germs and natural predispositions) in the theory of the different human 'races' and the move to a version of epigenesis with preformationist elements (but no germs) in the theory of the generation of organisms is explained by the specificity of the idea of 'race' itself. 'Races' are neither species nor variations, for Kant; that they, then, might be the result of the development of preformed germs, when species, variations and indeed individuals are not, is not self-contradictory. But the *need* for preformed germs or seeds in the theory of race – the need to distinguish the human races from each other *as preformed* in this way – is interesting. The germs make the distinction of race greater than the distinctions between varieties of the same species. Kant was committed to the idea of monogenesis[35] – of the unity of the human species – but 'races' are not species variations, despite the fact that they, like variations (and unlike species), may mix.[36] Here it is clear that cultural and political concerns drive the biological theory, at least in part.

The parthenogenesis of pure reason
Concerning the metaphor of epigenesis, however, commentators have tended to look to the biological theory as the final basis of explanation. But, despite its being the obvious reference in the metaphor, the biological theories of epigenesis, including Kant's own 'generic preformation', in fact offer little help in understanding the meaning of the metaphor for the *Critique of Pure Reason*. Prominent commentators – notably Phillip Sloan, Günter Zöller and John Zammito – have tried to map specific features of preformationism and epigenesis or Kant's 'generic preformationism' onto specific features of Kant's transcendental idealism, especially concerning either the status of the categories themselves or the *a priori* knowledge produced with them.[37] In a limited sense, this is not difficult to do. For example, we might think that the 'self-forming faculty' identified in the review of Herder is *reason*, as distinct from the faculty of understanding; in which case the categories could be understood as the limits to the self-forming power – limits to the production of knowledge. On this interpretation reason would be the epigenic force, with the categories the preformed limitations to it. But what does this teach us about transcendental idealism that we did not already know? Rather than explaining how the epigenesis metaphor illuminates anything for us about Kant's position, this interpretative approach tends to draw attention to aspects of Kant's theory of knowledge to *justify* the use of the metaphor. As Zöller concedes

(in the context of a criticism of an argument that fails to do this): 'Kant's notion of transcendental epigenesis has to be explained in accordance with the very doctrine that it is supposed to illustrate by means of analogy.'[38]

So how else might we approach the epigenesis metaphor? Granted that the contemporary debate on the biological theories is part of the manifest content of the passage that includes the epigenesis metaphor at B167, what is also latent there, and to what associative chains is it linked? What does the scientific context of the preformation–epigenesis debate *obscure* in the invocation of the epigenesis metaphor in the *Critique of Pure Reason* and what does an excavation of its relation to the other metaphors of generation, ancestry and birth reveal? What does a textual analysis reveal that the historical analysis in terms of biological theory misses?

We might first note that the epigenesis metaphor inevitably raises the question of the *origin* of the categories, even though that is, according to Kant's explicit remarks on the matter, outside of the problem field of the *Critique of Pure Reason*. That the categories are necessary for cognition is, Kant writes, a 'peculiarity of our understanding' for which no further ground can be found.[39] And to some extent the appeal to epigenesis confirms this. Especially in the form proposed by Blumenbach and part-endorsed by Kant, epigenesis was dominantly concerned with the forces or drives powering the organized development of the embryo rather than the explanation of the generation of the embryo itself at the moment of conception (the 'epi' in epigenesis means 'after'). As concerns natural science, this limitation would have recommended the theory to Kant. In the 'Critique of Teleological Judgment' Kant says that although we cannot rule out the possibility that 'organized natural products' are merely mechanically produced, it is certain that 'the mere mechanism of nature cannot provide *our cognitive power* with a basis on which we could explain the production of organized beings',[40] hence the need for us to think natural products through the idea of a purposive (intelligent) causality – the *regulative* idea of purposive organization. The question of the origin of all organization, Kant says elsewhere, lies '*outside* natural science, in *metaphysics*',[41] and the point holds for the origin of any particular product of nature. Thus the legitimate concern of natural science would begin after the act of generation according to purposive causality. As Shirley Roe puts it, Kant proposed that once one accepts organization as a teleological fact, 'one can proceed to explain on a mechanical basis how this organization functions and is maintained'.[42]

That might tempt us to say something similar about the fact of the categories, and to see the virtue of the epigenesis metaphor in its avoidance of the question of their origin. However, as the task of the Transcendental Analytic is not merely to accept the transcendental fact of the categories and then proceed to explain how these categories function in cognition, but also to justify the *necessity* – and hence the legitimacy – of the categories, to deny that their role in cognition is merely subjective or accidental, the question of their *origin* inescapably arises in the transcendental deduction, if only in negative form (they *do not* come from experience, they *are not* implanted from outside). This is what Frederick Beiser calls the ineliminable 'genetic' dimension of transcendental discourse.[43] Indeed the question of the origin of the categories is quite explicit in the introduction of the epigenesis metaphor, which first offers us an alternative to the idea of an empirical origin or an alternative to the idea that the origin of the categories lies in something *different in kind* from the categories themselves, as the 'epigenesis of pure reason' is contrasted first with *generatio aequivoca*, 'spontaneous generation', *not* with preformationism.

In one of the few references to epigenesis in Kant's notes on metaphysics – notes which reiterate the description of Locke as a physiologist, or as having a physiological method[44] – epigenesis is distinguished from preformationism via the distinction between educt and product:

Whether concepts are mere *educta* or *producta*. Preformation or genesis. (*Producta* either through physical (empirical) influence or through the consciousness of the formal constitution of our sensibility and understanding on the occasion of experience, hence *producta a priori*, not *a posteriori*.)[45]

Putting the passage from the *Critique of Pure Reason* together with this note allows us to see the main relevant distinction as that between empirical *a posteriori* production of concepts (*generatio aequivoca*, the production of the intellectual from the physical, or *influxo physico*[46]) and epigenic *a priori* production of concepts (*generatio univoca*, the production of the intellectual by the intellect, or *epigenesis intellectualis*).[47] If we have become accustomed to call *generatio aequivoca* 'spontaneous generation', this should not blind us to the fact that for Kant it is epigenesis as *generatio univoca* that is connected to the *spontaneous generation* of the pure concepts in the understanding (*epigenesis intellectualis*).

Indeed, the idea of a 'spontaneous generation' of the categories by the understanding imposes itself more and more when we look beyond the single reference to epigenesis in the *Critique of Pure Reason* to the wider set of metaphors of generation, birth and ancestry there. Contrasting the faculties of sensibility and understanding in the Introduction to the Transcendental Logic, Kant characterizes the former as 'the receptivity of our mind to receive representations insofar as it is affected in some way', while understanding is 'the faculty for bringing forth representations itself [*Vorstellungen selbst hervorzubringen*], or the spontaneity of cognition'.[48] Kant frequently talks of the 'origin' (*Ursprung*) of the categories in the understanding[49] and says that they 'spring pure and unmixed [*rein und unvermischt entspringen*] from the understanding', a fact which a little later requires, he says, the production of 'an entirely different birth certificate than that of an ancestry from experiences'.[50] Referring to them often as 'ancestral concepts' (*Stammbegriffe*)[51] Kant speaks of the need to 'bring [them] forth' (*hervorzubringen*) by a special act of the understanding;[52] they are, as the epigenesis passage itself says, 'self-thought'. In the Transcendental Doctrine of Method, Kant speaks of the possibility of synthetic *a priori* judgments in the same way, as 'this augmentation of concepts out of themselves [*diese Vermehrung der Begriffe aus sich selbst*] and the parthenogenesis [*die Selbstgebärung*], so to speak, of our understanding (together with reason), without impregnation by experience [*ohne durch Erfahrung geschwängert*]'.[53] As all of these quotations show, then, but the last shows most explicitly, the most insistent generative model evoked in the *Critique of Pure Reason* is in fact neither preformationism nor epigenesis but something much more like *parthenogenesis*, in the sense of a spontaneous production without fertilization or impregnation. The categories spring from the understanding as Athena sprang from the head of Zeus. Kant's earliest critic, Johann Georg Hamann, noted precisely this parthenogenesis of pure reason as part and parcel of Kant's 'violent, unjustified, wilful divorce' of sensibility and understanding: the 'mythology' of 'a new immaculate virgin'[54] and the miraculous birth of principles and concepts.[55] This, for Hamann, was *the* illusion at the heart of the *Critique of Pure Reason*.

But if parthenogenesis is the model for the generation of the pure concepts of the understanding, why is there no explicit reference to it among Kant's various analogies between theories of generation and theories of knowledge? For parthenogenesis was recognized among Kant's contemporaries (as it is today) as an existing method of reproduction – the method of the reproduction of aphids, for example.[56] Although there are no explicit references to parthenogenesis in the analogies between theories of generation and theories of knowledge, there are imaginative descriptions of what appear to be a version of it in the review of Herder and in the *Critique of Teleological Judgment*. If the philosophical concern of the passage which includes the epigenesis metaphor in the *Critique of Pure Reason* is to distinguish transcendental idealism as *generatio univoca* from empiricism as *generatio aequivoca*, the concern in these other texts is to distinguish between different kinds of *generatio univoca* – the *generatio univoca homonyma* of Kant's own generic preformationism and the possibility of *generatio univoca heteronyma* inherent in Herder's theory. To do so Kant entertains – in order to reject, and indeed to abhor – the possibility of continuity between species. In the review of Herder, Kant grants the possibility of describing nature in terms of 'the ladder of organizations' – the hierarchical categorization of species according to their similarities – but denies that this bespeaks any affinity between species:

> The smallness of the distinctions, if one places the species one after another in accordance with their *similarities*, is, given so huge a manifoldness, a necessary consequence of this very manifoldness. Only an *affinity* among them, where either one species would have arisen from the other and all from a single procreative maternal womb, would lead to *ideas* which, however, are so monstrous that reason recoils before them.[57]

In the 'Critique of Teleological Judgment' Kant notes that the resemblances between various natural forms reinforces the suspicion 'that they are actually akin, produced by a common original mother', and that the 'archeologist of nature', considering this,

> can make mother earth (like a large animal, as it were) emerge from her state of chaos, and make her lap promptly give birth initially to creatures of a less purposive form, with these then giving birth to others that became better adapted to their place of origin and to their relations to one another, until in the end this womb itself rigidified, ossified, and confined itself to bearing definite species that would no longer degenerate, so that the diversity remained as it had turned out when that fertile formative force ceased to operate.[58]

This, as Kant specifies in a footnote, is the idea of *generatio univoca heteronyma* – not absurd (unlike *generatio aequivoca*) but not met with in experience (unlike *generatio univoca homonyma*).

As Christine Battersby remarks, Kant's prose here is 'unusually vivid'.[59] The awful possibility that is being contemplated – effectively, self-forming and active matter – is imaginatively described in terms of a maternal (hence female) generative power, labouring apparently parthenogenically, without any mention of a paternal partner. And this parthenogenic description of a certain understanding of epigenesis is actually much closer to *generatio aequivoca* than Kant's footnote suggests. For the mechanistic epigenesis that Kant rejected was seen by some of those who propounded it as including a theory of spontaneous production. Buffon declared:

> My experiences demonstrate quite clearly that there are no preexistent germs, and at the same time they prove that the generation of animals and vegetables is not univocal. There are perhaps as many beings produced by the fortuitous mingling of organic molecules as there are [those] which can produce by a constant succession of generations.[60]

Thus we should have to say that what Kant is rejecting here is the parthenogenic epigenesis of a vital materialism, the initially unlimited fecundity and generative power of 'a single procreative maternal womb' or 'a common original mother' spilling offspring from her lap: the *naturally* generatively self-sufficient virgin mother, matter giving birth to form. Given that he rejects this, the model of parthenogenesis appropriated for the description of the generation of the categories seems, on the other hand, to be more like that of the *supernatural* virgin birth. But if a supernatural parthenogenesis provides the model for the mono-parental generation or spontaneous self-production of the categories out of the understanding, the generation of intellectual form itself, this is now a *masculine* parthenogenesis, if we assume – as the quotations lead us to – that the conventional gendering of the matter/form distinction as female/male is at work here.

The fantasy of pure reason

It is tempting to speculate that Kant's 'generic preformation' is the conjoining of the purposive masculine principle of form with the epigenic development of feminine matter according to causal laws. In a rare explicit reference to the different contribution of the sexes to generation, in *Religion within the Boundaries of Mere Reason* (1793/4), this gendered distribution seems to be confirmed.

In a discussion of the problem of the possibility of the transmission of original sin in the virgin birth Kant writes that

> according to the hypothesis of epigenesis, the mother, who descended from her parents through *natural* birth, would still be tainted with this moral blemish [original sin], and would pass it on to her child, at least half of it, even in a supernatural birth. To escape this consequence, therefore, we would have to assume the theory that the seeds [of the descendents] *pre-exist* in the progenitors, not, however, the theory that these seeds develop on the *female* side (for then the consequence is not escaped) but on the *male* side alone (not on the part of the *ova* but of the *spermatozoa*). So, since the male side has no part in a supernatural pregnancy, this mode of representation could be defended as theoretically consistent with the idea [of virginal birth].[61]

The model of supernatural parthenogenesis is the only model according to which the generation of the categories – like the immaculate conception – can remain 'pure'. Further, this model *seems* to avoid a problem that would dog the appeal to any theory of *natural* generation as a model for the production or epistemic status of the categories: the problem of *contingency*. To the extent that natural generation is a result of conception it involves contingency at its heart, a fact that, for Kant, opened the way for sceptical questions about the relation between the immaterial immortal soul and the body:

> The contingency of conception, which in humans as well as in irrational creatures depends on opportunity, but besides this also on nourishment, on government, on its moods and caprices, even on vices, presents a great difficulty for the opinion of the eternal duration of a creature whose life has first begun under circumstances so trivial and so entirely dependent on our liberty.[62]

Thus any appropriate metaphorical model for the production or epistemic status of the categories *as necessary* must be one that does without conception understood in terms of the contingency of fertilization. It must exclude any reference to an idea of conception that relies on an external fertilizing agent. As even the model of the virgin birth cannot avoid this (and ought by rights to be rejected for the same reason that the preformation model of divine implantation was rejected in the *Critique of Pure Reason*), the spontaneous, immanent generation of the pure concepts from within the understanding (*generatio univoca homonyma*) must be a self-sufficient parthenogenesis of the strictest and purest kind.

In itself, there is nothing especially odd about the metaphorical appeal to parthenogenesis, rather than an appeal to any other theory or mode of generation. But what moves this in the *Critique of Pure Reason* from the level of metaphor to that of fantasy is the imaginative appropriation – via a disavowal – of a form of generation coded as female to represent the intellectual power of the generation of form itself, coded as masculine. Although it is veiled by the prominence of the metaphor of epigenesis, and also by the concentration on the metaphor of epigenesis in the literature on Kant, this fantasy nestles in the lap of transcendental idealism. How can we be sure of the legitimacy of the 'self-thought' pure concepts of the understanding? Only if self-fertilizing 'father' understanding gives birth to them himself.

However, the fantasy of purity expressed in the idea of intellectual parthenogenesis is at the same time undermined by the ineliminably biological terms of the discourses of generation from which it is drawn. The biological metaphors indicate a stain on the purity of the *a priori* concepts, a blot from Kant's own hand that seeps through the pages of the *Critique of Pure Reason*. Hamann made this point more generally, pointing out that language, an impure condition of experience 'with no credentials but traditions and usage', necessarily remains unthought in the *Critique of Pure Reason*.[63] In fact this is a point about *languages*, rather than language as a general structure. As such, it is a point about the material conditions of thinking. More specifically, however, the biological metaphors in the *Critique of Pure Reason* unwittingly reveal the material conditions of reproduction for the transcendental productions and reproductions of the understanding and the imagination: the human condition, and empirical reproduction, of the transcendental subject.

Notes

1. Immanuel Kant, *Critique of Pure Reason*, trans. Paul Guyer and Allen W. Wood, Cambridge University Press, Cambridge, 1998, B167–8, pp. 264–5. (*Kritik de Reinen Vernunft*, Band 1, Suhrkamp, Frankfurt am Main, 1956.)
2. See, for example, Timothy Lenoir, 'Kant, Blumenbach, and Vital Materialism in German Biology', *ISIS*, vol. 71, no. 256, 1980, pp. 77–108.
3. Kant, *Critique of Pure Reason*, A651–2/B679–80, pp. 594–5. Immanuel Kant, 'Of the Different Races of Human Beings' (1775–77), trans. Holly Wilson and Günter Zöller ('Von der Verschiedenen Rassen der Menschen', *Werke*, Band VI: *Schriften zur Anthropologie, Geschichtsphilosophie, Politik und Pädogogik*, Insel-Verlag, Frankfurt am Main, 1964); 'Determination of the Concept of a Human Race' (1785), trans. Holly Wilson and Günter Zöller; 'On the Use of Teleological Principles in Philosophy' (1788), trans. Günter Zöller, all in Kant, *Anthropology, History and Education*, ed. Günter Zöller and Robert B. Louden, Cambridge University Press, Cambridge, 2007. See also Robert Bernasconi, 'Who Invented the Concept of Race? Kant's Role in the Enlightenment Construction of Race', in Bernasconi, ed., *Race*, Blackwell, Oxford and Malden MA, 2001.
4. See, for example, Kant, *Critique of Pure Reason*, A13/B27, p. 134; A81/B107, p. 213.
5. Johann Georg Hamann, *Metacritique on the Purism of Reason*, in Hamann, *Writings on Philosophy and Language*, ed. and trans. Kenneth Haynes, Cambridge University Press, Cambridge, 2007.
6. Kant, *Critique of Pure Reason*, A14/B28, p. 134; B2–3, p. 137.
7. Ibid., Aix, p. 100; A86–7/B118–9, pp. 220–21.
8. Ibid., B166–7, p. 264.
9. Ibid., B167–8, pp. 264–5.
10. Shirley A. Roe, *Matter, Life and Generation: Eighteenth-Century Embryology and the Haller–Wolff Debate*, Cambridge University Press, Cambridge, 1981, p. 1.
11. Phillip R. Sloan, 'Preforming the Categories: Eighteenth-Century Generation Theory and the Biological Roots of Kant's A Priori', *Journal of the History of Philosophy*, vol. 40, no. 2, April 2002, p. 232. In this Sloan follows Jacques Roger (*Les Science de la vie dans la pensée française du XVIIe siècle*, Armand Colin, Paris, 1963). On preformationism, see Roe, *Matter, Life and Generation*, pp. 3–5.
12. Albrecht von Haller, *Sur la formation du cœur dans le poulet* (1758), cited in Sloan, 'Preforming the Categories', p. 236.
13. See Helmut Müller-Sievers, *Self-Generation: Biology, Philosophy and Literature Around 1800*, Stanford University Press, Stanford CA, 1997, pp. 28–9; Günter Zöller, 'Kant on the Generation of Metaphysical Knowledge', in Hariolf Oberer und Gerhard Seel, eds, *Kant: Analysen–Probleme–Kritik*, Königshausen & Neumann, Würzburg, 1988, pp. 76–7.
14. On the sexual politics of the various versions of preformationism, see Eve Keller, *Generating Bodies and Gendered Selves: The Rhetoric of Reproduction in Early Modern England*, University of Washington Press, Seattle WA and London, 2007, esp. pp. 149, 154.
15. Roe, *Matter, Life and Generation*, p. 151.
16. Blumenbach (*Über den Bildungstrieb und das Zeugungsgeschäfte*, 1781), quoted in Müller-Sievers, *Self-Generation*, p. 43; Müller-Sievers's interjection. While it was true that Blumenbach's 'formative drive' was in itself inexplicable, so was Newton's force of gravity, and that had been no obstacle to its scientific acceptability and success. See Müller-Sievers, *Self-Generation*, p. 31.
17. Recent work, in particular that of John Zammito and Phillip Sloan, has demonstrated this complexity beyond doubt. See Sloan, 'Preforming the Categories'; John Zammito, 'Kant's Early Views on Epigenesis: The Role of Maupertuis', in Justin E.H. Smith, ed., *The Problem of Generation in Early Modern Philosophy*, Cambridge University Press, Cambridge, 2006; John Zammito, '"This Inscrutable Principle of an Original Organization": Epigenesis and "Looseness of Fit" in Kant's Philosophy of Science', *Studies in History and Philosophy of Science* 34, 2003.
18. Immanuel Kant, 'The Only Possible Argument in Support of a Demonstration of the Existence of God', in Immanuel Kant, *Theoretical Philosophy 1755–1770*, ed. and trans. David Walford with Ralf Meerbote, Cambridge University Press, Cambridge, 1992, p. 155.

19. Kant, 'The Only Possible Argument', p. 156. See also p. 157: 'the following alternatives seen unavoidable: either the formation of the fruit is to be attributed immediately to a divine action, which is preformed at every mating, or, alternatively, there must be granted to the initial divine organisation of plants and animals a capacity, not merely to develop [*entwickeln*] their kind thereafter in accordance with a natural law, but truly to generate [*erzeugen*] their kind.'
20. Ibid., p. 157. For a detailed discussion of interpretations of Kant's view in 'The Only Possible Argument', see Zammito, 'Kant's Early Views on Epigenesis, pp. 337–46.
21. See Sloan, 'Preforming the Categories', *passim*.
22. Kant, 'Of the Different Races of Human Beings', p. 90; see also p. 89.
23. Ibid., p. 90.
24. Kant, *Critique of Pure Reason*, A66/B91, pp. 202–3.
25. See Sloan, 'Preforming the Categories', p. 232.
26. Immanuel Kant, 'Review of J.G. Herder's *Ideas for the Philosophy of the History of Humanity*', trans. Allan W. Wood, in Immanuel Kant, *Anthropology, History and Education*, ed. Robert B. Louden and Günter Zöller, Cambridge University Press, Cambridge, 2007, pp. 139–40 ('Rezension zu Johann Gottfried Herders *Ideen*', in *Werke*, vol. VI).
27. Zammito, '"This Inscrutable *Principle*"', p. 88. See also Sloan, 'Preforming the Categories', p. 244.
28. Immanuel Kant, *Critique of Judgment*, trans. Werner S. Pluhar, Hackett, Indianapolis IN, 1987, §81, p. 305 n5 (*Kritik der Urteilskraft*, Suhrkamp, Frankfurt am Main, 1974).
29. Ibid., §81, p. 309.
30. Kant, *Lectures on Metaphysics*, trans. and ed. Karl Ameriks and Steve Naragon, Cambridge University Press, Cambridge, 1997, p. 385 (AK 28:684). On the distinction between educt and product, see Zammito, 'This Inscrutable *Principle*', pp. 90–91.
31. Kant, *Critique of Judgment*, §81, p. 309. See also Kant, *Lectures on Metaphysics*, p. 385 (AK 28:684): in the first case, of 'involution (of encasement)' – that is, preformationism – 'the human being is educt, in the second [case, epigenesis], product; if we have cause to assume the system of epigenesis, then we assume the human being as product', that is 'human beings are produced wholly new'.
32. Kant, *Critique of Judgment*, §81, p. 309.
33. Ibid., §81, p. 311.
34. Ibid., §81, p. 309.
35. See Alix Cohen, 'Kant on Epigenesis, Monogenesis and Human Nature: The Biological Premises of Anthropology', *Studies in History and Philosophy of Biological and Biomedical Sciences* 37, 2006.
36. See, for example, Kant, 'On the Use of Teleological Principles in Philosophy', p. 202.
37. Phillip Sloan claims that the preformationist basis is the crucial point, even in the B edition reference to epigenesis, as the relevant background is Kant's rejection of 'strong preformationism' or *individual* pre-existence theories, including the individual pre-existence of germs and predispositions. Sloan claims that Kant's use of the preformationist terms was not 'casual or non-technical, or only employed as loose analogies', and that the categories are to be understood as 'biological properties' (Sloan, 'Preforming the Categories', pp. 252, 245; see also pp. 250, 251–2.) But this interpretation leaves us unable to distinguish between the generic preformationism of transcendental idealism and the Lockean 'physiological' position that the passage at B167 explicitly rejects. Sloan does not accept this problem, arguing that although the categories are 'biological properties' they are not, however, 'merely preformed subjective biological characteristics that would be individually specific and implanted at the creation' (pp. 242, 245). But it is very hard to see how Sloan's claim that the categories are to be understood as 'biologically pre-existent within us' is consistent with the claim at B167 that the categories are 'self-thought *a priori* first principles of our cognition'; that is, Sloan's argument does not so much explain the epigenesis metaphor in the *Critique of Pure Reason* as deny it in favour of the preformationist element.

Günter Zöller interprets the epigenesis metaphor as a reference to the production of metaphysical knowledge or *a priori* cognitions rather than a reference to the production of the categories themselves. What is at issue is the production of synthetic *a priori* propositions – '*products* of the spontaneity of the intellect' – rather than the reproduction, *a posteriori*, of a pre-existing order (Zöller, 'Kant on the Generation of Metaphysical Knowledge', pp. 79, 74). Zöller thus stresses the analogy between the *spontaneity* of the intellect and the self-forming aspect of epigenesis (or the analogy between metaphysical knowledge and organisms as true products, the generation of something genuinely new). However, he acknowledges what is in fact most idiosyncratic in Kant's version of epigenesis at that time, namely the postulation of the germs and natural dispositions as 'a virtual preformation underlying actual epigenesis', and effectively identifies this aspect of the theory with the – albeit non-empirical – *a priori* facticity of the categories (pp. 89, 90).

John Zammito emphasizes the oddity of Kant's appeal to epigenesis in the *Critique of Pure Reason*, given that Kant did not ever accept an unqualified version of epigenesis and was highly critical of what he saw as its dominant tendency towards – or even identification with – vital materialism. Zammito speculates that it must have been the idea of an 'innate force' in epigenesis that attracted Kant: 'The categories themselves should not be seen as preformed, but only as produced spontaneously by an innate *capacity* or *power* – a "faculty" of the mind, whose own origin was utterly inscrutable' (Zammito, '"This Inscrutable *Principle*"', p. 92; see also Zammito, 'Kant's Early Views on Epigenesis', p. 347). Zammito's interpretation successfully picks out a specific feature of Kant's own epigenic theory of generation – the postulation of a self-forming faculty or power, akin to Blumenbach's *Bildungstrieb* or Herder's genetic force – and identifies this with the spontaneity of the faculty or power of the understanding. But his point is ultimately that the metaphor is strained and unilluminating (Zammito, '"This Inscrutable *Principle*"', pp. 92–3).
38. Zöller, 'Kant on the Generation of Metaphysical Knowledge', p. 87. Zöller (p. 84) criticizes A.C. Genova's interpretation of Kant's use of the epigenesis metaphor in terms of an anachronistic understanding of epigenesis as genetic constitution according to a Darwinian idea of evolution. See A.C. Genova, 'Kant's Epigenesis of Pure Reason', *Kant-Studien*, vol. 65, no. 3, 1974.
39. Kant, *Critique of Pure Reason*, B145–6, p. 254. It is Locke's 'physiology of the human understanding' that is said to be concerned with 'the explanation of the possession of pure concepts', in contrast to Kant's transcendental critique (Aix, p. 100; A86–7/B118–9, pp. 220–21.)
40. Kant, *Critique of Judgment*, §71, p. 269, my emphasis.
41. Kant, 'On the Use of Teleological Principles in Philosophy', p. 50.
42. Roe, *Matter, Life and Generation*, p. 151.
43. Frederick C. Beiser, *German Idealism: The Struggle Against Subjectivism 1781–1801*, Harvard University Press, Cambridge MA and London, 2002, p. 173.
44. Immanuel Kant, *Notes and Fragments*, ed. Paul Guyer, trans. Curtis Bowman, Paul Guyer and Frederick Rauscher, Cambridge University Press, Cambridge, 2005, notes 4851 (p. 195); 4866 (p. 197); 4893 (p. 198) (all 1776–78).
45. Ibid., note 4851 (1776–78), p. 194.
46. In the *Notes and Fragments* Kant refers to Locke's position as 'influxionism', the postulation of 'the outer causality (of influx)', or '*influxo physico*'. See notes 4893 (p. 198), 5988 (p. 323) (both 1783–84), and 4275 (p. 124) (1770–71), respectively.
47. Zöller ('Kant on the Generation of Metaphysical Knowledge', p. 83, referring to note 4859) points us to the idea of *epigenesis intellectualis* in Kant's *Notes*. In Zöller's words: 'Epigenesis as a concept pertaining to the epistemology of metaphysical knowledge is now characterised as "*epigenesis intellectualis*" thereby indicating the metaphorical use of the term with regard to a type of knowledge that originates in the intellect alone.' (This note is not translated in the Cambridge edition of Kant's *Notes and Fragments*.) I disagree that the issue in B167 concerns the production of *a priori* knowledge. It seems to me that the contrast with *generatio aequivoca* and Locke's empirical derivation of concepts suggests strongly that the issue concerns the production of the categories themselves.
48. Kant, *Critique of Pure Reason*, A51/B75, p. 193.
49. Ibid., for example at A57/B81, p. 196; A62/B87, p. 199.
50. Ibid., A67/B92, p. 204; A86/B119, p. 221.

51. Ibid., for example at A13/B27, p. 134; A81/B107, p. 213. 'Ancestral concepts' are contrasted with 'derivative concepts'.
52. Ibid., B111, p. 215.
53. Ibid., A765/B793, p. 656.
54. Kant's 'so to speak' (*so zu sagen*) legitimates Allen and Wood's translation of *die Selbstgebärung* as 'parthenogenesis' (when Kant does not say, for example, *der Jungfernzeugung*). Kemp Smith (Immanuel Kant, *Critique of Pure Reason*, trans. Norman Kemp Smith, Macmillan, London, 1933) translates *die Selbstgebärung* as 'spontaneous generation'; Müller-Sievers (*Self-Generation*, p. 49) translates it as 'self-delivery'. Note also that *Vermehrung* in this passage has as well the sense of 'breeding' or 'reproduction'.
54. Hamann, *Metacritique on the Purism of Reason*, pp. 212, 215.
55. See John R. Betz, *After Enlightenment: The Post-Secular Vision of J.G. Hamann*, Wiley-Blackwell, Chichester, 2009, p. 240.
56. See Müller-Sievers, *Self-Generation*, p. 29.
57. Kant, 'Review of Herder', p. 132. For a discussion of the context of this passage, see Zammito, *The Genesis of Kant's Critique of Judgment*, Chicago University Press, Chicago IL and London, 1992, pp. 109–206. In his response to Reinhold's comments on his review, Kant specifies ('Review of Herder', p. 135), in relation to this precise passage, that this recoil is 'the *horror vacui* of universal human reason … where one runs up against an idea in which *nothing at all can be thought*'. Are we any the wiser for that clarification?
58. Kant, *Critique of Judgment*, §80, pp. 304, 305. Kant is not the 'archeologist of nature' who thinks this; he merely reports the possible view of such an archeologist.
59. Christine Battersby, *The Phenomenal Woman: Feminist Metaphysics and the Patterns of Identity*, Polity Press, Cambridge, 1998, p. 75. Zammito (*Kant, Herder and the Birth of Anthropology*, University of Chicago Press, Chicago IL and London, 2002, p. 306) writes, in relation to passages such as these, that '[t]he very idea of emergence of evolution in our sense *frightened* [Kant].'
60. Buffon, *Histoire naturelle, générale et particulière* (1749), quoted in John Farley, *The Spontaneous Generation Controversy: From Descartes to Operin*, Johns Hopkins University Press, Baltimore MD and London, 1977, p. 24. Farley's account of the epigenic theories of the eighteenth century as, essentially, theories of spontaneous generation speaks against Zöller's claim that 'the theory of spontaneous generation had become obsolete well before Kant' (Zöller, 'Kant on the Generation of Metaphysical Knowledge', p. 75).
61. Immanuel Kant, *Religion Within the Boundaries of Mere Reason and Other Writings*, ed. Allen Wood and George di Giovanni, Cambridge University Press, Cambridge, 1998, p. 83. It is notable that Kant appeals here to pre-existent seeds, as in the theory of race, when such seeds played no part in the theory of 'generic preformation'. Once again, the appeal to seeds seems to occur when the theory needs to affirm a cultural, or this time moral, as opposed to purely biological, difference. As Alix Cohen has argued (in 'Kant on Epigenesis, Monogenesis and Human Nature'), both racial difference and sexual difference (which is here not conceptually distinct from gender difference) are for Kant teleologically determined according to Nature's intentions for the human species. Eduardo Mendieta has also shown how gender differences (again, not yet conceptually distinguished from sex differences) are assigned by Kant to anthropology in the same way as racial differences (Eduardo Mendieta, 'Geography Is to History as Woman Is to Man: Kant on Sex, Race and Geography', in Stuart Elden and Eduardo Mendieta, eds, *Reading Kant's Geography*, SUNY Press, Albany NY, 2011). The conjunction of sex, race and preformed seeds in Kant's work ought to be investigated further.
62. Kant, *Critique of Pure Reason*, A779/B807, p. 663.
63. Hamann, *Metacritique on the Purism of Reason*, p. 208.

2 Hegelian phenomenology and the critique of reason and society

PETER OSBORNE

> Abbot Terrasson has remarked that if the size of a volume be measured not by the number of its pages but by the time required for mastering it, it can be said of many a book, *that it would be much shorter if it were not so short.*
>
> Kant, Preface to First Edition, *Critique of Pure Reason*

Gillian Rose's *Hegel Contra Sociology* would be much shorter were it not so short. It is unashamedly, and sadly, an extremely difficult book; not just in terms of the complexity and subtlety of the position it puts forward, but, primarily, in terms of the way in which this position is presented. But it is, nonetheless, in many ways an important book. For it challenges, at a fundamental level, the generally accepted framework within which Hegel has been interpreted; and, in so doing, it challenges accepted beliefs not only about the relationship between Marx and Hegel, but also about the philosophical adequacy of Marxism and the redundancy of Hegelianism. It contains a densely argued and philosophically sophisticated piece of Hegel scholarship which is mobilized against all the prevailing tendencies of contemporary social theory, and it will be of particular interest to 'the materialist friends of the idealist dialectic'.[1]

In this essay my aim is twofold: (i) to produce an account of some central themes of the book, and, in particular, of the reading of Hegel around which it revolves; and (ii) to offer a provisional assessment of the standpoint it adopts, not so much with regard to the textual credibility of the interpretation of

Hegel from which it derives, as with respect to its immanent viability and more general implications. For Rose treats the conception of Hegelian phenomenology which she outlines as the only possible coherent theoretical basis for the development of a critical theory of subjectivity, culture and, hence, politics. She wants to appropriate aspects of Hegel's philosophy. The idea which the book develops is that the philosophical basis of Hegel's thought must be appropriated by Marxism if the latter is to be able to generate a critical politics. So it is the internal cogency of Rose's account of Hegel, rather than its historical veracity, which is important.

Hegel Contra Sociology announces itself as 'an attempt to retrieve Hegelian speculative experience for social theory',[2] and it concludes with a brief outline of a projected Hegelian social theory (labelled 'critical Marxism' – I will come back to this) as 'the exposition of capitalism as culture', 'a presentation of the contradictory relations between Capital and culture'[3] in the phenomenological (speculative) mode. In the meantime, it develops a philosophical critique of sociology and of Marxism, and a strikingly original interpretation of Hegel's thought which focuses on the sociopolitical significance of his idea of speculative experience.

The argument is that Marx's critique of Hegel is based on a Fichtean reading of his system which fails to grasp the true meaning of his concepts of actuality and spirit, and that in fact these concepts provide the theoretical basis for the conceptualization of the subjective mediations of objective social forms. Marx's own conception of practical materialism is seen as theoretically incapable of conceptualizing such mediations, since it involves abstract dichotomies between being and consciousness, and theory and practice, which can only be unified *abstractly* in an 'ought'. Without such mediations, the relation between *Capital* and politics is seen to be indeterminate. *Capital* gives an account of the objective determinations of social relations, but Marxism is seen to be theoretically incapable of utilizing this knowledge through a politics which accounts for how these social relations may be practically transformed *on the basis of their objective determinations*, because it cannot develop adequate concepts of subjectivity and culture.[4]

In what follows, I first give an account of Rose's understanding of Hegel, contrasting it with that on which Critical Theory is based, since (i) this is a standard interpretation, and (ii) Rose's reading of Hegel functions as a reformulation of the foundations of Critical Theory; then I discuss its implications for Marxism, and I discuss Rose's understanding of Marx. I conclude with a few comments of a general nature on the overtly 'philosophical' character of the project that Rose outlines. One of the most interesting things about the book is that, while it criticizes existing formulations of Critical Theory, it demonstrates and clearly endorses the explicitly 'philosophical' nature of its project.

Hegelian phenomenology and the radicalization of Kant's critique of reason

Hegel Contra Sociology is perhaps best understood as a response to Habermas's account of the development of German philosophy from Kant to Marx, which prepares the ground for his formulation of Critical Theory as a theory of knowledge-constitutive interests, and to the understanding of the idea of metacritique, as the radicalization of Kant's critique of reason, on which that theory is based.[5] It is this interpretation of the idea of metacritique which determines the meaning Habermas gives to the statement that 'a radical critique of knowledge is possible only as social theory'.[6] As we shall see, Rose's reading of Hegel involves a reinterpretation of this fundamental axiom of Critical Theory, which changes its orientation from a (at least formal) directedness towards Marx back towards Hegel.

Habermas's understanding of the idea of metacritique is elaborated by Garbis Kortian in his book *Metacritique: The Philosophical Argument* of *Jürgen Habermas* (1980). A brief examination of the different ways in which Kortian and Rose treat the concept of metacritique will serve to introduce Rose's position and to situate it in relation to Critical Theory. Kortian characterizes 'metacritique' as an argumentative strategy with reference to Hegel's *Phenomenology of Spirit*, which is taken to provide its paradigm.[7] He develops an account of the philosophical structure of Habermas's work in terms of the idea of metacritique, and he uses the difference in the form of the arguments that Hegel and Habermas use to determine the theoretical specificity of Habermas's work. Critical Theory generally – Habermas's work in particular – is presented as a response to the failure of Hegel's attempt at metacritique: 'Critical Theory is intended as the experience and expression of the failure of the Hegelian concept.'[8]

In agreement with Kortian's acceptance of a distinction between the epistemological structures of phenomenological and other forms of metacritical argument, but in opposition to his account of their difference, *Hegel Contra Sociology* presents a reading of Hegel which is built upon a claim for the epistemological superiority of the phenomenological form of Hegel's argument. Hegel's thought is counterposed to that of the advocates of Critical Theory, and of sociological thought generally (of which Critical Theory is seen to be an instance, despite itself), as representative of the only possible form of thought capable of superseding the dilemmas of Kantianism, which are taken to be reproduced within all sociological thought (and most strikingly in Habermas) because of its reliance upon Kantian forms of argumentation.[9] So while Habermas claims that his own work is genuinely metacritical, and that Hegel's is metaphysical – in its failure to eliminate all 'absolute' presuppositions – Rose claims that only Hegel has achieved genuine metacritique, and that Habermas's work remains Kantian. The basis of this claim is that Hegel has been almost universally misunderstood.

Kortian uses the term 'metacritical' to characterize the epistemological structure of a theory which is, broadly speaking, 'critical' in the sense in which Horkheimer uses the term; that is, which reflects upon the relation between the epistemic subject engaged in critique and the object criticized; which reflects upon the presuppositions of critique.[11] Kortian distinguishes, none too clearly, between genuine or 'radical' metacritique – 'the movement associated with the "meta" is only radical so long as it resolutely refuses any ... absolute position'[12] – and metacritique which fails to carry through the radicalization of critique which is its task[13] because it rests on some absolute presupposition, but which nonetheless presumably reveals some of the preconditions of critique. He places Hegel's *Phenomenology* in the latter group. This is the source of a certain amount of conceptual confusion since it means that the paradigmatic example of metacritique is a failed instance of that which it exemplifies. This is the result of defining it as an *intention*. But I think it is clear what Kortian is getting at.

Emphasizing the specificity of Hegel's thought, Rose restricts her usage of the term 'metacritique' to refer to that particular form of reflection on the presuppositions of theory developed by those who rejected Hegel's philosophy; that is, quasi-transcendental reflection – inquiry into the ontological or sociological preconditions of critique by transcendental argument. Habermas's theory of knowledge-constitutive interests is established by an argument of this kind. This kind of argument is *quasi*-transcendental because its results are both *a priori* (as the ground of critique) and seemingly naturalistic (as external to the mind). Consequently:

> The status of the relation between the sociological precondition and the conditioned becomes correspondingly ambiguous in all sociological quasi-transcendental arguments.[14]

In opposition to such an ambiguous form of argument, Hegelian phenomenology is presented as a form of cognitive activity which successfully radicalizes the critique of reason, which presents its social preconditions through a process of speculative self-reflection in which the exposition of critique and the derivation of its ground are united:

The exposition of abstract thinking and the derivation of the social institutions which determine it are completely integrated in the tracing of the education of self-consciousness at specific historical moments.[15]

The reason that Kortian does not distinguish phenomenological and quasi-transcendental arguments in this way is that his reconstruction of Habermas's argument shares the presuppositions of Habermas's thought. In this sense, it is less a reconstruction than a restatement. It presupposes the validity of the interpretation of Hegel from which Habermas starts out. This interpretation (which is a standard one) maintains that Hegel

> employs the radicalisation of critique, or this experience which he terms 'speculative', in the service of an absolute system of knowledge governed by the presupposition of the identity of thought and being.[16]

The *Phenomenology of Spirit* is taken to be grounded in idealist metaphysics. Rejecting this metaphysic, Habermas separates the idea of the self-reflection from the phenomenological form of its presentation. It is this abstraction that gives rise to the idea of metacritique which Kortian explicates.

Now, from the point of view of Hegel's thought, which Rose adopts, this abstraction of the idea of metacritical argument from its original form appears as a regression to that Kantian form of argument which separates off the subject from the object of critique, and defines their relation *abstractly*, in terms of a critical *method*. It was just this methodological conception of reflection which Hegel sought to overcome, because 'it takes for granted certain ideas about cognition as an *instrument* and as a *medium*, and assumes that *there is a difference between ourselves and this cognition*'.[17] The methodological appropriation of the idea of the self-reflection of knowledge robs it of its primary critical function. Metacritique, as opposed to phenomenology, is thus an essentially ambiguous enterprise which attempts to reveal the presuppositions of critique through the direction of the critical method towards previously neglected aspects of human existence.[18]

In Kortian's terms, we can say that the ambiguity of metacritically (quasi-transcendentally) established preconditions constitutes a failure on the part of those theories which are grounded on them to overcome, or to 'radicalize', critique. For their combination of *a priori* and naturalism gives them just that 'absolute' character which defines the objects of metaphysical thought. However, although they are philosophically unsatisfactory, Rose acknowledges the fact that such metacritical arguments can be extremely fruitful sociologically. Indeed, she argues that they are the method by which the basic paradigms of sociology were established. The first chapter of *Hegel Contra Sociology*, 'The Antinomies of Sociological Reason', gives a comprehensive, if condensed, historical account of the development of sociology in terms of its philosophical foundations in neo-Kantianism, which shows how a variety of sociological enterprises were established by different metacritical arguments, each designed to uncover different preconditions of neo-Kantian epistemology. Neo-Marxist sociology is also seen to exhibit this syndrome of reaction to, but incorporation within, neo-Kantianism. Although both attempted to overcome the philosophical problems of traditional sociology, it is argued that Lukács and Adorno in fact represent different positions within neo-Kantianism.[19] And Althusser is seen to combine neo-Kantian epistemology (his conception of science) with sociological metacritique (his theory of structures of social formation), and so to make 'all the classic neo-Kantian moves solely within a project of rereading Marx'.[20]

Rose's argument is that Hegelian phenomenology is the only way out of these philosophically inadequate forms of neo-Kantianism. The reason a way out is needed (although this is never actually made explicit in the text – an example of its unnecessarily enigmatic stance) is that, while neo-Kantian metacritique may be 'sociologically' (i.e. descriptively) adequate, its philosophical inadequacies make it *practically* impotent, because it is incapable of generating a social theory in which the ground of critique, of theory generally – objective social determinations – is conceived other than as distinct from, and externally related to, consciousness. It is incapable of giving rise to a social theory which grasps its object in terms of the subjective mediations through which it is experienced and reproduced, and through which it can be transformed. The argument for Hegelian phenomenology (as opposed to simply 'contra sociology') rests on two premisses: (i) that, despite almost universal belief to the contrary, Hegel's philosophy does not rely on the metaphysical presupposition of the identity of thought and being; that 'the fact that the Absolute alone is true, or the truth alone is absolute'[21] is not a *presupposition* of Hegel's thought at all: and (ii) that the philosophical foundations of Marxian materialism (as opposed to simply its sociological revisions) are themselves in some way Kantian or Fichtean in so far as they are not Hegelian.

Although a demonstration of the validity of this second premiss is attempted, briefly, at the end of the book (to which I will return), it is assumed from the beginning. For it is claimed, without argumentation, that Kant's philosophy of consciousness, with its theoretical contradictions and practical moralism, 'can *only* be criticised if the infinite is knowable'.[22] We are offered an *exclusive* choice between the possibility of Hegelianism and the impasse of an impotent Kantianism, since, accepting Kant's critical destruction of previous metaphysics, Rose, along with Hegel, recognizes that the infinite can only be knowable in its unity with the finite – that is, as the absolute.

This doctrinaire insistence on the exclusive theoretical option of Kant (and Fichte) *or* Hegel, reminiscent of the falsely exclusive choices offered by Lukács in his essays on aesthetics in the 1930s) but lacking their possible political vindication, is a theoretical flaw which has the unfortunate effect of closing the discourse articulated by the text at just that point at which it promises to become most interesting. It leaves the question of the theoretical value of the position outlined (which is always also a practical question) unexplored, by implicitly assuming that it is the only way out of a certain theoretical dilemma. The perspective within which that dilemma arises, and which determines its form (epistemology), is never itself questioned. The compositional structure of *Hegel Contra Sociology,* which combines philosophical argument with textual citation in a complex and often ambiguous manner, and its terse, assertive style, which at times borders on the cryptic, are the formal correlates of this refusal to consider, concretely, the general significance of the position it puts forward (which is essentially a refusal to open a dialogue with the reader).

Let us examine the argument put forward in defence of the first premiss (above) – the denial of any 'absolute' presuppositions in Hegel's thought. The bulk of *Hegel Contra Sociology* is devoted to its substantiation.

Rose's reading of Hegel, in conscious opposition to Marxist appropriations of his thought, revolves around her analysis of the roles played by that pair of concepts most often rejected, if not ridiculed, by those appropriations as representative of its systematic, and so idealist and ultimately theological, aspect. These are the concepts of the absolute and of speculation (in all its various forms as speculative thinking, speculative discourse, speculative experience, and, particularly important to Rose's interpretation, speculative rereading).

> Marxist sociology has mystified Hegel by making a distinction between a 'radical method' and a 'conservative system'. As a result of this artificial distinction, the centrality of those ideas which Hegel developed in order to unify the theoretical and practical philosophy of Kant and Fichte has been ignored.[23]

Rose sets out to reassert the centrality of these ideas. Her thesis is that 'Hegel's philosophy has *no* social import if the absolute cannot be thought',[24] since, as the unity of the finite and the infinite,[25] it represents the unity, and hence the difference, of actuality and possibility. So, how can the absolute be thought? What are the conditions of such a form of thought? And how can they be derived without being implicitly presupposed? That is, how can the transcendental circle, which involves the implicit presupposition of that which is to be deduced in the specification of that from which it is to be deduced, be avoided?[26] How can the absolute be shown to be thinkable without this being presupposed in the form of the assumption of the identity of thought and being?

The key to this set of problems is the idea of phenomenology.

> The only consistent way to criticise Kant's philosophy of consciousness is to show that the contradiction which a methodological, or any natural, consciousness falls into when it considers the object to be external, can itself provide the occasion for a change in that consciousness and in its definition of its object.[27]

The only way to criticize Kant (*within the problematic of modern epistemology*, one might add) is thus through a phenomenology which presents the forms of knowledge according to their own methodological standards, as they appear to consciousness, and which thereby presents 'the realm of appearance as defined by limited forms of consciousness'.[28] Such a presentation is a genuine radicalization of Kant's critique of reason because it involves no presuppositions about the nature of knowledge as it is presented in a series of diverse forms, other than the bare axiom that knowing is 'the being of something for a consciousness',[29] which is a necessary condition of *all* epistemology; a universally shared presupposition.

Such a presentation, Hegelian phenomenology, is possible, because of the unity of the processes of cognition and reflection within consciousness. As Hegel explains in the introduction to the *Phenomenology*,

> Consciousness examines its own self. ... [It] is, on the one hand, consciousness of the object, and on the other, consciousness of itself; consciousness of what for it is the True, and consciousness of its knowledge of the truth. Since both are *for* the same consciousness, this consciousness is itself their comparison; it is for the same consciousness to know whether its knowledge of the object corresponds to the object or not.[30]

The series of contradictory experiences which the observing (reading) consciousness undergoes as it progresses through the different historical forms of knowledge re-created in their determinate series by a phenomenology is seen by Rose to lead, by implication, to the concept of the absolute. It is argued that the experience of the contradictory nature of hitherto apparently valid forms of knowledge subverts the distinction between finite and infinite on which those forms – as different relations between consciousness and objects external to it – were based, and implies a notion 'which does not divide consciousess or reality into finite and infinite':[31] the absolute. As *implied*, however, the absolute is 'present but not yet known'. Only its *concept* is known. That it is present can be 'acknowledged but not stated',[32] since to state that it is present would suggest that it is present to consciousness (i.e. known), which it is not. This acknowledgement

> is not an abstract statement about the absolute, but an observation to which we have now attained, by looking at the experience of a consciousness which knows itself as an antithesis, as negative...[33]

So, the concept of the absolute is derived, by implication, phenomenologically. It arises out of Hegel's critique of Kant's epistemology. But the derivation of the concept is equivalent only to 'the attainment of the observation that the absolute is present'. We cannot yet think the absolute. How can this be done?

The absolute can *never* be 'thought' or 'known' in the ordinary sense of being a determinate object for consciousness (viz. Hegel's definition of knowledge, above), despite the title of the final chapter of the *Phenomenology*, because it is not a possible *object* of consciousness. It is not a possible object of consciousness because it is, by definition, beyond the opposition of consciousness and its objects, and 'consciousness is always this opposition between itself and its object'.[34] As 'implied' or 'alluded to', it cannot so much be 'thought' or 'known' as *experienced in a particular way*. It can be experienced negatively, or *speculatively*, as the formal unity of the multiplicity of contradictory experiences or relations by which it is implied. It is the production of such a form of experience of the absolute, which Hegel calls speculative thought, which Rose takes to be the purpose of a phenomenology.

In a phenomenology, a sequence of 'shapes of consciousness' is assembled 'in order to *see* the absolute by presenting the series of its determinations, of its misapprehensions',[35] both historically and contemporaneously. Because no one set of determinations, no one particular form of phenomenal knowledge, can grasp the absolute, philosophy is necessarily systematic. 'This idea of a whole which cannot be grasped in one moment or in one statement for it must be experienced is the idea of the system'.[36] But because the absolute is not a static totality, neither is the system through which it is presented. The essentially negative determination of the absolute means that its systematic apprehension is never-ending; it involves the continual re-cognition of phenomenal knowledge or prevailing forms of experience (which may themselves be changing) as speculative experience.[37]

As I understand it from Rose's exposition, phenomenal knowledge is re-cognized, speculatively, by the observing (reading) consciousness of a phenomenology in the following way. The presentation of forms of natural consciousness (that is, of forms of consciousness 'natural' to particular historical periods) as forms of phenomenal knowledge (that is, as part of determinate cultural configurations) leads the observing consciousness to see their series as necessary, and to see them as determined. The experience this consciousness undergoes is speculative; it is the experience of 'the transgression of the limit between the positive and its condition';[38] because the recognition of determination it involves explodes the distinction between the finite and the infinite which grounds the purely contemplative attitude of ordinary thought, which conceives of its objects as external to it.[39] It thus involves the concept of the absolute (as the unity of the conditions and the conditioned), in relation to which the prevailing form of phenomenal knowledge is revealed to be inadequate to its object (which is now conceived in its unity with, rather than as external to, consciousness).

So, speculative thought is the rethinking of phenomenal knowledge from the point of view of the absolute, the rethinking of phenomenal knowledge as inadequate knowledge of the absolute. As such it is a form of thought which acknowledges a lack of identity between the subject and predicate of propositions that represent phenomenal knowledge. Propositions, ordinarily construed, are taken to posit a false identity between the concepts with which they operate and the objects these concepts are used to represent, in so far as the logic of propositional grammar dictates that subject and predicate are conceived as independent prior to predication, and related by predication. From the perspective of the absolute, on the other hand, subject and predicate are determinations which 'acquire their meaning in a *series* of relations to each other',[40] and which are consequently not independent of each other, but in some way mutually constitutive. This leads to the idea of speculative (re)reading; the reading of propositions as *speculative* identities. In such 'speculative propositions',

> The subject of the proposition is no longer fixed and abstract with external, contingent accidents, but, initially, an empty name, uncertain and problematic, gradually acquiring meaning as the result of a series of contradictory experiences.[41]

Rose's interpretation of Hegel's system is thus that it is constituted by the phenomenological representation and speculative rereading of phenomenal knowledge, and gives rise to 'knowledge' of the absolute through the speculative *experiences* which it provokes. And these experiences are 'critical'. For example, in terms of moral and political consciousness, its speculative apprehension involves experience of the fact that ethical life (*Sittlichkeit*, a term used by Hegel to designate the unity of the spheres of morality and legality, the practical realm) is misrepresented by the prevailing cultural forms through which it is experienced and reproduced.

Although it is an essentially negative mode of cognition, which reveals the 'untruth' of phenomenal knowledge in all of its forms, speculative experience is positive in three ways: (i) purely formally, in so far as it involves determinate negation;[42] (ii) to the extent that it reveals the determination of the misapprehension which it uncovers (as we shall see, this is problematic); and (iii) in so far as the revelation of misapprehension contains, implicitly, the demand for a change in that which determines that misapprehension. I will examine the second and third of these 'positive' aspects of speculative experience, and the relation between them, in a moment, for this is the issue on which the way in which Rose's form of Hegelianism can contribute to the development of a critical Marxism rests. But first, I will quickly complete my account of Rose's position.

To sum up: according to Rose, the *Phenomenology of Spirit*, and any phenomenology for that matter,

> is not a teleological development towards the reconciliation of all oppositions between consciousness and its objects, to the abolition of natural consciousness as such, but a speculative presentation of the deformations of natural consciousness;[43]

> [it is] not the experience of consciousness recapturing its alienated existence, but the presentation of the formation of consciousness as a determination of substance, and (or rather *through*) consciousness' misapprehension of that determination;[44]

> ... not a success, but a *gamble*. For the perpetual occurrence of inversion and misrepresentation can only be undermined, or 'brought into fluidity', by *allusion* to the law of their determination...[45]

This open-ended interpretation of Hegelian phenomenology, and its culmination in speculative experience of the absolute, which Rose develops primarily through an examination of Hegel's Jena works, laying particular emphasis on the *System of Ethical Life* of 1802 as the first phenomenology,[46] is used to produce critical reading of most of Hegel's mature works.

The *Philosophy of Right* and the *Logic* are read as phenomenologies, as representative of the 'standpoint of consciousness'. (Accordingly, one might say that the *Logic* ends the *Phenomenology* rather than that the *Phenomenology* introduces the *Logic*. Whereas the former is a phenomenology of natural consciousness, the latter is taken to be a phenomenology of abstract, philosophical consciousness – a form of consciousness derived, historically, in the *Phenomenology*.) The *Aesthetics* is read as a 'philosophy', as representative of the standpoint of the absolute, of the collectivity. This is possible because the phenomenon it presents – art – is taken by Hegel to be historically transcended, to be 'no longer a formative, educative, political experience'.[47] The lectures on the philosophies of religion and history are read as methodologically mixed texts:

> In both lecture series there is no sustained phenomenology. Instead the 'standpoint of the absolute' is abstractly and repeatedly stated and contrasted with the standpoint of religious relation, difference, representation or consciousness. The two texts reveal the *aporia* of subjectivity: the subjective standpoint is criticised by means of the exposition of its formation; but the absolute is thought as subject.[48]

Significantly, there is no discussion of the *Encyclopaedia*.

It is a feature of Rose's interpretation that Hegel's phenomenologies are taken to involve 'speculative rereadings' of the propositions of phenomenal knowledge. Paradigmatically, these are the propositions of Kant and Fichte's philosophy, which is taken by Hegel to be the philosophical articulation of the prevailing forms of knowledge and experience, determined by the bourgeois property form. So 'speculative rereading' is a Hegelian or 'philosophical' equivalent to Marxian critique (in the sense of the critique of political economy – we can see here how Rose's reading of Hegel reformulates the philosophical foundations of Critical Theory). It is at once a demonstration of the inadequacy of a particular theoretical perspective to a particular object, and a 'critique' of the form of social relations which 'correspond' to that perspective in so far as they determine it. However, as we noted at the start of this article, Rose's claim for Hegelian phenomenology is much stronger than this. It is that it is the only philosophically adequate form of theory capable of critically conceptualizing subjectivity and culture. It is to this claim that I now want to turn.

Hegelian phenomenology and Marxism: the critique of society

There is an ambivalence in Rose's attitude to Marxism and to the question of the relationship between Hegelian phenomenology and Marxism, which reflects a crucial and unresolved ambiguity in her conception of phenomenology. This ambiguity is the result of a failure to resolve the tension within her account of Hegel's thought between its philosophical and sociopolitical aspects; the tension between its function as critique of reason and its function as critique of society. This, in turn, is a consequence of a failure to acknowledge the extremely limited sense in which a phenomenology can be socially critical, which is an effect of overestimating the cognitive value of speculative experience. Perhaps the strangest thing about *Hegel Contra Sociology* is that, while it gives probably the clearest account in English of the precise character of Hegelian speculation, it fails to grasp the significance of the limitations it so expertly delineates. As I suggested earlier, this is because it remains within the problematic of modern epistemology.

The ambiguity in Rose's conception of phenomenology (essentially an ambiguity in her conception of the sense in which it can lead to knowledge of the social determination of consciousness) is displayed in the statement that in phenomenologies

> the illusions and experiences of moral and political consciousness are presented in an order designed to show how consciousness may progress through them to *comprehension of the determination of ethical life*.[49]

On the basis of this claim it is further claimed that phenomenology is not only 'a presentation of political experience', but itself 'the definitive political experience'.⁵⁰ Marxism seems, very definitely, to have been *replaced*. But does speculative experience of the absolute really involve comprehension of the determination of ethical life? I think not. It involves only comprehension (in the politically crucial form of 'experience', it is true) of the fact that ethical life is determined. And this is a very different thing. A theory of this determination is still required. Only by exploiting this ambiguity in the phrase 'comprehension of the determination of ethical life' is Rose able to make such a strong case for Hegel.

This brings us back to the second and third 'positive' aspects of speculative experience noted above, to the question of the relation between the kind of determination revealed in speculative experience and possibility of real social change. For it is Rose's belief that a phenomenological social theory ('the exposition of capitalism as culture') is 'the only way to link the analysis of the economy to comprehension of the conditions for revolutionary practice'.⁵¹ Such a theory is labelled 'critical Marxism' because the 'analysis of the economy' involved is to be Marx's. There are two problems here: (i) the reduction of Marxism to 'the analysis of the economy', and (ii) the incorporation of any form of *analysis*, of *theory*, within a phenomenological 'presentation'. I will argue that an examination of the nature of speculative experience and its theoretical conditions reveals a fundamental incompatibility (though not inconsistency) between Hegelian phenomenology and Marxian critique. And that, consequently, phenomenology is incapable of fulfilling the theoretical expectations which Rose has of it. But, first, let us see how phenomenology is socially critical, in its own right.

Rose takes speculative experience to be 'critical' not just epistemologically, in its independence from presuppositions, but also, and *consequently* (and this is the problem), politically, in its orientation towards other philosophies and to society. It is critical in this latter, dual, sense because it involves the recognition of a form of mediation between consciousness and its objects which is not acknowledged either by other philosophies or by the existing forms of law and property relations to which these philosophies correspond. This recognition is taken to subvert both the validity of these philosophies and the legitimacy of the forms of social relation which condition them and sustain their credibility. Now, as we noted above, such negative criticism has a positive function, and it is here that a new problem arises which demonstrates quite clearly how limited is a social critique grounded in epistemology.

One of the positive functions of speculative experience is

> to make a different form of ethical life possible by providing insight into the displacement of actuality in those dominant philosophies which are assimilated to and reinforce bourgeois law and property relations.[52]

The problem is: (i) that this insight can contribute to the development of a new form of ethical life only in a minimal sense, and (ii) that merely to conceive of the possibility of a new form of ethical life is, on Hegel's terms, epistemologically unjustifiable. The contradiction within Hegel's project registered here takes us to the heart of Rose's understanding, and defence, of Hegel's concept of speculation.

The reason it is unjustifiable even to conceive of an alternative form of ethical life is that to remain critical epistemologically, consciousness must posit no form of relation between itself and its objects which does not arise 'naturally' out of its self-reflection upon the objects present to it in phenomenal knowledge. And, as we noted above,[53] Rose's 'materialist' appropriation of Hegel denies that the dialectic of consciousness is spontaneously self-generating, understanding it instead as the source of speculative experience. (Despite her description of Hegelian philosophy as 'the definitive political experience', in fact in contradiction to it Rose acknowledges the political impotence of philosophy when she says that the 'possibility of becoming ethical' depends on neither the recognition of determination, nor on any moral decision, but on a 'transformation of intuition'.[54]

The determination of which is, of course, by definition, beyond the individual consciousness.) So 'absolute ethical life' (the social ideal) is an 'unstatable' alternative.[55] What is more, even in this empty, abstract form it is unjustifiable.

Simply by virtue of being an alternative, Rose argues, however unspecifiable, the concept of the absolute 'contains an abstract imperative', a moment of *Sollen* ('ought'),[56] despite itself, despite its purely negative derivation. For once it has been derived it cannot but present itself to consciousness as an alternative. Ironically, it is precisely the need to avoid the 'abstractness' of a 'positive' alternative (one which is 'posited' by consciousness, and unrelated to the existing state of things) which leads Hegel to defend an unspecifiable alternative that is ultimately equally 'abstract' in so far as it too presents itself to consciousness as an 'ought' despite its phenomenological derivation.

But rather than rejecting the standpoint of consciousness as a starting point because of this contradiction, Rose acknowledges it and accommodates it within her exposition. It is here that the originality of her interpretation lies. Rejecting both 'right-' and 'left-wing' Hegelianism as attempts to resolve the contradiction by unjustifiably adopting one of its sides and neglecting the other, she embraces the contradiction as definitively characteristic of Hegel's thought, calling it 'the paradox of Hegel's philosophy of philosophy',[57] and taking it to show that an element of *Sollen*, of 'ought', of epistemologically unjustifiable striving for an alternative state of affairs, *must* be present in philosophy, and that this is quite consistent with Hegel's critique of Kant. This element of *Sollen* is taken to appear as a subjective limitation on speculative experience.

The argument is that once it has been acknowledged that the absolute cannot be thought (cannot become present to consciousness) through its objects[58] while the dichotomies that its concept transcends remain a feature of the world which our consciousnesses inhabit, 'we can think the absolute by acknowledging the element of *Sollen* in such a thinking',[59] speculatively.

This restatement of the idea of speculative experience from the point of view of its practical aspect reveals the unity of theoretical and practical reason in the unity of the epistemological and practical *limitations* from which speculative experience suffers. Such experience is presumably only subjectively limited in the sense that its objectively determined limitations appear as limitations *of* the subject.

So, 'thinking the absolute' speculatively is something of a pyrrhic victory, both sociologically and practically. For while the acknowledgement and explanation of an unjustifiable element of *Sollen* in speculative experience reasserts its theoretical consistency, it also serves to emphasize both its theoretical and practical impotence.[60] This is particularly clear from a comparison of Rose's description of Hegel's idea of the vocation of philosophy with her understanding of his philosophy.

Philosophy, we are told, has the vocation 'to present a notion of law to our abstract consciousness which will re-form ethical life without being re-formed by it'.[61] It 'urges *us* to transform ethical life by re-cognizing the law of its determination'.[62] This re-cognition, it is argued, 'commends a different way of transforming [it]'[63] from that of the arbitrary and tyrannical imposition of a new form without regard to determinations of the existing form – a mode of transformation paradigmatically represented by the Terror of the French Revolution, and taken to be theoretically articulated in the categorical imperatives of Kant's and Fichte's practical philosophies. But philosophy cannot specify *concretely* what this new mode of transformation is. And so, I would argue, it cannot bring about such a transformation. A '*notion* of law' will not transform anything.

Rose describes Hegel's new mode of transformation as 'transforming the specific determination in relation to the totality of its real possibilities'.[64] No further specification is possible, because of the law of the determination of ethical life whose formal recognition is seen to lead to recognition of the necessity of such transformation, the specific form of which would determine the mode of transformation, is, *by definition,* unknowable in any ordinary sense of the word 'know'. It can only be known as the negation of all forms of determination which presuppose the independence of condition from conditioned. Hegel thus 'commends' an 'unstatable' alternative, and 'urges' us to seek it through the transformation of determinations which are 'unspecifiable'! This is where Marxism comes in.

The attempted incorporation of Marxist theory within Hegelian phenomenology which Rose undertakes is necessitated by the fact that, despite indications to the contrary, Hegelian phenomenology is incapable of generating knowledge of the concrete determinations that give rise to the correlation between forms of consciousness and forms of social relations which it presents, and by the fact that such knowledge is necessary if speculative experience of the deformations of natural consciousness is to lead to a transformative practice based on (rather than simply against) objective social determinations. But there is a fundamental contradiction here. For the absence from Hegelian phenomenology of a *theory* of objective social determination is no accident. It is a consequence of a particular epistemological argument, the one from which the phenomenological form is itself derived.

This argument maintains that to avoid the ambiguity, and practical impotence, of quasi-transcendentally established, Kantian, metacritical theories of the social determination of consciousness, the standpoint of consciousness must be criticized *immanently.* In a phenomenology the critique of the standpoint of consciousness is achieved, exclusively, through its adoption; through its 'presentation' in a form designed to reveal its limitation. Such an adoption of the standpoint of consciousness is theoretically incompatible with any social *theory.* It involves the *presentation* of social forms (forms of social relation) in a form designated to provoke the reading consciousness into experiencing their determination of the forms of consciousness to which they correspond and along with which they have been 'presented'. It does not involve a social theory. 'Theory' is precisely what it rejects.

Rose's ambivalence towards Marxism centres on this problem of the status of theory, and of the theoretical status of Marxism. It is the result of her strident critique of the philosophical foundations of Marxism, as they are presented in Marx's early writings. Her argument is that because of the inadequacy of his conceptualization of the theory–practice relation, Marx 'misunderstood the relation between his own (later) discourse and the possibility of a transformed politics';[65] that he misunderstood the *meaning* of his own discourse. She does not object to the analysis in *Capital*, but to 'any presentation of that analysis as a comprehensive account of *capitalism*, ... any pre-judged, imposed "realisation" of that theory, any using it *as a theory, as Marxism*'.[66]

Now, it seems to me that what we have here is a straightforward confusion, and false identification, of the realms of theory and practice, in the idea of 'theory' which is presented. The idea of Marxism in the above quotation quite unjustifiably, and almost incomprehensibly, identifies the theorization of an object, as opposed to its 'presentation', with the 'pre-judged, imposed realisation' of some theory of how that object *ought* to be. No allowance is made for mediations between social theory and politics. And it is *assumed* that the theoretical structure of *Capital* is such that it takes social reality to be an 'object' and ignores the subjective aspect of its reproduction.

Rose's problem is that she has no other conception of theory. Marx is placed within the Kantian problematic on the basis of a cursory reading of a few early texts, in which his philosophical position is neither fully developed nor discussed at any length.[67] But this negligent treatment of Marx (compare it to the care lavished on the details of Hegel's most obscure works!) is not contingent. For Rose's maintenance of the subject–object problematic of modern epistemology, while it allows her to conceptualize the mediation of the objective within the subjective (phenomenologically), rules out the *possibility* of a theoretical mode in which the subjective is mediated within the objective, and *this* is the only possible form of a materialist theory of subjectivity, culture and politics, which aims to go beyond the mere recognition of the 'deformation' of existing forms of phenomenal knowledge to theorize their real determinations and possible modes of transformation. The Hegelian approach which Rose adopts excludes the possibility of an understanding of Marx.

Conclusion: the end of philosophy?

If *Capital* is not 'a comprehensive account of capitalism', or at least the beginnings of, and basis for, such an account, what is it? And how can it be of use to a theory which aims to present the contradictions between capital and culture, to expose capitalism as a culture? I do not think that there are answers to these questions which do not involve the abuse of basic hermeneutic standards in the reading of *Capital*. But where does this leave Hegel and Hegelian phenomenology?

The short answer to this question is 'outside Marxism'. Rose's critical Marxism' is incoherent. But her idea of Hegelian phenomenology is not. It is merely limited. It represents the end point of modern philosophy; a point at which the self-critique of epistemology has reached its limit, and from which it can progress no further, condemned to eternal repetition, the never-ending production of a speculative experience of society which remains trapped within the confines of the perspective it knows to be false.[68] For through her critical reading of Hegel, Rose has arrived at just that point at which Adorno, whose path was more tortuous, came to rest: recognition of the fact that the essential negativity of the dialectic of consciousness means that it can have no resting place, can secure no 'true' knowledge.[69]

But while the reiteration of such a position may clear our philosophical consciences, and represents a timely reminder of the fallacy of epistemological absolutism, it remains impotent in the face of contemporary reality.

Notes

An earlier version of this article was read to the Philosophy Society at Cambridgeshire College of Arts and Technology in February 1982. I would like to thank those present on that occasion, and Chris Arthur, for their comments on the draft.

1. Athlone Press, London, 1981. The strangeness of this phrase when taken outside of its strictly pedagogical context is particularly appropriate here, since it locates Rose's project most precisely while at the same time questioning its coherence. (For while historical materialists may be friends of the dialectic – practitioners, hopefully – are they 'friends' of the *idealist* dialectic?) The phrase at once asserts and subverts the idea of materialism. It raises the problem of subjectivity. By reconstructing the idealist dialectic as a dialectic of consciousness in the interests of materialism, Rose too raises the problem of subjectivity. However, as I hope to show below, by accepting the construction of such a dialectic *exclusively from the standpoint of consciousness*, despite the fact that material determinations are acknowledged, the phenomenological dialectic that Rose sanctions is incapable of solving this problem which it so acutely poses.

   One of the implications which can be drawn from such an understanding of Rose's text is that while the phrase 'materialist friends of the idealist dialectic' registers a central philosophical problem of materialism – the problem of subjectivity – it does so in terms of categories which give rise to it, but through which it cannot be solved. In this sense, Joe McCarney is right to use the phrase to define a particular theoretical task, but wrong to suggest that it can be used to define a problematic. The construction of a problematic within which the problem of which it is an index can be coherently posed is the task! I would therefore suggest that *RP* becomes not 'the house ;ournal of "the materialist friends of the idealist dialectic"', but the house journal of those concerned to deconstruct *and then reconstruct* the enigma of which that phrase is the mark. (Cf. J. McCarney's correspondence, *Radical Philosophy* 30, Spring 1982, pp. 51–2.)
2. *HCS*, p. 1.
3. *HCS*, p. 220.
4. *HCS*, pp. 214–20.
5. Cf. J. Habermas, *Knowledge and Human Interests*, 2nd edn, H.E.B., London, 1978, Part One, 'The Crisis of the Critique of Knowledge', pp. 1–63.
6. Ibid., p. vii.
7. Rose does not discuss Kortian's book, though she does refer to it in a footnote as 'an excellent discussion of Habermas' (*HCS*, p. 228 n181). Elsewhere it has been described as 'too static and one-sided' because of its attempt to 'thoroughly Hegelianise Habermas' (D. Kellner and R. Roderick, 'Recent Literature on Critical Theory', *New German Critique* 23, pp. 141–70; p. 165). But it is for just this reason that it is useful here. It highlights the originality of Rose's reading of Hegel and demonstrates its effect on the philosophical foundations of Critical Theory.
8. G. Kortian, *Metacritique*, Cambridge University Press, Cambridge 1980, p. 29.
9. Ibid., p. 32.
10. Cf. *HCS*, ch. 1, pp. 1–47.
11. Cf. M. Horkheimer, 'Traditional and Critical Theory', in *Critical Theory: Selected Essays*, trans. M.J. O'Connel, New York, 1972, pp. 188–243.
12. Kortian, *Metacritique*, pp. 29–30.
13. 'Metacritique is true critique, or rather, it is what critique becomes when it is made radical'. Ibid., p. 29.
14. *HCS*, p. 14.
15. *HCS*, p. 185.
16. Kortian, *Metacritique*, p. 30.
17. G.W.F. Hegel, *Phenomenology of Spirit*, trans. A.V. Hiller, Clarendon Press, Oxford, 1979, p. 47.
18. Kortian expresses this distinction very clearly when he says: 'It is precisely by virtue of what is articulated through speculative experience that the discourse of the speculative proposition is to be distinguished from theoretical enterprises which are content to bring together different positive fields, and to pass from one to another by a transference *(metaphopa)* which produces a synthesis in the metaphor and not in the concept.' Kortian, *Metacritique*, p. 28.
19. *HCS*, pp. 27–33.
20. *HCS*, p. 37.
21. Hegel, *Phenomenology of Spirit*, p. 47.
22. *HCS*, p. 44.
23. *HCS*, p. 42.

24. *HCS*, p. 42.
25. *HCS*, p. 47
26. For an account of the expositional, rather than strictly deductive, structure of transcendental arguments, cf. S. Körner, 'On the Impossibility of Transcendental Deductions', *Monist* 51, 1967.
27. *HCS*, pp. 45–6.
28. *HCS*, p. 46.
29. Hegel, *Phenomenology of Spirit*, p. 52.
30. Ibid., p. 54.
31. *HCS*, p. 46.
32. *HCS*, p. 158.
33. *HCS*, p. 181.
34. *HCS*, p. 153.
35. *HCS*, p. 181.
36. *HCS*, p. 182.
37. 'Absolute knowledge is a path which must be continually traversed.' *HCS*, p. 182.
38. The phrase is Kortian's. *Metacritique*, p. 28.
39. Rose's claim is that 'to see the determination in the act is to see beyond the dichotomy between act and non-act'. *HCS*, p. 205. The claim is crucial, for it is the experience of 'seeing the determination in the act', which it is claimed that only a phenomenology can give rise to, that is the basis of Rose's idea of political (educative) experience, which in turn is the basis of her critique of Marxism.
40. *HCS* p. 49.
41. *HCS*, p. 49. This 'Hegelian' semantics hardly seems as original as Rose appears to suggest.
42. By referring to the 'purely formal' positive aspect of determinate negation, I mean that it is positive in so far as it offers the limited truth about an object, that it is *not* some particular thing. I do not mean to imply that I agree with Hegel that a new form *immediately* arises, i.e. that the dialectic of consciousness is spontaneously self-generating (cf. Hegel, *Phenomenology of Spirit*, p. 51). Nor is Rose committed to this position. By construing spirit as a 'structure of recognition' rather than a metaphysical entity, she is absolved from the sin of making the Idea the subject of history. However, as we shall see, this undermines her claim for the political significance of phenomenology.
43. *HCS*, p. 150.
44. *HCS*, p. 152, parentheses added.
45. *HCS*, p. 159, first emphasis added.
46. *HCS*, pp. 59–73.
47. *HCS*, p. 121.
48. *HCS*, p. 106. It is not clear to me how Rose can account for those texts which 'think the absolute as subject' or 'adopt the standpoint of the collectivity' since they transgress the 'critical' rule of relentless negativity. It is for this reason that it only seems possible to understand her reading of Hegel as 'revisionist', for it seems to invalidate a number of his mature texts. Not that this is a bad thing, of course; to attempt to render all of Hegel's texts consistent with each other, and to defend them, would be a bizarrely ahistorical, and futile, enterprise.
49. *HCS*, p. 50, emphasis added.
50. *HCS*, p. 209.
51. *HCS*, p. 220.
52. *HCS*, p. 208. Indeed, Rose describes this as 'the overall intention of Hegel's thought'.
53. See note 42 above.
54. *HCS*, p. 65.
55. *HCS*, p. 202.
56. *HCS*, p. 78, parentheses added.
57. *HCS*, p. 78. .
58. While the absolute cannot ever be an object of consciousness, it is suggested that it could be 'known', 'naturally' in a society that was socially transparent in so far as each 'object' of consciousness, each piece of phenomenal knowledge, would contain and display its mediation of every other aspect of phenomenal knowledge, thereby giving the absolute in full, in a certain sense. This is the (purely formal) idea of absolute ethical life.
59. *HCS*, p. 204.
60. The, at least formal, theoretical consistency of Rose's position has not been grasped by other reviewers, who have accused her of falling back upon a left-Hegelian reading, and have then noted the inconsistency between such a position and other claims made for her reading. Such readings of Rose's text fail to get to grips with its central point, because they underestimate its subtlety. Berki, for example, thinking that he is arguing against Rose, concludes his review with the statement that Hegel 'emanates only "restlessness" but no direction', inferring from this 'he is not "contra sociology"'. But the whole point of Rose's reading is to show the compatibility of Hegel's 'restlessness' with his contrariness to sociology, and thereby to specify *precisely* the way in which Hegel's

thought is restless. Berki ignores rather than refutes Rose.

This kind of misunderstanding is compounded by Rose's use of the expression 'speculative thought', and her, at times unqualified, insistence that such 'thought' is thought *of* the absolute. It is most clearly revealed in the 'Yes, I did', 'No, you didn't' character of the exchange between Rose and Hawthorn on the question of whether Rose actually shows the absolute to be thinkable. As I argue here, Rose seems not to fully grasp the significance of her own position. (Cf. R.N. Berki, 'Thinking the Absolute', *TLS*, 23 October 1981, p. 1242; G.Hawthorn, *London Review of Books*, vol. 3, no. 21, and the exchange of letters between Rose and Hawthorn, *LRB*, vol. 3, no. 24.

61. *HCS*, p. 184.
62. *HCS*, p. 187.
63. *HCS*, p. 201, parentheses added.
64. *HCS*, p. 191.
65. *HCS*, p. 219.
66. *HCS*, p. 219.
67. The section on Marx, 'The Culture and Fate of Marxism', is only six pages in length. Apart from a reference to the *Grundrisse* to support the misleading claim that 'Marx saw the appeal of art as eternal and ahistorical' *(HCS*, p. 216), the latest text referred to is the 'Theses on Feuerbach', which is treated, quite unjustifiably, as if it were a definitive statement of Marx's philosophical position. In general, the issue of the 'philosophical' status of Marxism is treated as if it were quite unproblematic. (For a detailed, and brilliant, reading of Marx's texts up to 1848, which addresses the dual question of the meaning of philosophy for Marxism, and its fate within Marxism, see G. Labica, *Marxism and the Status of Philosophy*, trans. K. Soper and M. Ryle, Harvester Press, Brighton, 1980. Labica's insistence on *reading* Marx, in the fullest sense of that term, produces an account of his early writings which emphasizes the fact, and complexity, of the conceptual development they embody. Rose, on the other hand, both treats these texts as homogeneous and considers that they represent the philosophical framework in relation to which the later, 'economic' works acquire their meaning.)
68. Cf. *HCS*, p. 182: 'Absolute knowledge is a path which must be continually traversed.'
69. Cf. T. Adorno, *Negative Dialectics*, trans. E.B. Ashton, Routledge & Kegan Paul, London, 1973. Rose's own account of Adorno's thought *(The Melancholy Science*, Macmillan, Basingstoke 1978) provides an interesting point for a comparison of Adorno with Rose's Hegel.

3 The vertigo of philosophy: Deleuze and the problem of immanence

CHRISTIAN KERSLAKE

One of the few terminological constants in Deleuze's philosophical work is the word 'immanence', and it has therefore become a foothold for those wishing to understand exactly what 'Deleuzean philosophy' is. That this ancient and well-travelled notion is held to have been given new life and meaning by a Deleuzean approach is evidenced in much recent secondary literature on Deleuze, and, significantly, in one central theoretical section of Hardt and Negri's *Empire*, which takes up the theme of 'the plane of immanence'.[1] Yet on closer inspection it becomes clear that what is at stake in Deleuze's contribution to the history of this term is actually quite elusive. I will claim here that 'immanence', despite appearing to connote philosophical transparency, is in fact a *problem* for Deleuze; indeed perhaps it is *the* problem inspiring his work. Not for nothing does Deleuze suggest that 'immanence is the very vertigo of philosophy'.[2]

Can a preliminary definition of immanence be given at the outset? I would suggest that two features – one formal, the other ontological – are pre-eminent. Formally, a philosophy of immanence is a philosophy that does not appeal to anything outside the terms and relations constructed and accounted for by that philosophy. Ontologically, we might say that in a philosophy of immanence, *thought* is shown to be fully expressive of *being*; there is no moment of 'transcendence' of being to thought.[3] Such general criteria, however, could be said of a multitude of philosophies from early Greek cosmology onwards. By which criteria, then, could a philosophy be said to be 'more' immanent than another?

Hardt and Negri, by focusing explicitly on what they take to be an exhaustive opposition between immanence and transcendence, claim that there is something specifically modern about the notion of immanence. 'The primary event of modernity', they say, is 'the affirmation of the powers of *this* world, the discovery of the plane of immanence.'[4] For them, the characteristic of *this*-worldliness appears to sanction the step of equating immanence with materialism. Modernity achieves its apogee in the powers of affirmation liberated by Spinozism, rather than in the deepening of the powers of reflexivity and self-consciousness liberated by Kantianism. Indeed, they complain that the 'relativity of experience' introduced by Kant 'abolishes every instance of the immediate and absolute in human life and history. Why, however, is this relativity necessary? Why cannot knowledge and will be allowed to claim themselves to be absolute?'[5]

These words will seem strange to those coming from the Kantian tradition. Whilst the complaint is reminiscent of Hegel, the word 'immediate' suggests otherwise. Rather than raising the Kantian stakes as Hegel does, Hardt and Negri seem to retreat from them altogether. But, the post-Kantian might say, isn't it with Kant that the claim to immanence is first truly justified? The purpose of the Kantian critique is surely to ask *how* immanence is to be achieved, to ask how it is possible, and to secure it by right against the transgressions of theology and metaphysics. The ancient metaphysical idea of immanence must yield to the project of immanent critique. Hardt and Negri seem to suggest that immanence is something that can be *immediately* affirmed, without any prior investigation into its possibility. Things become odder still for the post-Kantian philosopher when Hardt and Negri suggest that although 'Hegel restores the horizon of immanence ... [this] is really a blind immanence', in which all activity is subordinated to a divine teleological order.[6] Again, it is easy to see how from a Hegelian perspective it is Hardt and Negri's notion of immanence that is blind, in that they are not concerned with the critical questions of the *justification* of structures of knowledge and action that occupy Hegel in the *Phenomenology* and serve to secure the Hegelian *right* to absolute immanence.

In this article I will claim that Deleuze's views on immanence are far removed from those espoused by Hardt and Negri, and in fact are much closer to the Kantian tradition than is generally suspected. I will also call into question Deleuze's apparent Spinozism regarding the question of immanence. Deleuze does hold that thought can immanently express being, but nevertheless he crucially holds to the Kantian distinction between thought and experience. This is also the key to situating Deleuze between Kant and Hegel: for Deleuze, to claim that the absolute is open to *thought* does not, as it does for Hegel, imply that it is open to *experience*.[7]

This said, I will also suggest that if the word 'immanence' appears continuously throughout Deleuze's work, this is not because it is a sign of a continuity of philosophical position, but because it designates the site of an enduring problem. When Deleuze finally comes explicitly to elaborate the notion of immanence in his late works, it has undergone radical change. This article will take an eccentric path because it attempts to reconstruct and defend Deleuze's early approach to immanence, as opposed to his final views. Despite the absence of explicit discussion of 'immanence' in his magnum opus *Difference and Repetition*, I claim that it is there that we find Deleuze's most defensible formulation of a new philosophy of immanence.[8]

Deleuze, Hyppolite and Hegel
In 1955 Deleuze wrote a review of his teacher Jean Hyppolite's book *Logic and Existence* in which he both makes clear how much he accepts of Hyppolite's reading of Hegel and provides the only published plan, to my knowledge, in which he lays out the aims of his future philosophical project.[9] Deleuze begins by

saying that Hyppolite's main theme is that 'Philosophy must be ontology, it cannot be anything else; but there is no ontology of essence, there is only an ontology of sense.'[10] He adds 'that philosophy must be ontology means first of all that it is not anthropology'. Let us first unfold Hyppolite's interpretation of this notion of sense.

The use of the word 'sense' (*Sinn*) does not seem especially central in Hegel's own work, but Hyppolite makes clear that he is identifying it with the more familiar 'notion', or 'concept' (*Begriff*). Why does he do this? While there is undoubtedly a Husserlian inspiration at work, this move also draws out the sense in which the concept in Hegel is a philosophical reality; it *expresses* reality. Hyppolite cites Hegel's *Lectures on Aesthetics*:

> Sense is this wonderful word which is used in two opposite meanings. On the one hand it means the organ of immediate apprehension, but on the other hand we mean by it the sense, the significance, the thought, the universal underlying the thing. And so sense is connected on the one hand with the immediate external aspect of existence, and on the other hand with its inner essence.[11]

For Hegel these two opposite meanings signify a common source; they signify that the universal will be generated in the sensible; that the universal concept and the singular intuition are two aspects of the self-differentiation of the absolute. The intelligible articulation of the structure of self-differentiation is what Hyppolite will call sense, while the movement itself can be called expression.[12] For Hegel, the problem with Kant's critique is that the concept remains too *external* to the thing itself: 'the categories are no fit terms to *express* the Absolute'.[13] Moreover, the concept as such is never merely possible in Hegel. A Kantian possible concept (e.g. of '100 thalers') is for Hegel not really a concept, but merely 'a content-determination of my consciousness';[14] that is, it is *merely* a representation. A concept, rather, is ultimately and intrinsically neither representational nor referential, but expressive of a reality. This couple sense/expression will be taken up by Deleuze. Both Hegel and Deleuze are against philosophies of representation because such philosophies claim to express what should be genuinely universal within a framework that remains *relative* to subjective representational experience (i.e. which has only been justified anthropologically), so that the concept of expression doesn't ever gain its full extension, and *thought* is denied its rightful access to *being*.[15] The notion of the thing-in-itself is symptomatic of Kant's contradictory position: he forbids himself to say anything determinate about it, yet insists that it has essential content for thought. Kant therefore is only partially aware of the transition to which he is midwife: 'from the being of logic to the logicity of being'.[16] For Hegel, there will ultimately be nothing outside the concept: absolute idealism will transparently and immanently express every aspect of being. It is for this reason that Hyppolite says that 'immanence is complete' in Hegel.[17]

Now, Hyppolite also gives primacy to the notion of sense because he wants to lay priority on the special character of the *Logic* in Hegel's system. For Hyppolite, the *Logic* is the expression of being itself; it is the high point of Hegel's system in which 'the concept, such as it appears in dialectical discourse, is [unlike in the *Phenomenology*] simultaneously truth and certainty, being and sense; it is immanent to this being which says itself.'[18] Hegel's logic is a logic of sense, in which the sense of being itself is said through the genesis of concepts produced by the philosopher.[19] Attempting to avoid the anthropomorphic view of Hegel promoted by Kojève, Hyppolite tries to restore the high metaphysical status of the Hegelian system. Hence, like Deleuze, his anti-humanism is an echo of the claims of classical philosophy. In an important passage for Deleuze, Hyppolite says that

> Hegel is still too Spinozistic for us to be able to speak of a pure humanism; a pure humanism culminates only in sceptical irony and platitude. Undoubtedly, the Logos appears in the human knowledge that interprets and says itself, but here man is only the intersection of this knowledge and this sense. Man is consciousness and self-consciousness, while at the same time natural Dasein, but consciousness and self-consciousness are not man. They say being

as sense in man. They are the very being that knows itself and says itself.[20]

The implication of Hyppolite's reading here is that the phenomenological and historical parts of Hegel's system are anthropological entries into the system. Hyppolite is influenced by Heidegger's 'Letter on Humanism': man is the 'place', the structural possibility that Being can reveal itself as such, and express its sense *through* 'man'. After man has been broken down and introduced into the absolute by the *Phenomenology*, the *Logic*, absolved of humanism, retraces the ideal genesis of the sense of being. This would be the meaning of Hegel's statement that the content of the *Science of Logic* 'is the exposition of God as he is in his eternal essence prior to the creation of nature and a finite mind'.[21]

In his review of Hyppolite, Deleuze affirms fully this reading of Hegel. Two passages are of particular importance. The first places Deleuze's development of the notion of difference explicitly within the context of Hegelian self-differentiation:

> [T]he external, empirical difference of thought and being [in the Kantian system] has given way [in Hegel] to the difference identical with Being, to the difference internal to the Being which thinks itself. ... In the *Logic*, there is no longer, therefore, as in the empirical, what I say on the one side and on the other side the sense of what I say – the pursuit of one by the other which is the dialectic of the *Phenomenology*. On the contrary, my discourse is logical or properly philosophical when I say the sense of what I say, and when in this manner Being says itself.[22]

Deleuze will never leave behind this image of a 'properly philosophical' discourse. That is, his philosophy will be a philosophy of the absolute; it will accept the move from the perspective of the limitations of knowledge in Kant to the claim that dialectical thought can express the absolute and in turn ground knowledge. Deleuze shares none of the reservations about Hegelian immanence that are exhibited by his fellow postwar French philosophers. He has no bad conscience about the notion of immanence and he does not construct a philosophy of difference in order to *subvert* immanence (and introduce some notion of 'irreducible otherness' into it), but rather in order to *fulfil* it – precisely as Hegel does. Our problem will be to explain how and why Deleuze returns to elements in *Kant* to carry out this aim. Deleuze concludes his review with some pregnant questions for Hyppolite after summarizing the mains claims of the book:

> Following Hyppolite, we recognize that philosophy, if it has a meaning, can only be an ontology and an ontology of sense. The same being and the same thought are in the empirical and the absolute. But the difference between thought and being is sublated in the absolute by the positing of the Being identical to difference which, as such, thinks itself and reflects itself in man. This absolute identity of being and difference is called sense. ... The richness of Hyppolite's book could then let us wonder this: can we not construct an ontology of difference which would not have to go up to contradiction, because contradiction would be less than difference and not more? Is not contradiction itself only the phenomenal and anthropological aspect of difference?[23]

We thus have four criteria laid out in 1955 for Deleuze's future philosophy. First, like Hegel, he believes that Kantian *critique* must at a certain point be subordinated to a *philosophical affirmation* of the logicity of being. Second, he affirms that as the philosophy of immanence concerns the absolute, therefore all differentiation found in it will be internal, self-generated, differentiation.[24] Third, this philosophy must be able to 'say its own sense', and, through this reflexive act, coincide with the sense of Being itself. Finally, we also have the suggestion that the absolute claims of Hegelian philosophy must be purified of dependence on phenomenal and anthropological content, and that this latter category, for some as yet unspecified reason, includes the concepts of contradiction and negation. The decisive problem for Deleuze's project will lie in consistently articulating the third criterion along with the others.

Now, if we look for an actualization of this project, we appear to find it not in *Difference and Repetition*, but in *Spinoza and the Problem of Expression*, also published in 1968. It is in Spinoza that

Deleuze finds the fullest flowering of an alternative model of immanent self-differentiation that remains faithful to the Hegelian schema, but that also presents a notion of difference without contradiction. However, the place of Spinoza in Deleuze's philosophy turns out to be extremely complicated, and he remains just as haunting and irresolvable a presence for Deleuze as he was for the work of the post-Kantians.

Spinoza and the 'best plane of immanence'

In the *Spinoza* book of 1968, Deleuze fashions a history of the philosophy of immanence, from the Neoplatonists through to Duns Scotus, which culminates in Spinoza. He also reaffirms in 1991 that it is Spinoza who sets out 'the "best" plane of immanence'.[25] I will claim shortly that the meaning of immanence has nevertheless undergone a radical shift between these dates.

Much of *Spinoza and the Problem of Expression* is concerned with the theological history of the notion of immanence. For Deleuze, Spinoza's contribution is to claim that there is no transcendent God, only a God immanent to nature, whose attributes must be conceived not as 'eminent' to natural attributes, but as 'univocally' sharing the same meaning. But once the *theological* issue of the identity of God with nature has been achieved in principle, one is still left with a set of purely *ontological* questions. How is the specific structure of this ontology to be defended? In what form will the nature of being express itself in thought? Why would Spinoza's philosophy be 'more immanent' than Hegel's, for instance, when Hyppolite has given strong reasons for affirming that immanence only becomes truly 'complete' in Hegel?

We come close to an answer if we follow Deleuze's attempt to enact a philosophical *construction* of absolute immanence in his reconstruction of the first part of Spinoza's *Ethics*. Deleuze presents an account of absolute difference that is formally coherent and provides a foil to the Hegelian view that difference is primarily negation, and that the self-differentiation of the absolute must be conceived in the form of a totality. I will only convey the gist of the argument here, as my aim is rather to assess its role and status in Deleuze's theory of immanence.

The first few propositions of the *Ethics* state that 'two substances having different attributes have nothing in common with each other' (E1P2), because an attribute is 'what the intellect perceives of a substance as constituting its essence' (E1D4), and a substance is 'conceived through itself' (E1D3).[26] Substances, moreover, cannot be distinguished from one another by their 'modes', but only by their attributes. No substance can therefore be in a relation of limitation or causality with another. We thus start with a bare plurality of substances with one attribute, each of which has nothing to do with the other. Deleuze points out that it would be incoherent to introduce a unifying, eminent substance 'behind' these substances-with-one-attribute. This would be a merely 'modal' or 'numerical distinction', as it would presuppose a *division* between substances that *share* something in common. This would go against the definition of substance, which therefore requires a rigorous logic of 'real distinction'.[27] The universality at work in this picture is distributive rather than collective; it concerns the 'each', rather than the 'all'. Spinoza's next big move is to argue that there can only be an absolute infinity of these really distinct substances-with-one-attribute.[28] But in this case, the notion of 'substance' should really be resituated at the level of absolute infinity itself; therefore the framework is now reconceived so that there is one substance *composed* of the set of really distinct *attributes*.[29] The attributes are *univocally* affirmed of the absolutely infinite substance; there is no transcendent genus or substance 'behind' them, to the extent that it is their univocal affirmation that constitutes their status as substance. Only the real distinction of the attributes, taken to infinity, dispels the need for an eminent unity, or a spurious collective totality of the components of the absolute. Only through this theory of 'real distinction', or pure difference, can Spinoza think absolute immanence, 'the absolute identity of Being and difference'.[30]

At strategic points in the book, Deleuze appears to imply that all the aspects of Hegelian immanence are to be found in Spinoza: expression, the absolute, self-differentiation, genetic method. However, for the presentation of absolute difference to be more than formally coherent, Deleuze would need to commit himself to an account of the relation between the logical (or formal) and the real. Immanence must be *realized*. In an important phrase, Deleuze claims to have revealed 'the only realized ontology'.[31] Now Spinoza's version of the realization of immanence fundamentally rests on a recapitulation of the traditional ontological argument ('it pertains to the nature of a substance to exist', E1P7). But will Deleuze himself rely on the ontological argument to fulfil the four criteria mentioned above for his own philosophy of immanence? There are three problems with this possibility.

1. Wouldn't Deleuze have to make more effort to defend this kind of ontological argument from well-known criticisms such as Kant's? For Kant, 'existence' cannot be predicated of the absolute in a formal argument, since to say that something exists requires an extra-logical moment (for instance the presence of an intuition). Now if Deleuze wishes to appeal to the expressivist theory of concepts mentioned earlier in relation to Hegel, then this would be circular, as the validity of that theory depends on a successful demonstration of an internal relation between being and thought. And while Hegel often speaks highly of the ontological argument, the weight of his theory of expression does not rest on a return to that argument, but on other more post-Kantian anti-sceptical arguments about the relation of thought and being, presented in the *Phenomenology*. Yet Deleuze wrote no *Phenomenology*; he has no 'introduction to the System'.

2. For Deleuze, the presentation of absolute difference is 'an *immediate* and adequate expression of an absolute Being that comprises in it all beings'.[32] To cite a phrase Deleuze uses

elsewhere, it involves a 'static genesis' of the structure of the absolute.[33] Hegel's *Science of Logic*, on the other hand, performs a 'dynamic genesis' of 'the logicity of being' in such a way that 'it says its own sense' (accounts for itself through the concepts it has generated) through the very movement of thought presented step by step in the book itself. The *Logic* therefore *enacts* the complete and immanent interpenetration of the logic of being with the logic of thought. For instance, the movement from being to nothingness and then to becoming at the start of the *Logic* is *simultaneously* a movement of thought in which the bare *thought of being* reveals itself to be *nothing* determinate. Moreover, it is also through this approach that Hegel completes his response to the Kantian critique of the ontological argument, by arguing that the notion of bare 'existence' or 'being' cannot be *conceived* without introducing some determinacy into it: to *be* is to *be something*.

Now Hegel's articulation of the logicity of being is, of course, only made possible by the claim that difference must be fundamentally understood as negation. We know that Deleuze disagrees with this, but is the necessary consequence of this disagreement that he also has to give up on a determinate and genetic account of the development of thought? If so, then he will have concomitant problems defending his account of immanence against Hegel's. Hegel manages to generate a lot of determinate possibilities out of the structure of negation: it is hard to see what determinate possibilities can be strictly generated from 'difference in itself'. In the Spinozist account, there is no direct movement from the real distinction of the attributes to the position that thought and extension are two of these attributes.

3. Let us return to the issue of the 'immediate' genesis of absolute immanence. Can Deleuze's formal demonstration of absolute difference *by itself* present a criterion of absolute immanence that can serve as a standard by which to criticize other philosophies of immanence as failures? It is sometimes suggested

that Hegelian immanence introduces an illegitimate transcendence by the mere fact of presenting an *order* for absolute self-differentiation, or by presenting this order as teleological (see the remarks of Hardt and Negri above). Although here a materialist impulse tends to confuse the argument (the animus being against any claim to hierarchy in the absolute), the idea seems to be that if only one appeals to the notion of immanence itself, as rigidly oppositional to transcendence, that is enough to dispel any spectres of God, teleology, and so on. Now, such an approach does not answer the questions above concerning the *realization* of immanence, which Hegel has arguably answered better. Nevertheless, might it not be possible to perform an initial theoretical *affirmation* of the structure of absolute difference that, by illuminating the mere formal possibility of a structure of difference that would avoid negation, opens the possibility of seeing reality in such a way? I believe this thought is definitely being ventured by Deleuze, but it is not clear that this is the path that could lead to 'the only realized ontology'. It is important to remember that Spinoza thinks he is *demonstrating* the structure of the absolute, and would be critical of any interpretation of 'affirmation' which suggested voluntarism. Spinozism is not a kind of inverted Pascalian wager by which one bets that a transcendent God does not exist. If absolute immanence is to be affirmed, it cannot be as a possibility, but as a *necessity*. And that requires that it defeat the other ontological possibilities.

We come here to a crossroads. On the one hand, it could be that the Spinozist argument is really a *model* of absolute difference that is put to work elsewhere by Deleuze in the service of another, more hidden, theory of immanence which will be able to compete with post-Kantian theories of immanence. On the other hand, it is equally clear that Deleuze did indeed go on to affirm the Spinozist theory of immanence as 'the best plane of immanence' in works such as *What is Philosophy?* Nevertheless, in the following passage it is clear that something has changed:

Spinoza was the philosopher who knew full well that immanence was only immanent to itself. ... He is therefore the prince of philosophers. Perhaps he is the only philosopher never to have compromised with transcendence and to have hunted it down everywhere. ... He discovered that freedom exists only within immanence. He fulfilled philosophy because he satisfied its prephilosophical presupposition. ... Spinoza is the vertigo of immanence from which so many philosophers try in vain to escape. Will we ever be mature enough for a Spinozist inspiration?[34]

First, the immanence/transcendence opposition is now taking on all the work. Moreover, this notion of transcendence is highly unusual in that it includes not only concepts of entities such as God, but even the notions of subject and object. As Deleuze elaborates in his last published article, the short opuscule entitled 'Immanence: A Life', both the subject and the object are not transcendental, but 'transcendent', whereas the field of immanence itself is 'an impersonal pre-reflexive consciousness, a qualitative duration of consciousness without self'.[35] Here Deleuze in fact appeals to the later Fichte, and he seems very close to the philosophy of pre-reflexivity found in Fichte by Dieter Henrich in his seminal article 'Fichte's Original Insight'.[36] However, the suggestion that 'immanence is related only to itself', yet must be considered to be pre-reflexive, is a difficult one, as how is the 'self-relation' supposed to be justified if it has *no* intrinsic connection with reflexive self-consciousness?

This leads us to the second change: immanence has become a *'pre-philosophical presupposition'*. Now, this move towards a late-Fichtean position has two major consequences for Deleuze's project. First, the apparent embrace of a featureless form of intellectual intuition raises problems with the continuing philosophical affirmation of 'difference' and 'multiplicity'. As we will see, Deleuzean 'dialectical difference' was elaborately and determinately worked out in *Difference and Repetition* in a way that is antagonistic to any reliance on some source of primal 'indifference'.[37] Second, Deleuze can no longer claim to have found 'the only realized ontology', because such a philosophy of immanence could never be *realized*; its pre-reflexivity precludes this. Thus we come to the conclusion that Deleuze's late affirmation of the Spinozist notion of immanence occurs at a huge cost: immanence is now a 'presupposition' that must be 'pre-philosophically' affirmed. And this surely amounts to a return to Fichte's criterion, that it depends on the kind of person one is whether one accepts this version of things.[38]

I have said that in *Spinoza and the Problem of Expression* immanence genuinely appears to be a matter of philosophical *construction*. I ventured that Deleuze's static genesis of absolute difference could provide a *model* for the construction of immanence itself. What was needed was an account of its critical validity in relation to other philosophies of immanence. The materials for this are present in *Difference and Repetition*.

Immanence and ideas in Kant

It is Deleuze's return to Kant in *Difference and Repetition* that provides the most powerful approach to a new philosophy of immanence. Kant's own 'plane of immanence' could be said to have two aspects. First, the implication of the whole project of a 'Critique of Pure Reason' is that reason can perform a critical operation *upon itself* – an immanent critique.[39] However, exactly how this reflexive act is to be accomplished is not clear. Kant at first seems to envisage that there is a pure element of reason that has 'its own eternal and unchangeable laws' and is a 'perfect unity' and that therefore provides the necessary vantage point for an auto-critique of human experience.[40] However, since the thrust of the first *Critique* is precisely to show the *dependence* of reason on the other features of cognitive functioning (such as sensibility and the understanding), Kant makes it clear at the protracted end of the work that the 'unity of reason' must be considered rather as a 'single supreme and inner *end*, which first makes possible the whole'.[41] That is, the fulfilment of an immanent critique systematically requires the teleological projection of an *actualized* unity of the diverse aspects of cognition. It turns out that the work of the *Critique of Pure Reason* is to be part of a metaphysics,[42] which 'is also the culmination of all *culture* of human reason'.[43] Metaphysics in turn is a part of 'philosophy', which is 'the science of the relation of all cognition to the essential ends of human reason (*teleologia rationis humanae*)'.[44]

The second aspect of Kantian immanence is much better known. Kant's method of transcendental argumentation secures an enduring restriction upon all the faculties and features of cognition so that they can only be legitimately used if they conform to the structure of experiential cognition. That is, their immanent use is justifiable, but their transcendent use is shown to be illegitimate. Kant's main use of the term 'immanence' is in fact with regard to the immanent use of the faculties of cognition.[45]

Two related questions are relevant here. First, the procedure of the self-critique of reason and the restriction produced and consolidated by that procedure are related in a mysterious way. The latter is by right the *result* of the former, but the former is the most obscure. If the wider method of the self-critique cannot be justified, then how can Kant say that he has strictly drawn the line between legitimate and illegitimate cognition? Second, it appears that Kant is guilty of using the notion of 'reason' equivocally. Reason acts as both the subject and object of critique, without it being made clear how reason (as subject) could save a bit of itself from its involvement with the other faculties of cognition (in its role as object of critique). These metacritical issues are encountered in one way or another by the post-Kantians, but the Deleuzean take on them is quite specific, and perhaps closer to Kant than the post-Kantians were prepared to go.

Kant's notion of immanent critique seems to involve an unstable oscillation between *noumenal* and *teleological* claims. In the first edition of the *Critique* Kant appears to affirm some kind of cognitive access to noumena, for instance in the section on noumenal freedom where the human being is said to be 'one part phenomenon, but in another part ... a merely intelligible object'.[46]

This echoes the distinction in the 'pre-critical' *Inaugural Dissertation* between 'things thought sensitively ... *as they appear*, while things which are intellectual are representations of things *as they are*'.[47] Nevertheless, as Kant elaborates his system (particularly under pressure of his development of the theory of inner sense, and of problems in the 'deduction' of freedom), he begins to shift all the metacritical weight of reason's power to criticize itself on to systematic teleology. The claims about the 'culture of human reason' are expanded in the *Critique of Judgment*, where the functions of experience and knowledge themselves are more explicitly tied up with purposive activity (for instance through the development of the notion of 'reflective judgment').

Now, in his philosophical works of the 1950s and 1960s, Deleuze too appears to appeal both to some kind of noumenal access and to a teleology of the cognitive faculties. On the one hand, Deleuze often comes across as a high rationalist. He argues in 1956 that it is only by

> determining the differences in nature between things ... that we will be able to 'return to things themselves'. ... If philosophy is to have a positive and direct relation with things, it is only to the extent that it claims to grasp the thing itself in what it is, in its difference from all that it is not, which is to say in its internal difference.[48]

With its quasi-Hegelian appeal to 'internal difference', this desire to 'return to things themselves' is by no means an echo of the trusted phenomenological maxim: on the contrary, Deleuze appears closer to resurrecting the rationalist project of returning to *noumena*. Elsewhere, Deleuze writes of attaining a 'truly sufficient reason' which will enable us to determine things in themselves in their internal difference.[49]

On the other hand, Deleuze is concerned in all of his works up until *Difference and Repetition* with the notion of teleology.[50] *Kant's Critical Philosophy* is an explicitly teleological reading of the structure of Kant's system. In an article on Kant's aesthetics from 1963, Deleuze writes that 'in the *Critique of Aesthetic Judgment*, Kant poses the problem of the genesis of the faculties in their primary free accord. He discovers an ultimate foundation, which is lacking in the other *Critiques*. Critique in general ceases to be a simple *conditioning*, to become a transcendental Formation, a transcendental Culture, a transcendental Genesis.'[51] It is at this point, however, that we can locate a crucial development of the Kantian position. In *Difference and Repetition* Deleuze attempts to push further the theory of the 'ends of reason' by reconstructing Kant's theory of Ideas of reason, so that the concepts of the understanding are seen to depend fundamentally on the orientation of cognition towards Ideas. My claim in what follows is that Deleuze fuses the noumenal and the teleological in his new notion of 'Idea', in such a way that he can legitimately claim that *thought* has access to noumenal being (while experience, understood in terms of recognition according to the generality of concepts, does not). This achievement of the immanence of thought to being, however, is achieved *critically* in Deleuze, rather than metaphysically, as in Kant.

To proceed it is necessary to bring out the general teleological structure of cognition present in Kant's work right from the first edition of the *Critique*. The basic aim of the Transcendental Deduction of Categories is to discover an a priori structure that grounds the connection between concepts (as 'functions of unity') and the sensible manifold. It is now recognized that the argument of this Deduction continues well into the 'System of the Principles of Pure Understanding'.[52] However, I would claim that the argument extends even further, right into the further reaches of the Transcendental Dialectic. In fact, it is precisely here that the general task of the Transcendental Deduction meets up with the metacritical status of the *Critique*, in the teleology of pure reason. Kant in fact is clear about the general importance of Ideas for the basic activity of cognition in the first edition of the *Critique* when he suggests at length that a third Deduction – a Transcendental Deduction of Ideas – is also necessary.[53] While the a priori forms of the understanding are often taken to be sufficient conditions for the 'coherence' of experience, Kant himself argues directly against such a view. Just as the Deduction of Categories was a response to the possibility that spatio-temporal 'appearances could after all be so constituted that the understanding not find them in accord with the conditions of unity', presenting a mere rhapsody or 'confusion' of sensations (the crucial passage at A90/B123), so does Kant admit that it is conceivable that 'among the appearances offering themselves to us there were such a great variety ... of content ... that even the most acute human understanding, through comparison of one with another, could not detect the least similarity.'[54] Kant now appeals to reason to finally ground the applicability of concepts to experience, and to ground the coherence of concepts in judgements in general. 'For the law of reason to seek unity is necessary, since without it we would have no reason, and without that, no coherent use of the understanding, and lacking that, no sufficient mark of empirical truth.'[55] Kant says that the understanding presents only a 'distributive unity' among appearances, without granting a 'collective unity'.[56] It is only by projecting a 'horizon' or guiding totality that the analytic unity of concepts can be used logically, in such a way that higher and lower 'functions of unity' *converge* with each other.[57] This would fulfil the fundamental requirement that is at the root of the Transcendental Deduction of the Categories. This horizon, says Kant, must 'direct the understanding to a certain goal respecting which the lines of direction of all its rules converge at one point'.[58]

However, obviously the collective unity (or totality) of appearances, as a '*focus imaginarius*', is precisely what can never be experienced as such, so the principle can only be regulative, not constitutive; that is, it is an Idea. Nevertheless, Kant insists that Ideas legitimately project a logical world, a *mundus intelligibilis*, of complete representation.[59] In fact, the Idea has an anomalous transcendental status: on the one hand, it is a peculiar kind of 'problematic concept', which itself does not conform to the usual criteria for concepts (it is not related to an intuition, nor does it serve as a tool for recognition).[60] On the other hand, it is a transcendental condition: it is thus a condition of the possibility of unity in a concept; it *gives* unity to a concept, by acting as the horizon in which unification can occur. Ideas themselves cannot be known (one cannot know God, or the self, etc.), but they are necessary conditions for the coherence of concepts (and therefore of knowledge and experience).

Two problems arise for Kant. First, how can Ideas be both particular concepts and conditions of concepts in general? Second, while the first stages of Kant's critique demonstrate the constitutive role of *pure forms* such as the categories of space and time, to go on to affirm the transcendental necessity of the Ideas involves affirming the necessity of *something unconditioned*. But what grounds this claim? How can this teleology be justified in such a way that it does not merely depend once more on a noumenal postulation about the 'essential ends of reason', or the structure of conceivability in general? On the other hand, if the ends of reason are merely 'regulative' for finite minds,[61] then how can *this* teleology be related to the teleology of reason necessary for the self-critique of reason itself to be possible? The weight Kant places on the 'outer limits' of the critique, on teleology, reason and the Ideas, is in danger of producing an implosion in the critical structure.[62]

The problematic field

Deleuze finds a way through these problems by exploiting the Kantian discovery that Ideas must be different in kind to concepts. Kant was on to something when he implied that Ideas are not themselves unified or objects of recognition. Deleuze's ingenious move is to take a peculiarly *literal* reading of Kant's statement that Ideas are 'problematic'. If Ideas are complete determinations, but concepts are general, then Ideas are problematic because they do not withstand coherent generalization: this is their quality, that they cannot be *recognized* or *experienced*. Nevertheless, they are in principle open to *thought*, as the necessary horizon of complete determination. Not only this, they are also essential to *motivate* knowledge at all.

> The fact is that [reason] alone is capable of drawing together the procedures of the understanding with regard to a set of objects. The understanding by itself would remain entangled in its separate and divided procedures, a prisoner of partial empirical enquiries or researches in regard to this or that object, never raising itself to the level of a 'problem' capable of providing a systematic unity for all its operations ... [it] would never constitute a 'solution'. For every solution presupposes a problem.[63]

This is really an echo of Kant's theme in the Preface to the second edition of the *Critique* that

> reason ... compel[s] nature to answer its questions. ... Reason, in order to be taught by nature, must approach nature with its principles in one hand, according to which alone the agreement among appearances can count as laws, and in the other hand, the experiments thought out in accordance with these principles.[64]

Knowledge itself is preceded by the posing of questions – that is, by thought.[65] Knowledge should not be understood as simply involving descriptions of states of affairs according to rules; rather, knowledge concerns solutions to problems. Therefore, established knowledge, or what permits recognition, is really nothing but the realm of established solutions.[66]

Kant does not spell out explicitly this difference in kind between Ideas and concepts. For him, one of the main criteria for the problematic 'horizon' is that it be *unified*. But is this a relevant criterion for the structure of problems? The criterion of *unity* is strictly speaking a function of the understanding. Concepts are 'functions of unity' and empirical cognition or knowledge is the locus of 'unification' through concepts. Kant is therefore presupposing the projected *unity* of Ideas only as a *telos* from the standpoint of knowledge – that is, from empirical representation. The power of Ideas is understood in terms of logical representation, in terms of a logical calculus that can only be a pale reflection and amplification of the realm of already established empirical concepts. However, *if* Ideas are to be thought primarily as problems (according to Deleuze's literal reading), this implies that they must already have their own consistency and form *as problems* that stand structurally outside achieved empirical knowledge, 'feeding' and conditioning knowledge. Any empirical knowledge is only 'determined by the conditions of the problem, engendered in and by the problem along with the real solutions. Without this reversal, the famous Copernican revolution amounts to nothing.'[67]

Deleuze proceeds to argue that Ideas can be conceived as already possessing the power to synthesize difference in themselves.[68] Again, this thought is familiar from Hegel: the Kantian dialectic is taken by Hegel to be the clue to the real extra-representational structure of the determinable world, a structure which lies beyond the 'concept' in the Kantian sense. Deleuze, too, is content to use the word 'dialectic' to describe the specific mode of differentiation for Ideas; Deleuze's account of problems is said to explore 'the dialectical half of difference'.[69] Also like Hegel, Deleuze believes that Kantian 'complete determination' is conceivable at the level of thought (if the correct means are used), even if it is not 'experienceable' as such by a finite being. Complete determination is reconceived by Deleuze as the ideal determination proper to a problematic field. However, contra Hegel, he excludes a dialectics of negation as the correct means to undertake an exhaustive determination of the Idea. As mentioned above in the first section, Deleuze believes that the form of contradiction is a 'merely phenomenal' aspect of difference itself. What can this mean?

Again one returns on the rebound from Hegel to Kant. For Kant, although concepts are 'functions of unity' in judgements, synthetic judgements are perpetually amplifying concepts, revising them according to the problem or Idea according to which they are 'focused'. As a result, concepts are ultimately indefinable.[70] The principle of contradiction in fact refers only to concepts that have already been established and given preliminary definitions, and serves as a rule of unity within experience. But due to the *de jure* immersion of the concept in the problematic field, in which established concepts and definitions can be broken down and reformed once a problem becomes transformed, the principle of contradiction has only relative significance. Hegel can thus with some justice be said to have failed to plunge deep enough into the nature of difference in the absolute. Instead, for Deleuze the Idea is determined according to a logic of structure, in which contradiction between terms that *actualize* the structure should not be confused with the relations and transformations set out in the structure itself. If the structure is taken purely in its 'pre-actual' state, as a set of ideal transformations, in which the elements are subject to reciprocal determination, then the contradictions that might arise between the actualized elements and relations remain undecided or unselected. In this pure state, of course, the problem can only be thought, not experienced, precisely because experience functions by means of conceptual recognition.

Such problematic structures may apply to particular fields of knowledge and experience, or may ground the question of what counts as knowledge itself. As an example of a particular structure, Deleuze sometimes refers to the Lacanian school's theories of psychic structure. Take the Oedipus complex: there are a number of possible positions in the structure (mother, father, female child, male child) which can be occupied ('identified' with) in various ways, and thus can become caught in various vectors of desire. The Oedipal structure 'itself' cannot be experienced, although it can be completely determined. If the identifications break down, pathology may ensue, as in Dora's case. Dora may begin to experience her identity as a 'problem', oscillating between subject positions.[71] While fantasy and dream may be able to give form to and sustain the transformations of thought, the introduction of the problematic field into experience itself, bound by the rules of conceptual recognition and a particular spatio-temporal structure, can only be deeply destabilizing, in Kantian terms a 'transcendent' exercise of one's faculties.

Such problematic structures must also extend to the most abstract philosophical levels. The criteria for knowledge itself are set up in response to the 'problem' of knowledge. Again, these criteria themselves cannot be 'experienced' or 'known', and the philosophical exploration of a problematic field cannot itself be judged by the standards of knowledge, as it sets those standards.

It is the sense of the *destination* of cognitive activity in a horizon that is to remain *by right* problematic that marks the singularity of Deleuze's extension of the teleology implicit in the Kantian Copernican turn. For Deleuze, indeed, the result of transcendental philosophy will *not* primarily be the dictum that all philosophy must conform to the conditions for the possibility of experience – that is, enact the *immanent use* of the structures of experience; in fact, Deleuze encourages their *transcendent use or exercise* (*exercice*), as it is precisely this that will critically reveal the limits of experience.[72] For Deleuze, all activities, both voluntary and involuntary, in which thought becomes caught up in a problematic field which undermines the structure of experience, go under the name of 'transcendental empiricism', a phrase which is analogous to the Hegelian notion of 'speculative experience'.[73] Hegel's view that the critical apprehension of limits requires that they be transgressed is thus taken up in a new way by Deleuze.[74] As is the case for Hegel, Deleuze's notion of immanence actually *requires* the transcendent use of the faculties, and the activity of thought beyond experience. But, unlike for Hegel, experience never becomes fully reconciled with thought.[75] This allows Deleuze the space to develop a new, non-Hegelian 'logic of sense' (Hyppolite's phrase) which attempts to express the paradoxical act of thinking problems. In *The Logic of Sense* Deleuze elaborates on the ability of problematic thought to perform an 'ideal genesis' of its own conditions, and thus to 'say its own sense'.

It is clear that Deleuze's potentiation of Kantian Ideas therefore involves an inversion of Kantianism. It is no longer that the empirical use of Ideas is a transcendental illusion; rather, it is our attempts to apply the rules of conceptual representation to problems and Ideas that is the real transcendental illusion.

For here, representation transgresses its own limits *and treats problems as concepts*. Kant had misinterpreted what he discovered: the real illusion is to interpret Ideas as concepts which lack an intuition, and not rather according to the specific logic of problematic, complete determination. Kant's claim that the realm of Ideas was ordered in the form of a purely logical world of representation is in fact an uncritical presupposition, which Deleuze critically rectifies.

Given the destination of cognitive thought in the Idea, the only choice for the critical philosopher is univocally to affirm problematicity as such. But what form can this take? It is at precisely this level that the Spinozist argument for absolute difference finds its true place. Absolute difference is shown to be formally coherent in the Spinoza book, but its existence could not be assumed without recourse to an ontological argument. As we saw, the procedure of 'starting' with absolute immanence risks falling back into 'pre-philosophical presupposition'. But, in fact, absolute immanence lies at the 'end' of the system, rather than at its beginning: it is the *telos* towards which cognition and critique move, and which must be philosophically affirmed. Now, the demonstration of the *formal* coherence of the thought of absolute difference gives us the right to replace the Kantian collective horizon, in which all Ideas converge in a presupposed unity modelled on the concept, with a truly, intrinsically differential horizon, whose only foundation is absolute difference without unity. Reason itself can be remodelled ('a truly sufficient reason'): it is no longer immediately considered to 'seek unity'. From the ideal notion of collective unity we move to a permanently *distributive* structure of reason. And while the Kantian 'common horizon' is shattered, chaos or indeterminacy does not ensue; rather, the splinters can assume a new formation.

This philosophical affirmation of 'the absolute identity of Being and difference' provides Deleuze with a novel ontological position between Kant and Hegel. For Kant, Ideas are *merely* problematic, 'merely ideal', while for Hegel the dialectical Idea is fully actual. However, for Deleuze Ideas are *essentially* problematic *in themselves*. Like Hegel, Deleuze will affirm that there is no noumenal reality that cannot potentially be captured by dialectical thought. Thought can indeed fully express being – but (contra Hegel) *only* through a (non-conceptual, non-negative) form of differentiation that remains intrinsically problematic for experience. Between Kant and Hegel, Deleuze's claim is that *Ideas, as problems, are constitutive*. That is, they are *univocally* affirmed of being itself, against the equivocity of Kantian reason.

So why does Deleuze insist that 'immanence is the very vertigo of philosophy'? There are perhaps both manifest and latent answers in Deleuze's work. The manifest answer is that immanence is the telos of reason, which, in its full differential and dispersive form, can only signify the undermining of experience on the part of reason. The latent answer invokes structural limits within the very notion of immanence. Since Deleuze's account of absolute difference does not allow for an immanent unfolding of determinate categories (in the way that Hegel's theory does), he must instead take a more crooked path to immanence, involving a complex mixture of transcendental (Kantian) and formal and ontological (Spinozist) argumentation. In other words, it is *because* Deleuze attempts to construct an immanent theory of difference which escapes the forms of negation and the concept that he must sacrifice the self-generating and self-validating features of Hegel's system of immanence, features that make it not only a philosophy *about* immanence, but a philosophy that demonstrates at every step its own immanence in its very writing and being read. How, then, is one to adjudicate between Deleuze's and Hegel's systems? Perhaps *this* question is closer to the 'vertigo of philosophy' Deleuze really had in mind, which may explain his attempts to move beyond his early system. The vertigo would be latent in the problematic notion of immanence itself.

Notes

1. Michael Hardt and Antonio Negri, *Empire*, Harvard University Press, Cambridge MA, 2000; Giorgio Agamben, 'Absolute Immanence', in *Potentialities*, Stanford University Press, Stanford CA, 2000; Alain Badiou, *Deleuze: The Clamor of Being*, trans. L. Burchill, University of Minnesota Press, Minneapolis, 2000; Daniel W. Smith, 'The Doctrine of Univocity: Deleuze's Ontology of Immanence', in M. Bryden, ed., *Deleuze and Religion*, Routledge, London, 2001.
2. This remark, first made in 1968 in *L'Idée d'expression dans la philosophie de Spinoza*, translated by M. Joughin as *Expressionism in Philosophy: Spinoza*, Zone, New York 1992, p. 180, is paraphrased in 1991 in *What is Philosophy?*, trans. G. Burchell and H. Tomlinson, Verso, London, 1994, p. 48.
3. Another factor, this time theological, might also be said to be pre-eminent: a philosophy of immanence would deny a God that was transcendent to nature. However, as I will suggest later, once this theological conception is analysed into its purely philosophical elements, it dissolves into the two features just mentioned.
4. Hardt and Negri, *Empire*, p. 71.
5. Ibid., p. 79.
6. Ibid., p. 82.
7. Alain Badiou dismisses without argument the very idea that Deleuze's work should be understood in terms of the post-Kantian project (*Deleuze: The Clamor of Being*, pp. 19, 45), claiming that Heidegger's return to the question of Being is more important for Deleuze: 'The question posed by Deleuze is the question of Being. ... Deleuze's philosophy is in no way a critical philosophy. Not only is it possible to think Being, but there is thought only insofar as Being simultaneously formulates and pronounces itself therein' (p. 20). But the latter formulation would hold for both Heidegger and Hegel, and it is not irrelevant that discussions of Kant and Hegel vastly outnumber discussions of Heidegger in Deleuze's work.
8. *Difference and Repetition*, trans. P. Patton, Athlone, London, 1994; *Différence et répétition*, PUF, Paris, 1968. Hereafter cited as 'DR', with English and French pagination respectively. The problematicity of Deleuzean immanence was correctly noted by Derrida in his obituary for Deleuze, where he laments the fact that he and Deleuze never had the philosophical encounter that they owed each other. 'My first question, I believe, would have concerned ... the word "immanence" on which he always insisted, in order to make or let him say something that no doubt still remains secret to us' (J. Derrida, 'Il me faudra errer tout seul', *Libération*, 7 November 1995, p. 38).
9. It is worth noting that the only dedicatee of any book by Deleuze is Hyppolite, 'in sincere and respectful homage', in *Empiricism and Subjectivity: An Essay on Hume's Theory of Human Nature*, trans. C. Boundas, Columbia University Press, New York, 1991.
10. Review reprinted in Jean Hyppolite, *Logic and Existence*, trans. L. Lawlor and A. Sen, SUNY Press, Albany NY, 1997, pp. 191–5. In his 1978 lectures on Kant, Deleuze describes how for Kant 'there is no longer an essence behind appearance, there is rather the sense or non-sense of what appears' (Seminar 1, p. 5; available at www.deleuze.fr.st). This signifies 'a radically new atmosphere of thought, to the point where I can say that in this respect we are all Kantians'. Philosophical method is no longer subject to the effort of either deriving the sensible from the ideal or the ideal from the sensible, and accommodating the one to the other; rather, the two are intrinsically correlated. A new approach is possible: as Deleuze says, 'something appears, tell me what it signifies or, and this amounts to the same thing, tell me what its condition is' (ibid.).
11. G.W.F. Hegel, *Aesthetics: Lectures on Fine Art*, trans. T.M. Knox, Oxford University Press, Oxford, 1988, pp. 128–9, quoted in Hyppolite, *Logic and Existence*, p. 24.
12. See C. Taylor, *Hegel*, Cambridge University Press, Cambridge, 1975, pp. 3–50, for an account of the Romantic legacy of the concept of expression in Hegel's writings. 'The universe reflects rational necessity in two ways; it conforms to it, and it expresses it. It can be seen as in a sense analogous to a statement' (p. 108).
13. *Encyclopedia Logic*, trans. W. Wallace, Clarendon Press, Oxford, 1975, #44, p. 72.

14. G.W.F. Hegel, *Lectures on the Philosophy of Religion*, one-volume edition, ed. Peter C. Hodgson, University of California Press, Berkeley, 1988, p. 184. Cf. *Encyclopedia Logic*, #51, pp. 84–5.
15. 'Mere representational thinking, for which abstraction has isolated them, is capable of holding the universal, particular and individual apart' (*Science of Logic*, trans. A.V. Miller, Humanities Press, New York, 1989, p. 620).
16. Hyppolite, *Logic and Existence*, p. 176.
17. Ibid.
18. Ibid., p. 35.
19. Ibid., p. 175.
20. *Logic and Existence*, p. 20.
21. Hegel, *Science of Logic*, p. 50.
22. Review of Hyppolite, *Logic and Existence*, p. 194.
23. Ibid., p. 195.
24. See, for instance, the appeal to the Hegelian distinction between 'external' and 'internal difference' in 'Bergson's Concept of Difference', trans. M. McMahon, in J. Mullarkey, ed., *The New Bergson*, Manchester University Press, Manchester, 1999, pp. 47–50. See also the reference to the '*Sich-unterscheidende*' in DR 117/154.
25. *What is Philosophy?*, p. 60.
26. B. Spinoza, *Ethics*, trans. E. Curley, Penguin, Harmondsworth, 1996. Standard referencing for Spinoza is used: 'E' for *Ethics*, followed by Part (1–5), then definition (D), axiom (A) or proposition (P) number.
27. Deleuze, *Expressionism in Philosophy*, pp. 34–9.
28. Infinity in Spinoza means non-limitation, so by absolute infinity Spinoza need only mean 'the set of whichever unlimited substances there are'.
29. 'When substance is absolutely infinite, when it has an infinity of attributes, then, and only then, are its attributes said to express its essence, for only then does substance *express itself* in its attributes', Deleuze, *Expressionism in Philosophy*, p. 42.
30. Deleuze, Review of Hyppolite, *Logic and Existence*, p. 195.
31. DR 303/387.
32. Deleuze, *Expressionism in Philosophy*, p. 175; stress mine.
33. On genesis, see DR 191/247; on static genesis, see *The Logic of Sense*, trans. Mark Lester with Charles Stivale, Athlone, London, 1991, pp. 109–26.
34. *What is Philosophy?* p. 48; stress mine.
35. 'Immanence: A Life', trans. N. Millett, *Theory, Culture, Society*, vol. 14, no. 2, p. 3.
36. 'The possibility of reflection must be understood on the basis of this primordial essence of the Self. ... A gap, perhaps even an abyss, opens up between the "Self" and what makes the Self intelligible' (D. Henrich, 'Fichte's Original Insight', trans. D. Lachterman, *Contemporary German Philosophy* I, 1982, pp. 22–3). The texts of Fichte referred to by Deleuze are the post-1800 *Introduction to the Blessed Life*, and the 1797 Introductions to the *Wissenschaftslehre*, but Deleuze indicates that he is referring to the Introductions only in so far as they elaborate the 'intuition of sheer activity; not a matter of existence, but of life' ('Immanence: A Life', p. 6), and thus refers to the post-1800 Fichte.
37. On 'indifference', see DR 276/354.
38. J.G. Fichte, 'First Introduction to the *Wissenschaftslehre*', in *Introductions to the Wissenschaftslehre*, ed. D. Breazeale, Hackett, Indianapolis IN, 1994, #5, pp. 15–20.
39. In the Preface to the *Critique of Pure Reason* (trans. P. Guyer and A. Wood, Cambridge University Press, Cambridge, 1997) (hereafter cited as 'CPR', followed by first and second edition pagination), Kant writes of the demand 'that reason should take on anew the most difficult of all its tasks, namely, that of self-knowledge' (CPR Axi).
40. CPR Axii–xiii.
41. CPR A833/B861; stress added.
42. CPR A841/B869.
43. CPR A851/B879.
44. CPR A838–9/B866–7.
45. Cf. CPR A297/B313, A308/B365.
46. CPR A546/B574.
47. I. Kant, *Theoretical Philosophy 1755–1770*, trans. D. Walford, Cambridge University Press, Cambridge, 1992, p. 384, Ak. 2: 392.
48. 'Bergson's Conception of Difference', p. 42. This 'difference from all that it is not' does not of itself lead to a Hegelian (or quasi-Hegelian) formulation in terms of determinate negation. The 'all' here may refer to a set of mutually incompatible things, in which case nothing would be gained and much would be missed by characterizing difference as negation.
49. *Nietzsche and Philosophy*, trans. H. Tomlinson, Athlone, London, 1983, p. 49. Cf. DR 57/80, 154/200.

50. Of course, rationalism and teleology are often to be found together (in Leibniz, for instance), but Deleuze even finds a crucial dependence on teleology in Hume, through focusing on Hume's one-off reference to 'a kind of pre-established harmony between the course of nature and the succession of our ideas' (*Enquiry Concerning Human Understanding*, Clarendon Press, Oxford, 1975, pp. 54–5). The last chapter of Deleuze's *Empiricism and Subjectivity* is devoted to purposiveness, while the books on Nietzsche, Kant, Bergson and Proust all have significant teleological dimensions.
51. 'L'idée de genèse dans l'esthétique de Kant, *Revue d'Esthétique* 16, 1963, p. 121. In *Nietzsche and Philosophy* Deleuze also develops the Kantian theme of a 'transcendental culture' (pp. 133–41).
52. See H. Allison, *Kant's Transcendental Idealism*, Yale University Press, New Haven CT, 1983, p. 172.
53. CPR A669/B697.
54. CPR A654/B682. This possibility also provides the motivation for the *Critique of Judgment*. See particularly the First Introduction: 'For although experience forms a system in terms of *transcendental* laws, which comprise the condition under which experience as such is possible, yet empirical laws might be so *infinitely diverse*, and *the forms* of nature which pertain to particular experience *so very heterogeneous*, that the concept of a system in terms of these (empirical) laws must be quite alien to the understanding, and that the possibility – let alone the necessity – of such a whole is beyond our grasp. And yet for particular experience to cohere thoroughly in terms of fixed principles, it must have this systematic coherence of empirical laws as well' (*Critique of Judgment*, trans. W. Pluhar, Hackett, Indianapolis IN, 1987, First Introduction, p. 392/203). The main difference between the first and third *Critique*s here is that in the former Kant does not yet admit the possibility that the *forms* as well as the content of nature might be infinitely diverse. Cf. CPR A654/B682.
55. CPR A651/B680.
56. A644/B672; cf. A583/B611.
57. A658/B686.
58. A644/B672.
59. CPR A659/B687.
60. See CPR A254/B310: 'I call a concept problematic that contains no contradiction but that is also, as a boundary for given concepts, connected with other cognitions, the objective reality of which can in no way be cognized.' Although Kant will state that there are only three Ideas (Self, World and God), I will focus on the minimal definition of Ideas as outlined here, in order to facilitate comprehension of the Deleuzean transformation of Kantian Ideas.
61. See CPR A568/B596f., A643/B671f.
62. As the 'First Introduction' to the *Critique of Judgment* shows, Kant begins to move towards affirming an attempt to bring the previously regulative nature of Ideas within a constitutive systematic teleology: 'the concept of experience [would be understood] *as a system in terms of empirical laws ...* Unless this is presupposed, particular experiences cannot have thoroughly lawful coherence, i.e. empirical unity' (pp. 392–3/203). In the *Opus posthumum* this move is finally embraced.
63. DR 168/218–19.
64. CPR Bxiv.
65. Deleuze continually emphasizes the Kantian distinction between thought and knowledge: see *Proust and Signs*, trans. R. Howard, Athlone, London, 2000, p. 97; *Nietzsche and Philosophy*, pp. 93, 172–3.
66. By stating that Ideas are *unknowable*, 'Kant does not mean that Ideas are necessarily false problems and thus insoluble but, on the contrary, that true problems are Ideas, and that these Ideas do not disappear with "their" solutions, since they are indispensable conditions without which no solution would ever exist' (DR 168/219).
67. DR 162/210.
68. Chapter 4 of *Difference and Repetition* is entitled 'The Ideal Synthesis of Difference', but translated by Patton as 'Ideas and the Synthesis of Difference'.
69. DR 221/285. The other half is 'aesthetic' difference. Both 'halves' involve non-Hegelian accounts of difference. As well as the 'exploration of the two halves of difference', part of Deleuze's project in *Difference and Repetition* is to attempt to construct a kind of schematism between dialectical Ideas and aesthetic intensities. On schematism, see DR 218/281, 328/282; and 'La méthode de dramatisation', in *Bulletin de la Société francaise de Philosophie*, vol. 61, no. 3, 1967, pp. 95–6.

70. CPR A728/B756f. See also Kant's statement that analytic unity in concepts presupposes synthetic unity (B133n.).
71. DR 316n17/139n. Cf. J. Lacan, *Seminar III: The Psychoses*, trans. R. Grigg, Routledge, London, 1993, pp. 170–80, for Lacan's theory of 'problems' with relation to Dora.
72. 'Transcendent exercise' is often erroneously translated as 'transcendental exercise' in the English edition of *Difference and Repetition*.
73. I borrow the term from G. Kortian, *Metacritique*, Cambridge University Press, Cambridge, 1980, p. 37. Hegel remarks that the *Phenomenology* is 'the Science of the *experience* which consciousness goes through' (*Phenomenology of Spirit*, trans. A.V. Miller, Oxford University Press, Oxford, 1977, p. 21; cf. p. 56), but the *recollection* of this experience 'for us' (ibid.) can also be called an experience; hence 'speculative experience'. As I have been suggesting, for Deleuze the notion of 'experience' remains in its Kantian signification, and should not be confused with dialectical thought.
74. 'No one knows, or even feels, that anything is a limit or defect, until he is at the same time above and beyond it. ... A limit or imperfection in knowledge comes to be termed a limit or imperfection, only when it is compared with the actually present Idea of the universal, of a total and perfect' (Hegel, *Encyclopedia Logic*, #60, pp. 91f). The notion that the Idea is 'actually present' is clearly the controversial one in Hegel.
75. It is important to note that Deleuze changed his mind on this issue by the time of *Anti-Oedipus* (1972), trans. R. Hurley et al., Athlone, London, 1984. There he reaffirms a traditional Kantian account of the 'immanent use' of syntheses, as opposed to recommending their transcendent use. We are presented with three syntheses of the unconscious (connective, disjunctive and conjunctive), which secure 'a transcendental unconscious defined by the immanence of its criteria' (p. 75), and permit the denunciation of illegitimate metaphysical uses of the syntheses ('psychoanalysis has its metaphysics – its name is Oedipus'; ibid.). However, by reversing his earlier account, and returning to a traditional reading of Kant, Deleuze encounters new problems. Why, for instance, should we accept that these three syntheses are adequate to the unconscious, if their immanence is only stipulated? The interweaving in *Difference and Repetition* of the theory of the syntheses of repetition with the theory I am describing here seems more sophisticated.

DISOWNED ENLIGHTENMENTS

4 Feminism and the Enlightenment

PAULINE JOHNSON

The recent turn taken by feminist theory towards a critique of the spirit of humanism would have surprised Simone de Beauvoir and the early delineators of the concerns of 'second wave' feminism. According to *The Second Sex*, feminism is an expression of humanism in a quite straightforward sense.[1] Indeed, the main feminist message of *The Second Sex* is the assertion that women must be considered first and foremost as human beings. According to the standpoint of *The Second Sex* the oppression of women appears as a denial, in a specifically discriminatory sense, of their right and task as human beings to freely choose their own identity and destiny. For Beauvoir, feminism meant the demand that women should cease to be stultified by their culturally imposed femininity and should, along with men, enjoy the human task and responsibility of making *themselves*. According to *The Second Sex*, 'what peculiarly signalizes the situation of woman is that she – a free and autonomous being like all human creatures – nevertheless finds herself in a world where men compel her to assume the status of the Other.'[2]

In recent times, however, feminism has developed a powerful unmasking critique of the image of the human which underpins Beauvoir's analysis of the oppression of women in modern society. As Lloyd points out, the Sartrean ideal of humanity as transcendence, as the drama of a self-choosing subject, is not, as it claims, a universal ideal. The Sartrean ideal used by Beauvoir is, 'in a more fundamental way than Beauvoir allows, a male ideal'.[3] On this recent account, the Sartrean ideal of transcendence is clearly formulated as an exhortation to the masculine self to transcend or overcome the threat of a supposed feminine state in which the mere facticity or 'given' character of the body engulfs the self.

Today, it seems, feminism has lost its former innocent reliance on the claims to universality and gender-neutrality made on behalf of images of a common humanity. Indeed, contemporary feminism has played a crucial part in developing an unmasking critique of those images of universal human aspirations and priorities upon which its own disclosure of the oppressed humanity of modern women once rested. Harding describes feminism's new reflective and critical relationship to descriptions of a universal humanity in the following terms:

> What we took to be humanly inclusive problematics, concepts, theories, objective methodologies, and transcendental truths are, in fact, less than that. Indeed, these products of thought bear the mark of their individual creators, and the creators in turn have been distinctively marked as to gender, class, race and culture.[4]

In particular, as Harding goes on to show, modern feminism has in recent years played a crucial part in a developing ideology-critique of the claims to universality made on behalf of a Western conception of human reason. Feminism has joined with other perspectives in modem cultural criticism to expose this concept of reason as a mere' thing of this world' embodying the norms, values and priorities of particular historio-cultural practices.

The distinctive participation of contemporary feminism in a broad-based critique of the claims of a sovereign reason appears symptomatic of the growing theoretical and ideological maturity of this vital social movement. There is, moreover, a considerable consensus within the recent feminist literature about the necessity and the general direction of this unmasking critique. An important dispute has arisen, however, over the question of the meaning, the consequences, of this critique for contemporary feminism itself. Certain feminists have supposed that the critique of the claims of transcendent reason establishes modern feminism on the path of counter-Enlightenment.[5] This position maintains that feminism requires a fundamental break from an Enlightenment commitment to the cause of reason and truth, which is exposed as nothing more than a distorted and disguised will-to-power. There are, however, those for whom feminism's unmasking critique of Western constructions of a sovereign reason cannot be understood as an invitation to an anti-Enlightenment posture. Harding, for example, endorses feminism's debunking critique of the ways in which Western constructions of the power of reason systematically embody the norms and priorities of a male-dominated culture. Yet for her this critique in no way heralds feminism's own break from the commitments of the Enlightenment.[6] Lovibond too has suggested that feminism now needs to take stock of its deep indebtedness to the 'emancipatory metanarratives' of Enlightenment.[7]

The following essay investigates aspects of this disputed interpretation of the relationship between contemporary feminism and the so-called project of Enlightenment. The argument is that current attempts to sever feminism's ideological ties with the Enlightenment rest on a basic misinterpretation of the character and spirit of Enlightenment. These feminisms have misconstrued the character of the Enlightenment on two counts. First, their critique is typically aimed at a caricature of the historical Enlightenment. Their repudiation of the Enlightenment influence is based on a portrait of the legitimating temper of seventeenth-century rationalism and fails to acknowledge the anti-dogmatic spirit which progressively emerged in eighteenth-century intellectual life. The first two parts of the essay argue that this fundamental misconstruction of the spirit of the historical Enlightenment has distorted feminism's understanding of its own Enlightenment legacy. The vital difference in the temper of these two periods is then illustrated by a comparison between the limitations of Astell's seventeenth-century feminism and the radicalism of Wollstonecraft's late-eighteenth-century version.

Second, the suggestion that contemporary feminism can be understood as an anti-Enlightenment posture indicates a failure to grasp the essential meaning of Enlightenment as an unfinished cultural project. This interpretation of Enlightenment has mistakenly reduced the dynamic, ongoing, self-critical process of Enlightenment thinking to a set of fixed principles and doctrines. Perhaps the most forceful expression of Enlightenment thinking as the aspiration which has infused the whole spirit of modernity is still to be found in Kant's famous essay 'What is Enlightenment?' Enlightenment, Kant tells us, is 'the emergence of man from his self-imposed minority. His *minority* is his incapacity to make use of his own understanding without the guidance of another.'[8] Thus understood, Enlightenment means only a commitment to an ongoing critique of prejudice and to the historical production of a self-legislating humanity. This commitment which has threaded its way through the intellectual trajectory of modernity exists as a living, dynamic aspiration which is fundamentally irreducible to any single formulation. So it seems that the acknowledgement of feminism's own Enlightenment character by no means signifies its assimilation to any pre-existing goals and perspectives. On the contrary, feminism's current critique of Enlightenment formulations appears as another vital episode in the unfolding of the Enlightenment project itself. Feminism's discovery of the prejudices built into the various articulations of this project is nothing more than an extension and clarification of the meaning of the Enlightenment.

Enlightenment, it is argued, needs to be viewed not just as a one-sided epistemology, nor as the legitimating ideology of certain interests within eighteenth-century society.[9] Enlightenment, said to have produced as its 'crowning achievement' a modern culture of humanism, is not reducible to any single interpretation of the character of its goals and perspectives. The final part of the essay outlines modern feminism's own character as a specific, dynamic interpretation of the meaning of modern Enlightenment. It indicates some of the ways in which the meaning of contemporary Enlightenment and modern feminism come together. Both criticize existing social practices and attempt to reveal the radical social possibilities existing in the present. Feminism, I suggest, needs to understand itself as a vital part of this movement pushing back the frontiers of existing social possibilities. This concluding section of the essay points to feminism's place within a contemporary historicized understanding of Enlightenment aspirations.

Images of Enlightenment in contemporary feminism

A certain interpretation of the postmodern 'turn' in contemporary feminism is up for review here. Basing itself on a totalizing and abstract critique of Enlightenment rationalism, this brand of postmodern feminism construes modern reason as a guilty normalization of a set of prejudices whose influence is uniformly felt throughout every aspect of contemporary culture. Jardine's *Gynesis: Configurations of Women and Modernity*, which seeks to jettison the entire legacy of the 'humanist and rationalist eighteenth century', is a typical example.[10] Hekman also looks upon postmodern feminism as a fundamental break from a 'homocentric' Enlightenment tradition. She sees a fundamental unity of purpose between feminism and postmodernism. Both 'challenge the epistemological foundations of Western thought and argue that the epistemology which is definitive of Enlightenment humanism, if not of all Western philosophy, is fundamentally misconceived'. Both, she goes on, 'assert consequently that this epistemology must be displaced, that a different way of describing human knowledge and acquisition must be found'.[11]

To Hekman and Jardine, Enlightenment embodies that colonizing spirit of scientific rationalism which has, in the context of modern-day epistemological disputes, reappeared in the form of positivism and empiricism. Hekman distinguishes her own feminist critique of Enlightenment from those postures which see in Enlightenment rationalism a privileging of the 'male' values of domination, rationality and abstraction, against which they assert the claims of the supposed female values of nurturing, relatedness and community.¹² To Hekman, feminism is a vital participant in a contemporary challenge to the so-called epistemological attitude of Enlightenment. 'Enlightenment', on this account, means the oppressive, universalizing assertion of certain, dogmatically assumed truth claims. Feminism, by contrast, sides with a hermeneutic sensitivity to the conditioned, interpretative character of all knowledges. Against an Enlightenment 'epistemology' defined as the study of knowledge acquisition that was accomplished through the opposition of a (masculine) knowing subject and a known subject, a modern feminist approach 'entails the attempt to formulate ... an explanation of the discursive processes by which human beings gain understanding of their common world'.¹³

The shared presumption of Jardine, Hekman and Flax is that feminism's critique of Enlightenment suggests an opposition, in principle, between two competing ideologies, Flax, for example, sees in contemporary feminism and in Enlightenment the clear and irreconcilable opposition of two ideological competitors. In her view, despite an understandable attraction to the (apparently) logical, orderly world of Enlightenment,

> feminist theory more properly belongs in the terrain of postmodern philosophy. Feminist notions of the self, knowledge and truth are too contradictory to those of the Enlightenment to be contained in its categories. The way(s) to feminist future(s) cannot live in reviving or appropriating Enlightenment concepts of person or knowledge.¹⁴

In particular, Flax points out that contemporary feminism is deeply opposed to an Enlightenment construction of a sovereign reason which it exposes as resting on a 'gender rooted sense of self'.¹⁵ On this account, the motto of the Enlightenment, *sapere aude* – have courage to use your own reason – confers an alleged normative universality on the supposed attributes of a modern masculine subjectivity. The attributes of passionate sensibility and intuitive understanding, associated with a socialized femininity, can only appear as impediments to be overcome in the development of the self-legislating Enlightenment personality.

According to this kind of interpretation of the significance of feminism's critique of Enlightenment, Enlightenment appears only as a repressive epistemology whose grip must be broken in order to assert the excluded claims of the different and the marginal.[16] The prehistory of a feminist epistemology comes to appear as the repetitious logic of a totalitarian opposition between mind and body, reason and passion, reflection and intuition. What emerges is a portrait of a masculinized rational faculty which remorselessly identifies itself and its power of universalizing abstractions with human agency itself. The claims of the passions, of nature and of the uniquely individual appear as the mere objects of reason's limitless will to mastery. Because in the 'paradigm of Western reason' the human subject is identified with her/his own subjective reason, all difference is suppressed and an ascribed masculine psychology is conferred with an alleged normativity.

It is, then, a particular interpretation of contemporary feminism's critique of Enlightenment which is up for review here. The disagreement is not with those feminist critiques which seek only to unmask the various ways in which Western constructions of the power of reason systematically embody the norms and priorities of a male-dominated culture. To the extent that a contemporary feminism understands itself as an immanent critique which seeks to rescue the emancipatory intent of Enlightenment from the various prejudices which cling to its 'master narratives', there is no argument. The disagreement is, rather, with those for whom this critique of the 'Western Paradigm of Reason' is seen to impose the necessity for separating contemporary feminism by radical surgery from the influence of Enlightenment thinking.

The Enlightenment interpretation proposed below suggests, as already mentioned, that the anti-Enlightenment turn in contemporary feminist thinking involves two major misconceptions about Enlightenment. First, the feminist assault on the normalizing claims of Enlightenment thinking frequently rests on a frozen image of seventeenth-century rationalism, overlooking the progressive turn away from this interpretation of the Enlightenment which occurred throughout the eighteenth century. Second, this particular misconstruction of Enlightenment is indicative of a more general misperception which confuses a *specific* meaning given to the ideal of a self-legislating humanity by the historical Enlightenment itself with the open-ended, dynamic interpretation of this ideal which has become the meaning of contemporary Enlightenment.

The historical Enlightenment and its project

While Gay has properly warned against any attempt to treat the Enlightenment as a compact body of doctrine, he discovers, nevertheless, a distinctive cultural climate in eighteenth-century intellectual life. Despite the conflicting interpretations of the object of the newly discovered 'science of man', the historical Enlightenment agreed on the ultimate self-responsibility of each individual. 'Whatever the *philosophes* thought of man – innately decent or innately power-hungry, easy or hard to educate to virtue – the point of the Enlightenment's anthropology was that man is an adult dependent on himself.'[17]

Cassirer finds, however, that d'Alembert's description of his own age as the 'century of reason' and the 'philosophic century' is too imprecise to capture the distinctive intellectual climate of eighteenth-century intellectual life.[18] Cassirer and others point out that this self-description meant something quite specific to eighteenth-century intellectuals. Namely, although they assume that there is unity, simplicity and continuity behind all phenomena, d'Alembert and his eighteenth-century colleagues do not fall into the snares of the 'spirit of the systems' upheld by the seventeenth-century rationalists.[19] In the great metaphysical systems of the seventeenth century, reason is in the realm of the 'eternal verities' of 'those truths held in common by the human and the divine mind'. The eighteenth century takes reason in a different sense. 'It is no longer the sum total of "innate ideas" given prior to all experience, which reveal the absolute essence of things. Reason is now looked upon as rather an acquisition than as a heritage.'[20]

Markus has suggested that for the eighteenth century 'reason' appeared in what are, from a contemporary point of view, two rather incompatible guises.[21] In the first place, the eighteenth-century intellectuals constructed a specifically critical construction of the power of reason understood as the critique of prejudice. Reason, on this account, assumed the negative character of critique. Reason concerned itself with the attempt to destroy the irrational 'superstitions' of the age, seen as the cause of all its ill.[22] On this construction, reason meant that newly born capacity to understand the world-views of others not dogmatically from the standpoint of the supposed 'eternal verities' discovered by reason but, rather, as particular world-interpretations expressive of a diversity of cultural experiences. The eighteenth-century intellectuals, it has been said, discovered the concept of culture; they were the first to identify that now commonplace conception of the 'fashioning' of humans by their society. The critique of prejudice contrived to establish an anti-dogmatic insight into the social-institutional supports behind a diversity of belief systems.

And yet the Enlightenment construction of reason, as, in Cassirer's phrase, a 'heritage', also gave a particular *positive* understanding of the character of the rational life. In this positive construction, reality described an objective, albeit secular, set of principles capable of guiding humanity's progress towards an enriched, fulfilled and harmonious social life. The eighteenth century's image of the rational character of the 'city of the future' modelled on 'nature's plan' suggested that the high Enlightenment was unable to countenance the absolute relativization of the cultural accomplishment of historical periods and societies. As Markus points out, this concept of rationality evoked a normative standard, a positive conception whereby the contributions of the diverse cultural products of other societies and epochs to the promotion of the rational, the harmonious and balanced life could be assessed.[23] So the destructive power of critique was to clear the way to a new rational social order, ruled no longer by mere prejudice and superstition but by the 'highest' considerations of the well-rounded, harmonious development of human potentialities. Jacob and other major interpreters of the period particularly emphasize that high Enlightenment figures like Voltaire sought an order in society and government, modelled after the new scientific conception of the orderly and balanced universe.[24]

Modern feminism's antipathy towards the anthropological underpinnings of an eighteenth-century understanding of the rational life is clear. The Enlighteners' supposition that the new rational society could be modelled after the principles of nature meant that traditional social arrangements continued to have powerful sanction. And yet this eighteenth-century understanding of the rational life meant also a new departure in the development of the modern image of the self; an understanding which, in fact, shares common ground with contemporary feminism's own critique of a one-sided rationalist conception of the self.

To the Enlighteners, the secular principle of human perfectibility or self-improvement emerged as the clear successor to the rationalists' one-sided vision of reason's war on the unruly passions. Against the narrow asceticism of seventeenth-century morality, the Enlighteners' understanding of the good, the rational life encompasses the rehabilitation of the sensuous passions as a vital, creative force. Diderot, for example, insists that under the tutelage of reason's power of discrimination, a 'natural' sensuous love serves to unfold hitherto unrealized capacities for happiness and virtue in the personality of the lover.[25] And Émile's journey of self-development is radically incomplete without the love of his partner Sophie.[26]

Luhmann has emphasized that the rehabilitation of the passions evident in the Enlighteners' image of the rational, happy life is indicative of the inauguration of the modem concept of personality itself.[27] He points out that the psychology of the seventeenth century still worked with the old concepts of temperament and humour which allowed no room for personal development. This only changes in the course of the eighteenth century at which point people are conceived as being changeable, capable of development, still unperfected. In the context of this new understanding of personality, marital love, a love based on 'tender confidence' and esteem, was given a vital place in the Enlighteners' image of the virtuous, happy and rational life. Fairchilds describes the new libertarian meaning of the Enlightenment's understanding of personality as follows:

> In the face of centuries of Christian asceticism, the Enlightenment propounded the possibility of individual happiness on earth in the face of centuries of Christian disparagement: the Enlightenment rehabilitated the passions, including romantic love and sexual desire, as essential elements in such happiness.

The discussion so far has been particularly concerned to differentiate some aspects of the notion of rationality typical of the high Enlightenment from the rationalism seen to characterize seventeenth-century intellectual life. Jacobus and other main interpreters of this period emphasize that the increased radicalism, the specifically critical character of an eighteenth-century understanding of the notion of rationality, was by no means a uniform or unambiguous development.[29] Nevertheless, I would argue, there are important differences between the self-understanding of these two periods which need to be taken on board in the efforts of contemporary feminism to assess its own relation to Enlightenment. The anti-Enlightenment turn in contemporary feminism, as we have seen, challenges what it has construed as the essential dogmatic spirit of Enlightenment thinking; it has focused particularly on its supposed one-sided rationalism and on its metaphysical pretensions. This image overlooks the important new critical spirit, the anti-dogmatic construction which came to infuse the conception of Enlightenment throughout the eighteenth century, although this cultural commitment to the critique of prejudice laid down by the Enlighteners was, as noted, constrained by their own positive, normative conception of the character of the rational life.

Modern feminism can gain useful insights into both the radicalism and, from its own contemporary point of view, the fundamental limits of the Enlighteners' image of the rational life, by considering the focus given to this image in Wollstonecraft's *A Vindication of the Rights of Woman*. A brief comparison between Wollstonecraft's late-eighteenth-century feminism and the more conservative standpoint espoused in Mary Astell's late-seventeenth-century feminism illustrates important discontinuities between the two constructions of the power of reason outlined so far. Moreover, serious tensions which pervade the core of Wollstonecraft's feminism can be traced to limitations within the Enlighteners' own inaugural vision of the Enlightenment project.

Enlightenment feminism: Astell and Wollstonecraft
The Enlighteners' image of the rational life was quite plainly not intended to include women. Rousseau's Sophie, 'made for man's delight', is esteemed only for her contribution to the self-development of her mate Émile. Contemporary feminist scholars have rightly drawn attention to the deep misogynistic currents which inform the perspectives of main intellectual figures in the Enlightenment. Fox-Genovese, for example, points out that, 'as heirs to the time-honoured notions of female inferiority, Enlightenment thinkers normally continued to view women as weak, troublesome, shrewish, false, vindictive, ill-suited for friendship, coquettish, vain, deceitful and in general lesser humans.'[30]

Yet, despite this failure to challenge an overtly patriarchal legacy, the Enlighteners' deliberations on the character of the rational life opened up hitherto unsuspected possibilities for the development of a far-reaching feminism. Wollstonecraft's feminism moved beyond a mere politics of anti-discrimination, which calls only for an end to the exclusion of women from existing social priorities, to demand for women a vital place in setting the agenda for life in the 'City of the Future'. The Enlighteners' image of the rational life which emphasized the harmonious development of the individual's many-sided possibilities opened up a new creative dimension in Wollstonecraft's late-eighteenth-century feminism.

To appreciate the novel radicalism of Wollstonecraft's feminism, it is useful to compare her Enlightenment standpoint with the limitation of a feminism which had already surfaced in the seventeenth century. Astell's *A Serious Proposal to the Ladies* made explicit seventeenth-century feminism's identification with the rationalist's war on the degraded and unruly passions.[31] Aptly described as 'Reason's Disciples', Astell and her friend Elizabeth Elstorb placed great faith in the power of reason to expose the triviality, the moral unseriousness, of the conventions governing the lives of the new bourgeois women. The seventeenth-century feminist accepted her unpopular task as the upholder of the 'rules of reason' against a gross, unrestrained life guided only by the pursuit of sensuous enjoyment. Astell explains the plight of the seventeenth-century feminist as the defender of reason against the unruly, untutored passions thus:

> Custom has usurped such an unaccountable Authority, that she who would endeavour to put a stop to its arbitrary sway, and reduce it to Reason is in a fair way to render herself the butt for all the fops in Town to shoot their impertinent censures at.[32]

In the first instance, Astell's feminism voiced the protest of middle-ranking and upper-class women at their effective loss of status and power in the new bourgeois society. Although the newly emerging bourgeois society certainly provided this class of women with substantial grievances, by its insistence on the rational legitimation of all social practices, it offered also the main ideological preconditions for the articulation of an early feminist standpoint. Writing on marriage in the year 1700, Mary Astell asked:

> If Absolute Sovereignty be not necessary in a State how comes it to be so in a Family? Or if in a Family why not in a State; since no reason can be alleg'd for one that will not hold more strongly for the other.[33]

Luhmann and others have, however, pointed to the essentially conformist character of the seventeenth-century construction of the power of reason.[34] To the seventeenth-century European, it seemed that the rational life ultimately meant the observance of the rules and norms of the social environment against the tyranny of the unruly passions. And this seventeenth-century image of the rational life which conditioned Astell's feminism placed serious limitations on the radicalism of her protest. Astell's feminism was simply not equipped to interrogate in any essential way the priorities of her society. *A Serious Proposal* could only demand an end to the systematic exclusion of women from the seeming fruits of an intellectual culture monopolized by men. Astell's feminism called for the end to the universality of women's exclusion from the elevated 'life of the mind' and their systematic relegation to the 'Trifles and Gaities' of the marriage estate.[35]

On first inspection, the standpoint of Wollstonecraft's *A Vindication* appears as merely the renewal of the perspective already established in *A Serious Proposal*. Mary Wollstonecraft clearly emerges as another of 'reason's disciples'. Wollstonecraft's demand that the society recognize women as 'reasoning creatures' meant, however, something different and rather more radical than was implied in the feminism of her seventeenth-century counterparts. To Wollstonecraft, the barbarousness of the lives of bourgeois women does not appear simply in the denial of any intellectual life to the women newly herded into the trivialities of the domestic sphere. The tragedy of the situation appears, more precisely, in the deplorable waste of women's potential to lead a life guided by the aspiration towards self-improvement and human perfectibility. The Introduction to *A Vindication* announces Wollstonecraft's intention to 'consider women in the grand light of human creatures, who, in common with men, are placed on this earth to unfold their faculties'.[36] So it is the standpoint of 'improvable reason' which provides Wollstonecraft with the platform from which to challenge the unnaturalness and irrationality of the lives of women of her own class.

A late-eighteenth-century figure, Wollstonecraft has at her disposal a specifically critical construction of the meaning of the rational life: a construction which affirms as its reigning value the norm of the balanced development of all the individual's faculties into the self-directing adult personality. In the first instance, this image of the rational life appears as the platform for Wollstonecraft's scornful critique of the futility of the lives of bourgeois women in the newly depoliticized sphere of the household. To Wollstonecraft, bourgeois society had meant the creation of a whole class of women dehumanized and enslaved by their dependency. Wollstonecraft's feminism protests at the debilitating, one-sided development of women's human capacities in a bourgeois domestic life.

> Taught from their infancy that beauty is woman's sceptre, the mind shapes itself to the body, and roaming around its gilt cage, only seeks to adore its prison. Men have various employments and pursuits which engage their attention, and give character to the opening mind; but women, confined to one and having their thoughts constantly directed to the most insignificant parts of themselves, seldom extend their views beyond the triumph of the hour.[37]

Denied the opportunity to develop a range of human potentials, the personalities of women could only become horribly distorted and impoverished.

Clearly, Wollstonecraft had no more stomach for the idleness and mere sentimentality which dominated early bourgeois domestic life than had her seventeenth-century predecessors. What is quite new, however, is her conviction that our efforts to build an enriched and decent social life could be informed by an attempt to redeem those traces of a humanistic ethic presently locked within the distortions of bourgeois domesticity. Wollstonecraft despises the prison-house of bourgeois domesticity with its futile and trifling preoccupations. And yet it is less the type of concerns nourished by the new bourgeois family that Wollstonecraft finds so repugnant than their one-sided and hence distorted form. In the bourgeois family the humanistic image of relations with others based on a 'tender confidence' only makes its distorted appearance as an irrational romantic love fanned by 'vain fears and fond jealousies'.[38]

What needs to be stressed here is that the standpoint of 'improvable reason' does not simply articulate a judgement on the trivial irrationality of the lives of the new bourgeois women. It is also an invitation for a vital, creative participation in opening up new life possibilities for the enriched self-legislating personalities of the future. To Wollstonecraft, this creative dimension of the standpoint of 'improvable reason' suggests that a domestic ethic of affectionate care and duty towards particular others presently languishing in the artificial sentimentality of the private sphere is worthy of redemption as a public ethic. Wollstonecraft supposes that the bourgeois family both provokes and expresses a need to which it cannot adequately respond. The privatization of the ethic of care and responsibility for particular others appears in the particular context of the bourgeois family in the unstable and distorted guise of transitory and possessive love. To Wollstonecraft, this need for relations of care and responsibility for others finds its most appropriate expression in the friendship which is to her 'the most holy band of society'.[39] Wollstonecraft's feminism preserves, then, the ideal of active citizenship. Far from conceiving the realm of private activities as a sphere which needs to be protected from political interference, Wollstonecraft encourages the politicization of those perspectives and needs presently contained within a repressive private sphere. Ursula Vogel comments on this visionary aspect of *A Vindication*:

> The role which we commonly identify as belonging in the private sphere, Mary Wollstonecraft perceives as a constitutive element of citizenship. Stripped of their familiar association with intimate affections, and merely personal interests, the tasks of the mother obtain the dignity of public virtues.[40]

Condorcet, too, argued for the 'admission of women to the rights of citizenship' on the basis of the civic importance of their' gentle and domestic virtues' and on the basis of the distinctive character of their reasoning powers, seen by him as an expression of their specific interests and aspirations.

> Women are not governed, it is true, by the reason of men. But they are governed by their own reason. Their interests not being the same as those of men through the fault of the laws, the same things not having the same importance for them as for us, they can (without lacking reason) govern themselves by different principles and seek a different goal.[41]

An evaluation of the utopian aspect of Wollstonecraft's programme is not particularly relevant here. 'What is of concern is the peculiar radicalism of her feminism, which supposes itself to have not merely grievances at systematic patterns of discrimination experienced by bourgeois women, but a vital positive contribution to make to discussions over the character of the rational life. Where Astell's feminism had demanded only an end to women's systematic exclusion from the life of 'reasoning creatures', Wollstonecraft appealed to the standpoint of 'improvable reason' to demand the participation of the distinctive voice of women in unfolding the meaning of the rational, happy life.

Reiss offers a very different interpretation of the radicalism of *A Vindication*. On his account, Wollstonecraft was prevented from arguing a truly revolutionary case

> because she argued *within* Enlightenment rhetoric, for the extension of equality without regard (at least) to gender. Wollstonecraft was asserting women's right to catch up with men, in the same way that Tom Paine (for example) argued that the enfranchisement of the dispossessed – whether colonials, the poor, or the aged must catch up with that of proprietors. It was always a matter of the right to participate in the system, not of the need to change it.[42]

Here Reiss discovers only one aspect of the main trends in what is, from a modem point of view, Wollstonecraft's highly contradictory feminism. As previously argued, Wollstonecraft is not afraid of upholding those qualities with which education and circumstance supposedly endow women as vital ingredients in the fully humanized, improved personality.[43] In her view, bourgeois women have been constrained by a life dedicated to the cultivation of the sensibilities. And yet, as the following passage suggests, Wollstonecraft's feminism targets only the dehumanizing, one-sided character of those 'feminine' qualities produced by bourgeois domesticity.

> 'The power of the woman,' says some author, 'is her sensibility'; and men, not aware of the consequence, do all they can to make this power swallow up every other. Those who constantly employ their sensibility will have most: for example, poets, painters, and composers. Yet, when the sensibility is thus increased at the expense of reason, and even the imagination, why do philosophical men complain of their fickleness?[44]

Wollstonecraft's critique of modern gender relations had at its disposal an image of the improved, many-sided personality. Accordingly, her feminism recognizes a positive contribution from a different feminine voice in setting the agenda for life in the 'City of the Future'. Wollstonecraft does not, however, manage to sustain this perspective. The appeal to an Enlightenment construction of the rational social life also makes way for a legitimating perspective on an existing gendered bifurcation of private and public roles construed as nature. In this case, we see that Wollstonecraft is not calling for a recognition of the distinctive voice of women as active citizens in establishing the character of new social forms. She seeks only a reappraisal of the public significance of the private duties presently performed by bourgeois women in the domestic sphere. Women, Wollstonecraft remarks, 'may have different duties to fulfil; but they are human duties, and the principles that should regulate the discharge of them ... must be the same'.[45] At such points, the radicalism of her challenge to the new bourgeois social arrangement which severed the lives of middle-class women from the new public sphere is seemingly overwhelmed by a naturalistic patriarchal ideology.

Despite its own overt radicalism, Wollstonecraft's feminism is haunted by a historically understandable, naturalistic construction of the gendered character of social tasks and duties. In this capacity her feminism does nothing to challenge the priorities and the practical arrangement of her society. It merely calls for the recognition of the vital importance of 'womanly' duties in the realization of a harmonious, balanced social life.

So, in Wollstonecraft's feminism, we see the aporetic manifestation of the two dimensions of an Enlightenment construction of the character of the rational life discussed earlier. On the one hand, Wollstonecraft employs the Enlightenment construction of the rationality of the balanced, harmonious life and personality as the vehicle for her positive feminist critique of both the one-sidedness of the lives of bourgeois women and the one-sidedness of public discussions over the content of the good, the rational social life. Whilst women are denied the exercise of all their human faculties in the 'gilt cage' of bourgeois domesticity, so too there is insufficient public recognition of the humanizing ennobling potentials of those virtues of 'tender confidence' and 'gentle forbearance' supposedly nurtured by the intimate sphere. On the other hand, Wollstonecraft's feminism does not attempt to challenge the seeming naturalness of a gendered division of labour.[46] In its positive construction, 'rationality' loses its critical power as an interrogation of existing social arrangements from the standpoint of the neglected claims of a diversity of human potentials. Seen, rather, as a vision of a balanced, orderly social life, a vision whose rationality is authorized by the supposed order of a harmonious universe, the Enlightenment appeal to reason has the effect of sanctioning an existing way of life. To the extent that it works uncritically within the aporia of this understanding of the character of rationality, Wollstonecraft's feminism cannot itself entirely escape a naturalistic ideology which imposes an essential status on the culturally acquired roles and interests of modern women.

Feminism and the unfinished project of Enlightenment
The naturalistic ideology which plagues *A Vindication* appears as a manifestation of the anthropological foundations of Wollstonecraft's typical Enlightenment vision of the rational social life. Despite the eighteenth century's stress on humanity's unique capacity for self-improvement, this enterprise is still seen to be circumscribed and shaped by man's anthropological nature. The Enlightenment had not yet fully achieved the historical consciousness which was to emerge in the nineteenth century. Human attributes continue to be seen largely as fixed anthropological traits. Far from suggesting the pursuit of historically posited goals and objectives, the idea of the rational life appeared to the eighteenth-century Enlightenment as the revelation of nature's own plan. Hazard points out that it was supposed that the light of reason would discover nature's plan and once this was fully illuminated all that remained was to conform the new society to it.[47] The capacity for the rational life was viewed in terms of eliminating the obstacles to the natural unfolding of 'human capacities', in the light of an anthropological discovery rather than as an affirmation of a historical project or task.[48]

The eighteenth-century anthropology according to which reason appears as an inherent capacity in the individual and truth the revelation of nature's plan was unable to discover its own legitimating prejudices. These would only become apparent with the historicized perspective which was to emerge in the nineteenth century. From the point of view of a historicized consciousness, the Enlighteners' suppositions that the new rational society could be modelled after the principles of nature ultimately suggested the failure of the historical Enlightenment's capacity to sustain a commitment to the cause of a self-legislating humanity. The *philosophes* were not yet able to formulate the Enlightenment project as a commitment to radical democracy which recognized concrete individuals as the arbiters of their own wills and needs. As Markus explains, the Enlightenment philosophers' search for the 'truth' of a rationally unified secular culture 'able to discover and to impose a unique direction towards human perfection upon all processes of change occurring in a dynamic society ultimately means the failure of the historical Enlightenment itself with respect to its own emancipatory vision'.[49]

Although it remained to later generations of Enlightenment thinkers to diagnose the root causes of the failure of the historical Enlightenment, the seeds of its own self-critique were already unwittingly implanted in the aporias of Enlightenment's feminism. The democratic impulses of Wollstonecraft's feminism, which saw her calling for a recognition of the distinctive voices of women in any discussion of the character of life in the 'City of the Future', was now in conflict with her endorsement of an anthropology which construed an imposed gender division of labour as an expression of a natural order. Yet, in the final analysis, the anthropological underpinnings of her Enlightenment understanding of the rational life meant that traditional social arrangements continued to have a powerful sanction. In particular, as Jane Rendall points out, the Enlightenment's attack on the seventeenth century's concept of a divinely ordered patriarchal family was replaced by an equally repressive legitimating ideology of the family as a pre-political web of natural relationships.[50]

The twentieth century shattered the optimism nursed by eighteenth-century European philosophy. The extravagant expectations harboured by Condorcet and others that 'the arts and sciences would promote not only the control of natural forces but would also further understanding of the world and of the self, would promote moral progress, the justice of institutions, and even the happiness of human beings', have all but disappeared.[51] With Markus, Bauman and others. Habermas clearly acknowledges the failure of the eighteenth century to free itself from the grip of dogma and prejudice. It seems equally clear, however, that our present capacity to unmask the failure of this early formulation of Enlightenment is precisely evidence of the continuing, vital relevance of this open-ended cultural project to contemporary social life. As Bauman sees it, the failure of the historical Enlightenment to implement its own project does not mean that the project itself was abortive and doomed. 'The potential of modernity is still untapped and the promise of modernity needs to be redeemed.'[52]

So an assertion of modern feminism as an episode in Enlightenment thinking recognizes feminism's own necessary participation in this, as yet radically incomplete, open-ended project of cultural criticism. Feminism takes its vital and distinctive place in the project described by Kant as the future-oriented optimism that people could emerge from their self-imposed minority to legislate for themselves. It remained for later generations of thinkers inspired by the historical Enlightenment to historicize and radically democratize the meaning of this task. Whereas the Enlighteners had appealed to the 'truth of nature' to *impose* a direction towards human perfection, the spirit of the Enlightenment since that time has sought to maintain the emancipatory temper which sees human beings as the creators of their own social world on the basis of the needs and the aspirations of concrete individuals themselves. This spirit was encapsulated in the broadening nineteenth-century demand for constitutional reform, republicanism and finally social revolution and radical democracy.

As already suggested, Kant's essay 'What is Enlightenment?' still stands as a classical interpretation of the broad cultural meaning of the Enlightenment as the ongoing, still radically incomplete project of modernity. Kant's essay underlines that Enlightenment exists only as a human task or goal. We live, he says, not in an enlightened age but in an age of Enlightenment. The historical Enlightenment vision of a self-reliant humanity capable of legislating for itself must be embraced as the arduous task of every modern individual. The Enlighteners showed that Enlightenment required nothing but freedom, in particular 'the freedom of man to make public use of his reason at all points'.[53]

On this account, Enlightenment means the freedom of self-legislation in those matters of public import which transcend the realm of the mere private duty of the citizen. In the end, Kant suggests that, whilst Enlightenment remains a cultural and individual task, it also and at the same time identifies the original vocation of human nature itself. Nature, he comments,

> has evolved the seed for which she cares most tenderly, namely the propensity and the vocation for independent thinking: this gradually works back on the mentality of the people (whereby they become little by little more capable of the freedom to act) and also eventually even on the principles of government, which finds it advantageous to itself to treat people who are now more than machines in accordance with their dignity.[54]

Enlightenment is a historical project guided by a regulative idea to be constantly recharged with contemporary historical content.

Kant's view of Enlightenment is a call for a radical emancipation from the dogmas of the past and for practical autonomy. This is a call that has resounded down to our own time. The call was heard by Kant's contemporaries who applied Kant's critical method to his own philosophical presuppositions. Each succeeding generation of Enlightenment has submitted the certitudes of its own milieu to the same critical questioning in order to re-marshal the energies and redefine the contemporary meaning of Enlightenment, thus making another advance down the road that Kant had designated. Each unveils a new dimension of the problem and a new terrain on which the battle for freedom and reason needs to be prosecuted in order to realize our historically accumulating sense of human dignity.

Modern feminism is similarly best understood as occupying this kind of double relation to Enlightenment thinking. On the one hand, modern feminism clearly cannot ignore its own continuity with the Enlightenment tradition. It preserves the Enlightenment's emancipatory vision in which human beings are affirmed as the determinators of their own social world. In particular, modern feminism is properly understood as an interpretation of a contemporary historicized understanding of Enlightenment. Feminism today typically repudiates all Enlightenment formulations which turn on an appeal to an impartial reason and to an eternal and normatively conceived human nature. Modern feminism appears as a vital moment in a contemporary interpretation of the cause of Enlightenment as a commitment to the cause of radical democracy.

The affirmation of feminism's own Enlightenment character does not, it must be stressed, suggest its assimilation to any fixed set of doctrines and principles. As its critic, modern feminism unmasks the failures of the various episodes in the Enlightenment tradition to adequately interpret the meaning of the Enlightenment project. The narrow rationalism of seventeenth-century metaphysics, the naturalizing constructions of the Enlighteners themselves, the so-called gender-blindness of Marxian categories as well as liberalism's own construction of an abstract 'rights-bearing' subject have all been appropriately targeted by contemporary feminism.

Yet, as a critic of the Enlightenment tradition, modern feminism is also and at the same time a manifestation and an interpretation of Enlightenment. Feminism constantly seeks to push back the legacy of our entrenched prejudices to reveal new social possibilities in the present. Ever since Wollstonecraft, feminists have affirmed their commitment to a qualitatively expanded interpretation of the meaning of Enlightenment. Modern feminism has consistently attempted to expose the prejudices embedded within those definitional constructions of the human subject called upon in the various formulations of the meaning of Enlightenment. Contemporary feminism has, moreover, attempted to open up our understanding of those activities and actions deemed the proper subject for public discussion and expression. The familiar feminist call for the politicization of the personal sphere is one instance of feminism's vital and distinctive contribution to an ongoing process of immanent critique in which generations of Enlightenment thinkers have opened up new terrains which need to be encompassed in a commitment to radical democracy. Modern feminism is a qualitative expansion of the contemporary Enlightenment project. It relies unquestioningly on no pre-existing interpretations but offers its own unique, still developing, interpretation of Enlightenment understood as a broad-based programme for critique and social change promoting the social recognition of diverse human potentials and ways of life.

Notes

1. S. de Beauvoir, *The Second Sex*, Penguin Books, Harmondsworth, 1972.
2. Ibid., p. 29.
3. G. Lloyd, *The Man of Reason: 'Male' and 'Female' in Western Philosophy*, Methuen, London, 1984, p. 101.
4. S. Harding, *The Science Question in Feminism*, Open University Press, Milton Keynes, 1986, p. 15.
5. See, for example, A. Jardine, *Gynesis: Configurations of Women and Modernity*, Cornell University Press, New York, 1985; S. Hekman, *Gender and Knowledge: Elements of a Post-modern Feminism*, Polity Press, Cambridge, 1990; J. Flax, 'Post-modernism and Gender Relations in Feminist Theory', in L. Nicholson, ed., *Feminism/Postmodernism*, Routledge, London, 1990, pp. 39–63.
6. S. Harding, 'Feminism, Science and the Anti-Enlightenment Critiques', in Nicholson, ed., *Feminism/Postmodernism*, pp. 83–106, p. 99.
7. S. Lovibond, 'Feminism and Postmodernism', *New Left Review* 178, November–December 1989, pp. 5–29.
8. I. Kant, 'What is Enlightenment?', in *Kant on History*, ed. L.W. Beck, Bobbs-Merrill, Indianapolis IN, 1963, p. 3.
9. See M.C. Jacob, *The Radical Enlightenment: Pantheists, Freemasons and Republicans*, George Allen & Unwin, London, 1981. Jacob offers a very illuminating account of the diversity of intellectual trends at play throughout the eighteenth century.
10. Jardine, *Gynesis*, p.20.
11. Hekman, *Gender and Knowledge*, p. 1.
12. Ibid., p. 5.
13. Ibid., p. 9.
14. Flax, 'Post-Modernism and Gender Relations in Feminist Theory', p. 42.
15. Ibid., p. 43.
16. See, for example, E. Grosz, 'Feminism and Anti-Humanism', in A. Milner and C. Worth, eds, *Discourse and Difference: Post-Structuralism, Feminism and the Moment of History*, Centre for General and Comparative Literature, Monash University, Melbourne, 1990, pp. 63–75.
17. P. Gay, *The Enlightenment: An Interpretation*, Volume 1: *The Rise of Modern Paganism*, Alfred Knopf, New York, 1966, p. 174.
18. E. Cassirer, *The Philosophy of the Enlightenment*, Beacon Press, Boston MA, 1951, p. 13.
19. See J. d'Alembert, Introduction to *Preliminary Discourse on the Encyclopaedia of Diderot*, Bobbs-Merrill, Indianapolis IN, 1963, p. xxxv.
20. Cassirer, *The Philosophy of the Enlightenment*, p. 13.
21. G. Markus, 'A Society of Culture: The Constitution of Cultural Modernity', paper presented to *Thesis Eleven* conference, Melbourne; in G.Robinson and J. Rundell, eds, *Rethinking Imagination*, Routledge, London, 1994, pp. 15–29.
22. Ibid.
23. Ibid.
24. Jacob, *The Radical Enlightenment*, p. 104.
25. D. Diderot, *The Encyclopaedia*, trans. and ed. S. Gendzier, Harper Torchbooks, New York, p. 97.
26. J.-J. Rousseau, *Émile*, trans. Barbara Foxley, Everyman, London, 1969.
27. N. Luhmann, *Love as Passion: The Codification of Intimacy*, Polity, Cambridge, 1986, p. 99.
28. See S. Spenser, ed., *French Women and the Age of Enlightenment*, Indiana University Press, Bloomington, 1984, p. 98.

29. See Jacob, *The Radical Enlightenment*.
30. E. Fox-Genovese, 'Property and Patriarchy in Classical Bourgeois Political Theory', *Radical History Review*, vol. 4, nos 2–3, 1977.
31. M. Astell, *A Serious Proposal to the Ladies*, London, 1696.
32. M. Astell, quoted in H. Smith, *Reason's Disciples: Seventeenth Century Feminists*, University of Illinois Press, Urbana, 1982, p. 63.
33. M. Astell, *Reflections Upon Marriage*, London, 1700, quoted in J. Mitchell, 'Women and Equality', in A. Phillips, ed., *Feminism and Equality*, Blackwell, Oxford, 1987, p. 31.
34. See, for example, Luhmann, *Love as Passion*, p. 94.
35. See R. Perry, *The Celebrated Mary Astell: An Early English Feminist*, University of Chicago Press, Chicago, 1986, pp. 79–80.
36. M. Wollstonecraft, *A Vindication of the Rights of Woman*, Norton, New York, 1967, p. 58.
37. Ibid., pp. 82–3.
38. Ibid., p. 122.
39. Ibid.
40. U. Vogel, 'Rationalism and Romanticism: Two Strategies for Women's Liberation', in J. Evans et al., eds, *Feminism and Political Theory*, Sage, London, 1986, pp. 31–2.
41. N. de Condorcet, 'On the Admission of Women to the Rights of Citizenship', in K.M. Baker, ed., *Condorcet: Selected Writings*, Bobbs-Merrill, Indianapolis IN, 1976, pp. 97–8.
42. T. Reiss, 'Revolution in Bounds: Wollstonecraft, Women and Reason', in L. Kauffman, ed., *Gender and Theory: Dialogues on Feminist Criticism*, Blackwell, Oxford, 1989, pp. 11–41, p. 21.
43. See, for example, passages from Wollstonecraft, *A Vindication of the Rights of Woman*, Norton edition, pp. 43, 110.
44. Ibid., p. 110.
45. Ibid., p. 92.
46. See ibid., p. 115.
47. P. Hazard, *European Thought in the Eighteenth Century*, Hollis & Carter, London, 1954, p. xvviii.
48. See G. Markus, 'Concepts of Ideology in Marx', *Canadian Journal of Political and Social Theory*, vol. 7, nos 1–2, 1983, p.86ff.
49. Ibid., p. 86.
50. J. Rendall, *The Origins of Modern Feminism*, Macmillan, London, 1985.
51. J. Habermas, 'Modernity versus Post-modernity', *New German Critique* 22, Winter 1981, pp. 3–15, p. 9.
52. Z. Bauman, *Legislators and Interpreters: On Modernity, Postmodernity and Intellectuals*, Polity, Cambridge, 1987, p. 191.
53. Kant, 'What is Enlightenment?', p. 10.
54. Ibid., p. 15.

5 Will the real Kant please stand up: The challenge of Enlightenment racism to the study of the history of philosophy

ROBERT BERNASCONI

This article poses the question of racism in philosophy. I will be referring to the racism that we often find in the texts of some of the most eminent figures of the history of Western philosophy, particularly Locke and Kant. They seem to express racist views that appear to us, but not apparently to them, to run counter to the ethical principles that they themselves proclaimed. However, the focus of this article is not so much on their racism, but on our ways of addressing it, or, more often, our ways of not addressing it. My question is whether there is not an institutional racism within contemporary philosophy that emerges in our tendency to ignore or otherwise play down their racism while we celebrate their principles. It is to my mind shocking to see how little thought contemporary philosophers give to this issue, although there are definite signs that there is now at least a recognition of the problem, just as the sexism of so much philosophy is also now being more carefully scrutinized.[1] Because the details of both Locke's and Kant's racism are now more readily available to anybody who wants to know about them than they were even three or four years ago, it is important to think about what difference they might make to the way these thinkers are discussed and taught. In other words, we must explore the possibility, which some people may want to dismiss too quickly as a symptom of political correctness in the academy, that these investigations raise serious and difficult philosophical questions that we need to attend to as a matter of urgency.

The unwillingness of philosophers generally to confront, for example, the failure of Locke and Kant to oppose the African slave trade does not arise out of a healthy refusal to engage in tabloid philosophy, but represents both a moral and a philosophical shortcoming.

I should make it clear at the outset that I do not understand this article as offering reasons not to read them. In spite of my best efforts to avoid giving precisely this impression, some people have assimilated my efforts to the way that certain scholars attempted to use the facts of Heidegger's involvement with National Socialism as a way to expel him from the canon: according to Gilbert Ryle, because Heidegger was not a good man, he cannot have been a good philosopher.[2] But I have never used that argument, nor sought to apply any variation of it to the works of Locke or Kant. My point is not that we should now bypass these thinkers, but that, given their unquestioned importance, such that we cannot afford not to read them, we should make their racism a further reason to interrogate them. In other words, because they were unquestionably major philosophers whose impact lives on outside the academy as well as in it, their racism has a particular claim to our attention. This is what makes Kant's racism more philosophically interesting than that of Christoph Meiners, for example. So how should we address the racism of Locke and Kant? I will detail three initial tasks, but this is not intended as an exhaustive list.

The first task is to research, acknowledge and address philosophically the racism of canonical philosophers in such a way that it is seen in relation to the larger body of their work. This includes raising the question of how the racism of these thinkers relates to their philosophy. For example, Frege was strongly anti-Semitic, but it is hard to draw a connection between his anti-Semitism and his philosophy. Heidegger's involvement with National Socialism raises serious questions that cannot be evaded by any philosophical assessment of his work, but his anti-Semitism, although undeniable, is not so easily associated with his philosophy, although an argument along these lines can be formulated. The case against Heidegger quite properly relies on the fact that he was at work in a crucial time period when the question of the fate of the Jews could not be evaded, but at other times other moral questions impose themselves. Slavery was one of these. Western philosophy has been and is still largely in denial about its racism, not least because most specialists tend to be defensive about the thinkers on whom they have devoted years of study.

Take Locke, first. It is true that Locke scholars for a number of years have recognized the need to address the question of his leading role in the administration of British colonial activities and his investment in the slave trade through the Royal African Company, as well as the Company of Merchant Adventurers, who operated in the Bahamas, but the consideration of these topics is still largely the preserve of historians and political theorists, as if they raised no philosophical questions.[3] Although the precise role that Locke played in writing *The Fundamental Constitutions of Carolina* is unknown and may never be settled, it seems that, when that document grants to slaveholders 'absolute power and authority' over their Negro slaves, the reference to 'power' was added to the manuscript in his own handwriting to read: 'Every Freeman of Carolina shall have absolute power and Authority over his Negro slaves, of what opinion or Religion soever.'[4] The point of the specific article of the *Fundamental Constitutions* was to resolve the question of whether conversion to Christianity on the part of the slave would jeopardize the slaveholder's interest in his property. But Locke's intervention in 1669 was continuous with his insistence in the *Second Treatise of Government* that subjection to 'absolute, arbitrary, power' defines slavery.[5] With reference to power, the terms 'absolute' and 'arbitrary' are used by Locke virtually interchangeably.[6] And yet, as a generation of scholars have now repeatedly observed, the chapter 'Of Slavery' in the *Second Treatise* clearly excludes chattel slavery of the kind practised in Carolina, because it is restricted to captives in a just war.⁷ Locke must have recognized that what he said about legitimate forms of slavery in the *Second Treatise* contradicted the conditions he helped to establish for Negro slaves in Carolina. And the fact that 'Slaves bought with Money' by planters in the West Indies make an appearance in the *First Treatise* shows that he was perfectly capable of relating his political theory to conditions outside England, when it helped his argument.⁸ Nevertheless, most commentators on Locke take it for granted that what needs to be explained is merely a contingent, anomalous, aberrant Locke behind which lies the benign far-sighted liberal Locke, the Locke of whom Lockeans are proud to be the heirs.

Turning to Kant, it is hard to know whether the fact that Kant scholars waited for non-specialists like Emmanuel Eze and me to raise the issue of Kant's racism was because these scholars did not know the full range of Kant's works very well – which would be somewhat damning if true – or because they persuaded themselves that there was nothing here worth discussing.⁹ In any event, Kant's essays on race were acknowledged by philosophers until the Second World War, and it was only after that time that recognition of their existence seemed to be confined to non-philosophers, such as Leon Poliakov and George Mosse, who included reference to Kant in their books on the background to the Holocaust.¹⁰ It is true that some philosophers, and not just historians of science, when writing on the 'Critique of Teleological Judgment', saw that some of the central problems addressed in that work were first formulated by Kant in his essays on race.¹¹ However, the racism that is apparent in those essays, as in his lectures on anthropology and on physical geography, was almost never brought into relation with his teleology, his moral philosophy or his essay on universal history, in spite of the obvious question that they raised: how could his racism coexist with his moral universalism?¹²

Discussions of the racism of Enlightenment philosophers are often met by the response that the philosopher in question – it does not really matter who it is – simply shared the assumptions of the time. This suggests a second task: one must recognize the importance of context for an understanding of these philosophers. To assess their remarks one needs to know the range of views being expressed at the time in which they wrote. This exercises a form of external control on our judgements. The 'child of his time' defence cannot be used until we research what their contemporaries thought and particularly how their contemporaries responded to them. Although there does not appear to have been a thoroughgoing public debate about the legitimacy of chattel slavery until some time after Locke's death, we do know that he was familiar with a debate, involving one of his former students, over the question of whether Christians can be enslaved, a question that concerned planters fearful about the impact on their investment of missionary efforts among slaves.[13] Blumenbach objected to some of Kant's racial remarks against the Tahitians as unfair.[14] Concern about Kant's racism is not therefore a 'new concern', the product simply of sensibilities that have only recently surfaced. This part of the inquiry is important because it makes it possible to decide whether or not an interpretation is anachronistic.[15]

A third and somewhat related task is to inquire into their sources, paying particular attention to the selection of sources. What did they know, when did they know it, and what could they have easily known had they wanted to? To my surprise, in raising these questions I have made the kind of historical discoveries that one would have thought specialists in the area would have known long ago. My earlier discussion of Locke's insertion of the term 'power' in the *Fundamental Constitutions of Carolina* is a case in point. Even though the fact that Locke had a role in the drafting of this document has been widely known, so far as I am aware no scholars focused on the evidence that Locke added the term 'power' until I did.[16] Similarly, I find it surprising that Kant scholars would not have noticed that Kant had alternative accounts of the character of Africans at his disposal from that 'On the Use of Teleological Principles in Philosophy', and that when he characterized the freed Negroes of America and England as – like the Gypsies in Germany – unwilling without exception to work, he deliberately gave credence to the account provided by James Tobin of the pro-slavery faction rather than that proposed by James Ramsay, a prominent opponent of slavery, although both were equally available to him in the same periodical.[17] Kant was well aware of the problem of alternative sources and explained why in his review of Herder's *Ideas*: one could prove whatever one chose to prove.[18] But that is why Kant's own choices must be carefully examined. Kant's failure to express disapproval of the chattel slavery of Africans, either in his published works or, so far as I can tell, in his lectures, has to be understood in the context of the fact that this was one of the most prominent moral issues of his day.

Excising contradictions

These three tasks – identifying the problematic statements of these thinkers that are prima facie racist, locating them in the context of their works and the broader historical context, and establishing their sources – are basic tasks that intellectual historians would perform as a matter of course, although they involve scholarly and historical skills that philosophy graduate programmes, for the most part, do not spend much effort in developing among their students. By contrast, many philosophers, even historians of philosophy, seem not to care about these tasks, because they are intent on taking the problem into a different sphere. Historians of philosophy tend for the most part to isolate Locke, Kant and Hegel from the historical realities which nurtured them and to which they responded. Furthermore, whole volumes of their works are disregarded. In short, the basic rules of good history are disregarded. For largely historical reasons, the study of the history of philosophy in the English-speaking world has much more to do with maintaining its philosophical legitimacy in the face of the very narrow conception of philosophy that came to prominence in the period immediately after the Second World War than with meeting the standards that would establish its credentials as history.

For fifty years or so historians of philosophy have believed that they can write a work in the history of philosophy and brazenly rewrite the arguments of the canonical philosophers, if they think they can improve on what those philosophers had managed for themselves. For example, Bernard Williams in the preface to his book on Descartes explains that because Descartes' work was inevitably and essentially 'ambiguous, incomplete, imperfectly determined by the author's and his contemporaries' understanding', he would take it upon himself to write a 'rational reconstruction of Descartes' thought'.[19] The history of ideas, he explained, is 'an historical enquiry and the *genre* of the resulting work is unequivocally history', but the history of philosophy faces 'a cut-off point, where authenticity is replaced as the objective by the aim of articulating philosophical ideas'.[20] Clearly the casualty of such efforts is an understanding of the historical dimension of a philosopher's work and I believe that this leaves anyone who takes this route ill-equipped to address the question of the coexistence in the same thinker of both racism and moral universalism, which is why they tend to ignore one or the other, usually the racism. This approach allows philosophers to persist in presenting racism as no more than a surface feature of a philosophy, in contrast with moral universalism, which is a philosophical thesis that, as such, will always trump racist particularism.

What is a philosopher who believes that arguments are the base currency of philosophy to do in the face of a bad argument or a contradiction in some text by a major historical philosopher? Whereas some academics seem to gain some satisfaction from exposing the errors of a Plato or a Kant, and for many of them this seems to be all the satisfaction they need, Williams seems to advocate that one simply pick and choose, add and subtract, until one arrives at what the philosopher should have said. If the problem is that a thinker appears to contradict himself or herself, then one can always drop one of the competing claims. The rule is that one saves the proposition that is most worth saving, and it is only a slight extension of this practice to drop all claims that are in the least bit embarrassing, whether there is a contradiction or not. What remains is the 'authentic' doctrine of the philosopher in question. We are served a new, slimmer, more elegant Kant, after he has undergone liposuction and had the surplus removed. This is quite normal philosophical practice, which is why no eyebrows are raised when it is applied to Locke's role in writing *The Fundamental Constitutions of Carolina*, Kant's insistence on the racial superiority of whites, and, for that matter, Hegel's exclusion of Africa, China and India from history proper. What remains is a benign, sanitized philosophy.

Although most commentators choose to excise the racism from the philosopher in question in the way I have just described, a few have begun to address the contradiction between racism and moral universalism. They have found that sometimes imputing a racist position to the thinker renders them more coherent and serves to defend their philosophical credentials. So when trying to explain why Locke accepted the idea that blacks could be slaves, but seems at the same time not to have wanted Native Americans to be slaves, Barbara Arnell simply concludes that the former were for him 'less than human', although she seems to have no direct evidence for choosing that particular formulation.[21] Consider also the example of James Farr's essay on the problem of slavery in Locke's political thought.[22] Following his recognition that Locke's theory positively condemns seventeenth-century slave practices even though Locke invested in the African slave trade and was involved in legislation concerning it, Farr asks: 'are there other grounds in Locke's political thought that *would* justify seventeenth century slavery?' His answer is as follows: '*I fear* that there just are no other grounds. In particular, Locke was not a racist in the strong sense required to justify slavery.'[23] Farr seems to be saying that it would be better that Locke had been a consistent racist than that he be caught contradicting himself. Or, more precisely, it seems that Farr would prefer evidence that Locke was a racist in a strong sense than that he was inconsistent, where being a strong racist means having 'both an *empirical* theory that explains black racial inferiority and a *moral* theory that justifies enslavement because of racial inferiority'.[24] I do not accept Farr's account, which identifies strong racism neither with strength of feelings, nor with the character of actions, but with explicit theories. Nor do I believe that he has exhausted the historical evidence. But my interest here is that Farr, who was not a philosopher, nevertheless wants, above all, a Locke who is free of contradiction. Of course, had Farr been a philosopher of the kind that is all too familiar, he could have simply disregarded the evidence of Locke's investment in the slave trade and in its institutionalization by declaring that this was not the real Locke. Indeed, he could also have disregarded any empirical theory on the grounds that it was not the real Locke either, as happens when philosophers read Kant.

This can most easily be illustrated by reference to Thomas Hill and Bernard Boxill's recent essay, 'Kant and Racism'. I applaud their essay as one of the few serious treatments of the topic, but I regard it as symptomatic of the failings I identify as endemic to predominantly analytic approaches to this topic. Hill and Boxill's strategy is to distinguish at the outset Kant's philosophical theses from his empirical claims, to which they assimilate his 'racist and sexist beliefs and attitudes'. This allows them to segregate what they call his 'basic ideas (e.g. the central and more foundational claims in the three Critiques and the *Groundwork*)' from the 'separable parts' of that philosophy, which are 'independent of the basic ideas and perhaps falsely believed to be derivative' from them, and from particular illustrations.[25] In other words, they operate by making distinctions. So long as there is no necessary connection between the 'racist and sexist beliefs and attitudes' and what they identify as his main philosophical claims, then this provides them with the basis for saying that, if Kant writes racist remarks, it is not the real Kant who does so.

So who is the real Kant? The 'real Kant' apparently is not the historical Kant but, rather, the author only of his 'central philosophical principles'. The real Kant is defined not by texts so much as by select ideas that contemporary Kantianism finds valuable. So Kant's teleology is discarded because contemporary philosophers are sceptical about it and because it appears to be separable.[26] The emphasis is on constructing a Kant that can meet the demands we place on a contemporary moral theory, including providing resources against racism. But it is striking that even within these very restricted accounts of Kant, the name Kant is still made to do all the work, and the theory remains parasitic on a brand name whose status largely derives from texts that are now for the most part ignored. I am thinking of the fact that for the generations immediately after Kant it was the *Critique of Teleological Judgment* that was regarded as his true accomplishment. It is almost impossible for anyone taught Kant by a contemporary Kantian to make sense of most of what Schelling, Hegel or Hölderlin had to say in praise of him, let alone the majority of their criticisms. For example, at the beginning of 1795 Hölderlin wrote to Hegel that he regarded the way in which Kant united mechanism with the purposiveness of nature to contain 'the entire spirit of the system'.[27] That is to say, the version of Kant taught in history of philosophy courses today has been developed to protect Kant against the criticisms levelled by his immediate successors, thereby making the writings of the latter appear arbitrary and idiosyncratic. The real Kant is the version of Kant that approximates most closely to what the philosophers who propose this construction recognize as the truth. The real Kant is the true Kant because common sense, freedom from contradiction, and, where possible, freedom from racism, are introduced as hermeneutic principles even where they contradict the historical evidence. What one often finds is anything but the much-vaunted analytic necessity; what one finds is pick and mix. Kant himself is damned: his racist attitudes are judged to be incompatible with his basic principle of respect for humanity in each person. But 'the deep theory' is salvaged to live and fight racism another day.[28]

The point of contention here is not the racism of the historical Kant, which Hill and Boxill concede, but how philosophers can come to a better understanding of how racism operates, the better to understand and so combat it. Hill and Boxill believe that in spite of his racism, Kant's moral theory 'can serve as a reasonable framework for addressing contemporary racial problems, provided it is suitably supplemented with realistic awareness of the facts about racism and purged from associations with certain false empirical beliefs and inessential derivative theses'. But the problem of the coexistence of what they deem to be Kant's racist attitudes and his philosophical ideas incompatible with those attitudes is not pursued. This is all the more surprising because their defence of Kant as a philosophical resource to address racism and particularly their defence of 'reasonable deliberation and dialogue to address racial problems' leads them to argue for an examination of racism in terms that I fully endorse. This is what they say: 'such use of reason must be informed by an adequate understanding of the empirical facts about racism, its genesis, its stubbornness, its hiding-places, its interplay with other factors, and the most affective means to combat it.'[29] My response is that if one indeed wants to address racism, then investigating Kant's racism in its coexistence with cosmopolitanism would have been a good place to start. One finds there an influential, articulate racism whose genesis, stubbornness, self-deception, and interplay with its opposite that is there to be studied. But how is this to be done?

One's answer to this question will depend on how we already think of racism, which is why I applaud the publication of Boxill's recent anthology on this issue, in which the essay 'Kant and Race' is to be found. Reliance on a narrow definition of racism has led to a society which is obsessed almost exclusively with the task of avoiding saying certain things, especially policing certain types of essentialist remarks about racial inequality, while doing nothing to address, for example, inequalities in access to education, health care and economic well-being, as well as life expectancy, as they correlate with racial identity. If one wanted to address those questions, in terms of both diagnosis and remedy, Kant's philosophy has, particularly in the curtailed versions now popular among Kantians, much less to recommend it than some other philosophies, and that too belongs under the topic of Kant and racism. And I might add that, although arguments drawn from Kant could be used to combat racism, historically they seem to have had little impact – as a study of, for example, debates about the abolition of slavery confirms.

The analytic approach relies heavily on the assumption that the appropriate hermeneutical task in this context – the primary imperative – is to resolve the contradiction between racism and universalism in these philosophies, either by amputating one limb of the contradiction or by supplying a missing premiss. As Michel Foucault notes in *The Archeology of Knowledge*, both philosophers and historians have tended to operate on the assumption that the discourses they analyse possess coherence and that we all speak to overcome the contradictions of our desires, our influences and the conditions under which we live.[30] However, if, as Foucault suggests, we challenge that assumption, then the contradictions I have identified in Locke and Kant, far from being mere surface phenomena that can easily be surgically corrected, are perhaps better understood dialectically, although Foucault would not have liked the idea.[31]

Take the parallel and more familiar case of the contradiction between the American Declaration of Independence's proclamation of human equality and the practice of sexual discrimination and chattel slavery which the Founding Fathers continued to underwrite. The claim is still often made that the Declaration of Independence in some way entailed the emancipation of slaves and it was only a matter of time before the inference would be drawn and the United States would become the place it was destined to be. But another way to reconcile the Declaration's statement of the equality of human beings with the racist practices of the country was to declare *The Negro a Beast*, as one author insisted at the end of the nineteenth century.[32] These alternative ways of resolving the contradiction are indeed opposed, but, from what I am here calling provisionally a dialectical perspective, it can in addition be seen that that opposition is sustained by their mutual adherence to the words of the Declaration. The Declaration of Independence, understood as an expression of a society sustained by a racially based slavery, called for both a universalism and a more explicit racism than had hitherto existed. To that extent it is possible to see these rival positions as nevertheless mutually supporting each other, in so far as they both work to sustain the space that makes possible their opposition.[33] This allows some insight into the coexistence of moral universalism and racism in Kant, as I hope now to show by taking up a problem identified by Robert Louden in his recent book *Kant's Impure Ethics*.

Cosmopolitan prejudice

Louden quotes a passage from Kant's *Conflict of the Faculties* where Kant writes that 'all peoples on earth ... will gradually come to participate in progress'. Louden's gloss is that 'Kant is logically committed to the belief that the entire human species must eventually share in the destiny of the moral species: moral perfection.' This leads Louden to identify Kant as a gradualist. Louden quotes a statement from the *Reflections*: 'we must search for the continual progress of the human race in the Occident and from there spreading around the world.'[34] It sounds no better in context. The previous sentence, the first of the note, which unfortunately Louden does not cite, reads: 'The oriental nations would never improve themselves on their own.'[35] The problem is that attributing gradualism to Kant seems to raise more questions than it resolves: given his view of the permanency of racial characteristics, including talents and dispositions, and given his opposition to colonialism and race mixing, one still has no answer to the question of how 'the entire species' would progress. Hence Louden explains, according to a formula that is more familiar than illuminating, although Kant is logically committed to the idea that the entire species progresses in perfection, he is not personally committed. My hypothesis is that Kant's cosmopolitanism – his search for a purpose in human history – made his racism even more pronounced because the racial inferiority he already recognized now struck him as an offence against all humanity, an offence against this very cosmopolitanism. When we read in Kant's 'Idea for a Universal History with Cosmopolitan Intent' that Europe will probably give law to the rest of humanity, we should hear not only pride but frustration directed against the other races from a man who elsewhere will complain that the white race alone of all the races contains 'all impulses and talents'.[36]

When philosophers today find in Kant's cosmopolitanism a resource for their own thinking, they need to be more aware than they are of the different ways in which it is severely compromised, at least in its original formulation. The cosmopolitanism that is today taken to be an appropriate response to nationalism, or what some people like to call tribalism, is very different from Kant's cosmopolitanism because the latter was formulated not as an antidote to nationalism, let alone racism, but as an answer to the question of the meaning of human history. Kant could see purposefulness at work in nature, but he could not see anything comparable in human affairs, which, by contrast, seemed arbitrary.[37] A universal history with cosmopolitan intent addressed that problem, but at a clear price. Henceforth, to be lazy was not merely to be less deserving – a judgement that, from Locke's perspective, would be damning enough, as it would threaten God's plan by running counter to his command 'to increase and multiply'. It was also to infect or compromise the very idea of humanity as Kant conceived it.

Kant expressed this concern in a number of places, most notably in his review of Herder's *Ideen* and in the *Critique of*

Judgment. From Herder's perspective, all people contributed to the idea of humanity, but in Kant's time laziness was not only a fault of select individuals; it was also widely regarded as a racial characteristic of, among others, Africans, Gypsies and South Sea Islanders. On Kant's account, their dispositions, like their other racial features, were the product of the effect of the climate on the germs (*Keime*) of their ancestors, a climate so benign that it gave them no reason to do anything but enjoy Nature's largesse. Hence the question of why they existed. This same question of purposefulness that is at the heart of Kant's conception of cosmopolitanism is also at the heart of his concept of race. What makes Kant's concept of race so distinctive is its reliance on the teleological principle for judging nature in general as a system of ends. As I mentioned, Kant wrote in his review of Herder's *Ideen* that one can use the empirical evidence to give either a favourable or an unfavourable account of people like the Tahitians. But if history is to be read as if it has the meaning that he believed should be attributed to it, then there is no choice. Kant saw the Tahitians as by nature less talented and so, although they may be better suited to survive their particular climate, their role in human progress was problematic.

From a dialectical perspective, Kant's stature as a philosopher derives from the way he helped to articulate and thereby helped to produce a radical transformation of the philosophical landscape, a shift in our way of conceiving ourselves and the world, something like what certain philosophers of science sometimes call a paradigm shift. But this is invisible to an analytic approach. Cosmopolitanism as a philosophy of history embodies a new basis for prejudice: hatred, distrust or incomprehension in the face of those who, by refusing to assimilate to European ways, do not contribute to the march of humanity towards cosmopolitanism. This renders them in some sense less human. Hence believers in a certain form of reason renounce with all the zeal of religious believers those whom they see as refusing what reason demands of them. Then universalists in the name of 'all' attack those who seek to maintain their difference. A new more virulent strain of prejudice has germinated as a side effect of the new version of universalism. Theoretical racism does not only take the form of believing in polygenesis or a simple biological destiny. Racism is more often to be found in moral gradualism, geographical determinism, or in the gesture which demands 'become like us' and which adds *sotte voce* 'you can never become like us because you are not one of us'.[38] Cosmopolitanism in at least some of its versions is a constituent form of such racisms, not its contrary, which is why we need to be on our guard to recognize racism in the concrete – that is to say, in context. If analytic reasoning establishes that there is no necessary connection between Kant's caricature of Africans and his cosmopolitanism,[39] it can do so because it can choose to reformulate his cosmopolitanism so as to establish this result. That saves cosmopolitanism, but it does nothing to throw light on how racism operates within major philosophical texts, let alone exploring ways to combat it.[40]

With his introduction of a more rigorously defined concept of race, Kant opened up a new space for thinking: he took it into new territory. And then his thinking stopped. One could attribute this to cowardice or laziness, but it is more likely that, because this was new territory, he did not know what to think. Those who came after him worked within the space he opened up. He never resolved the problem of how to reconcile his belief in cosmopolitanism with his racism, but this left a dangerous legacy, one which he occasionally glimpsed. To the question of how 'the entire species' might progress, he responded: 'It appears that all of the Americans will be wiped out, not through the act of murder – that would be cruel – but they will die out.... A private conflict will emerge among them, and they will destroy each other.'[41] Kant, it must be remembered, was a defender of Native Americans against their exploitation through colonialism. But it is clear from this statement that when he referred to the entirety of humanity he did not mean everybody. Indeed, in note 1520 of the *Reflexionen zur Anthropologie* Kant wrote in a somewhat sinister way: 'All races will be extinguished ... only not that of the Whites.'[42] But how would that take place? Kant explicitly opposed genocide as a solution, and commentators agree that that was not an option for him. In one place in *The Racial Contract* Charles Mills writes, 'I'm not saying that Kant would have endorsed genocide.'[43] It is a throwaway line, much like Paul Gilroy's similar remark in *Against Race*: 'he [Kant] does not himself conceive of genocide or endorse its practice against Negroes, Jews, or any other variety of peoples.'[44] Nevertheless, Kant needed to reject it explicitly only because it suggested itself as a solution to the problem of reconciling a specific conception of progressive cosmopolitanism with a belief in the inequality of the races that threatened to frustrate it.

Forgetting history

I readily concede that most analytical philosophers will find little, if anything, here to threaten moral universalism or cosmopolitanism as they understand it. It is for them enough simply to observe that they can formulate versions of these positions that do not entail racism. I also recognize that my call for a re-examination of the way that the study of the history of philosophy operates threatens a practice so thoroughly established that to many of its adherents it is obvious. When charges of sexism and racism are levelled against a canonical philosopher they can easily be dismissed as the result of a failure to understand the task and procedures of the history of philosophy. But perhaps it is time to put that task and those procedures in question so as to challenge a history of philosophy that takes itself so seriously as philosophy that it forgets that it is also supposed to be history. Whenever a thinker is defended by use of the 'central arguments defence' the risk is that, in trying to marginalize the criticism, philosophy itself is rendered less and less central because it comes to be more and more restricted. In other words, the price to be paid for defending some of the major philosophers of the

Western tradition against charges of racism is that we diminish philosophy as an activity more generally. Ultimately ill-conceived defences of these philosophers do more to damage the place of philosophy in our culture than any of the evidence brought against them. Philosophers are not and never have been as divorced from historical reality as their defenders are forced to make them: Locke was proud of the fact that he was a practical man and not just a thinker; however embarrassed we might now be about some of his activities, we do not serve ourselves by dismissing their relevance to an understanding of his thought. By teaching slimmed-down versions of these thinkers – the so-called 'real Kant' rather than the historical Kant – we contribute to the illusion that all that matters is the annunciation of fine principles.

My point is not to deny or dismiss the need we feel to address the contradictions in a philosopher, particularly when the contradiction arises in the context of moral issues. When this problem arises for us in the context of studying the life and works of philosophers to whom we feel especially indebted in our own thinking, the urge to find a resolution is particularly strong. Nor would I deny that there is much to be learned from these exercises. But if the analytic philosopher has a way of separating off the question of the racism of great philosophers from what is considered to be their authentic doctrines, thereby suppressing the problem in a way consistent with his or her overall philosophical stance, the continental philosopher has a different strategy: he or she is prone to offer ever more fanciful interpretations, turning the transgression into its opposite.[45] However, to the extent that I believe that so-called continental philosophy or, more precisely, dialectical philosophy is ultimately better equipped to address these issues than analytic philosophy because it is less prone to sacrificing the complexity of the issues to the distorting lens of false clarity and abstraction from historical reality, then it is so much the worse for continental philosophy, because it has largely failed to do so.

But let me end on a conciliatory note with what might be agreed by good-minded representatives of both approaches. Hill and Boxill close their essay by recognizing that 'confident, complacent, well-positioned white people' will find it difficult to do what they know to be right and indeed still more difficult to know what is right.[46] The cure to self-deception, in so far as there is one, lies, they argue, in listening to what others with different viewpoints, attitudes and emotions say and indeed designing institutions to help us do so, institutions which would allow reason to do its work. I believe that this is a most significant recommendation which would, if it was widely adopted, change what is taught under the name philosophy, as well as the way it is taught, and in a way that ultimately will impact on the question of whether philosophy in the future addresses a broad audience or an increasingly narrow one.[47]

Notes

1. I talk exclusively about racism in this article because I believe it should be treated in its uniqueness, just as sexism or homophobia should be, although I grant that at various points they intersect. Indeed, I will focus primarily upon anti-black racism, although prejudice against other races and groups is also rampant in the works under consideration.
2. *Times Higher Educational Supplement* 850, 17 February 1989, p. 12.
3. John Dunn considered Locke's silence on the Europeans' use of Africans as chattel slaves an 'immoral evasion'. John Dunn, *The Political Thought of Locke*, Cambridge University Press, Cambridge, 1969, p. 175 n4. See also Geraint Parry, *John Locke*, George Allen & Unwin, London, 1978, p. 70.
4. 'The Fundamental Constitutions of Carolina', *North Carolina Charters and Constitutions 1578–1698*, ed. Mattie Erma Edwards Parker, Carolina Charter Tercentenary Commission, Raleigh, 1963, p. 164. On the question of Locke's authorship, see J.R. Milton, 'John Locke and the Fundamental Constitutions of Carolina', *The Locke Newsletter* 21, 1990, pp. 111–33. Milton does not draw specific attention to the phrase on which I am here focusing, but the conclusion that he considers it to be in Locke's hand is unmistakable if one compares what he says with Parker's edition of the manuscript changes.
5. John Locke, *Two Treatises of Government*, ed. Peter Laslett, Cambridge University Press, Cambridge, 1988, p. 284 (henceforth *TT*).
6. See Nicholas Jolley, *Locke: His Philosophical Thought*, Oxford University Press, Oxford, 1999, pp. 211–12.
7. *TT*, pp. 283–5, 322–3, 382–3.
8. Ibid., pp. 236–8.
9. Emmanuel Chukwudi Eze, 'The Color of Reason: The Idea of "Race" in Kant's Anthropology', in Katherine M. Faull, ed., *Anthropology and the German Enlightenment*, Bucknell University Press, Lewisburg PA, 1995, pp. 200–241; and Robert Bernasconi, 'Who Invented the Concept of Race?', lecture first delivered in 1995, published in Robert Bernasconi, ed., *Race*, Blackwell, Oxford, 2001, pp. 11–36. Also R.

Bernasconi, 'Kant as an Unfamiliar Source of Racism', in Julie Ward and Tommy Lott, eds, *Philosophers on Race*, Blackwell, Oxford, 2002, pp. 145–66. See also Robert B. Louden, *Kant's Impure Ethics*, Oxford University Press, Oxford, 2000, pp. 93–100; Thomas E. Hill and Bernard Boxill, 'Kant and Race', in Bernard Boxill, ed., *Race and Racism*, Oxford University Press, Oxford, 2001, pp. 448–71. Allen W. Wood defers to Louden in *Kant's Ethical Thought*, Cambridge University Press, Cambridge, 1999, pp. 338–9. It is striking that Hill and Boxill themselves characterize the debate as one provoked by 'non-Kantians' ('Kant on Race', p. 448).

10. Léon Poliakov, *The Aryan Myth*, trans. Edmund Howard, Barnes & Noble, New York, 1996, pp. 171–3. George Mosse, *Toward the Final Solution*, University of Wisconsin Press, Madison, 1985, pp. 30–31, 73. One of the few philosophers to show an interest in these essays after the Second World War was Gabrielle Rubel. See the selections translated in *Kant*, Oxford University Press, Oxford, 1963, pp. 98–100, 150–52, 184–9. However, this could be judged to be merely a continuation of an interest begun almost forty years earlier in *Goethe und Kant* (Selbstverlag, Vienna, 1927) and 'Kant as a Teacher of Biology' (*The Monist* 41, 1931, pp. 436– 70).

11. For example, J.D. McFarland, *Kant's Concept of Teleology*, University of Edinburgh Press, Edinburgh, 1970, pp. 56–68; Peter McLaughlin, *Kant's Critique of Teleology in Biological Explanation*, Edwin Mellen Press, Lewiston NY, 1990, pp. 29–32; Manfred Riedel, 'Historizismus und Kritizismus: Kant's Streit mit G. Forster und J.G. Herder', *Kant-Studies*, vol. 72, no. 1, 1981, pp. 41–57.

12. The question was raised briefly by Nathan Rotenstreich in 1979, but seems not to have been pursued further for almost twenty years. 'Races and Peoples', in *Practice and Realization*, Martinus Nijhoff, The Hague, 1979, p. 100.

13. Locke had in his personal library a copy of Rev. Morgan Godwyn's *The Negro's and Indians Advocate, Suing for Their Admission into the Church: or a Persuasive to the Instructing and Baptizing of the Negro's and Indians in our Plantations*, London, 1680. See John Harrison and Peter Laslett, *The Library of John Locke*, Oxford University Press, Oxford, 1971, p. 144. *The Fundamental Constitutions of Carolina* had already pronounced on this issue. I am working with Anika Simpson on a more detailed treatment of Locke's relation to the enslavement of Africans, in which among other things the question, neglected here for lack of space, of the legitimacy of using a term like 'racism' with reference to Locke is raised.

14. F.W.P. Dougherty, *Commercium epistolicum J.F. Blumenbachii. Aus einem Briefwechsel des klassischen Zeitalters der Naturgeschichte*, Niedersächsische Staats- und Universitätsbibliothek Göttingen, Göttingen, 1984, p. 189.

15. Hill and Boxill, 'Kant on Race', p. 448. In an earlier, longer version of this essay I also addressed Hegel's racism. The issues raised are ultimately no different in his case; it suffices to refer briefly to the parallels. On the question of whether the charge of racism was an anachronism, G.E. Paulus publicly attacked Hegel's *Philosophy of Right* at the time of its publication for its Eurocentrism. 'G.E. Paulus', *Vorlesungen über Rechtsphilosophie*, vol. 1, ed. Karl-Heinz Ilting, Frommann, Stuttgart-Bad Cannstatt, 1973, p. 372. See further R. Bernasconi, 'With What Must the Philosophy of History Begin?' *Nineteenth Century Contexts* 22, 2000, pp. 171–201. On Hegel's outrageous distortion of his sources in an attempt to justify violence against Africans, see R. Bernasconi, 'Hegel at the Court of the Ashanti', in Stuart Barnett, ed., *Hegel after Derrida*, Routledge, London, 1998, pp. 45–6. Finally, for a discussion of Hegel that takes a similar form to that I have found among some Kant scholars, see Darrel Moellendorf, 'Racism and Rationality in Hegel's Philosophy of Subjective Spirit', *History of Political Thought*, vol. 13, no. 2, Summer 1992, pp. 243–55. Moellendorf judges that 'Hegel's account of spirit makes his racism possible not necessary' (p. 249). Furthermore, 'Hegel's racism is not contradictory to his more general theoretical views, nor does it follow from them, rather it is compatible with them' (p. 249). But this begs the question as to what 'the fundamental claims' (p. 244) are, just as Moellendorf asserts that Hegel's racism can be traced 'to the general ideology of the nineteenth century' (p. 244) without investigating either Hegel's use of

his sources or his contribution to the formation of that ideology.
16. See R. Bernasconi, 'Locke's Almost Random Talk of Men', *Perspectiven der Philosophie* 18, 1992, p. 316 n4.
17. I. Kant, 'Uber den Gebrauch teleologischer Principien in der Philosophie', *Kants Werke*, Akademie Ausgabe, Walter de Gruyter, Berlin, 1923, vol. VIII, p. 174n; trans. Jon Mark Mikkelsen, 'On the Use of Teleological Principles in Philosophy', in Bernasconi, ed., *Race*, p. 54 n4. See Bernasconi, 'Kant as an Unfamiliar Source of Racism', pp. 148–9. Subsequently, I found that Monika Firla-Forkl had already made the same observation: 'Philosophie und Ethnographie: Kants Verhältnis zu Kultur und Geschichte Afrikas', in *XXV Deutscher Orientalistentag*, ed. Cornelia Wunsch, Franz Steiner Verlag, Stuttgart, 1996, p. 439 (henceforth all references to the Akademie Ausgabe of Kant are abbreviated as *AA* followed by the volume number).
18. *AA* VIII, p. 62.
19. Bernard Williams, *Descartes: The Project of Pure Enquiry*, Penguin, Harmondsworth, 1978, p. 10.
20. Ibid., p. 9.
21. Barbara Arneil, *John Locke and America*, Oxford University Press, Oxford, 1996, p. 127.
22. James Farr, '"So Vile and Miserable an Estate": The Problem of Slavery in Locke's Political Thought', *Political Theory*, vol. 14, no. 2, 1986, pp. 263–89.
23. Ibid., p. 264; my stress.
24. Ibid., p. 278.
25. Hill and Boxill, 'Kant on Race', p. 448.
26. Ibid., pp. 452, 456, 462–3. I am not challenging the thesis 'that objections to Kant's teleological claims are not of themselves ground for dismissing his emphasis on reason in his basic moral and political theories' (ibid., 463). My inquiry operates at an entirely different level.
27. See *Briefe von und an Hegel*, vol. 1, ed. J. Hoffmeister, Felix Meiner, Hamburg, 1969, p. 20.
28. Hill and Boxill, 'Kant on Race', pp. 467, 449.
29. Ibid., pp. 449, 467.
30. Michel Foucault, *L'Archéologie du savior*, Gallimard, Paris, 1969, p. 195; trans. A.M. Sheridan Smith, *The Archeology of Knowledge*, Tavistock, London, 1972, p. 149.
31. I employ the word 'dialectical' provisionally here because, although this term is now fraught with ambiguity, the basic insight into the reciprocal relation that ties contradictory terms, an insight widespread in so-called continental philosophy, first became pronounced in Hegel's dialectical philosophy.
32. Charles Carroll, *The Negro A Beast*, American Book and Bible House, St Louis MO, 1900). Lest I be misunderstood, I should make it clear that I am not, of course, suggesting that the idea that the Negro was a Beast was a proposition that Kant could ever have allowed. Kant wrote his essays on race in large part in an effort to exclude this possibility and, indeed, further to secure the unity of the human species.
33. Recognition of this fact at some level may have been what led some abolitionists to challenge the Declaration of Independence, but in so far as the Declaration defined the space of discourse this option could not be sustained politically. See Robert Bernasconi, 'The Constitution of the People: Frederick Douglass and the Dred Scott Decision', *Cardozo Law Review*, vol. 13, no. 4, 1991, pp. 1281–96.
34. *AA* VII, p. 89; *AA* XV1, p. 789, both quoted in Louden, *Kant's Impure Ethics*, p. 105.
35. *AA* XV, p. 788. See also *AA* XXV, p. 840.
36. *AA* VIII, p. 29; *AA* XXV/2, p. 1187.
37. *AA* VIII, p. 17.
38. Hence my surprise at finding Joseph McCarney defend Hegel from the charge of racism on the grounds that he was, rather, a geographical determinist: *Hegel on History*, Routledge, London, 2001, p. 143. Indeed, it is even suggested that 'a firmer theoretical basis for the fundamental equality of human beings than Hegelian spirit provides can scarcely be conceived' (ibid., p. 145).
39. I should be clear that I am not using the term 'analytical philosophy' as a synonym for 'Anglo-American philosophy'. I mean, rather, those philosophers committed to a form of thinking that leaves no room for synthesis, holism or dialectic, while recognizing that analysis nevertheless plays an indispensable role in these other ways of thinking. But it should not go unnoticed that the approach to the history of philosophy that I am here describing as analytic has its roots in a certain reading of Kant.

40. For an invaluable contribution to a historical understanding of cosmopolitanism, see Pauline Kleinfeld, 'Six Varieties of Cosmopolitanism in Late Eighteenth Century Germany', *Journal of the History of Ideas* 60, 1999, pp. 505–24.
41. *AA* VIII, p. 35; *AA* XXV, p. 840.
42. *AA* XV/2, p. 878.
43. Charles Mills, *The Racial Contract*, Cornell University Press, Ithaca NY, 1997, p. 72.
44. Paul Gilroy, *Against Race*, Harvard University Press, Cambridge MA, 2000, p. 60.
45. For example, Jacques Derrida, *De l'esprit*, Galilée, Paris, 1987; trans. Geoffrey Bennington and Rachel Bowlby, *Of Spirit*, University of Chicago Press, Chicago, 1989. Derrida argues for a reading of 'spirit' in Heidegger that neglects the connotations of the word at that time. See R. Bernasconi, 'Heidegger's Alleged Challenge to the Nazi Concepts of Race', in James E. Faulconer and Mark A. Wrathall, eds, *Appropriating Heidegger*, Cambridge University Press, Cambridge, 2000, pp. 50–67.
46. Hill and Boxill, 'Kant and Race', p. 470.
47. In a more thorough treatment I would need to address the philosophical canon and philosophers' resistance to multiculturalism as well as the racial constitution of the average philosophy department, including its student body. On the latter, see Leonard Harris, '"Believe it or Not" or the Ku Klux Klan and American Philosophy Exposed', *Proceedings and Addresses of the American Philosophical Association*, vol. 68, no. 5, May 1995, pp. 133–7. On the former, see Robert Bernasconi, 'Philosophy's Paradoxical Parochialism: The Reinvention of Philosophy as Greek', in Keith Ansell-Pearson, Benita Parry and Judith Squires, eds, *Cultural Readings of Imperialism*, Lawrence & Wishart, London, 1997, pp. 212–26. I should stress that I do not mean to deny the existence of a significant number of philosophers who have at some cost long raised these issues and advocated a re-examination of the canon. Nor would I deny that for much of my career I have been unambiguously part of the problem, until some of my students woke me from my dogmatic slumber.

6 Exchange on Hegel's racism

JOSEPH McCARNEY & ROBERT BERNASCONI

REPLY TO BERNASCONI

Robert Bernasconi's article in *RP* 117 has harsh and important things to say about some philosophical heroes of the Enlightenment, especially Kant, and it deserves serious critical attention.[1] This response is not directly concerned with the central claims of the article but with a marginal, though still significant, aspect: its treatment of Hegel. It will be argued that Bernasconi has overreached himself here and that Hegel should be moved out of the range of his criticism. To show this would in one way do Bernasconi a service, for it would allow what is truly integral to his case to stand out more clearly. It must be admitted, however, that, as is perhaps only to be expected, his dealings with Hegel cannot simply be excised without affecting the rest. They reflect back on the main project, suggesting grounds for viewing it with a certain reserve.

It seems all too easy to cite considerations that should have induced Bernasconi to be more discriminating in his targets. If, for instance, Kant, as he claims, failed 'to express disapproval of', while Locke 'accepted', black slavery, Hegel's considered verdict stands in sharp contrast.[2] It can be given in a formulation that is familiar to Bernasconi since he quotes it elsewhere: 'reason must maintain that the slavery of the Negroes is a wholly unjust institution, one which contradicts true justice, both human and divine, and which is to be rejected.'[3] This judgement might surely have sufficed of itself to give Bernasconi pause in claiming that the issues raised by 'Hegel's racism' are 'ultimately no different' from those raised in the case of Kant.[4] The subject of anti-black racism needs, however, to be taken a little further since it is the primary focus of Bernasconi's article.

A starting point is provided by a reference to my book, *Hegel on History*. Bernasconi expresses surprise at finding me 'defend Hegel from the charge of racism' on the grounds that he was a 'geographical determinist'.[5] It would be pointless to dwell here on the fact that this is but one strand of the defence, not, as Bernasconi implies, the whole of it. The same is true of the fact that I do not actually use the term 'geographical determinist' of Hegel, preferring to speak of his 'geographical materialism'.[6] What is worth dwelling on is the fact that Hegel's geographical thesis is understood and applied by him with an impartiality that, so far from providing a cloak for racism, seems incompatible with it. The relevant claim is that in some regions of the globe, nature, in the form of terrain or, more especially, climate, presents too great an obstacle to the development of spirit. This is no less true of the 'frigid' than it is of the 'torrid' zone: 'The frost which grips the inhabitants of Lapland and the fiery heat of Africa are forces of too powerful a nature for human beings to resist, or for spirit to achieve free movement.'[7] Thus, these forces are too powerful for human beings in general – for white Europeans no less than for black Africans. It is, one might say, ironic that, as we now know, Africa was the birthplace of Hegelian spirit, of the distinctively human consciousness he interpreted through that concept, and remained its sole home for all but a small portion of its life on earth. Hegel would, however, have had no difficulty in showing this truth the respect he habitually accords the findings of science. Among many other indications there is the claim, hard to square with 'geographical determinism', that the Greeks derived the materials for the development of their art and religion from, among other non-European sources, Egypt, while Egypt 'probably received its culture from Ethiopia'.[8] On the strength of these observations Hegel might reasonably be regarded as a precursor of 'Black Athena'. It is at the very least odd to find a thinker who inclines in that direction accused of being an anti-black racist.

Hegel's account of the Greeks deserves a closer look, for it constitutes virtually a hymn to racial impurity. Thus, he insists that it is 'superficial and absurd' to suppose that their 'beautiful and truly free life' could arise as 'the development of a race [*Geschlecht*] keeping within the limits of blood relationship and friendship'. On the contrary, the Greeks developed themselves from 'a *colluvies*, a conflux of the most various nations [*Nationen*]', and the beginnings of their cultural development are connected with 'the advent of foreigners' in Greece.[9] The terminology is significant here. In Hegel's standard usage a 'nation' is a group united by common descent, in accord with the kind of fact of etymology to which he attaches great significance, 'the derivation of the word *natio* from *nasci*' (to be born).[10] Thus, 'nation' may be seen as cognate with, perhaps as a narrower specification of, 'race'.

The important point for present purposes is that a 'nation' has to be distinguished from a 'people' (*Volk*). A people is a 'spiritual individual', a community constituted through a distinctive form of spirit; that is, a distinctive form of consciousness and self-consciousness, 'its self-consciousness in relation to its own truth, its essence', or what might broadly be termed its culture.[11] Hegel makes the relevant point by telling us that in so far as peoples are also nations, 'their principle is a natural one'.[12] Thus, we are in touch once more with an aspect of the distinction between nature and spirit, a distinction that belongs to the very architecture of his thought and has an especially crucial role in the philosophy of history. For history is precisely, in one aspect at least, the escape of spirit from nature, its overcoming of all natural determinants such as common descent or blood relationship. As is to be expected, it is peoples and not nations, spiritual and not natural entities, who are the vehicles of this process. Indeed, groups whose principle is a natural one, such as nations, tribes, castes and races, cannot as such figure as historical subjects. It follows that, for Hegel, there literally cannot be a racist interpretation of history. History is an object which can never be brought into focus through racist categories, and racism is incompatible with historical understanding.

Turning from Hegel's philosophy of history to his philosophy of right yields a smaller range of material combined with an even clearer enunciation of anti-racist principle. The key idea is that in the modern state '*A human being counts as such because he is a human being*, not because he is a Jew, Catholic, Protestant, German, Italian, etc.'[13] It is, rather obviously, the case of the Jews that is most pertinent at present. In this passage, as elsewhere, Hegel is setting himself against the most powerful form of racism of his time and place. This manifested itself in, for instance, the fulminations of J.F. Fries against 'the Jewish caste' and in the movement to exclude the members of this 'caste' from civil and political rights. In the face of such tendencies, Hegel insists that 'Jews are primarily human beings', adding that the demand for their exclusion has 'proved in practice the height of folly' while the way in which governments, and more particularly the Prussian government, have acted in this regard has proved 'wise and honourable'.[14]

It is curious that Bernasconi, in his dealings with 'Hegel's racism', allows him no credit for his stand as a principled opponent of anti-Semitism. The oddity is the greater if one contrasts his treatment with that of Heidegger. The issue at stake on each side of the contrast is that of the supposed connection between philosophy and racist views. Where Heidegger is concerned, Bernasconi is tentative and circumspect: 'his anti-Semitism, although undeniable, is not so easily associated with his philosophy, although an argument along these lines can be formulated.'[15] In dealing with Hegel such judiciousness is cast aside, though an argument to connect his alleged racism with his philosophy would be at least as difficult to formulate.

Bernasconi formulates no such argument while tending to proceed as if he had. It may possibly be symptomatic in this regard that he is content just to situate disparagingly, by prefacing with an astonished 'it is even suggested that', the claim made in *Hegel on History* that Hegelian spirit provides an unrivalled theoretical basis for 'the fundamental equality of human beings'.[16] There is, of course, no reason why he should engage in particular with my statement of the case for Hegelian spirit. Yet he surely needs to engage seriously with that case in some form. For, on the face of it, to speak of the fundamental equality of human beings is simply to spell out what that spirit plainly implies. It is, after all, the spirit whose 'substance ... is freedom', a substance to be achieved only 'through the freedom of each individual' since 'we know ... that all human beings as such are free, that the human beings as human being is free'.[17] To note this is to be brought in contact with what Bernasconi calls 'moral universalism', an aspect of the legacy of the Enlightenment which Hegel accepted and took forward. Bernasconi constructs a vigorous, sceptical rhetoric around this doctrine, once again without providing an argument on the key question, its supposed inner link with racism. What he does instead is to focus on the seemingly related idea of Kantian 'cosmopolitanism' and offer an argument against that. He then simply runs the two ideas indifferently together as a couplet, 'moral universalism or cosmopolitanism'.[18]

This procedure would be unsatisfactory even if the argument against cosmopolitanism were more persuasive. All it essentially relies on, however, to establish the link with racism is a supposed biographical fact about Kant. The 'hypothesis' is that his cosmopolitanism 'made his racism even more pronounced because the racial inferiority he already recognized now struck him as an offence against all humanity, an offence against this very cosmopolitanism'.[19] What is needed, however, is a theoretical argument about concepts, not an appeal to individual psychology. The problem would scarcely be worth noting were it not for the example set for Bernasconi by Hegel's stance on the same issue. For Hegel distinguishes between the two Enlightenment doctrines now in question, and in retaining the one while rejecting the other suggests at least the germ of a rational ground for his preference. He does so, significantly, in the section of the *Philosophy of Right* cited earlier, in close proximity to its celebration of the inclusiveness of the modern state. What is suggested there is that cosmopolitanism represents a fake, merely abstract, universalism, a 'fixed position' of false homogeneity that abstracts, in particular, from 'the concrete life of the state' with its variety of peoples and their defining spirits.[20] Bernasconi might have found in this at least a model for the kind of argument against cosmopolitanism he requires.

A different kind of point should be made by way of conclusion. It is prompted by the wholly admirable sense that pervades Bernasconi's writing of the practical significance of ideas, and, more specifically, by the contrast he alludes to between the real world of racist injustice and oppression and that of contemporary discourse about racism.[21] In part the point consists simply in questioning the wisdom in this context of a strategy of damning the Enlightenment even in its highest flights of moral universalism. The mention of Heidegger should be enough to suggest that the precedents here are not encouraging, and that a Hegelian balance and realism in this area might serve the cause of anti-racism better. The point may be put in a more general form. This involves the view that, however hard to articulate, there is an indispensable distinction of some kind to be acknowledged between what belongs to the structure of a philosophy and what does not, between contingent facts about the lives and opinions of some Enlightenment thinkers and what is of the essence of Enlightenment philosophy. Bernasconi's work is a salutary reminder of the complexity of such a distinction, specifically of the dangers of relying on it for a facile airbrushing of the great figures of the past. It also suggests, however, the dangers of an answering facility on the other side.

The distinction in question is needed because, without it, disreputable opinions or even incidental remarks, instead of being judged to be incompatible with the logic of a philosopher's position, a sad decline from her best insights, are liable to engulf the whole. Our anti-racist critique will then end up proving far too much. The test it proposes is one that Hegel will certainly not pass, not least in view of what I have called the 'obnoxious and shocking' character of his aspersions on non-European peoples, with their residue of 'cultural prejudice, complacency and arrogance'.[22] Neither, however, just to consider the spectrum of his nineteenth-century successors, will Marx, Mill or Nietzsche. Indeed, it is doubtful whether many European thinkers whose opinions and attitudes were formed before, say, the 1970s would emerge unscathed. The entire canon of Western philosophy from Aristotle to Wittgenstein is likely to stand convicted. This is to render the history of philosophy in a paranoid style that seems to mirror, at least in its monocular obsessiveness, the fantasies of the racists.

This outcome may be tolerable for the historians themselves, confirming them in their role as the valets to whom, in Hegel's epigram, no man is a hero. They may even enjoy the frisson of making their own, and our, flesh crawl with frightful stories, secure in the inner conviction that, ensconced in the liberal academy, they cannot themselves fall victim to the evils they so readily conjure up. For the actual victims of racism, however, the implications are different. Such an intellectual construct cannot possibly empower but rather serves to crush them under the weight of history. Those whom it empowers can only be the racists, conveying to them the assurance that the entire tradition of Western philosophy is, whatever surface protestations it may make, really on their side. The whiff of a kind of treason of the clerks hangs in the air here. A proper sense of clerkly responsibility would require them instead to deny racism the least shred of intellectual legitimacy or credibility and exhibit it as the vicious stupidity and unreason it is. In that task Hegel should, as this discussion has tried to show, be recognized as a resourceful ally.

JOSEPH McCARNEY

Notes

1. Robert Bernasconi, 'Will the Real Kant Please Stand Up: The Challenge of Enlightenment Racism to the Study of the History of Philosophy', Chapter 5 above.
2. Ibid., pp. 15, 16.
3. G.W.F. Hegel, 'Prefatory Lectures on the Philosophy of Law', trans. Alan S. Brudner, *Clio*, vol. 8, no. 1, 1978, p. 68. See Robert Bernasconi, 'Hegel at the Court of the Ashanti', in Stuart Barnett, ed., *Hegel after Derrida*, Radical Philosophy 119, May/June 2003, Routledge, London and New York, 1998, p. 58.
4. Bernasconi, 'Will the Real Kant Please Stand Up', n15.
5. Ibid., n38.
6. Joseph McCarney, *Hegel on History*, Routledge, London and New York, 2000, p. 144.
7. G.W.F. Hegel, *Lectures on the Philosophy of World History: Introduction*, trans. H.B. Nisbet, Cambridge University Press, Cambridge, 1975, pp. 154, 155, translation slightly modified.
8. G.W.F. Hegel, *The Philosophy of History*, trans. J. Sibree, Dover, New York, 1956, pp. 237, 201.
9. Ibid., pp. 226–7. For the original text, see G.W.F. Hegel, *Vorlesungen über die Philosophie der Geschichte*, ed. E. Moldenhauer and K.M. Michel, *Theorie Werkausgabe*, vol. 12, Suhrkamp, Frankfurt am Main, 1970, pp. 278–80.
10. Hegel, *Lectures*, p. 56.
11. Ibid., p. 96, translation modified. For the original text, see G.W.F. Hegel, *Die Vernunft in der Geschichte*, ed. J. Hoffmeister, Felix Meiner, Hamburg, 1955, p. 114.
12. Hegel, *Lectures*, p. 55, translation modified; *Die Vernunft*, p. 64.
13. G.W.F. Hegel, *Elements of the Philosophy of Right*, trans. H.B. Nisbet, Cambridge University Press, Cambridge, 1991, p. 240.
14. Ibid., pp. 295–6.
15. Bernasconi, 'Will the Real Kant Please Stand Up', pp. 129–30.
16. Ibid., n38.
17. Hegel, *Lectures*, pp. 54–5, translation modified.
18. Bernasconi, 'Will the Real Kant Please Stand Up', p. 145.
19. Ibid., pp. 18–19.
20. Hegel, *Elements*, p. 240.
21. Bernasconi, 'Will the Real Kant Please Stand Up', p. 141.
22. McCarney, *Hegel*, pp. 142, 151.

RESPONSE

Some of Joseph McCarney's criticisms of my 'Will the Real Kant Please Stand Up' arise only because he misidentifies the issue I discuss there. As I explain in my opening paragraph, I wrote the essay to call into question the way philosophers today address – or often fail to address in a serious way – the racism of some of the most exalted figures of the history of Western philosophy. I make it clear that the aim of the essay is not to establish the racism of those figures, although I do rehearse some of the evidence for the convenience of readers not familiar with my earlier essays on the subject. It is our racism, not theirs, that my essay primarily addresses. Or, more precisely, I am concerned with the institutional racism of a discipline that has developed subtle strategies to play down the racism of Locke, Kant and Hegel, among others, with the inevitable consequence that, for example, in the United States philosophers are disproportionately white. So if, as McCarney puts it, I tend to proceed as if I had formulated an argument linking Hegel's 'alleged'(!) racism with his philosophy, this is because I have done so elsewhere, as I explain in note 15.

However, even if my essay in *Radical Philosophy* does not focus on Hegel's racism, I am happy to take this opportunity to defend what I have said elsewhere about it, not least because McCarney's response to 'Will the Real Kant Please Stand Up' exemplifies many of the tendencies I want to expose. McCarney objects to my statement in note 15 that the issues raised by Hegel's racism are 'ultimately no different' from those raised in the case of Kant, but he misses the target when he attempts to counter this claim by showing that Hegel, unlike Locke and Kant, explicitly opposed slavery.[1] The paragraph to which that note is attached is not about slavery, but about the tendency of analytic philosophers to ignore historical evidence when they interpret philosophical works from past eras. My point is not that Kant's racism is the same as Hegel's, but that their racism, however different, raises the same set of issues for us today, not least because philosophers tend to use the same strategies to avoid addressing their racism.

One of the most common of these strategies is to ignore the specifics of the historical context, while at the same time proclaiming, without appeal to historical evidence, a 'child-of-his-time' defence. There is, in other words, lip service to history, but no attempt to follow through on it. McCarney himself is not immune to this tendency. On McCarney's account, Hegel's superiority over Locke and Kant is established on the basis that he alone explicitly attacked the African slave trade. But it is entirely illegitimate for McCarney to juxtapose the different treatments of slavery in Locke, Kant and Hegel, as if they were contemporaries. Hegel's rejection of chattel slavery does not have the same meaning that it would have had, had it been written in a different period. When Hegel denounced slavery, the decisive questions, at least among Europeans, were less whether slavery should be abolished and more how and when it should be abolished and whether this episode in European history should be allowed to undermine its sense of its own moral superiority. In fact, Hegel was clear both that chattel slavery should be abandoned only gradually and that the enslavement of blacks should be regarded in retrospect as a necessary moment in the transition towards a higher stage of development.[2] In my view, this places Hegel on the wrong side of the debate to which he was actually contributing, a debate of genuine political significance at the time he was writing.

Things only get worse when we turn to Hegel's use of the travel literature of his day in order to establish his portrait of Africans in the *Lectures on the Philosophy of History*. In *Hegel on*

History, McCarney defends Hegel by blaming his sources, even while showing himself to be willing to concede that the 'histrionic temptations of the lecture theatre' may have led him to select 'the most lurid and blood-curdling of the tales available to him'.[3] But in 'Hegel at the Court of the Ashanti', which I cite in note 15, I show that Hegel cannot be portrayed as a victim of his sources. Hegel's portrait of blacks as cannibals was not simply a stereotype that Hegel unthinkingly repeated. I demonstrate, I believe for the first time, that the stories Hegel told his students about Africans were his own invention, in so far as he took published accounts and exaggerated the details. For example, whereas Hegel's source records that the king of Ashanti crushed the bones of his dead mother in rum and water, he reported that the bones were washed in blood.[4] Hegel also included other stories, especially about cannibalism and mindless massacres, that either are without any known source or are greatly exaggerated. McCarney has read my essay on Hegel's distortion of his sources: he refers to it indirectly in his response but he does not take the opportunity either to answer my argument or to modify his defence. Indeed, it does not even lead him to pause when he presents us with a Hegel who respects the findings of science. The idea that Hegel's racist portrayal of Africa can be excused because it simply followed the best knowledge of the day cannot be sustained and has been perpetuated only because historians of philosophy have not done their homework. That McCarney explicitly persists in the image of a Hegel who follows the best scientific evidence, when I have shown the contrary, is troubling.

    The purpose of the stories Hegel fabricated about Africans was to support his contention that they were not yet ready for freedom. He manufactured a case against Africans to support his claim that slavery had improved blacks. It is always possible that McCarney thinks that this has nothing to do with Hegel's philosophy, and, while I am inclined to think that this is hardly a marginal question for a philosopher for whom freedom is such a central concept, I concede that, for a certain style of philosophizing, it is a matter of course to eliminate what is subsequently regarded as embarrassing. This is another of those strategies that in 'Will the Real Kant Please Stand Up' I identify as a way of playing down a philosopher's racism. To be sure, from that perspective, which has already turned its back on the historical philosopher, there is no clear criterion by which to decide what is or is not integral. So, rather than debate the importance of this case, let me introduce another which is even harder to dismiss and which again runs directly counter to McCarney's interpretation.

McCarney understands Hegel to have said that 'groups whose principle is a natural one, such as nations, tribes, castes and races, cannot figure as historical subjects'. My problem is not with that claim as such, but with McCarney's suggestion that it follows that for Hegel 'there literally cannot be a racist interpretation of history'. But it is not enough to notice that, for Hegel, the subjects of history are peoples. It is also relevant that he believes that only certain races produce peoples. Indeed, not all races even divide into specific national spirits.[5] Furthermore, in my essay 'With What Must the Philosophy of History Begin?', I explain that this was why Hegel judged that history proper begins only with the Caucasian race.[6] As I cite this essay in the same note, note 15, to which McCarney takes such exception, I would have expected him, in his response to my essay, to address the textual evidence that Hegel uses race as a category to exclude all but Caucasians from being historical subjects in the full sense. Even if McCarney was unaware of the clear textual evidence that I have marshalled in support of this interpretation, I would have thought that the notorious exclusion of Africa proper from world history would have alerted him to it. But this is not part of McCarney's Hegel. McCarney writes: 'For history is precisely, in one aspect at least, the escape of spirit from nature, its overcoming of all natural determinants such as common descent or blood relationship.' Contrast that with what Hegel himself wrote: 'each particular principle of a people is also subject to natural determining'.⁷ In *Hegel on History* McCarney writes that 'a firmer theoretical basis for the fundamental equality of human beings than Hegelian spirit provides can scarcely be conceived'.⁸ I would suggest that a firmer theoretical basis might have been found had Hegel had a different account of nature's relation to spirit than the one he actually had.

Instead of debating my textual arguments about Hegel's racism, McCarney fantasizes about a Hegel who 'might reasonably be regarded as a precursor of "Black Athena"'. This assertion is made on the strength of Hegel's observation that the Greeks derived the development of their art and religion from, among other non-European sources, Egypt, while Egypt 'probably received its culture from Ethiopia'.⁹ However, it should be recalled that one of Martin Bernal's major claims in the first volume of *Black Athena* is that the thesis of an Egyptian source for Greek culture, the 'Ancient Model', was first seriously challenged between 1815 and 1830, especially by Karl Otfried Müller in the 1820s.¹⁰ Hegel was writing at a time when the idea that Egyptian art and religion was one of the sources of Greek art and religion was still very much alive. I am therefore at a loss to know what McCarney means when he describes Hegel specifically as a 'precursor' of this view. What is clear is that Hegel was having trouble reconciling the widely shared admiration of his day for things Egyptian with the growing tendency to try to correlate the hierarchy of civilizations with a hierarchy of races, given that the ancient Egyptians were at that time widely thought of as black. The African component of Egypt is very much in evidence in Hegel's discussion, even while he insisted that Egypt did not belong to Africa proper.

Locke, Kant and Hegel did not simply reflect the prejudices of their time. They reinvented those prejudices by giving racism new forms. Locke played a role in formulating the principle that masters have absolute power and authority over the Negro slaves at a time when the form of North American slavery was far from having been decided. Kant was the first to offer a scientific definition of race, and he himself appealed to this idea of race in order to legitimate prejudices against race mixing. Hegel was a *precursor* of the mid-nineteenth-century tendency to construct philosophies of history organized around the concept of race, such as we find in Robert Knox and Gobineau. The fact that Locke, Kant and Hegel also played a role in formulating emancipatory ideas constitutes the problem I am concerned with. It does not make it disappear. This is because the annunciation of fine principles – the philosopher's stock in trade – is no guarantee that one is not at the same time undermining or negating those principles.

I do not see that as an indirect result of my work in this area 'the actual victims of racism' will be crushed by racists newly empowered to learn that the entire tradition of Western philosophy is on their side. Nor do I share the vision McCarney's final paragraph conjures up, according to which attention to racism within the Western philosophical canon will lead scholars to adopt a paranoid approach to the history of philosophy that will result in them becoming 'secure in the inner conviction that, ensconced in the liberal academy, they cannot fall victim to the evils they so readily conjure up'. I do not share that vision because philosophers for the most part seem already to have that inner conviction about themselves, while ignoring the institutional racism of their discipline. I thought it was clear that I presented the failings of Locke, Kant and Hegel to encourage us to think harder about our own philosophical procedures, not in order to generate self-satisfaction. I am sorry that McCarney did not accept my invitation.

ROBERT BERNASCONI

Notes

1. Robert Bernasconi, 'Will the Real Kant Please Stand Up', Chapter 5 above, n15.
2. G.W.F. Hegel, *Vorlesungen über die Philosophie der Weltgeschichte*, ed. Johannes Hoffmeister, Felix Meiner, Hamburg, 1955, p. 226; trans. H.B. Nisbet, *Lectures on the Philosophy of World History*, Cambridge University Press, Cambridge, 1975, p. 184.
3. Joseph McCarney, *Hegel on History*, Routledge, London, 2000, p. 143.
4. Robert Bernasconi, 'Hegel at the Court of the Ashanti', in Stuart Barnett, ed., *Hegel after Derrida*, Routledge, London, 1998, p. 46.
5. G.W.F. Hegel, *Enzyklopädie der philosophischen Wissenschaften* III, Theorie Werkausgabe 10, Suhrkamp, Frankfurt, 1970, p. 65; trans. William Wallace, *Philosophy of Mind*, Oxford University Press, Oxford, 1971, p. 47.
6. Robert Bernasconi, 'With What Must the Philosophy of World History Begin? On the Racial Basis of Hegel's Eurocentrism', *Nineteenth Century Contexts* 22, 2000, pp. 183–4. I address an argument that is remarkably similar to McCarney's at pp. 187–8.
7. Hegel, *Vorlesungen über die Philosophie der Weltgeschichte*, p. 187; trans. *Lectures on the Philosophy of World History*, p. 152, translation modified.
8. McCarney, *Hegel on History*, p. 145.
9. Hegel, *Vorlesungen über die Philosophie der Geschichte*, Theorie Werkausgabe 12, Suhrkamp, Frankfurt, 1970, p. 248; trans. J. Sibree, *The Philosophy of History*, Dover, New York, 1956, p. 201.
10. Martin Bernal, *Black Athena*, vol. 1, Rutgers University Press, New Brunswick NJ, 1987, p. 31.

7 The philosopher's fear of alterity: Levinas, Europe and humanities 'without Sacred History'

ANDREW McGETTIGAN

> Europe, that's the Bible and the Greeks. It has come closer to the Bible and to its true fate. Everything else in the world must be included in this. I don't have any nostalgia for the exotic. For me Europe is central.
>
> Emmanuel Levinas, 1986[1]

Those who have sought resources in Levinas for a project of anti-racism have been confounded by some of his comments about non-Western cultures: 'the exotic'. In addition, many of his advocates have been confused by the metaphysical apparatus assembled in support of the valorization of the 'face' (*le visage*): these features tend to be understood biographically or as functionless remnants of religious beliefs and personal prejudices.

This article attempts to demonstrate that the two problems – metaphysical apparatus and unpalatable comments – are fundamentally connected through Levinas's conception of transcendence. The failure to foreground paleonymy in his writing means that the systematic reconfiguration of terms such as 'face', which transforms its everyday sense, goes unaddressed. The 'face' is not a physical countenance; it is an interpretation, beyond philosophy and phenomenology, tied to a particular historico-cultural formation: the 'culture issued from monotheism'. This has the consequence that the special *idea* of the face of the Other (*Autrui*), as encounter with the idea of the Infinite, in drawing from one particular culture, is not open to all other cultures; it is not a universal possibility. My strong claim will be that the problematic of the face is at root mobilized in a valorization of the Judaeo-Christian legacy against those who come from outside 'the West'.

There is a misapprehension when 'alterity' in Levinas's work is understood simply as difference.

For him, it marks a positive plenitude that breaks with Being. In this regard, intra-ontic difference would be encompassed by knowledge and hence merely part of 'the Same'. Infinite responsibility remains a metaphysical gesture. In the essays contemporaneous with *Totality and Infinity*, alterity references *height*, the *better*, 'trans-ascendence' and as such depends on determining the value of the individual in the possibility of effectuating the infinite beyond the finite.[2] It should be stressed at the outset that the present essay does not circumscribe *Otherwise than Being*, a work that operates with a different temporality and largely eschews the vocabulary of 'metaphysics' and 'exteriority' found in the first book.[3]

Here, I reconstruct the context for *Totality and Infinity* by bringing together Levinas's writings on anthropology and Judaism with the more familiar 'philosophical' text, so as to illuminate the axis of 'Sacred History' in its exemplariness.[4] Only by reading these texts together can the importance for Levinas of a philosophically reconfigured religious inheritance be located as it interrelates with and qualifies his phenomenology, such that the differentiation of 'philosophy' and 'eschatology' may be comprehended.

Humanity with and without Sacred History
In 'Jewish Thought Today' (1961), Levinas lists three conditions marking the novelty of the contemporary world-historical situation. Alongside the defeat of anti-Semitism and the foundation of the State of Israel, he includes 'The arrival on the historical scene of those underdeveloped Afro-Asiatic masses who are strangers to the Sacred History that forms the heart of the Judaic-Christian world.'[5] Besides the belated entry into history

of Africa and Asia, a tenet of Levinas's philosophy of history that connects him through Franz Rosenzweig to Hegel,[6] we should attend to the claim that 'Sacred History' differentiates the West as a monotheistic formation.

The specificity of this formation means that even Marxism must be understood as a Judaeo-Christian legacy, which under Mao is 'lost in the vastness of these foreign civilizations and impenetrable pasts'. The universality of its principles are blocked by a cultural and historical inheritance sufficiently foreign for Levinas elsewhere to describe it as 'lunar or Martian'; notoriously, a 'yellow peril' which, as a 'spiritual' peril,[7] threatens the 'new-found authenticity of Israel' (*JTT*165).

Given the centrality of the critique of Western philosophy in terms of its violent conceptuality and will to totality, Caygill writes on this 'fear of Asia': 'Levinas might have been expected ... to confront Europe and its dangerous metaphysics with new sources of universality and freedom drawn from the East. That he does not even contemplate this step is one of the many mysteries of this tormented text' (*L&P* 183). Such an expectation would ally Levinas with the thoughts offered by Merleau-Ponty in 'Everywhere and Nowhere', where the 'Orient' could serve as a 'sounding-board' through which 'we learn to estimate what we have shut ourselves off from by becoming Western'.[8] But the darker problem is that Levinas has given us enough material in his writings on anthropology (and Merleau-Ponty) to come to see that these prejudices, repeated in a later article pointedly entitled 'Beyond Dialogue',[9] have supporting theories. We are obliged to ask what a cultural formation is for Levinas, such that the 'gaze of Asia', a 'religious collectivity that is ... built around different structures', can help Jews and Christians 'rediscover their kinship' (*JTT* 165).

First, some context: Levinas's formative training in Neo-Kantianism and phenomenology occurs in a period where the philosophical concept of the nation is at the forefront of academic concerns.[10] Second, Levinas, again through Rosenzweig, has strong connections to Hermann Cohen, for whom the notion of 'peoples' (*Völker*) as spiritual entities is central, the Jewish people being exemplary for humanity as a whole. Derrida noted the importance of Fichte for Cohen, in that the former 'discovered that the social Self is a national Self' and hence allowed thought to go beyond Kant through the formation of a *Geisteswissenschaft* – a 'human science' that would study the particularities of different *Volkgeister*.[11] That is, the transcendental is no longer understood as universal – there are different experiential structures for different societies, cultures and peoples.[12]

Third, Husserl, who appears to be Levinas's dominant interlocutor in this context, had, in his late writings, differentiated 'humanities' in the plural –*Menschheiten* as distinct from *Menschentum* – according to their historicities or 'historicalities' (*Geschichtlichkeiten*).

> Historical mankind does not always divide itself up in the same way in accordance with [the category of historicity]. We feel this precisely in our own Europe. There is something unique here [in Europe] that is recognized in us by all other human groups, too, something that, quite apart from all considerations of utility, becomes a motive for them to Europeanize themselves even in their unbroken will to spiritual self-preservation; whereas we, *if we understand ourselves properly*, would never Indianize ourselves, for example. I mean that we feel (and in spite of all obscurity this feeling is probably legitimate) that *an entelechy is inborn in our European civilization which holds sway throughout all changing shapes of Europe and accords to them the sense of a development toward an ideal shape of life and being as an eternal pole.* ... The spiritual *telos* of European humanity, in which the particular telos of particular nations and of individual men is contained, *lies in the infinite, is an infinite idea* toward which, in concealment, the whole spiritual becoming aims, so to speak.[13]

I flag here the two key aspects of this particular European historicality that will persist in Levinas: the idea of the infinite, in metaphysical Desire, and the idea projected into the infinite future, the prophetic time of sacred history produced through 'fecundity' (*TI* 301, 306). This doubling of the infinite is taken to distinguish the West from Asian cultural formations. That said, it is important to appreciate why Levinas repudiates the notion of entelechy. For Levinas, there is no 'History' governed by a *telos*. Humanity is not the site of such a production in spite of itself (*TI* 72–3) ('an inward maturation of reason *common to all*' [*TI* 219]). Consequently, there is no linear scale on which historical societies are located in a hierarchy and no value that attaches to humanity per se. Here, Levinas's essay on Lucien Lévy-Bruhl illuminates the notions of participation and separation found in *Totality and Infinity*.[14]

With respect to cultural formations, for Levinas, Lévy-Bruhl's achievement is to undermine the universal claims for transcendental subjectivity – that the investigation into 'our' conditions of possibility of experience are the conditions of possibility for any experience whatsoever. 'Lévy-Bruhl questions precisely the supposed necessity of those categories for the possibility of experience. He describes an experience which mocks causality, substance, the reciprocal determination – such as space and time – of these conditions for 'all possible objects'.[15] The categories of Aristotle and Kant do not apply to those 'participating';[16] they belong to cultural formations that have accreted above that primitive form – the 'given' depends upon a prior 'wresting' that sensation performs on inchoate being. Such an engagement with concrete environments and landscapes is anterior to and *orients* representation, which appears *after* in the formation of egoism *qua* separation.[17]

In this way, Levinas takes Lévy-Bruhl to have 'ruined representation' as the central philosophical category and to have overturned the notion of exteriority as neutral being.[18] It follows, then, that there is no linear history to humanity, no historical totality, because there is a plurality of 'modes of existing', discrete 'mentalities', which differ radically in their fundamental encounter with the world and do not reduce to each other.

Cultural totalities are national, ethnic and religious and marked by fundamental ideational differences. Such an understanding can be found throughout Levinas's writings. It underlies his 'Reflections on Hitlerism' where the German is distinguished from the Judaeo-Christian:

> It is to a society in such a condition that the Germanic ideal of man seems to promise sincerity and authenticity. Man no longer finds himself confronted by a world of ideas in which he can choose his own truth on the basis of a sovereign decision made by his free reason. He is already linked to a certain number of these ideas, just as he is linked by his birth to all those who are of his blood. He can no longer play with the idea, for coming from his concrete being, anchored in his flesh and blood, the idea remains serious.[19]

These comments on the 'German' are transmuted later into the 'pagan' or 'barbarian'. In 'Place and Utopia', Levinas details the three main spiritual formations.[20]

1. Pagan: seeks the satisfaction of the self before the other. Rooted in Being and Fate, it is egoist and unconcerned if it usurps another's place in the sun.
2. Christian: marked by the utopian rejection of this world in favour of the life to come.
3. Jewish: concerns itself with 'ethical action' which 'does not flee from the conditions from which one's work draws its meaning' – that is, this world.

Regarding the last, Levinas appears close to Rosenzweig's contention that the Jewish people attests to a collective meta-historical experience – a different way of experiencing time.[21] Indeed, Levinas's own essay on Rosenzweig contains the startling claim that 'Judaism is alive and true to the degree that it stays close to God, while Christianity is alive and true ... to the extent that it marches into the world and penetrates it.'[22] As outrider to 'ethical action', the 'Christianization' of the world repeats Husserl's 'Europeanization' and prepares the opposition of freedom to fate, while the 'pagan' appears to gloss all cultures that fall outside this monotheistic front. Crucially, these differences do not simply relate to historical *content*: 'Sacred History' determines a different temporality and historicality.

'Teaching': the revaluation of religious sources

'Jewish Thought Today' indicates the basis for treating Judaism as exemplary. It underscores the 'novelty' of the Western reconsideration of the Talmud: it is 'no longer treated archaeologically or historically but as a form of teaching' (*JTT* 161). As a cultural repository, its value escapes from 'outmoded theology or simple folklore'.[23] 'Teaching' here connects to the Neo-Kantian discussion of Lehre – variously translated as 'doctrine', 'teaching', 'study' and so on, but signifying a body of experience handed down. This unique source is reconfigured for its pertinence to current and future conditions. Cohen's *Religion of Reason out of the Sources of Judaism* is exemplary here,[24] while the pervasive themes can also be seen in Walter Benjamin's earliest writings.[25]

Much weight is accorded to Levinas's claim to be teaching Hebrew to Greek philosophizing, but it is in this notion of 'teaching' that such translation can be seen as a two-way process. To use a different register: Levinas argues that certain concepts taken from Judaism now achieve a new legibility in the disenchanted, desacralized modern world: this secularization is a necessary condition for the ethical response to the other.[26] As Robert Gibbs puts it, 'The desacralization of the world is what allows that full translation of the relations to God to become realized in our relations with other people.'[27] The reconfiguration of religious teaching only occurs after a necessary 'atheism' where all 'myths' are purged: 'Everything that cannot be reduced to an inter-human relation represents not the superior form but the forever primitive form of religion' (*TI* 77, 79). Levinas has no belief in a personal God, posits no afterlife, and constantly translates the content of the biblical text and commentaries into philosophical language.

The ethical begins beyond atheism when religious teaching is distilled to philosophical, not to say Kantian, ideas. What remains of 'monotheism' is the idea of the infinite (double genitive). As he writes in 'Meaning and Sense', the 1964 essay that positions his world-view in contrast to Merleau-Ponty and structuralist anthropology: 'The revealed God of our Judeo-Christian spirituality maintains all the infinity of his absence, which is in the personal "order" itself.'[28]

These ideas are not straightforwardly part of philosophy; in *Totality and Infinity* they form what Levinas terms 'eschatology'. Philosophically reduced 'teaching' takes these religious contents as legitimate starting points for orientation.[29] Where philosophy *qua* phenomenology runs up against the limit of being, the break-up of totality, eschatology serves as a supplement.

> Without substituting eschatology for philosophy, without philosophically 'demonstrating' eschatological 'truths,' we can proceed from the experience of totality back to a situation where totality breaks up, a situation that conditions the totality itself. Such a situation is the gleam of exteriority or of transcendence in the face of the other [*le visage d'autrui*]. (*TI* 24)

Both Stella Sandford and Caygill have noted that the encounter with the Other as an idea of the infinite is irreducible to a phenomenological analysis[30] – Levinas's 'exteriority' cannot be posited from a phenomenological position. The 'gleam' of exteriority is already an eschatological *interpretation*, or in Levinas's terms a 'vision' aiming beyond the break-up of totality.

> The first 'vision' of eschatology (hereby distinguished from the revealed opinions of positive religions) reaches [*atteint*] the very possibility of eschatology, that is, the breach of the totality, the possibility of a *signification without context*. The experience of morality does not proceed from this vision – it *consummates* [*consomme*] this vision; ethics is an optics. (*TI* 23, translation modified)

For Levinas, eschatology is neither revealed nor deduced from within philosophy. Its validity as a set of orienting ideas comes from its inheritance, from its centrality to the monotheistic cultural formation. To 'envisage' the face as the encounter with the idea of the Infinite, as the commencement of *Illeity*,[31] exceeds phenomenological or philosophical description: Illeity as idea redeems a distinct mode of phenomenality – the enigmatic, absent trace in the face. To understand why eschatology is an interpretation, one can compare the account of the encounter with the Other (*Autrui*) in *Totality and Infinity* with that of Sartre's *Being and Nothingness*.[32]

In Part Three, "Being-for-Others", Sartre radically separates the experience of the Other as subject (*autrui-sujet*) from the identification of a particular *object* as another subject (*autrui-objet*). While seeming to deflate the traditional problem of other minds, he rescues the case for a direct experience of the other as subject (*autrui-sujet*): the experience of being-seen, in particular, the experience of shame (*BN* 256 ff.). As a result, the look, or gaze (*le regard*), is preserved phenomenologically as a particular, ambivalent experience of that which is in the midst of this world and beyond this world at the same time – this is transcendence (*BN*270).[33]

Where Sartre is forced to present the other-as-subject as out of reach ('what is certain is that I am looked-at: what is only probable is that the look is bound to this or that intra-mundane presence' [*BN* 277]), Levinas, in eschatology, interprets this out-of-reach as an absence or withdrawal indicating the beyond.

> The face is abstract.... But the abstractness of the face is a visitation and a coming which *disturbs* immanence without settling into the horizons of the World. Its abstraction is not obtained by a logical process starting from the substance of beings and going from the individual to the general. On the contrary, it goes toward those beings but does not compromise itself with them, withdraws from them, ab-solves itself. Its wonder is due to the *elsewhere* from which it comes and into which it already withdraws.... And Sartre will say that the Other (*Autrui*) is a pure hole in the world – a most noteworthy insight, but he stops his analysis too soon. The Other proceeds from the absolutely Absent, but his relationship with the absolutely Absent from which he comes *does not indicate, does not reveal,* this *Absent*; and yet the *Absent* has a meaning in the face. (*MS*59–60)

Instead of existential nothingness, the ideas of eschatology overwrite this nothingness as the absence which spurs metaphysical 'Desire' for the infinite. That is, the face as *Autrui*, as better, 'a relation to surplus' (*TI* 22–3), is already an idea impinging on phenomenological results, but an idea to which monotheism entitles 'us'.

Or, consider 'Illeity', which renders a God no longer onto-theological. Distinct from the third party (*le tiers*) who interrupts the intimacy of the face to face, Illeity designates the 'third person, who in the face has already withdrawn from every revelation and every dissimulation ... it is the whole enormity, the whole inordinateness, the whole infinity of the absolutely Other, which eludes treatment by ontology' (*MS* 61). Paradoxically, this absence prompts an envisioning of a positive transcendence, which, as idea, would be redeemed through ethical practice.

The idea of the face
Levinas suggests that I often pass indifferently before another person and do *not* feel the gaze (*MS* 52). For the trace of the face to appear, the ordinary experience must be 'jostled' by a presence that is not integrated into the world: a presence that can be effaced by 'humble chores' and 'commonplace talk' (*MS* 47):[34] 'It is not the interlocutor our master whom we most often approach in our conversations, but an object or an infant, or a man of the multitude, as Plato says' (*TI* 70).

Not all others are encountered as Other. It is the great failure of the English-language reception of Levinas to posit without justification a token – token correspondence between the other as object (*Autre*) and the face of the Other (*Autrui*). It fails for the reasons given by Sartre. Levinas's characteristic idea of first philosophy lying in the ethical relation generated by the face-to-face encounter with the Other has generally been understood in a familiar humanist, anti-bureaucratic sense: it is in a fundamental personal contact that I am struck by my commonality with the other. But this reading completely neglects Levinas's putative transcendence.

The 'face' is not an individual countenance. The face is not a physiological characteristic distilled from phenomenological description through which I recognize members of a genus. The face confounds ontology and interrupts phenomenology (*MS* 61) in a manner 'no transcendental method could corrupt or absorb' (*MS* 56). The particular, liminal experience of teaching through a master, who brings me more than I contain, prompts the positing of exteriority in remoteness and height – those qualities drawn from monotheism become ideas.

> Is the ideality of the ideal reducible to a superlative extension of qualities, or does it lead us to a region where beings have a face, that is, are present in their own message? Hermann Cohen (in this a Platonist) maintained that one can love only ideas; but the notion of an Idea is in the last analysis tantamount to the transmutation of the other [*Autre*] into the Other [*Autrui*]. (*TI* 71)

It should be stressed that there is no pre-existing realm of transcendence to which the subject is granted access in the encounter. The 'beyond' (the 'region' of the face) does not designate any *Hinterwelt* (this would be to collapse back into onto-theology [*MS* 60]). Instead, the desire for the infinite instigates ethics as the production of the beyond. The encounter with the master, who does not belong to my 'plane'(*TI* 101), is the spur to the production of transcendence beyond being.[35] As Stéphane Mosès insists, the '*geste spéculatif*' of Levinas lies precisely in this conception of the infinite being produced from out of this liminal experience,[36] for which *Autrui* should be reserved.

In turn, *Autre*, in its ethical determination, refers to the idea of fraternity: a pluralism of separated, external beings. In the section of *Totality and Infinity* entitled 'The Other and the others' (*Autrui et les autres*), Levinas argues that the epiphany of the face opens humanity: the experience of the third party in the eyes of the other, which becomes the Il of Il-leity, produces a whole new experience of humanity. This human fraternity is invoked over and above biological species being, but as it does so it exceeds phenomenological evidence (*TI* 213–14). The face comes from beyond the world of meaning and commits me to fraternity in referring to the 'third party' of Illeity, 'whom in the midst of his destitution the Other (*Autrui*) already serves'. But it is important to note that the encounter with *Autrui* is the prior condition of possibility for the valorization of *les Autres*, such that the latter are understood as a pluralism, not as members of a genus. These ideas are transformative: the pluralism produced in ethics is hooked back onto phenomenological experience as interpretation, not description.

Here, we must strictly reject the current conflation of the idea of the Other as *Autrui* with the more familiar idea of respect for the way in which the other person (*Autre*) exceeds my cognitive appropriations. Levinas consistently rejects the possibility of merely reflecting upon, acknowledging or recording the otherness of the other in favour of the need to effectuate transcendence which would thereby justify the encounter with the face of the Other.

Acknowledgement of the inability of comprehension to exhaust the particular individual in front of me merely records the break-up experienced by philosophy *qua* phenomenology. This is precisely the trap Simon Critchley falls into when he describes the face (or, worse, the other's eyes) as a 'palpable infinity that can never exhaust one's curiosity'. Even if such respect is engendered in a conversing that is 'actively and existentially engaged in a non-subsumptive relationship',[37] it fails to grasp the production of transcendence intended by Levinas in ethics. The emphasis on the non-subsumptive is purely negative; it does not get out of Being. In this regard, it would read Levinas either as espousing the false infinite of the 'ought'[38] or the account of intersubjectivity given in Husserl's Fifth Cartesian Meditation: both explicitly rejected by Levinas himself. The indefinable order of transcendence, as positive plenitude, is, for Levinas, not the indefinite extension of being. Instead he insists:

> The I is not a contingent formation by which the same and the other, as logical determinations of being, can in addition be reflected *within a thought*. It is in order that alterity be produced *in being* that a 'thought' is needed and that an I is needed. The irreversibility of the

relation can be produced only if the relation is effected by one of the terms as the very movement of transcendence, as the *traversing* of this distance, and <u>not</u> as a recording of ... this movement. 'Thought' and 'interiority' are the very break-up of being and the production (not the reflection) of transcendence. We know this relation only in the measure that we effect it; this is what is distinctive about it. Alterity is only possible starting from *me*. (*TI* 39–40)

The alternative of acknowledgement runs the risk of neglecting the universal being the particular being incarnates[39] – the 'beatific contemplation' of the other is 'idolatry' (*TI* 172). Such is the secular variety of the 'unctuous, consoling religion' at variance with the transformation wrought by the production of the infinite.[40]

The supposed 'superiority' and 'generosity' of Western thought

Wherein lies the superiority of such ideas? In so far as it presents a morality, Levinas's 'religion' offers itself as a corrective to Western nihilism: 'Morality does not belong to culture: it enables one to judge it; it discovers the dimension of height. Height ordains being' (*MS* 57). The idea of fraternity is premissed upon the monotheistic concept of alterity *as* height, the human as potential image of God, in opposition to a notion of alterity *as* difference that would be premissed upon a 'saraband of innumerable and equivalent cultures' (*MS* 58). Western thought is privileged in so far as it contains the germ of this value given to the individual as the finite site of the incarnation of the Infinite.

In *Signs*, Merleau-Ponty had taken up the results of Claude Lévi-Strauss's work in anthropology to advance the thesis that different cultures are multiple expressions of being on the same plane, with no one culture having direct or privileged access to eternal ideas. Universality is then understood as a practice of translation that leads to the 'lateral interpenetration' of cultures. Explicitly challenging this conception, Levinas's 'Meaning and Sense' recognizes the value of such an 'ontology of decolonization' (*MS* 44) but grants more importance to the consequent *disorientation*. No constructive principle is left in place which can give an orientation to existence – nihilism or the 'pure indifference of multiplicity' is the result (*MS* 45).[41]

Apparently, Merleau-Ponty had taken the 'generosity' of Western thought too far and forgotten its task of overcoming 'the infantilism of purely historical cultures', which had never understood themselves until the advent of anthropological science made of them an object (*MS* 58). What is that generosity? The willingness to see the *abstract* in other cultures – to accord them the dignity of being equals.

Introducing a distinction between the plurality of cultural meanings (*significations*) and the need for a single, orientating *sense* (*sens*), Levinas concludes that desire for exteriority and the beyond, as found in monotheistic culture, provides such a sense in the midst of the variety of cultural totalities: 'the Other dispels the anarchic sorcery of the facts' (*TI* 99). The Other orients being because it creates a value that drives and elevates practical reason, such that it is no longer satisfied with being and so aims at the beyond.

Again, an echo of Husserl is apparent. From as early as the 1911 essay 'Philosophy as Rigorous Science', Husserl was concerned to differentiate European, philosophical science from the plurality of historical *Weltanschauungen*.[42] As the only cultural form to be a 'culture of ideas', to set itself infinite tasks, 'capable of an absolute self-responsibility on the basis of absolute theoretical insights',[43] science, if taken up explicitly, assumes the form of an ethical ideal capable of unifying humanity and fending off the barbarism. While Levinas continues to support the 'excellence of Western science' (*MS* 58), and repeats Lévy-Bruhl's insistence on 'primitive', as opposed to 'savage', minds,[44] he does not subscribe to the notion that the idea of *science* can provide an adequate ethical ideal in the face of the events that scarred the twentieth century. Instead, *fraternity* is accorded that task.

In structuralist anthropology, the excessive generosity of the West puts its own privilege in question. But, for Levinas, it is precisely here that its special contribution to the world is revealed. The argument in 'Meaning and Sense' proceeds in transcendental fashion by asking: what is the condition of possibility for constructing a flat ontology of cultural meaning? It concludes that *orientation to the Other*, the excellence of the Judaeo-Christian legacy, underlies structuralist ontology.

> For there does exist the possibility of a Frenchman learning Chinese and passing from one culture into another, without the intermediary of an esperanto that would falsify both tongues which it mediated. Yet what has not been taken into consideration in this case is that an *orientation* which leads the Frenchman to take up learning Chinese instead of declaring it to be barbarian (that is, bereft of the real virtues of language), to prefer speech to war, is needed. One reasons as though the equivalence of cultures, the discovery of their profusion and the recognition of their riches were not themselves the effects of an orientation and of an unequivocal sense in which humanity stands. One reasons as though the multiplicity of cultures from the beginning sunk its roots in the era of decolonization, as though incomprehension, war and conquest did not derive just as naturally from the contiguity of multiple expressions of being. (*MS* 46)

Let me spell out three points:

1. The recognition of the richness of cultures and the suggestion that they are equivalent, depends upon an orientation to the Other; a *sense* of the status of humanity.
2. The veiled suggestion to the anthropologist is the following: we have seen that your interest in these other civilizations and cultures depends on an orientation towards the other. However, does the culture you examine *itself* reveal or valorize this orientation? The example of Chinese is not innocent given the passages referenced earlier and the insinuation that Chinese might be a barbarian language is neither retracted nor qualified. Robert Bernasconi observes that Levinas seems unaware that the Chinese also learn to speak French.[45]
3. War does not only spring from a logic directed towards totality and domination. War also springs from the friction of contiguity with other civilizations. Difference cannot be valorized per se, if war is to be avoided. Peace does not just

require the recognition of difference, but the orientation to the other: the *sens unique* which can ground peace. The Other as instantiating height, not the other as different.

Peace and ethical illusion

> Of peace there can only be an eschatology. (*TI* 24)

Even if the ideas associated with metaphysical desire for the Infinite are ethical and foreign to China, it may still not be clear why Levinas takes them to be superior. It must be stressed that there is no epistemological privilege accorded to these ideas. Levinas explicitly touches on the affinity between these ideas – variously glossed as 'metaphor', 'illusion', 'aspiration' – and delirium (*TI* 49). 'The power of illusion is not a simple aberration of thought, but a movement in being itself. It has an ontological import' (*TI* 240). In this case, its import lies in producing the beyond, an illusion that 'constitutes a positive event'(*TI* 55).

Some might baulk at this emphasis, but the face as eschatological interpretation commences from 'metaphor' as the 'marvel of language'. Philosophy and certain human sciences might try to reduce its power by drawing up a list of its sources, but this practice cannot 'destroy its intention': 'lucidity does not abolish the beyond of these illusions' (*MS* 56). If the beyond established is not simply to repeat onto-theology, or be determined by being, it must be a human, subjective production. It is because of this projection that Levinas describes the metaphysical as an 'aspiration for radical exteriority' – ethics is defined by its 'transcendent intention' (*TI* 29): 'the beyond which the metaphor produces has a sense that transcends (its origin); the power to conjure up illusions which language has must be recognized' (*MS* 56). The face is not the discovery by the West of a pre-existent truth.

The courthouse for eschatology is not the limits of theoretical reason or phenomenological description. The key lies in the ability of the idea of fraternity to orient peace. As in Neo-Kantianism, the idea is originary (*ursprünglich*) in that it sets the test it itself must undergo: it orients the task (*Aufgabe*) of practical philosophy on which it depends for its justification or validity. The excellence of the West would be located in a potential that must be manifested such that the other cultures of the world follow that example and Europeanize. That is, the belief in the superiority of monotheism's ideas can only be verified in attempting to produce it. As such, orientation is speculative: a form of bootstrapping described in *Otherwise than Being* as 'levitation' that has no other guarantee than its own activity:[46] 'to be worthy of the messianic era one must admit that ethics has a meaning, even without the promises of the Messiah'.[47]

The bottom line is peace. *Pace* Caygill, but via a different route, *Totality and Infinity* is an 'immense treatise on hospitality and war' (*L&P* 209 n2). Orientation is directed to the production and generalization of the prophetic vision of peace, averting the possibility of war (*MS* 46) – that this is best produced by eschatology is the gauge at the heart of Levinas's Occidentalism.

To recap, in so far as they exceed philosophical support, the ideas of the face and fraternity draw their power from the monotheism that informs Western culture. Rendered into Infinite Ideas, they form an eschatology that orients ethics, whose value, above other cultures and their particular ideas, lies in the ability to produce a politics directed to peace. This hypothesis can only be tested historically through this very production – it is fundamentally speculative. Or, as Cohen puts it, 'There will be no peace among nations unless our example is followed.'[48]

The Infinite and Asia: the influence of Rosenzweig

What sources support Levinas's prejudice against China and Asian thought? Given that he undertook no research himself, the obvious source is Rosenzweig's *The Star of Redemption* (on this score, itself a repository of third-hand banalities), where Eastern thought is compared to idolatry,[49] a charge repeated by Levinas.[50] The debt is recognized in the Preface to *Totality and Infinity*: 'We were impressed by the opposition to the idea of totality in Franz

Rosenzweig's *Stern der Erlösung* (*Star of Redemption*), a work too often present in this book to be cited'(*TI*28).

Reading the first part of *The Star of Redemption*, one is swiftly struck by the repeated oppositions between concepts inherent to Judaism and Christianity and those of the Chinese and Indian religions. The Judeo-Christian legacy is valorized by virtue of a conceptual superiority: the ideas of God, world and human are defined by the specific interrelation of transcendence and immanence and the concept of historical time.[51] For Rosenzweig, the experience of the 'face' (*das Gesicht*) of the other in language is not open to those dwelling within Asian cultures, for they have an inadequate conception of the relation between immanence and transcendence: the voice of the other cannot be heard – they flee the 'face of the living God for abstraction'.[52] In the Hindu conception of a world of veils, which reduces human reality to appearance, he sees too much separation between transcendence and immanence – nothing of value can appear *in this world*. In the Buddhist and Confucian conception of a world of excessive variation, he finds only a throng of spirits multiplying – an excess of mixing between immanence and transcendence.[53] If the transcendent is too fully merged into the world then there is only a negotiation through its infinity nothing of value can be extracted from this proliferation. In short, Buddhist and Hindu metaphysics are presented as polar opposites, but from which there is the same result – *the human individual is not the root of value.* The weakness of India and China for Rosenzweig is that they are unable to live beyond the immediate present, since history for those cultures is simply the passage of various contingent arrangements the future cannot be the site of meaning by which to guide the transformation of the present. In contrast, the history of the Judaeo-Christian West has been formed by a more complicated interaction of immanence and transcendence – according to the Bible, humanity was made in the image of God – and it finds itself suspended between the animal and the divine. This, combined with the concept of prophetic time, produces a wholly different culture, a wholly different past. Prophetic time signals the specific biblical temporality whereby revelation is not given once and for all as edict to follow, but as prophecy, giving signs that must be discerned in the future to come.[54]

As in Levinas, a unique concept of humanity rests with messianic monotheism: it is not present in other traditions whose own ideas can be encompassed by the Greek dimension of Europe.[55] For Levinas, these cultures cannot teach us, they bring nothing that we do not already contain: 'You can express everything in Greek. For example, you can say Buddhism in Greek.'[56]

In his essay on racism in the history of philosophy, 'Will the Real Kant Please Stand Up', Bernasconi identifies three tasks for any writing to be adequate as intellectual history.[57] These are:

1. 'identifying the problematic statements of these thinkers that are prima facie racist';
2. 'locating them in the context of their works and the broader historical context';
3. 'establishing their sources'.[58]

While that essay fails to think through its historicist apparatus, and its convenient valorization of the potential virtues of 'continental' practice, I have tried to situate Levinas's writings in the suggested manner. While Levinas's comments on Asia have been well known for some time, they have been separated from the 'serious' work. Bernasconi himself has attempted to effect this wall by differentiating occasional comments from philosophical texts: 'it would be a mistake to assume that the philosophical texts conceal behind their complexity the same appalling message that is said so directly in the interviews.'[59]

Here I have demonstrated that the views expressed in those pieces, whose sheer frequency should be underscored, do not 'run counter' to Levinas's ethics – if Levinas's radical, *metaphysical* transformation of that term is appreciated. Indeed, I have argued that the 'idea of the face', the spur to ethics, is fundamentally tied to a theory of separated cultural totalities which circumscribes the particularity of its obligating force. Levinas fears a valorization of alterity that would not orient around the transcendence resulting from 'Sacred History' distilled into ideas. To repeat, the alterity of height is distinguished from an alterity of difference. For Levinas, contiguity without orientation will lead to wars worse than those witnessed in recent history.

In light of this, I can share neither Bernasconi's suggestion that Levinas's work 'contains the most promising resources for addressing the enigma of persecution, hatred, and violence', nor Judith Butler's idea that Levinas can help to reanimate the 'human' in the 'humanities'.[60] the structure of 'what binds us morally' can find in Levinas only a representation of a specific religious tradition. Given the complacency with which Levinas rests on his shaky sources,[61] his philosophy evinces the easy, armchair belief in superiority which is constitutive of prejudice and discrimination: the claims for Judaism lack any form of independent testing beyond backing it – fidelity and ignorance trump science.

This leaves me to conclude with two questions. First, why have the philosophical readings of Levinas missed the, admittedly troubling, notion of transcendence and instead reduced his work to more familiar ideas? To paraphrase Kierkegaard: what does this 'mollifying exegesis' signify? Second, is it possible to break with an idea of the West, given the particular investments that underlie 'continental' or 'modern European' philosophy? Breaking with Bernasconi's forensic model of prosecution and apology, which fails to reflect on the privilege of latecomers, might not the challenge be not only to portray these writings in their own context, but to represent ourselves in, and our ties to, that same context? Is Western philosophy simply one cultural formation among others limning its own borders? What would it entail to act otherwise? These fundamental questions challenge the particularity of all philosophizing and cannot be avoided given current institutional and world-historical conditions. That the formative figures of twentieth-century thought offered solutions that we would now disavow does not mean that the problem to which those solutions were addressed is illusory.

Notes

Earlier versions of this article were presented to the Research Seminar of the Centre for Research in Modern European Philosophy, Middlesex University; the Human Sciences Seminar, Manchester Metropolitan University; and the 'Levinas and the Political' conference, Purdue University, Indiana. My thanks to Stella Sandford, Peter Osborne, Tim Hall, Nick Lambrianou, Peter Hallward and David Cunningham for commenting on the various drafts.

1. 'Emmanuel Levinas' (1986), in Florian Rötzer, *Conversations with French Philosophers*, trans. Gary E. Aylesworth, Humanities Press, New Jersey, 1995, pp. 57–65, p. 63.
2. Emmanuel Levinas, *Totality and Infinity: An Essay on Exteriority* (1961), trans. Alphonso Lingis, Duquesne University Press, Pittsburgh, 1969, p. 35;hereafter *TI*.
3. The specific relation to *Otherwise than Being* involves the reconstruction of a different systematic structure as Levinas introduces the concepts and ideas of diachrony, psyche, hostage and the nazirate. The key influence on this latter book is the notion of *Urimpression* found in Husserl's *Phenomenology of Internal Time Consciousness*. Emmanuel Levinas, *Otherwise than Being or Beyond Essence* (1978), trans. Alphonso Lingis, Kluwer Academic, Dordrecht, 1991. Edmund Husserl *Phenomenology of Internal Time Consciousness* (1905–1910), ed. Martin Heidegger, trans. James S. Churchill, Indiana University Press, Bloomington,1964.
4. In this regard, I respect two of the protocols expounded by Howard Caygill's *Levinas and the Political* (Routledge, London, 2002); hereafter *L&P*. 'Instead of separating Levinas's "philosophical" and his "Jewish" writings ... the importance of the relationship between "Israel" and the State of Israel in Levinas's thought makes it essential to insist on them being read together. And finally, given the inseparability of reflection on the political from political events, it is vital to pursue as far as possible a disciplined chronological exposition of the development of Levinas's thought and to avoid the luxury of the anachronistic pursuit of thematic parallels that is enjoyed by many commentators' (*L&P* 2–3).
6. Emmanuel Levinas, 'Jewish Thought Today' (1961), in *Difficult Freedom – Essays on Judaism*, trans. Seán Hand, Athlone Press, London, 1990, pp. 159–66, p. 160; hereafter/*TT*.
7. See Franz Rosenzweig, *The Star of Redemption* (1919), trans. William W. Hallo,Notre Dame Press,Notre Dame, 1985.
8. 'The yellow peril! It is not racial, it is spiritual. It is not about inferior values; it is to do with a radical strangeness, which is alien to all the density of its past, from where no voice with familiar inflection filters: it comes from a lunar or Martian past.' Emmanuel Levinas, 'Le Débat Russo-Chinois et la dialectique' (1960), in *Les Imprevusdel'histoire*, Fata Morgana,Montpellier,1994, pp. 170–73, pp. 171–2.
8. Maurice Merleau-Ponty, 'Everywhere and Nowhere', trans. Richard C. McCleary, in *Signs* (1960), Northwestern University Press, Evanston IL, 1964, pp. 126–58, p. 139.
9. Emmanuel Levinas, 'Beyond Dialogue' (1967), in *Alterity and Transcendence*, trans. Michael B. Smith, Athlone Press, London, 1999, pp. 79–89.
10. For the German context, see Hans Sluga, *Heidegger's Crisis: Philosophy and Politics in Nazi Germany*, Harvard University Press, Cambridge, MA and London, 1993. For the dominance of Neo-Kantianism in the France of the early twentieth century, see Vincent Descombes,*Modern French Philosophy*(1979), trans. L. Scott-Fox and J.M. Harding, Cambridge University Press, Cambridge, 1980, and the discussion in Caygill's first chapter, especially *L&P* 9ff.
11. Jacques Derrida, 'Interpretations at War: Kant, the Jew, the German' (1989), trans. Moshe Ron, in *Acts of Religion*,ed.

Gil Anidjar, Routledge, New York and London, 2002, pp. 137–88, pp. 174–5.
12. See Book One of Part III of *The Star of Redemption*.
13. Edmund Husserl, 'The Vienna Lecture' (1935) in *The Crisis of European Sciences and Transcendental Phenomenology: An Introduction to Phenomenological Philosophy*, trans. David Carr, Northwestern University Press, Evanston, 1970, pp. 269–99, p. 275; emphases added.
14. Emmanuel Levinas, 'Lévy-Bruhl and Contemporary Philosophy' (1957), trans. Michael B. Smith and Barbara Harshav, in *Entre nous: Thinking-of-the-other*, Continuum, London and New York, 2006, pp. 34–45. Lévy-Bruhl is referenced at *TI* 234 and *TI* 276.
15. 'Lévy-Bruhl and Contemporary Philosophy', p. 35, translation modified.
16. 'The pure form of time is unknown to primitives, the instants each have their own different potential, in contrast to the homogeneity of the form of time (in Kant).' Ibid., p. 42, translation modified. Compare the foregoing to the critique of 'empty, homogeneous time' in Benjamin's 'Theses on the Philosophy of History' (trans. Harry Zohn, in *Illuminations*, Fontana Press, London, 1973, pp. 245–55). In this regard, see Nickolas Lambrianou, 'Neo-Kantianism and Messianism: Origin and Interruption in Hermann Cohen and Walter Benjamin', in Peter Osborne, ed., *Walter Benjamin: Critical Evaluations in Cultural Theory*, 3 vols, Routledge, London, 2004.
17. Levinas, 'Lévy-Bruhl and Contemporary Philosophy', pp. 42–3.
18. Ibid., pp. 36, 41.
19. Emmanuel Levinas, 'Reflections on the Philosophy of Hitlerism' (1934), trans. Séan Hand, *Critical Inquiry* 17, Autumn 1990, pp. 62–71, p. 64.
20. Emmanuel Levinas, 'Place and Utopia' (1950), in *Difficult Freedom – Essays on Judaism*, trans. Seán Hand, Athlone Press, London, 1990, pp. 99–102.
21. Commenting on 'Reflections on Hitlerism', Caygill writes: 'Each [pagan and Christian civilization] has its own way of structuring time, in particular historical time; each has its own understanding of destiny and freedom and both have their opposed "predeterminations or prefigurations of their adventure in the world"' (*L&P* 32).
22. Emmanuel Levinas, 'Franz Rosenzweig' (1965), trans. Michael B. Smith, in *Outside the Subject*, Athlone Press, London, 1993, pp. 49–66, p. 62.
23. Emmanuel Levinas, 'Space is Not One-dimensional' (1968), in *Difficult Freedom*, pp. 259–64, p. 262.
24. Hermann Cohen, *Religion of Reason Out of the Sources of Judaism* (1919), trans. Simon Kaplan, Frederick Ungar, New York, 1972. Here, religion is a 'new extension' of the concept of man, as individual, and humanity, which mark the limit of traditional ethical understanding (ibid., pp. 19–32). It teaches ethics to say 'Thou' to 'he'.
25. 'However, the original and primal concept of knowledge does not reach a concrete totality of experience in this context, any more than it reaches a concept of existence. But there is a unity of experience that can by no means be understood as a sum of experiences, to which the concept of knowledge as teaching [*Lehre*] is *immediately* related in its continuous development. The object and content of this teaching [*Lehre*], this concrete totality of experience, is religion, which, however, is presented to philosophy in the first instance only as teaching [*Lehre*].' Walter Benjamin, 'On the Program of the Coming Philosophy' (1918), trans. Mark Ritter, in *Selected Writings: Volume 1 – 1913–1926*, ed. M. Bullock and M. Jennings, Belknap Press of Harvard University Press, London, 1996, pp. 100–110, p. 109.
26. Crucially, reason is taken to have entered world history with the democratic revolutions of the eighteenth century. In essays such as 'Messianic Texts', he argues that Jews are no longer excluded from political or state history and as a result messianic thinking is *no longer* appropriate. Emmanuel Levinas, 'Messianic Texts' in *Difficult Freedom*, pp. 59–96. As noted by Caygill, part of Levinas's valorization of technology is that it shows us that the gods are of this world (*L&P* 154).
27. Robert Gibbs, *Correlations in Rosenzweig and Levinas*, Princeton University Press, Princeton, 1992, p. 165.
28. Emmanuel Levinas, 'Meaning and Sense' (1964), trans. Alphonso Lingis (revised by Simon Critchley and Adriaan T. Peperzak), in *Basic Philosophical Writings*, ed. Adriaan T. Peperzak, Simon Critchley and Robert Bernasconi, Indiana University Press, Bloomington

and Indianapolis, 1996, pp. 33–64, p. 64; hereafter *MS*.
29. Kant's essay 'What is Orientation in Thinking?' (1786), trans. H.B. Nisbet, in *Kant: Political Writings*, ed. Hans Reiss, Cambridge University Press, Cambridge, 1991, pp. 237–49, proves the precursor for this question of religion and orientation in thought. See also Nickolas Lambrianou's doctoral thesis for a thorough discussion of orientation in Cohen, Rosenzweig and Benjamin. Nickolas Lambrianou, 'Origin and Becoming: Anticipation, Orientation and Creatureliness in the Work of Walter Benjamin, Hermann Cohen, Franz Rosenzweig and Hugo von Hofmannsthal', Ph.D., Birkbeck College, University of London, 2006.
30. Stella Sandford, *The Metaphysics of Love: Gender and Transcendence in Levinas*, Athlone Press, London and New Brunswick, 2000, p. 124. See *L&P* 99ff. for a discussion of the 'excessive' character of ethics which exceeds the noetic–noematic structure of intentional analysis.
31. The term is introduced in 'Meaning and Sense'.
32. Jean-Paul Sartre, *Being and Nothingness: An Essay on Phenomenological Ontology* (1943), trans. Hazel E. Barnes, Routledge, London, 1969; hereafter *BN*.
33. It should be noted that the crucial experience differs for the two writers: Sartre emphasizes the shame of being caught in a compromising act; Levinas, the shame of encountering a master who 'brings me more than I contain'.
34. In 'Space is not One-Dimensional' (p. 300 n1), he observes that people can close themselves off from such encounters by 'translating them into banal language'. This should be directly related to Heidegger's discussion of the chatter of they-talk.
35. Here Derrida's concerns over the persistent spatiality of Levinas's metaphors are of central importance. Jacques Derrida, 'Violence and Metaphysics', in *Writing and Difference* (1967) trans. Alan Bass, Routledge, London, 2001, pp. 97–192, pp. 139–46.
36. Stéphane Mosès, *Au-delà de la guerre: trios études sur Levinas*, Éditions de l'éclat, Paris and Tel Aviv, 2004, pp. 15, 102.
37. Simon Critchley, 'Introduction' to *The Cambridge Companion to Levinas*, ed. Simon Critchley and Robert Bernasconi, Cambridge University Press, Cambridge, 2001, pp. 1–32, pp. 27, 12.
38. 'Hegel thus formulates the bad infinite: "Something becomes an other: this other is itself somewhat; therefore it likewise becomes an other, and so on ad infinitum. This Infinity is the wrong or negative infinity; it is only a negation of a finite: but the finite rises again the same as ever, and is never got rid of and absorbed." ... In the situation we have described the other ([*Autre*] does not become likewise an other [*Autre*]; the end is not reborn, but moves off, at each new stage of the approach, with all the alterity of the Other [*Autrui*].' Note the difference between the alterity of the different *Autres* compared to the alterity of *Autrui*. Levinas, *Otherwise than Being*, p. 193 n34.
39. Emmanuel Levinas, 'Is Ontology Fundamental?' (1951), in *Basic Philosophical Writings*, pp. 1–10; p.7.
40. Levinas, 'Franz Rosenzweig', p. 55.
41. As he confirms in the interview with Rötzer: 'Naturally there were first-rate thinkers like Claude Lévi-Strauss. People read him with great interest, but no norms for thinking came out of it.' Rötzer, 'Emmanuel Levinas', p. 57.
42. Edmund Husserl, 'Philosophy as Rigorous Science' (1911), trans. Quentin Lauer, in *Phenomenology and the Crisis of Philosophy*, Harper & Row, New York, 1965, pp. 71–147.
43. Husserl, 'The Vienna Lecture', p. 283.
44. In his essay on Lévy-Bruhl, Levinas notes that the privilege of Occidental reason comes not from the cogito (a transcendental or universal argument) but from the *independence from history* that its thought has achieved. Levinas, 'Lévy-Bruhl and Contemporary Philosophy', p. 43.
45. Robert Bernasconi, 'Who is My Neighbor? Who is the Other? Questioning "the Generosity of Western Thought"', in *Ethics and Responsibility in the Phenomenological Tradition* (Ninth Annual Symposium of the Simon Silverman Phenomenology Center), Duquesne University Press, Pittsburgh, 1992, pp. 1–31, p. 22.
46. Levinas, *Otherwise than Being*, p. 170.
47. Emmanuel Levinas, *Ethics and Infinity: Conversations with Philippe Nemo* (1982), trans. Richard A. Cohen, Duquesne University Press, Pittsburgh, 1985, p. 114.
48. §41 *Deutschtum und Jugendtum*, cited by Derrida, 'Interpretations at War', p. 183.
49. 'The living "gods of Greece" were

worthier opponents of the living God than the phantoms of the Asiatic Orient. The deities of China as of India are massive structures made from the monoliths of primeval time which still protrude into our own times in the cults of "primitives."' Rosenzweig, *The Star of Redemption*, p. 35. And a later aside: 'at least the gods of myth *lived*' (ibid., p. 38).
50. 'It is probably because it evokes Greece that idolatry can still be preferred to something else! But idolatry also encompasses all the intellectual temptations of the relative, of exoticism and fads, all that comes to us from India and China, all that comes to us from the alleged "experiences" of humanity which we would not be permitted to reject.' Emmanuel Levinas 'And God Created Woman', in *Nine Talmudic Readings* (1970), trans. Annette Aronowicz, Indiana University Press, Bloomington and Indianapolis, 1990, pp. 169–76, p. 176.
51. This summary of Rosenzweig is synthesized from three brief sections: 'Asia: The Unmythical God' (pp. 35–8); 'Asia: The Non-Plastic World' (pp. 57–60); 'Asia: Non-Tragic Man' (pp. 73–6).
52. Ibid., p. 36. Incapable, therefore of pluralism, leading Levinas to repeatedly make reference to 'masses' and 'hordes' when referring to Asia and Africa.
53. This notion of China overflowing with spirits (ibid.,p. 35) may underlie Levinas's references to the 'density of China's past'.
54. Rosenzweig specifically categorizes Islam as *pagan* because of its once-and-for-all-time revelation in Mohammed; Judaism would also share this structure were it to rest with the Pentateuch. Indeed Islam is described as a *pagan plagiarization* of Judaism, with Mohammed 'taking over' revelation but neglecting the proper presuppositions of prophecy (ibid., p. 116) so that the Koran is only a 'magical miracle' and Allah (who is not God) only an 'oriental despot'(ibid., p. 118).
55. Rosenzweig glosses Eastern thought in terms of 'Primitive Atheism', 'Primitive Phenomenalism', and 'Primitive Idealism'.
56. Rötzer, 'Emmanuel Levinas', p. 63.
57. Robert Bernasconi,'Will the Real Kant Please Stand Up: The Challenge of Enlightenment Racism to the Study of the History of Philosophy', *Radical Philosophy* 117, January/February 2003, pp. 13–22.
58. Ibid., p. 15.
59. Bernasconi, 'Who is my Neighbor? Who is the Other?', p. 14.
60. Ibid., p. 2; Judith Butler, 'Precarious Life', in *Precarious Life: The Powers of Mourning and Violence*, Verso, London and New York, 2004, pp. 128–51.
61. See Gibbs, *Correlations in Rosenzweig and Levinas*, pp. 119, 145–6.

Peter Rabbit and the Grundrisse

Rosa and Charley Parkin

There can be no such thing as an innocent reading of the *Tale of Peter Rabbit*. As that most percipient analyst of the later manuscripts, Enid Blyton, puts it: 'We must pose this work the question of the specificity of its object, its relation to its object. The only reading of *Peter Rabbit* which speaks to us through the congealed layers of the past-becoming-present is a symptomatic reading - a reading in which we listen attentively to Beatrix Potter's silences.'[1]

So much is of course clear to the average reader of this epochal work, this work which has not only transformed our collective perceptions of rabbitness (*Kaninchenlichkeit*) but which has contributed a new chapter to the political economy of the cabbage patch. It is our contention in this brief monograph that *Peter Rabbit* marks a watershed in Potter's philosophical development, a distinct epistemological rupture from the earlier problematic of the Herne Bay manuscripts (above all, *The Tale of Squirrel Nutkin* and *Jemima Puddleduck*). Nothing more tellingly illustrates the completeness of this scientific metamorphosis than the contrast between the rather schematic hermeneutics of the Nutkin-Puddleduck period and the sure grasp of the principles of comparative political economy manifested in Peter Rabbit. The dramatization of the conflict between Peter and Mr. McGregor in the celebrated garden scene brilliantly pinpoints, in a so brief episode, those acute contradictions and levels of overdetermination characteristic of pre-capitalist cabbage production. The revelatory instance (Potter's favoured methodological device) is that 'moment' when Mr. McGregor, chasing Peter from the garden, seizes the rake and aims a blow at the fleeing creature. Through an inspired stroke of transformative symbolism, in which the *essence* of the rake changes from that of tool to that of weapon, Potter lays bare the irresolvable antagonisms of a sub-feudal order in which the role of producer and the role of warrior are indissolubly linked yet totally incompatible in their binary opposition.

It is quite clear from our reading of the unpublished drafts and revisions of the early manuscripts that Mr. McGregor is to be understood as an embodiment (*Träger*) of that class of small peasant proprietors from whom baronial landlords extracted in direct and unmediated forms surplus value in the dual forms of military service and corvée labour.[2] However, we must state quite emphatically that despite certain surface similarities the role of Mr. McGregor in the productive process is *not* to be equated with that of the Seven Dwarfs, as so many theorists from Schumpeter onwards have argued. The extraction of surplus from the productive labour of the Seven Dwarfs by the Royal household (Snow White) was a *mediated* political form, though ultimately backed up by terror, which is a condition more akin to the Asiatic mode of production than to sub-Feudalism. Failure to appreciate this crucial distinction has led to quite understandable confusion among the readers of these works - though unfortunately we cannot go into the important question of whose self-interests are in fact being served by these not accidental attempts at mystification and concealment.

The thesis we wish to advance is that the entire episode between Peter and Mr. McGregor, quite apart from the 'rake' scene is decisive in marking a conjuncture in the transformation of Peter Rabbit from an object of history to the real subject of history. It is precisely at that 'moment' when Peter is threatened by the 'rake' that he gets his blue jacket caught on the fence, and can only make good his escape by abandoning

INTERLUDE

8 *Peter Rabbit* and the *Grundrisse*

ROSA AND CHARLEY PARKIN

There can be no such thing as an innocent reading of *The Tale of Peter Rabbit*. As that most percipient analyst of the later manuscripts, Enid Blyton, puts it:

> We must pose this work the question of the specificity of its object, its relation to its object. The only reading of *Peter Rabbit* which speaks to us through the congealed layers of the past-becoming-present is a symptomatic reading – a reading in which we listen attentively to Beatrix Potter's silences.[1]

So much is of course clear to the average reader of this epochal work, this work which has not only transformed our collective perceptions of rabbitness (*Kaninchenlichkeit*) but which has contributed a new chapter to the political economy of the cabbage patch. It is our contention in this brief monograph that *Peter Rabbit* marks a watershed in Potter's philosophical development, a distinct epistemological rupture from the earlier problematic of the Herne Bay manuscripts (above all, *The Tale of Squirrel Nutkin* and *Jemima Puddleduck*). Nothing more tellingly illustrates the completeness of this scientific metamorphosis than the contrast between the rather schematic hermeneutics of the Nutkin–Puddleduck period and the sure grasp of the principles of comparative political economy manifested in *Peter Rabbit*. The dramatization of the conflict between Peter and Mr McGregor in the celebrated garden scene brilliantly pinpoints, in so brief an episode, those acute contradictions and levels of overdetermination characteristic of precapitalist cabbage production. The revelatory instance (Potter's favoured methodological device) is that 'moment' when Mr McGregor, chasing Peter from the garden, seizes the rake and aims a blow at the fleeing creature. Through an inspired stroke of transformative symbolism, in which the *essence* of the rake changes from that of tool to that of weapon, Potter lays bare the irresolvable antagonisms of a sub-feudal order in which the role of producer and the role of warrior are indissolubly linked yet totally incompatible in their binary opposition.

It is quite clear from our reading of the unpublished drafts and revisions of the early manuscripts that Mr McGregor is to be understood as an embodiment (*Träger*) of that class of small peasant proprietors from whom baronial landlords extracted in direct and unmediated forms surplus-value in the dual forms of military service and corvée labour.[2] However, we must state quite emphatically that despite certain surface similarities the role of Mr McGregor in the productive process is *not* to be equated with that of the Seven Dwarfs, as so many theorists from Schumpeter onwards have argued. The extraction of surplus from the productive labour of the Seven Dwarfs by the Royal household (Snow White) was a *mediated* political form, though ultimately backed up by terror, which is a condition more akin to the Asiatic mode of production than to sub-feudalism. Failure to appreciate this crucial distinction has led to quite understandable confusion among the readers of these works – though unfortunately we cannot go into the important question of whose self-interests are in fact being served by these not accidental attempts at mystification and concealment.

The thesis we wish to advance is that the entire episode between Peter and Mr McGregor, quite apart from the 'rake' scene, is decisive in marking a conjuncture in the transformation of Peter Rabbit from an object of history to the real subject of history. It is precisely at that 'moment' when Peter is threatened by the 'rake' that he gets his blue jacket caught on the fence, and can only make good his escape by abandoning it. Again, in this capsule statement, we have Potter's brilliant portrayal of the self-emancipatory act – the shedding of the 'jacket' conveys to us of course the throwing off of servile, anthropomorphic status imposed by the structures-in-dominance of the ideological state apparatus. It is during Peter's tearful monologue in the potting shed that the full significance of his act comes home to him: that is, that he has finally and irrevocably entered the realm of history as a reflexive agent. From this moment on he will be marked out by his kinsmen, Flopsy, Mopsy and Cottontail (who chose to remain in the ever-pregiven structure of the warren) as a figure of destiny: the singular and heroic figure for which all Potter's earlier works have in a sense prepared us.

None of the previous manuscripts matches the theoretic grandeur and philosophic *presence* of *Peter Rabbit* – including the much overrated *Tale of Mrs Tiggy-Winkle*, which, notwithstanding Lukács's extravagant assertions to the contrary, still bears the unmistakable traces of the Herne Bay period.[3] It is quite clear from a synoptic reading of the Preface to the second edition of the Czech translation of *Tiggy-Winkle*, published *after* the final (Putney) draft of *Peter Rabbit*, that Potter expresses serious reservations about the internal structure of the argument. There is a tacit recognition of the failure to give full weighting to those forces bearing upon Mrs Tiggy-Winkle's actions, which can only be accounted for as a result of the overdetermination of conjunctive instances within the given totality of the farmyard. What this does in effect is to present us with a completely dehistoricized hedgehog-subject.[4] It is impossible to imagine Potter falling into this same trap in any of her later analyses of precapitalist economic formations.

Our attempt to produce a correct reading of *Peter Rabbit* deliberately poses the problem of what it is to *read*. Only in answering this question can we feel confident in our task of rescuing Potter's contribution to science from the hands of those who seek to reduce this work virtually to the level of a fairy tale.

Notes

1. Enid Blyton, *Lire le Peter Rabbit,* Maspero, Paris, 1968.
2. See Nicos Poulantzas, 'Hegemony, Surplus and Unproductive Labour in the Cabbage Patch: A Reply to Miliband', *New Left Review* LXIV, 1970.
3. G. Lukács, 'Weltgeist, Naturgeschichte und Symbolsbegriffe bei *Frau Tiggy Winkle*', *Beatrix-Potter studien* VIII, 1956.
4. Adorno's biting comment is here very much to the point: 'The thought to which a positive hypostasis of anything outside the immanence of the dialectic is forbidden, overshoots the subject with which it no *longer* simulates as being one.' T. Adorno, *Spasms*, Frankfurt, 1972. This passage could have been written specifically with Mrs Tiggy-Winkle in mind.

/female/age 24/
activity: high/
reason: inappropria[te]
content/status: bloc[ked]

BETRAYALS

9 Oedipus as figure

PHILIPPE LACOUE-LABARTHE

It is probable, or at the very least plausible, that Western humanity now models itself on two figures or types – two 'examples', if you like. They appear to be antagonistic (or are at least supported by antagonistic discourses), but their antagonism also binds together, and founds, their kinship, as each of these figures or types claims to provide an exclusive representation of humanity as such.

The first of these figures is the older and obviously the more powerful in terms of its social, political and historical effects: the figure of the worker, in the sense in which it was expressly designated and thematized by Ernst Jünger, but also in the sense that it is supported by the entire social metaphysics of the nineteenth century, and especially by the thought of Marx in its entirety. Under its influence or impact, the essence of humanity – *humanitas* – recognizes itself, understands itself and tries to realize itself as the subject of production (the modern *poiesis*) in general or as the subject of *energy* in the strict sense: energy that is applied and put to work. In this figure, 'man' is represented as worker.

The second figure is less obvious, even though its figural or mythical determination is no less clear. This does not mean that its effects are less powerful, but it does mean that, thanks to a structural necessity, they are concealed: they are inscribed in the element of history and politics (but not society) in a less immediately readable manner. They have a kind of 'infra' or 'hypo' ('sub') status, and therefore pertain more clearly to the order of the *subjectum* in general. I refer, of course, to the figure of Oedipus in the sense that, ever since Freud, 'Oedipus' has been the name of desire, and in the sense that the figure of Oedipus represents the subject of desire. Which necessarily means: desire as subject. Desire is not the opposite of labour in the same way that consumption is the opposite of production. That crude opposition has had its day. But the fact that desire, like production, is consumed may mean that desire itself is a form of production or energy. It was probably a mistake to speak of a libidinal economy. I do not know if that was enough to reach the unique root from which the antagonism between desiring man and working man springs, or should spring. And nor do I know if we now have, given the current state of affairs, the ability to find that root. I would, however, like to take a step in that direction. Just a step, or in other words a very first step.

Heidegger has the distinction of having begun to deconstruct the figure of the Worker.[1] In doing so, he began to deconstruct the figural in general, or to deconstruct everything that modern ontology elevated to the rank of *Gestalt*, figure or type, when, abandoning its claim to be an onto-theology, it transformed itself into an onto-anthropology or, as I have suggested elsewhere, an onto-typology.[2] This figure or type is, making due allowance for the reversal of transcendence into 'rescendence' (the expression is Heidegger's) that we can observe in Feuerbach and Marx as well as Nietzsche, a strict equivalent to the Platonic *idea*. The figure or *Gestalt* of the Worker is understood by Heidegger as being one of the modes in which the essence of technology is deployed, or in other words as one of the modes of *Ge-stell*. The word designates the unity of coming together of all the modes of *Stellen*, 'formulating' or '(re)presenting' in general, from *Vorstellung* to *Gestalt*. It therefore designates being in its last *envoi*.

No such deconstruction of the figure of Oedipus has been attempted. It is usually ignored as a figure and viewed solely as a structure. The deconstruction of the Oedipal structure was and is still necessary. Just as it was necessary for the Freudian interpretation of the myth to be rigorously delineated. And yet it is perhaps just as necessary to look at the very simple, almost anodyne, gesture whereby Freud appropriates a mythical name and erects it into a concept, a schema or, as I believe, a figure. After all, that gesture is no more innocent that the gesture whereby Nietzsche decides to make Zarathustra the figure of the Will to Power (and the spokesman for the Eternal Return). And it is all the less innocent in that Nietzsche is never very far behind Freud. The question I would like to raise is therefore as follows: what necessity was Freud obeying when he turned to Oedipus and elevated him to the rank of figure? Just what was it that this mythical or post-mythical figure supported that made Freud think of appropriating it?

Freud himself is quite explicit about the many good reasons for recognizing the history or prehistory of desire in the myth. He also makes it perfectly clear that the mythical in general has to be resolutely taken into account. On the other hand, he never takes the trouble to re-examine the apparent spontaneity of his major gesture: subsuming everything to do with his discovery under the name of Oedipus and thus making that name the emblem of psychoanalysis itself because that name can be regarded as the name of the very subject of the unconscious. And yet the gesture was not without its consequences.

The suspicion – or rather the hypothesis – I would like to put forward is therefore this, and it can be formulated without too many precautions: the reason why Oedipus has become a figure in this way is that Oedipus could take on the status of a figure. A figure is not simply what it signifies or what we say it means. A figure is a figure only because it *imposes itself* as such and because it can have that *position*, or in other words the position of an *idea* that has been inverted or reversed. A figure necessarily has an ontological status in the metaphysical sense of that term. To put it in different terms: the fact that Oedipus is a figure is none of Freud's doing, or not just Freud's doing. It is the result of an ontology that pre-exists Freud, and that may also provide a support for what he always described as the fortuitous outcome of pure research.

The question is therefore: what predisposed Oedipus to take on the status of a figure? What authorized Freud's gesture? And my hypothesis – though it is merely a first hypothesis – is as follows: before becoming, no doubt jointly and severally, the figure of desire *and* science, Oedipus was already a figure; perhaps not the figure of desire, but certainly the figure of science. Oedipus was a figure in philosophy, and the figure of philosophy. Which probably means that Oedipus was also the figure of a desire: the desire for what philosophy, because of the very name it gives itself, claims to take as its object: 'love'. *Sophon* is one of the words, but not the only word, that the Greeks used for 'knowledge'. And perhaps – who knows? – loving means desiring.

There appears, in other words, to be a prehistory of 'the Oedipus'. A philosophical prehistory of 'the Oedipus'. Oedipus seems to have been considered the philosophical hero par excellence: the man in whom, or the man in whose destiny, all the inner meanings of the West's spiritual quest come together in a symbolic sense; he appears to have been recognized as the initial or tutelary hero of our history and our civilization. Within that history and within that civilization, the West is therefore described as 'Oedipal'. The name 'Oedipus', which is one of his names or at least one possible translation of his name, appears to have been a name for the West.

Just now, I alluded to a determinate moment in our history or in the history of thought. Truth to tell, and although this occurred before the sudden rise of psychoanalysis, Oedipus or the name 'Oedipus' entered philosophy somewhat late in the day. So late, in fact, that his entrance coincided with the moment when philosophy was beginning to believe that its end was near, that the questions that it had brought into being over two thousand years ago were on the point of receiving a definitive answer, or in short that a certain history, if not history itself to the extent that it was the history of thought, was coming to an end or a finish: the 'programme' had been completed. That is why Oedipus, who, for the Greeks themselves and at the inaugural moment of our history was the incarnation of the archaic, and referred to the darkest realms of a prehistory, became in reality, when philosophy appropriated him, a figure of the end and of completion. Or, which amounts to the same thing, he is, henceforth, the definitive figure of origins: Oedipus is the man in whom and according to whom the destiny of the West was sealed for ever.

This is the moment when philosophy finds its most 'appropriate' name outside itself (and, for instance, no longer recognizes itself, or recognizes itself less and less, in the name of Socrates). This is the moment, that is, when philosophy begins to seek its symbolic mark in its oldest antagonist – myth – and in doing so finds that it can board it for inspection. The moment when philosophy goes in search of a figure is the moment in its history that follows the most serious *crisis* that has ever affected philosophy: this is the moment that follows Kant's *critique* of metaphysics, and it sees philosophy attempting, no doubt for the first time, to find a new self-confidence and to restore itself to what it once was by overcoming the apparently final verdict that Kant had pronounced against it. Oedipus therefore appears at a truly tragic moment – it is the destiny of philosophy, or metaphysics to be more accurate, that is at stake – and, as in the myth, he appears in order to resolve a crisis. He appears like a *pharmakos*, and with all the ambivalence that surrounds that ritual character. It so happens that the crisis is 'symbolic': it is a crisis within thought. But perhaps – who knows? – the social crisis reflected in the myth is no longer a symbolic crisis. Perhaps the symbolic crisis that occurs in philosophy at the end of the eighteenth century is very directly related to the immense political crisis that threw Europe into upheaval after the French Revolution. The Schlegels of this world, at least, made no distinction between the two.

Aristotle

How did Oedipus' entry into philosophy come about? Why and how did philosophy go in search of him or seek him out? What was it that he represented that made him the incarnation of the hope that the crisis could be resolved, or that a model for its resolution could be found?

Truth to tell, Oedipus was already present within philosophy prior to this late moment – or, perhaps, before this terminal phase in philosophy in the strict sense which, for us, begins with German idealism. The name was already in circulation – and had been for a very long time; at least since Aristotle. I think that we have to dwell on this for a moment; otherwise we are in danger of failing to understand the meaning of the 'Oedipal operation' undertaken by German idealism.

It was indeed Aristotle – and you know how long his authority held sway over thought – who made Sophocles' *Oedipus Rex* what might be described as the definitive model for tragedy, the tragedy par excellence, or the tragedy of tragedies. He does so in the *Poetics*, which, as you know, attempts to define the specificity of tragedy within that specific form of *mimesis* known as the theatrical or the dramatic, or in other words the (re)presentation of human actions (the representation of a *mythos*). Aristotle introduces the question of its *telos*, its intended goal or final purpose. In his opinion, *mimesis* itself, which is 'natural to all men' and therefore truly human, has a very specific function: that of teaching us to see and 'theorize' (and here there is an obvious link with 'theatre'). *Mimesis* predisposes us to think and to know; it has a philosophical vocation. But it does not just have a theoretical function; or, rather, that theoretical function is also an economic function (with knowledge, an economy, if not the economy itself which is established): *mimesis* is also capable, according to Aristotle, of making bearable the sight (and this again is a matter of 'theory') of what we would find repulsive in the real world. The representation of, say, a corpse is bearable. In more general terms, the spectacle of death frightens us less than death itself and allows us to look at it (and therefore to think about it). Bataille will use this as an argument against Hegel. This function, which is the direct corollary of the theoretical function, is none other than *katharsis* – purgation or purification, not that the distinction matters greatly here (it is always a matter of driving out evil). *Mimesis* in fact acts like homeopathic medicine; to shift register, it functions like a sacrifice that uses a simulacrum or subterfuge to drive out social violence by spectacularly projecting the violence and murderous desires onto an animal. It is because it is theoretico-theatrical that *mimesis* is cathartic and, if you like, that it can provide a cure. We are within the space of what Jacques Derrida calls 'economimesis'.[3]

The exemplary instance of economimesis is tragedy, which is in Aristotle's view the highest form of art. And within tragedy it is illustrated in exemplary fashion by Sophocles' *Oedipus Rex*. For tragedy is, according to Aristotle, the social or political art par excellence (which should be understood as meaning the art that deals with the essentials of human *praxis*) and its task it to drive out the evil that affects human relations. That is why it plays simultaneously upon the two basic passions implicit, because of their very possibility, in any human relationship: fear, which is the passion inspired by the dissolution of the social bond, by unbinding or dissociation; and pity, which is in contrast the passion that inspires social relations, if not – as Rousseau thought – the primal passion of sociality. The tragic spectacle must discharge – in the sense that Freud will use that term, which derives directly from Aristotle – fear and pity. (This is easy to understand when it comes to fear, but much less so when it comes to pity. But if we reread Freud's *Massenpsychologie*, we find that an excess of love poses at least as great a threat to the social body as hatred.) This is why the tragic spectacle must (re)present a myth that can bring about this (twofold) discharge, or in other words the actions of a man who can inspire both fear and pity. The true tragic hero must, in other words, be both – and simultaneously – frightening and touching. He must inspire fear and still, because he inspires fear, make us feel compassion. He must therefore be a being who bears within him a basic contradiction, if not the basic human contradiction that is the enigma of humanity. He must therefore be, for the same reason and in his very identity, both a monster (the incarnation of evil) and a poor wretch (goodness itself). The tragic, defined in the true sense, comes about, that is, when guilt (responsibility for a sin) and innocence come together in one and the same being; when the myth is based upon the figure of contradiction, oxymoron (innocent guilt) or even paradox (the greater the guilt, the greater the innocence and vice versa). That is why the story of Oedipus, who pays the price for a sin he has committed without knowing it – who quite simply pays the price for his non-knowledge and whose desire for knowledge reveals the horror of his destiny – is the tragic myth at its highest degree of perfection.

All these things are well known. I recall them only to point out that, from philosophy's point of view, what is in play here explains not only why, until Nietzsche and Freud (and even until Heidegger after them), *Oedipus Rex* was regarded as the model for tragedy, but also why philosophy was able to seize hold of the myth, make it its own and promote Oedipus to being the very figure of philosophy. There are two main reasons for this – and they are certainly not the only ones.

On the one hand, the very structure and finality of tragedy, as analysed by Aristotle, this whole theoretico-cathartic mechanism (of knowledge and salvation) and therefore this economic mechanism, predispose tragedy to fulfil the two great functions of philosophy (Aristotle's rival was quite right about this): the theoretical and the practical, or, if you prefer to put it that way, the speculative and the ethico-political.

In that respect, it is not at all surprising that for the young Nietzsche, for example, the insistent recall of the Oedipal motif went hand in hand with the definition of philosophy as 'the doctor of culture' and with the political hope that tragedy would enjoy a renaissance in the modern West (and in Germany).

On the other hand, and what is more important, the fact that tragedy is already politically oriented implies that tragedy is the site for the revelation of the very essence of knowledge and the inspiration behind the desire for knowledge: the encounter with contradiction. In general. And that, it appears to me, is the basic reason why Oedipus reappears in philosophy at the moment when philosophy, in the person of Kant, reveals the contradictions to which human reason is exposed when it goes beyond its own limits, goes beyond the limits of finite experience and attempts to take up a position beyond the sensible world, or in the metaphysical as such, in order to tell the truth about the world, the soul or God, when, taking the model (or following the example) of the tragic hero, it becomes guilty of *hubris* – insolence and transgression. Oedipus – and this is the last gasp of metaphysics – makes it possible to think contradiction's being-thinkable. It represents a model for the solution of what Kant called the 'antinomies'. And because this kind of 'solution' is what constitutes the dialectic as such or speculative logic, Oedipus will be regarded as the dialectical hero or, which amounts to the same thing, the speculative hero.

Let me attempt to demonstrate this briefly.

Schelling

The singular honour of reintroducing Oedipus – and the question of the tragic along with him – into philosophy falls to Schelling. The gesture is contemporary with the first beginnings of German idealism, and therefore with the moment of the flowering of early Romanticism (the Romanticism of Jena). It is not unrelated to Friedrich Schlegel's philological work on Greek tragedy. It takes place at the time when Hegel, Hölderlin and Schelling were all beginning their philosophical work. The question confronting them was obviously the question bequeathed them by Kant, or, in a word, the critical question: is metaphysics, as elaborated from Plato to Leibniz and Spinoza, still possible? Or is the *subject* of thought – the Cartesian *cogito* on which all the metaphysics of the Moderns is based – subordinated to so many conditions as to be denied any truly metaphysical knowledge from the outset?

According to Schelling, who deals with this problem in a little book entitled *Letters on Dogmatism and Criticism* (1795), the debate within metaphysics that is initiated by Kant essentially comes down to the problem of freedom. To put it very schematically, Kant's critique declares that the problem of freedom, or the metaphysical problem of freedom, is insoluble, because there is no way of proving either that freedom is possible, or that it is impossible and that the rule of natural necessity is absolute. In order to solve this problem we would have to be able to adopt the position and viewpoint of God. Those are the terms bequeathed us by Spinoza. We would, in other words, have to accede to the Absolute Knowledge which alone can decide whether man is completely subordinate to the order of things and natural determinism, whether he is hemmed in by the sphere of objectivity, or whether he is, on the contrary, capable, in so far as he is a subject, of escaping the mechanism of the world and acceding to freedom. According to Schelling, the most basic philosophical contradiction is the very contradiction – which Kant took to extremes – between the objective (necessity or nature) and the subjective (freedom). And what is at stake here is, in his view, the possibility of the absolute subject, or, in other words, the possibility of the Absolute as subject.

Now there is a solution to this seemingly insurmountable contradiction. And the solution is given by Greek tragedy in its presentation of the myth of Oedipus. This is how the tenth and last of the letters that make up Schelling's book opens. It is a text to which I have already referred elsewhere.[4]

> It has often been asked how Greek reason could put up with the contradictions of its tragedy. A mortal who is destined by fatality to be a criminal struggles *against* fatality and yet he receives a terrible punishment for a crime for which destiny was responsible! The *reason* for this contradiction, or what makes it bearable, lay deeper than where it was being sought: it lay in the conflict between human freedom and the power of the objective world. When that power was a superpower (a *fatum*), the mortal must necessarily lose and yet, as he did not lose *without a struggle*, he had to be *punished* for his very defeat. The fact that the criminal, who was defeated only by the superpower of destiny, was *punished* implied that the recognition of human freedom was a *tribute* to freedom. Allowing its hero to

struggle against the superpower of destiny was Greek tragedy's way of paying tribute to human freedom; in order not to cross the barriers of art, it had to ensure that he was *defeated* but, in order to compensate, through art, for the humiliation of human freedom, he also had to undergo *punishment* ... for the crime committed by *destiny*. The great idea was to accept that ... [he] could consent to being punished for an *inevitable* crime in order to demonstrate his freedom through the loss of that freedom and to founder thanks to a declaration of the rights of free will.

This is a speculative interpretation of the 'innocent guilt' of Oedipus, as analysed by Aristotle. By struggling against the unavoidable, or in other words against the destiny (the most rigorous form of necessity) that is responsible for his crime, the tragic hero brings about his own downfall and voluntarily chooses to expiate a crime of which he knows himself to be innocent and for which he should, in any case, have paid the price. Innocent guilt or the deliberate, gratuitous courting of punishment: that is the solution to the conflict or contradiction. In the face of the objective world against which he is powerless, and of which he is no more than a part or a cog, in the face of the formidable 'machine' known as destiny, the subject demonstrates his freedom by accomplishing of his own accord, or voluntarily, what the machine demands of him. He manifests his freedom not simply by accepting necessity (an old solution which has no 'efficacy'), but through 'the very loss of his freedom'. He knows that he is innocent and is destiny's plaything (he knows that he did not know he was committing a sin), but it is he himself who strives to know who committed the sin and who freely accepts his condemnation by destiny.

We have here the schema and matrix for dialectical logic itself: the negative (the loss of freedom) is converted into the positive (the realization of freedom) thanks to exacerbation of the negative itself (courting punishment, the will to lose freedom). The dialectic deals with the paradox of contradiction or, in other words, identity. Whilst identity presupposes, if it is to exist, being identical to itself, identity is always both self-identity and its opposite. Which also means that alterity – including the most extreme alterity, or contradiction – is potentially an identity. No matter whether the 'supersession' is named or not (in Schelling's text it goes by the name of the 'barriers' inherent in art, or in other words the conditions specific to (re)presentation, *Darstellung* or *mimesis*), identity, Self-realization is always possible in the form of the work of the negative, or rather, in the present case, its reduplication. And it is because identity is thought of in terms of the Self, ipseity or *Selbstheit* that only a metaphysics of the subject can claim to resolve the paradox of the Same. When, conversely, the paradox remains a paradox, or when extreme difference is preserved, we stray beyond the limits of such a metaphysics in one way or another. This is probably the case in some of Diderot's work; it is also the case, in a clearer way, in Hölderlin. The dialectical operation – and it is an operation – is intended from the outset to safeguard the Self and the subject. That is why it can begin with the problematic of freedom. And that is also why, in its unfolding and as an unfolding, it is no accident, and not by chance, that the speculative dialectic recounts the history – in the twin senses of *mythos* and *Geschichte* – of a subject. Of the Subject itself as *subjectum*: foundation and being. The truth of the dialectic is the subject as possibility of the (re)presentation of identity to the self: self-consciousness, according to Hegel. But the strange thing is that, in the present case, it is another form of representation – *Darstellung* and not *Vorstellung*, or in other words theatricality and *mimesis* – that allows us to think its truth. If, as Bataille thought,[5] we have here an irreducible necessity, then the dialectic, in so far as it is the truth of the onto-theological, is a determinate interpretation or a determinate effect of a mimetology that is older and deeper down than the discourse on being. But I cannot follow that line of inquiry here.

Hegel

I am not at all certain that Schelling's first operation explains why, a few years later (and shortly after Hölderlin had in his turn offered a mimetologically inspired interpretation of *Oedipus Rex*, though it is marginal to dialectical-speculative thought in the strict sense of that term), Hegel should have chosen the character of Oedipus to be the very symbol of the act of philosophizing and, in doing so, elevated him to the rank of the figure of the philosophical for our entire era. For Hegel was indeed the first to promote Oedipus to the rank of figure.

The operation – for it is another interpretation – is relatively famous. To put it briefly, as going into detail is out of the question here, the episode takes place in the lectures on history given in Berlin, or in other words in the *Philosophy of History*. Here, Hegel sets out to demonstrate how the subject or Spirit gradually emerges, moment by moment, from its non-knowledge (ignorance, superstition, magic, confused religions and all the forms of the non-knowledge of the self), wrests itself away from or escapes the materiality that submerges it, gradually wins its own essence (which is to be knowledge, intellection – and self-knowledge) by freeing itself from its sensory and corporeal servitude, and succeeds in accomplishing and realizing itself as such. Once more, this is a question of freedom. This history of Spirit is history *tout court*; the meaning of history, in other words, is none other than the realization of Spirit and the accomplishment of the metaphysical. It begins, as we know, in the 'night of time' and its very trajectory is symbolic: it moves from West to East, from Orient to Occident, from an ancient and far off China to the Greece where philosophy (self-consciousness) sees the light of day, after having traversed India, Mesopotamia and Egypt. In a word, its trajectory follows that of the sun: the philosophy of history is a heliology.[6]

In this context, Oedipus intervenes when Hegel attempts to explain, still using the same metaphysical symbolism, how this transition from Egypt to Greece takes place. It is, of course, the transition from symbol to concept or idea that allows Spirit to reach its zenith. Egypt, explains Hegel, is the eve of Spirit's awakening: in its sun worship (heliophilia), Egypt senses the essence of Spirit; in its cult of the dead and its belief in metempsychosis, it senses the meaning of the immortality of the soul, or the idea that the human subject is the absolute and 'possesses infinite value'. But this is no more than a presentiment, and it does not succeed in expressing itself. In Egypt, writes Hegel, spirit still remains 'trapped in stone', in materiality and in sensuality. Egypt's discourse on truth, consciousness and man is infirm and is still infantile (*infans*); it does not speak the true language of Spirit, or the *logos*. It expresses itself through symbols carved on stones, through statues and mysterious monuments, in representations of the divine that remain half animal. This is why Egypt is the land of contradiction: in Egypt, Spirit struggles against that which enslaves it – the sensible, the corporeal, materiality and animality – but if it is to break loose and free itself, it must take one more step.

It is the Greeks who take that step, and it is the philosophical (metaphysical) step itself. This is inscribed in their mythology, but still in a symbolic form. And it is inscribed there twice. Its first inscription comes about when it transpires that the Greeks have a god who symbolizes the solution to the Egyptian enigma of the divine: in Egypt, the divine is the enigma itself. That enigma is none other than the enigma of truth. Hegel refers here to the inscription that could once be read in the goddess Neith's sanctuary in Saïs. It read: 'I am that which is, that which was, and that which will be; no one has lifted my veil.'[7] Hegel immediately thinks that this is a metaphor for truth, unveiling or *aletheia*. But the inscription goes on: 'The fruit which I have produced is helios.' Hegel comments: 'This lucidity is Spirit – the sun of Neith the concealed night-loving deity. In the Egyptian Neith, truth is still a problem. The Greek Apollo is its solution: his utterance is *"Man, know thyself"*.' The (Greek) solution to the (Egyptian) enigma or the solution to the mystery of truth is therefore Spirit as self-consciousness. The legend in the sanctuary in Saïs is deciphered by the inscription on the pediment of the temple of Apollo in Delphi, and it will fall to Socrates to make it philosophizing's imperative. Somewhat earlier than

Hegel, as it happens, Hölderlin had a similar intuition in a short story entitled 'The Disciples in Saïs'. After a long journey, the hero of this tale of initiation reaches the sanctuary of Neith and lifts the veil covering the statue of the goddess. And what he sees is himself, or his own image. He himself is – the subject in general is – the secret of truth. And this is what Hegel says: the truth about the truth is the Self.

Now this same step is taken for a second time outside Egypt (the Orient) and it is Oedipus who takes it – at least to the extent that the mythical sequence about the Sphinx is deciphered in a similar way. This is what Hegel says:

> Wonderfully, then, must the Greek legend surprise us, which relates that the Sphinx – the great Egyptian symbol [*Bild*] – appeared in Thebes, uttering the words 'What is it which in the morning goes on four legs, at midday on two, and in the evening on three?' [You will notice that this too is a solar trajectory.] Oedipus, giving the solution, *Man*, precipitated the Sphinx from the rock. The solution and liberation of that Oriental Spirit ... is certainly this: that the Inner Being of Nature is Thought [Spirit], which has its existence only in the human consciousness.[8]

Oedipus is, then, the man who solves the Egyptian riddle by replying: the truth or the secret is the subject (Spirit as subject). And this, according to Hegel, is the answer given by knowledge in general. The answer is man to the extent that he knows himself, that he is 'self-consciousness'. And this is why Oedipus articulates the first sentence, or rather the first word, of philosophy: 'Oedipus ... thus shows himself to be possessed of knowledge.'[9] That is one of his names; this is one of the translations or interpretations of the name 'Oedipus'. Oedipus answers only with – gives only – his name: 'I, who have seen, am the one who knows.' That is the name of the philosopher.

It is true that Hegel qualifies this 'Praise of Oedipus' with some serious reservations: 'good philosopher' that he is, he not only remains discreet about the Oedipal scandal (the parricide and especially the incest) but also, and this is a sign of a disturbing 'ambivalence', notes that Oedipus' 'abominations' mean that his figure remains in darkness. In a word, he is not too much of a Socrates to rectify and correct Oedipus' example. But the fact that he is not too much of a Socrates also means that something Oedipal secretly overdetermines the exemplarity of Socrates: Socrates resurrects the figure of Oedipus only because he himself is a tragic figure – the figure of the 'innocent guilty man' – and the hero of a philosophical (re)presentation who borrows at least the dialogical form from tragedy. Socrates is Socrates only in so far as he is the truth of Oedipus. That is why he will repeat Oedipus' 'Delphic' answer and will place the entire philosophical West – until Hegel, that is – under the sign of self-consciousness.

In a note on Gide's *Oedipe* – the Oedipus who Gide has say that, whatever the riddle of the sphinx might be, he is resolved to answer 'man' – Walter Benjamin remarks that something happens to Oedipus between the moment when he appears for the first time on the stage of Dionysus' theatre and when he appears to us, in our era: 'Very little', he says, 'But it is of great importance. *Oedipus conquers speech.*' Recalling the definition of the tragic hero that he has borrowed from Rosenzweig ('The tragic hero has only one language that is proper to him: silence'[10]), he then goes on: 'For Sophocles remains silent, almost silent. He is a bloodhound on his own trail, complaining about the harsh treatment meted out to him by his own hand. We find no thought, no reflection, in his discourse.' The tragic hero was, in other words, pure lamentation. He said nothing. He was immured in the riddle of his own pain, and the theatre resounded only with his lamentations and screams. Those are the lamentations and screams that, on a different stage, philosophy transforms into language, into *logos*, in order to recognize in them its own language: the *logos*. But the operation has taken 2,200 years – 2,200 years for the West to discover that it was Oedipal, and for it to be able to speak the discourse Oedipus could not speak. To develop his phrase, or rather to expand his one-word answer into a phrase. Or into his name. And that phrase is the dialectic itself: Absolute Knowledge.

Nietzsche and Freud

But this also means that Oedipus' accession to speech is very late in occurring. Oedipus becomes the figure of philosophy only when philosophy is coming to an end, only when its discourse is becoming exhausted. Paradoxically, Oedipus becomes philosophy's spokesman – and he is a verbose spokesman – only when philosophy is beginning to lose its voice and speaks only in languages that have become detached from it. And it is, perhaps, here that the Hegelian symbolic reaches its limits: it is quite possible that the sun that rises in Egypt – where 'the colossal statue of Memnon resounds at the first glance of the young morning sun'[11] – reaches its zenith in the sky of Greece, but then it immediately begins to set and to begin its westward trajectory. That is why Oedipus, who is the figure of a dawning Greek knowledge, is also the figure of a truly Western knowledge: the last knowledge. It is therefore not his hostility towards Hegel that explains why Nietzsche, that 'latecomer', should choose to call Oedipus 'the last philosopher' – who is, as it happens, also the last man.

I am thinking of a rather surprising text by Nietzsche: a fragment written shortly after his study of tragedy. It is a sort of short philosophical prose-poem. Oedipus, who is now alone, is talking to himself – as though he were two people. He is about to die, and it is with the echo of his own voice that he bemoans his own fate, rather as though he were the posthumous (or 'preposthumous', as Musil would have put it) incarnation of self-consciousness.

Let me paraphrase part of this text. Oedipus describes himself as the 'last philosopher' because he is the last man. No one but himself speaks to him, and his voice sounds to him like that of a dying man. He requests an hour's communion with the beloved voice, with the last breath of the memory of all human happiness. Thanks to that voice, he can cheat his loneliness and enter an illusory multiplicity and love because his heart refuses to believe that love is dead. His heart cannot bear the shiver of extreme solitude, and forces him to speak as though he were two men... And yet he can still hear the beloved voice. *Someone is dying outside him, the last man in the world. The last sigh is dying with him, a long alas whispered to him by the most wretched of the wretched: Oedipus.*

That the old Oedipus could be the figure of an exhausted self-consciousness that is dying; that this final discourse could take the paradoxical form of an interminable soliloquy in which the psyche speaks to itself (this is the last possible form of dramatic dialogue) at the very moment of its death; that there should be this voice that resonates almost beyond death and that death should divide the voice of the subject – perhaps it is this (or at least this is the hypothesis I would like to propose) that in some way opens up the space in which Freud *too*, probably without realizing it, encounters Oedipus. What I mean is that perhaps it is this that allows Oedipus to go on representing beyond or beneath the way consciousness relates to itself through self-presence, or beyond self identity a desire to know of which consciousness knows nothing, and of which it can know nothing. Perhaps it is this that allows him to reach a place (if it is a place) where by becoming absent from himself, forgetting himself as such, he emerges from himself, externalizes himself within the self, divides and becomes cut off from himself. Strangely enough, Nietzsche evokes forgetfulness in an early draft of this fragment, and speaks of the terrible solitude of the last philosopher, who is paralysed by the Medusa. Vultures hover over him. And he begs nature to let him forget.

But it is true to say that the figure Nietzsche is thinking of is, rather, that of Prometheus, or the figure which, from Feuerbach and Marx to Jünger, and even the Heidegger of 1933, overdetermines the figure of the Worker – and therefore a certain interpretation of *technē* that is not shared by Nietzsche. And still less is it shared by Freud. That Nietzsche should have 'failed to choose' between the names Oedipus and Prometheus is not, however, immaterial by any means. This 'failure to choose' does not concern only the mythical figuration of the 'last philosopher'. The last philosopher – like all the mythical figures invoked by Nietzsche, from Dionysus and Empedocles to Zarathustra – concerns the determination of (modern) man in his essence. It so happens that, for Nietzsche, the essence of man could be designated by the name 'Oedipus', rather than the name 'Prometheus'. The implications of this 'preference' are perhaps still incalculable.

You can already see the point I am trying to make for the moment: Freud's Oedipus is always reduced to the problematic of desire. It is said, with some justification, that Oedipus is, in Freud's view, the emblem of desire's destiny, and that the myth of Oedipus, as read in what we now know to be a tendentious way (or at least a lacunary way, as is any mythological reworking of a myth), simply supplies the model for the familial structuration of desire – and the tragic structuration of the unconscious. But if we place a unilateral emphasis of this aspect of the way Freud deals with the figure and the myth – and if, in doing so, we also simplify the way he deals with it – we fail, despite certain of Lacan's specific caveats, to notice that, for Freud, Oedipus is the incarnation of what he has embodied for philosophy, at least from Hegel onwards: the desire to know (or, to be more accurate and to use the Nietzschean term, the drive – *Trieb* – to know). And when Oedipus is at stake, the status of Freud's 'science' is also at stake.

To take only one well-known example. It can be found in the second of the *Three Essays on the Theory of Sexuality* ('Infantile Sexuality'), at the beginning of section 5 on 'The Sexual Researches of Childhood'. It consists of two short paragraphs:

The Drive for Knowledge
At about the same time as the sexual life of children reaches its first peak, between the ages of three and five, they also begin to show signs of the activity which may be ascribed to the drive for knowledge of research. This drive cannot be counted among the elementary instinctual components, nor can it be classed as exclusively belonging to sexuality. Its activity corresponds on the one hand to a sublimated manner or obtaining mastery, while on the

other hand it makes use of the energy of scopophilia. Its relations to sexual life, however, are of particular importance, since we have learnt from psychoanalysis that the drive for knowledge in children is attracted unexpectedly and intensively to sexual problems and is in fact possibly first aroused by them.

The Riddle of the Sphinx
It is not by theoretical interests but by practical ones that activities of research are set going in children. The threat to the bases of a child's existence offered by the discovery or the suspicion of the arrival of a new baby and the fear that he may, as a result of it, cease to be cared for and loved, make him thoughtful and clear-sighted. And this history of the drive's origin is in line with the fact that the first problem with which it deals is not the question of the distinction between the sexes but the riddle of where babies come from. (This, in a distorted form which can be easily rectified, is the same riddle that was propounded by the Theban Sphinx.)[12]

There is, then, such a thing as a drive for knowledge, and Freud says of it that it is 'a sublimated manner of obtaining mastery' (and it might perhaps in that sense be said to be 'Promethean'), and that it 'makes use of the energy of scopophilia', or in other words theoretical desire itself. Freud, who uses the word 'theory' in a rather weak sense, is no doubt pointing out that this interest in sexual problems is not theoretical (even though he notes in truly Aristotelian manner that children's drive for knowledge is aroused by them). Even so and even before the problem of the distinction between the sexes arises, it is quite simply the question of origins that stimulates the first search for knowledge: the great riddle of birth, and that is the very riddle that is propounded by the Theban Sphinx.

For Freud, Oedipus is, then, the figure of knowledge – of seeing and knowing; of the theoretical in the true sense. Similarly, in a related register which also concerns the entire psychoanalytic mechanism, tragic theatricality is still the model for the cathartic apparatus. Oedipus, in other words, is the emblem of desire but he also represents the man who solves the riddle of desire and interprets his destiny. For many people – if not the *Massen* – today, the so-called 'subject of psychoanalysis' is the form in which the philosopher lives on. Or lives on as a posthumous being, if the 'last analyst' really has not been born.

You are not unaware that Freud's consulting rooms and his desk were cluttered up with Egyptian figurines and statuettes, for which Freud appears to have had a real passion. Today, it is thought that we can simply dismiss this as a survival of some old idolatry; the rather strange attachment of the 'agnostic' to these archaic divinities is seen as a symptom of some lingering belief in the world of myth. We have often heard it said, from Lévi-Strauss to Girard, and now by many others, that psychoanalysis is no more than a mythology. But who knows? Perhaps the old Theban scene was in fact being re-enacted in its philosophical interpretation. Who knows? Perhaps this was Freud's way of symbolizing his determination to solve the riddle. Perhaps he was re-enacting, in his own way, the very scene of the philosopher, of the man possessed by a desire to know. What is at issue is, after all, the meaning of the strange 'exodus from Egypt' that was to be Freud's daily adventure and permanent exile. For there must have been something of an 'exodus from Egypt' for a man who, towards the end of his life, identified so strongly with Moses. Was that 'something', without him really knowing it (or without him wanting to know it), the decision to pursue the philosophical project, to inscribe in the tradition of knowledge, once more to begin – yet again – the destiny of Greece (which is not without a secret kinship with the Jewish destiny). Or is he taking over from a tradition that is dying out, that has become exhausted? Is he setting himself up as a rival and imaging a possible new beginning that extends beyond? Is he in search of a new discovery, and will he find it if he can find the final and definitive solution to the riddle of the Western adventure of knowledge? And is he facing up to the risks implicit in this new knowledge, and is he better at doing so than the Greeks? It would take a lot of time and patience to get anywhere with these questions. And perhaps simply asking them is still an Oedipal gesture: King Oedipus (still) has one eye too many.

Having said that, the fact that the Freudian figure of Oedipus (the oedipal) has finally been victorious – as I think we can argue – and has been able to compete, in what is now a worldwide struggle, with the (Promethean) figure of the Worker presupposes that, over and beyond the opposition – if that is what it is – between desire and work, there is something that makes this struggle, this 'encounter', possible. Given the current state of play, I have no more than a vague suspicion of what it is. It is based upon some allusive suggestions from Heidegger – who, as we know, never took Freud's discovery into consideration. For many reasons. But he did, as we also know, at least briefly subscribe to the mythology – the onto-typology – of the Worker, and he did overcome, for the space of a few months, Nietzsche's inability to choose between Oedipus and Prometheus.

It so happens that there is a Heideggerian Oedipus. A figure of Oedipus can, that is, be found in Heidegger, in a passage from the 1935 *Introduction to Metaphysics* (written over a year after the break with National Socialism). The passage appears in a section where, in a discussion of 'the limitation of being', Heidegger reworks the distinction between being and appearance:

> For the thinking of the early Greek thinkers the unity and conflict of being and appearance preserved their original power. All this was represented with supreme purity in Greek tragic poetry. Let us consider the *Oedipus Rex* of Sophocles. At the beginning Oedipus is the saviour and lord of the state, living in an aura of glory and divine favour. He is hurled out of this appearance, which is not merely his subjective view of himself but the medium in which his being-there appears; his being as murderer of his father and desecrator of his mother is raised to unconcealment. The way from the radiant beginning to the gruesome end is one struggle between appearance (concealment and distortion) and unconcealment (being). The city is beset by the secret of the murderer of Laius, the former king. With the passion of a man who stands in the manifestness of glory and is a Greek, Oedipus sets out to reveal this secret. Step by step, he must move into unconcealment, which in the end he can bear only by putting out his own eyes, i.e. by removing himself from all light, by letting the cloak of night fall round him, and, blind, crying out to

the people to open all doors in order that a man may be manifest to them as what he *is*.

But we cannot regard Oedipus only as the man who meets his downfall; we must see him as the embodiment of Greek being-there, who most radically and wildly asserts its fundamental passion, the passion for the disclosure of being, i.e. the struggle for being itself. In his poem *'In lieblicher Bläue blühet'*, Hölderlin wrote keen-sightedly: 'Perhaps King Oedipus has an eye too many.' This eye too many is the fundamental condition for all great questioning and knowledge and also their only metaphysical ground. The knowledge and the science of the Greeks were this passion.[13]

The story of Oedipus does not simply symbolize or (re)present the destiny of *aletheia*, or the unveiling of being (in which case, the West is more Oedipal than ever); because his determination is so savage, Oedipus is the figure of the Greek *Dasein* to the extent that it embodies the basic and inaugural 'passion' of the West: the passion for knowledge. That is what Heidegger was trying desperately to show the Germans at that time, and that was the meaning of his political discourse: they were his heirs. Now for Heidegger, as he explains at length in his commentary on the famous chorus about man from *Antigone*, it is the word *technē* that originally allowed the Greeks to think about 'knowledge'. Here, Oedipus is none other than the figure of *technē*. Now that Heidegger's political adventure is over, Oedipus occupies exactly the same position as the figure of Prometheus in the Rectorship Address. Heidegger makes the same shift as Nietzsche, but this time it is more explicit: it concerns the meaning of the word *technē*, and the word has at least two meanings. And it therefore concerns the essence of metaphysics. And we can also see how this interpretation of *Oedipus Rex* basically reveals the truth of the mythico-philosophical use – both Hegelian and Nietzschean – of the figure of Oedipus. Oedipus has nothing to do with the subject (self-consciousness), or in other words with knowledge (theory) as subject; but it has everything to do with knowledge as *technē*, and that is the starting point for the whole of Western metaphysics. And that is why modern technology is the Oedipal realization of the metaphysical.

Is this why the two rival figures of our day have something in common? Is the Worker, like Oedipus, a figure and (re)presentation of *technē*? Does the same knowledge secretly animate both the labouring animal and the desiring animal, and does it run through both political economy and libidinal economy? If that is the case, we require more than a complete re-evaluation of both socialism and psychoanalysis, their metaphysical status and their scientific destination (or pretensions). We must solicit and displace an entire opposition and the interpretation of that opposition. It is, after all, the major antagonism of our times.

It remains, then, for us to ask what 'knowledge' might mean from now on. And to ask what the name Oedipus might mean. Perhaps one day we will understand that a certain desire for knowledge – or the desire of a certain knowledge – definitely has something to do with the curious limp that has affected the Western gait ever since the Greeks.

TRANSLATED BY DAVID MACEY

Notes

This text was first delivered as a lecture at Brown University (Providence, USA) in November 1983; this essay was excluded from the English translation of Lacoue-Labarthe's *L'Imitation des modernes* (Galilée, Paris, 1986).

1. Martin Heidegger, 'On the Question of Being', trans. William McNeill, in *Pathmarks*, Cambridge University Press, Cambridge, 1998.
2. 'Typographie', in Sylviane Agacinski, Jacques Derrida, Sarah Kofman and Philippe Lacoue-Labarthe, *Mimesis: des articulations*, Aubier–Flammarion, Paris, 1975; translated as ch. 1 of Philippe Lacoue-Labarthe, *Typography: Mimesis, Philosophy, Politics*, Harvard University Press, Cambridge MA, 1989.
3. Jacques Derrida, 'Economimesis', trans. Richard Klein, *Diacritics*, vol. 11, no. 2, Summer 1981.
4. 'La Césure du spéculatif', in *L'Imitation des modernes*, Galilée, Paris, 1986; translated as ch. 4 of *Typography*.
5. Georges Bataille, 'Hegel, Death and Sacrifice', trans. Jonathan Strauss, in Allan Stoekl, ed., *On Bataille*, *Yale French Studies* 78, 1990.
6. Jacques Derrida 'White Mythology', in *Margins – Of Philosophy*, trans. Alan Bass, University of Chicago Press, Chicago, 1982. See also Bernard Pautrat, *Versions du soleil*, Seuil, Paris, 1971.
7. G.W.F. Hegel, *The Philosophy of History*, trans. J. Sibree, Dover, New York, 1956, p. 220.
8. Ibid.
9. Ibid., pp. 220–21.
10. Walter Benjamin, *The Origin of German Tragic Drama*, trans. John Osborne, New Left Books, London, 1977, p. 108.
11. Hegel, *The Philosophy of History*, p. 199.
12. Sigmund Freud, *Three Essays on the Theory of Sexuality*, in *On Sexuality*, Pelican Freud Library, Volume 7, Penguin, Harmondsworth, 1977, pp. 112–13; translation modified to read 'drive' for *Trieb*.
13. Martin Heidegger, *An Introduction to Metaphysics*, trans. Ralph Manheim, Yale University Press, New Haven CT and London, 1987, pp. 106–7.

Generations of feminism

LYNNE SEGAL

> Politics makes comics of us all. Or we would weep.
>
> Sheila Rowbotham[1]

I have been thinking for some time now about political generations.[2] Indeed, I began my last book, *Straight Sex*, with a reflection upon the enduring impact of those formative moments which first enable us to make some sense of the world, and our place within it – an unjust and shabby world, whatever our personal circumstances. Such moments remain all the more powerful if, like many of my own generation who became students in the 1960s, you have hoped – with whatever levels of scepticism and self-mockery – to participate in the making of history. They leave their mark, even as changing times cause one to rethink, perhaps even to renounce, one's formative political presumptions. Yet, what often leaves erstwhile political crusaders with little more than mournful and confusing feelings of loss and regret – whatever our capacities for irony – is the way in which new narratives emerge as collective memories fade, writing over those that once incited our most passionate actions.

So it has been with Women's Liberation, that second wave of feminism which arose out of the upsurge of radical and socialist politics in the late 1960s. It grew rapidly as a mass social movement, peaking in the mid-1970s before dissolving as a coherent organization by the end of that decade. If only indirectly, it affected the lives of millions of women. Now, however, a quarter of a century later, the sparse amount of thoughtful scholarship analysing the distinctiveness of that movement struggles for attention amidst a glut of texts delineating its contemporary academic progeny – largely scornful of its rougher parent, and the motley basements, living rooms, workplaces and community centres in which it was hatched. This is not just a female Oedipal tale, as disobedient daughters distance themselves from their mothers' passions, seeking recognition for themselves. It is also a sibling affair, as feminists contend with each other: fearful, perhaps, of being overlooked should we fail to keep abreast of new theoretical fashions; or unable to admit the tensions and contradictions of past attachments.

A small band of feminist historians, mostly in the USA, who *are* trying to recapture the diversity of the movement in which they participated, declare that they cannot recognize themselves, or others, in what they see as the distorting accounts of Women's Liberation circulating in contemporary feminism. Rosalyn Baxandall and Linda Gordon, for example, are gathering material for a multi-volume collection of literature from the movement in the United States. They are joined by others interested in archiving the local histories of Women's Liberation, such as Patricia Romney, documenting a group of fifty women of colour based in New York and Oakland, California, who – with other Black activists in the 1960s and 1970s – became the forgotten women who 'fell down the well' (as Carolyn Heilbrun puts it) in subsequent rewritings of Women's Liberation as exclusively white.[3]

These historians are aware of the dangers of their proximity to their own research, of how memories are muted or reshaped by subsequent perspectives and interests – whether one's own, or those of younger recorders. At a symposium on the history of Women's Liberation in the United States, Margaret (Peg) Strobel recounted that even when rereading her *own* diaries and letters she is amazed at their failure to match her current recollections of the events she has recorded there.[4] Reading our histories through the interpretations of others can be more unsettling again. Contemporary texts reviewing recent feminist history provide sobering examples of how the past is inevitably read through the concerns of the present, often invalidating earlier meanings and projects and erasing their heterogeneity. The displacement of former struggles and perspectives, however, is all the more disconcerting when contemporary theorists start off from a critical fascination with problems of 'experience', 'memory' and the 'silencing' of other voices, alongside a formal abhorrence of binary logics and apparent scepticism about generalization of all kinds. Yet, it is precisely the reckless generalization and false contrasts which astonish me when I read accounts of the distance self-proclaimed 'nineties' feminism has travelled from Women's Liberation, and what now appears newly homogenized as 'seventies' feminism.

Dubious contrasts

A British collection, *Destabilizing Theory*, edited by Michèle Barrett and Anne Phillips, was put together to highlight what it refers to as 'the gulf between feminist theory of the 1970s and 1990s'. It opens with the conviction: 'In the past twenty years the founding principles of contemporary western feminism have been dramatically changed, with previously shared assumptions and unquestioned orthodoxies relegated almost to history.'[5] Perhaps so. But just what is being dispatched here? Was it all of a piece? And is it equally anachronistic for contemporary feminists?

'Seventies' feminism is criticized for its 'false certainties'; its search for structural causes of women's oppression (indeed for its very notion of 'oppression'); its belief in women's shared interests (and its very attachment to the notion of 'women' or 'woman'); and so forth.[6] 'Nineties' feminism, in contrast, has replaced what is seen as the naive search for the social causes of women's oppression with abstract elaborations of the discursively produced, hierarchical constitution of an array of key concepts: sexual difference in particular, binary oppositions in general, and the hetero/sexualized mapping of the body as a whole. However, it does tend to have a few generalizations of its own, not least its totalizing dismissal of 'seventies' feminism, and the reduction of dissimilar projects to common ground.

A somewhat similar tension can be found in a parallel American collection aiming 'to call into question and problematize the presumptions of some feminist discourse': *Feminists Theorize the Political*, edited by Judith Butler and Joan Scott, which, like the British text, was published in 1992.[7] Its introductory essay shows greater caution in drawing comparisons between different phases of feminism, and it is more aware that contrasting 'postmodern' feminism with an earlier 'modernist' feminism buys into precisely the conceits of modernity itself, sharing all its enthusiasm for identification with the 'new' and overconfident renunciation of the 'old'. (Although it is surely a hostage to fortune to insist, on the opening page, that '"poststructuralism" indicates a field of critical practices that cannot be totalized.'[8]) Circumspect and equivocal as Butler characteristically is, always preferring the interrogative to the more vulnerable affirmative mode, her influential writing is always *read* as primarily deconstructive, privileging regulatory semiotic or semantic issues around 'subjectivity', 'identity' and 'agency', in insisting, as she does here, that 'To recast the referent as the signified, and to authorize or safeguard the category of women as a site of possible resignifications is to expand the possibilities of what it means to be a woman and in this sense to condition and enable an enhanced sense of agency.'[9] Butler is certainly right to stress that 'what women signify has been taken for granted for too long'. But, in calling for 'the conditions to *mobilize the signifier* in the service of an alternative production', she delineates a project that is distinctly distanced from the close attention to social *structures*, *relations* and *practices* which an earlier feminist project prioritized in pursuit of political-economic restructuring, and the transformation of public life and welfare. Butler even suggests here: 'Paradoxically, it may be that only through releasing the category of women from a fixed referent that something like "agency" becomes possible.'[10]

Only? However 'fictitious' or 'fixed' the category of women, feminists did once manage successfully to mobilize *them* (and not just signifiers) onto the streets and into campaigns in support of demands for nurseries, reproductive rights, education and skill training; to assist women fighting discrimination at work, violence at home, militarism worldwide; to work within Third World development projects; found the women's health movement, and so on and so forth: just as if 'something like "agency"' – women's agency – was there all along. A feminism that seeks *primarily* to re-theorize subjectivity is one that is incommensurate with, as well as distanced from, the perspectives and practices of Women's Liberation. It is simply *not* the same project, however sympathetic to those earlier goals someone like Butler may be. As others have noticed, the commitment to heterogeneity, multiplicity and difference underlying recent feminist theorizing can anomalously disguise a hegemonizing dismissal of theoretical frameworks not *explicitly* informed by poststructuralism.[11] Joan Scott exemplifies this form of exclusion of theoretical diversity when attacking 'resistance to poststructuralist theory' as resistance to 'theory' itself: 'Since it is in the nature of feminism to disturb the ground it stands on, even its own ground, *the resistance to theory* is a resistance to the most radical effects of feminism itself.'[12]

Here is the problem. Contemporary feminist theorizing rarely acknowledges the time and the place of political ideas. It addresses only abstract *theories* and their refutation. It operates with an idea of the history of feminism as the evolution of academic theory and debate. Tellingly, both the British and the North American feminist collections I have mentioned offer their readers a full index of *names* – in which, incidentally, extraordinarily few of the influential feminist names of the 1970s appear – but no index of *topics*. In the recent Blackwell textbook *Feminist Thought*, by Patricia Clough, dedicated to 'Women Around the

World Resisting Oppression, Domination, and Exploitation', there *is* a context index, but interestingly neither hint nor whisper of abortion or reproductive rights, housework, childcare, nurseries, welfare provision, immigration, marriage, the family, poverty, the state, employment, trade unions, healthcare or violence against women. There *is* pornography, autobiography, film theory, literary criticism, Woman, Native, Other. However you cross-reference it, just a few aspects of women's actual resistance 'around the world' seem to have gone missing.[13] Almost no effort is made in these texts to refer back to the activities and goals of Women's Liberation, only an attempt to contrast theoretical positions as ideal types.

The reason is, of course, that this is an easy way to *teach* feminism as an academic topic. But you cannot translate the time of theory and its fashions into political history without absurd caricature. Thus early Women's Liberation becomes, for example, a 'feminism of the subject', when it was not a theory about subjectivity at all. It is almost always described as a theory of equality rather than of difference, when it was neither of these things – the one usually presented as merely an inversion of the other. Both of these descriptions miss the point. Women's Liberation in its heyday was a *theory and practice of social transformation*: full of all the embroiled and messy actions and compromises of political engagement. It endlessly debated questions of priorities, organization and alliances in the attempt to enrich women's lives (heatedly discussing the varied – often opposed – interests of different groups of women). In the process, it transformed the very concept of the 'political', giving women a central place within it.

My sense of the recent history of feminism, in particular of the socialist-feminist strand of Women's Liberation flourishing in the early 1970s, conflicts with Julia Kristeva's often cited stagist mapping of three generations of feminist thought, in her famous essay 'Women's Time', first published in 1979. There she depicts the first wave of feminism as a time when women, using a 'logic of identification', pursued liberal, egalitarian ends, followed by the emergence of a militant second phase, which rejected all 'patriarchal' thought and practice, attempting to create 'counter societies' constructed around mythical notions of womanhood. This is the now familiar account of 'equality' feminism *followed by* a strictly alternative, 'difference' feminism: with women first seeking inclusion in, and later exclusion from, the masculine symbolic order. Drawing on Derrida, Kristeva proposes a *third* generation of feminism which is critical of the binary of sexual difference itself. Yet, as I hope to show, although they never used the rhetoric of deconstruction, this is precisely where many second-generation feminists came in. The contrasts are not as significant as recent retellings suggest.

Rowbotham's 'seventies' feminism

In my view, the most useful – and perhaps the only meaningful – way to think about the similarities and differences between different generations of feminism is by reflecting upon what defines a political generation and what smashes its hopes and dreams. On an International Women's Day march in the early 1970s, Sheila Rowbotham carried a placard that read: 'Equal Pay is Not Enough. We Want the Moon.' (File under equal-rights feminism? Perhaps not. Is the moon here a symbol of female difference? I think not.) We got neither, as she wrote a decade later; but the radical heritage of Women's Liberation continues, she argued, whenever feminists work to realize the dream 'that all human beings can be *more* than present circumstances allow'.[14] That vision is not one of equal rights. It was called 'socialism' and it was being reshaped to service feminism.

I want, for a moment, to focus on Sheila Rowbotham's writing, as she has been one of the most careful chroniclers (and continuing exponents) of Women's Liberation in Britain, in the hope that it may be, as she puts it, 'neither falsely valued nor undervalued', but that feminists might reflect back upon 'the hurly-burly of battle, draw clarity from real muddles and learn from our mistakes'.[15] (Dream on!, one might feel, in these new mean-spirited times.) Since memories only find resonance at certain times, Rowbotham adds, if you 'ignore the humdrum you fall into arrogance'.[16] It was Rowbotham, one of the many inspirational voices of 1970s' feminism, who proposed the very first Women's Liberation conference in Britain at Ruskin College in 1970; importantly for my purposes here, her books were read by tens of thousands of feminists in the 1970s. They were hugely influential in the initial years of Women's Liberation. Rowbotham would be criticized, early on, as representing a 1970s' feminism, unformed by psychoanalysis or structuralism.[17] Today, of course, her failures would be seen as an inattention to poststructuralism or 'postmodernity' – that paradoxical twist of modernity, contrarily repudiating linear narratives while depending on one.

Joining the game of textual analysis, I recently reread some of Rowbotham's books from the 1970s and early 1980s: something I do often to prevent my own long-term memories from dissolving (there seems nothing to be done about the crashing of short-term memory). Ironically, what is extraordinary about Rowbotham's writing is usually quite the reverse of what critics of 1970s' feminism imagine. It conveys an openness, a chronic *lack* of certainty, an almost infuriating tentativeness, reiteratively asserting: 'What we have developed through action and ideas has always to be subject to reassessment'; or 'I am too encumbered by the particular to move with grace and delicacy between subjective experience and the broad sweep of social relationships.'[18]

From her earliest reflections, Rowbotham describes the search for the roots of women's subordination as a 'perilous and uncertain quest'.[19] Her texts always stress what she calls 'the differing forms and historically specific manifestations of the power men hold over women in particular societies'.[20] They focus sharply on the diversity and situational specificity of women: whether of class, race, employment, domestic situation (although not at first, as she herself soon notes self-critically), sexual orientation: 'Our own indications are only tentative and incomplete ... Women's liberation is too narrow in social composition to comprehend the differences between middle class and working class, black and white, young and old, married and unmarried, country and townswomen.' Moreover, she writes in 1972, 'it is clear that most of the isolated gains we can make can be twisted against women and that many partial gains are often a means of silencing one group at the expense of another.'[21] She emphasizes the role of language as one of the crucial instruments of domination:

> As soon as we learn words we find ourselves outside them ... The underground language of people who have no power to define and determine themselves in the world develops its own density and precision ... But it restricts them by affirming their own dependence upon the words of the powerful ... There is a long inchoate period during which the struggle between the language of experience and the language of theory becomes a kind of agony.[22]

Ignorant of 'poststructuralism' Rowbotham may have been (writing these words in the early 1970s, in her mid-twenties), but not so ignorant, I would suggest, of the issues it addresses.

She tussles (a favourite word) endlessly with the problems of relying on direct experience, seeing it as both a strength and a weakness – again not so unlike, but less theoretically fine-tuned than, the recent essay by Joan Scott on the same topic in the collection from the USA mentioned above.[23] She continually affirms the pointlessness of attempting to pin down the nature of either 'women' or 'men', adding that 'All revolutionary movements create their own ways of seeing ... But this is a result of great labour.'[24] Her writing, like the forces which drew many women together in the early years of Women's Liberation, reflects the radical Left (largely Marxist) thought of the day: 'An emergent female consciousness is part of the specific sexual and social conjuncture, which it seeks to control and transform.'[25] So, while questions of subjectivity and identity are not ignored (and, when they appear, they are quite as shifting, provisional and contingent as any postmodernist might desire), the goal is always to transform society, to make it a better place for all its members, especially the neediest, and, in her words, 'gradually accumulate a shared culture of agitation'. She writes:

> There is democracy in the making of theories which set out to rid the world of hierarchy, oppression and domination. The act of analysis requires more than concepts of sex and class, more than a theory of the subject, it demands that in the very process of thinking we transform the relations between thinker and thought about, theory and experience ... Analysis is not enough alone, for we enter the beings and worlds of other people through imagination, and it is through imagination that we glimpse how these might change.[26]

Many 1970s' feminists have recalled, like Rowbotham, the imaginative leap when they first began to turn outwards to other women, generating an almost open-ended desire for solidarity with just those women they had hitherto distanced themselves from: 'The mainspring of women's liberation was not a generalised antagonism to men but the positive assertion of new relationships between women, sisterhood.'[27] Socialist feminists argued that while capitalist societies had changed the relative power and privileges of men, they had also consolidated women's inferior status, along with that of a multitude of other historically subordinated groups – predominantly along racialized and ethnic lines. So while it was not *inconceivable* that women might gain equality with men in existing capitalist societies, this would require such deep levels of cultural, economic and political change that they would already have become societies which were fundamentally different from any we have known.[28]

The state, in socialist-feminist analyses like those of Elizabeth Wilson or Mary McIntosh, was seen as not strictly 'patriarchal', but serving to regulate, and occasionally to restructure, the often contradictory and conflicting needs of a male-dominated market economy and the still intrinsically patriarchal arrangements of family life.[29] It was from such analyses that they set about shaking out and making visible the separate and distinct needs and interests of women (kept hidden by familial rhetoric);

campaigned against state policies and discourses which defined and enforced women's dependence on men; demanded an end to social neglect of women and children at risk from men's violence; fought for more and better social provision and community resources – all the while seeking alliances with other oppressed groups. Strategic priorities were usually paramount, whether making demands on the state or the trade unions, and even when elaborating utopian visions of communities and workplaces compatible with choice and flexibility, where the needs of all dependent people would not be hidden away in idealized, yet neglected and isolated, often impoverished, family units.[30]

This socialist-feminist strand of Women's Liberation, chronicled in books like Rowbotham's *The Past Is Before Us*, remained until the mid-1980s an active and influential source of ideas and strategies for promoting women's interests, usually working in diverse radical and reformist coalitions with other progressive forces.[31] However, the frustration and defeats of a second term of Conservative rule (1983–87), which targeted and weakened precisely those nooks and crannies in local government, resource centres and collective spaces that feminists (and other radicals) had managed to enter, gradually exhausted not only the political hopes but even the dreams of many. In recalling the early achievements of the women's movement in relaunching feminism, we also need to consider its limitations. But the precarious presumptions and faltering visions of the 1970s' feminism I knew have, as I see it, little to do with dogmatic certitudes, conceptual closure, binary thinking, identity politics or false universalism, and much more to do with the floundering fortunes of grassroots or movement politics in harsh and unyielding times.

And I am *not* forgetting the many painful clashes, at the turn of the 1980s, as a strengthening Black feminism challenged Eurocentrism in the priorities of much white socialist-feminist analysis, which privileged sexism over racism and ignored the particularities of ethnic difference. But trying to learn to listen to, and act upon, Black feminist perspectives was not initially a decisive factor in the fading away of socialist-feminism. On the contrary, Black feminists then occupied the same political spaces, and pursued largely similar or parallel strategic campaigns for expanding the choice and resources open to Black women and their families. The political limitations they saw in what they defined as 'Euro-American' feminism, at that time, as Valerie Amos, Gail Lewis, Amina Mama and Pratibha Parmar made clear in 1984, was that it has 'contributed to an improvement in the material situation of white middle-class women often at the expense of their Black and working class "sisters" ... The power of sisterhood stops at the point at which hard political decisions need to be made and political priorities decided.'[32]

The death knell of the 1970s' feminism I dwelt within was not simply the fallout from internal conflict and divisions, whether over race or sexuality – much as they turned feminist political spaces into stressful combat zones. Rather, coming together as agitators, of whatever sex, race or ethnic specificity, to pursue goals which require, among other things, a more egalitarian and caring world, brought us up against a ferocious, if contradictory and erratic, political opponent – something a new generation of officially licensed theorists, turning inwards rather than outwards, often prefer to ignore altogether. Over the last two decades, the ever more deregulated, ever more universalized, interests of capital have produced deepening social inequalities, nationally and internationally. In the process, they have ensured a significant increase in women's poverty. Meanwhile the fickle, unintended effects of market forces and new technologies, alongside the arduously pursued, intended consequences of feminist thought and campaigning, have ensured more paid work, autonomy and choice for *other* women, at least in the First World (as well as more insecurity for some men).

Twenty years ago it would have been hard to find a single self-respecting feminist in Britain who had not trekked out to the Grunwick factory in West London, in support of the predominantly Asian women on strike, or at least considered such action. In the 1990s, as Melissa Benn has noted, it would be hard to find a self-respecting feminist who had even *heard* of the predominantly Asian women on strike at Burnsall in Birmingham over an almost identical set of issues: refusal of union recognition, low pay and the use of dangerous chemicals; or who would have contemplated supportive action, if they had.[33] For sure, Rowbotham and like-minded socialist-feminists, working to help organize support for women in struggle against the harshest effects of global market forces, had for a while a certain naivety about the nature and potential of 'revolutionary' movements. The legacy of 1970s' feminism, seen as a movement of social transformation aiming to increase the power and self-determination of women everywhere, is contradictory and diverse. But serious consideration of its full significance is grievously absent in recent appraisals.

Theoretical assaults

There is another twist in this tale of two generations of feminism. In terms of the later writing over of earlier feminist narratives, the painful irony is that just as deconstruction and other forms of poststructuralism imprinted themselves on the academic feminism which had graduated from its lowly 1970s' birthplace in adult education into professional status in the universities – promoting conceptual uncertainty, political indeterminacy and subjective fluidity – opposing forms of feminist fundamentalism, moral certainty and psychic essentialism now really were entrenching themselves as the wisdom of the more accessible activist feminism of the 1980s. The voices of feminism – like those of Robin Morgan and Andrea Dworkin – which survived and intensified in the new decade were no longer analysing the specific historical contexts, shifting institutional arrangements, particular social practices or multiple discourses securing women's inequality and marginality. Instead, they denounced the ageless dominance of 'masculine' values over 'feminine' ones. A new and complacent romance around the feminine took precedence as essentially nurturing, non-violent and egalitarian; there was an accompanying condemnation of men and masculinity as ineluctably dominating, destructive and predatory, rooted in the performance of male sexuality.

It was this form of so-called 'cultural feminism' that I criticized in *Is the Future Female?* in the late 1980s. The original subtitle of my book, 'Arguments for Socialist Feminism', was rejected by my publisher, Virago Press, as already too unpopular to promulgate, leading to the more neutral 'Troubled Thoughts' of its published subtitle.[34] Politically, Dworkin and MacKinnon ushered in the simplistic and reductive anti-pornography campaign as the single most visible and highly funded feminist struggle in recent years. The pessimistic corollary of the rejection of historical specificities in this feminist discourse is the dismissal of the significance of women's political struggles and victories: 'Our status as a group relative to men', MacKinnon declared, 'has almost never, if ever, been much changed from what it is.'[35] Without buying into backlash anti-feminism, or the howls of anguish we currently hear from and about men, I think we might agree that this is not a very accurate picture of the gender changes and turmoil that have occurred throughout this century, and especially of the shake-ups over the last three decades. Meanwhile, as the 1980s progressed, it was either those, like Catharine MacKinnon, who offered some version of an increasingly totalizing and sanctimonious feminism (clinging to the moral high ground of women's marginality and helplessness), or others, like Camille Paglia, with equally totalizing inversions of this position (caricaturing feminism as prudish and puritanical) who found favour with the media. Neither offered any challenge to traditional gender discourses.

It is hard to summarize the illuminations and provocations of academic feminism's current embrace of poststructuralist critiques of universalizing thought and emancipatory narratives without courting the danger of homogenizing contemporary theorizing, much as it has erased the complexities of 1970s' feminism. The appropriation of poststructuralist priorities would inspire what has become known as 'feminist postmodernism' – although this conceptually confused and confusing label would not be accepted by all those placed under its banner. At least three separate strands of thinking are usually lumped together under this heading – deriving from Lacan, Derrida and Foucault, respectively – despite their very different implications for feminism.

The first and for a while the most influential post-Lacanian strand, often simply called 'French feminism', restricts its focus to the idea of sexual difference effaced by the spurious unity or wholeness of the Western 'subject' (Man): the white, male bourgeois subject of history who hides behind the abstract universals of the philosophical tradition. It stresses the need to fracture the universal or humanist self through attentiveness to its repressed or marginalized other: 'feminine' difference. Subversively imagined and rewritten as positive, the decentred side of the silenced and repressed 'feminine' is thought to enable women to 'foresee the unforeseeable', and escape the dichotomous conceptual order in which men have enclosed them.[36] This new focus upon images of female corporeality has been seen by its exponents as presenting a fresh purchase on the old essentialism debate, transcending earlier forms of historical, sociological or psychoanalytic anti-essentialist arguments. The 'feminine feminine', Luce Irigaray and Hélène Cixous suggest, can emerge only once women find the courage to break out of the male imaginary and into a female one; once women begin to speak and write their sexuality, which is always plural, circular and aimless, in contrast to all existing singular, linear and phallocentric, masculine forms of symbolization.[37] Such feminist reclaiming of the body unfolds here as always culturally and psychically inscribed female experience, not anatomical destiny, and is perhaps best seen as a form of aestheticized, high modernist, 'avant-gardism'.[38] It is nevertheless still narrated in terms of a *universal* corporeal subjectivity for women.

The attraction of such difference theory, which allows the feminist to speak 'as a woman', is obvious. The revaluing of those aspects of women's lives and experiences previously ignored or demeaned in male-centred theorizing was, and remains, crucial to feminist research and practice. But there is still a problem which it cannot easily tackle (even if we ride with its own cheerfully embraced contradictions), once we turn from the academic to the political realm. As I have argued elsewhere, it is precisely ideas of sexual difference encompassing the experiences supposedly inscribing our distinctive 'femaleness' which most dramatically *divide*, rather than unite, feminists attempting to fight for women's interests.[39] It is easier for women to join forces around issues on the currently unfashionable economic front (demanding parity in wages and training), or social policy (demanding more and better publicly funded welfare resources), than it has ever been for women to unite around issues of sexuality and the meanings we attach to the female body. Creatively exciting as the project of reimagining female corporeality has proved to be to some feminists,[40] its neglect of issues of class, race, ethnicity and other forms of marginality as equally constitutive of women's subjectivity and destiny has seemed exclusionary and disempowering to other feminists. Such criticism has been most forcefully expressed by Black and ethnic minority feminist theoreticians – from Gayatri Spivak to Barbara Christian or Deborah McDowell.[41] Some academic feminists like to quote Gayatri Spivak in support of their view that women today must 'take "the risk of essence" in order to think really differently'.[42] Spivak herself, however, has reconsidered her earlier suggestion for a 'strategic' use of a positive essentialism. Since such a move is viable only when it serves 'a scrupulously visible political interest', she now warns: 'The strategic use of essentialism can turn into an alibi for proselytizing academic essentialisms.'[43] And it has.

Spivak leads us to the second, more rigorous, Derridean strand of feminist poststructuralism, which is critical of the monolithic Lacanian version of difference theory. It questions all universalizing or totalizing theoretical tendencies, deconstructing every discursive patterning of the self, including that of 'woman'.[44] Here, in tune with the input of Black, Third World, lesbian and other feminisms, every generalization about women, including the feminist search for the causes of women's subordination or any generalized expressions of women's difference – whether seen in terms of responsibility for child-rearing, reproductive and sexual experience, men's violence, phallogocentric language, a female imaginary, or whatever – is regarded with suspicion. This position is summed up by Donna Haraway:

> There is nothing about being 'female' that naturally binds women. There is not even such a state as 'being' female, itself a highly complex category constructed in contested sexual scientific discourses and social practices ... The feminist dream of a common language, like all dreams for a perfectly true language, of a perfectly faithful naming of experience, is a totalizing and imperialistic one.[45]

Haraway wants to replace this dream with her own one of 'a powerful infidel heteroglossia ... building and destroying machines, identities, categories, relationships, spaces, stories', seeking a place for women in a future 'monstrous world without gender'.[46] Her dream is full of playful optimism about the future. For other more strictly deconstructive feminists, however, there is no theoretically defensible affirmative position, but only a reminder of the limits of concepts, as Spivak explains: 'the *absolutely* other cannot enter into *any* kind of foundational emancipatory project'.[47] Such a deconstructive feminism certainly avoids the perils of generalizations about female subjectivity. But it courts the danger that its own interest in endlessly proliferating particularities of difference, and the partial, contradictory nature of women's identities, endorses a relativity and indeterminacy which works to undermine political projects.

The third, Foucauldian, strand of poststructuralist feminism returns us to the body – to its 'sexuality' rather than to sexual difference – but only as a site or target of ubiquitous technologies of classification, surveillance and control. Foucault's warning that oppositional discourses are inevitably caught up in the relations of domination they resist has been important in highlighting the traps facing emancipatory movements: of reproducing rather than transcending traditional frameworks of subjection. And his arguments about meaning and representation have proved particularly productive for lesbian and gay theorists. Here, feminists can learn much from Foucault's insights about the genealogy of discursive regulation, but next to nothing about how organized resistance might impinge on such all-encompassing regimes of power, other than through the discursively disruptive, micro-political strategies favoured by some lesbian theorists.

Judith Butler, for example, suggests ways of making 'gender trouble' by subverting the masculine/feminine binary producing sexuality as heterosexuality. Emphasizing the multiplicity of sexual acts which occur in a non-heterosexual context can, she concludes, disrupt and disturb dominant heterosexual/reproductive discourses, 'through hyperbole, dissonance, internal confusion and proliferation'.[48] But, despite its influence on some feminists, others respond with sheer bewilderment or exasperation at what they see as the staging of battles at a strictly semiotic level.[49] And while some 'queer theorists' have understood Butler to be suggesting a type of individual transgressive 'performance' as the most relevant way of undermining existing gender dynamics, it is an interpretation she herself now rejects.[50] Meanwhile, some feminists have used Foucault to reject earlier feminist analysis of power in relation to key structural and institutional sites. Again, as often noted, the problem here is that it discourages analysis of *where* and *how* women are best placed to combat the authority and privilege men commonly wield over them – by entering those sites which are most expedient or have proved receptive to change, and supporting strategies to undermine or transform those which remain most rigid and resistant to change.[51]

Political agendas

Poststructuralism, especially in its Derridean and Foucauldian forms, has provided feminists with fresh (if not unique) conceptual tools for problematizing identities and social differences. It usefully emphasizes their hierarchically imposed and coercive nature, and the multiplicity of intertwining, destabilizing and exclusionary discourses or narratives in which subjectivities are historically enmeshed. It suggests the possibility (however difficult) of categorial re-significations or reconfigurations, as well as the need for acceptance of paradox and contradiction in conceptualizing change. Feminists need to pay heed to the normativities and exclusions of discourse, especially as they construct differences between women. But in a world of intensifying inequality, any concern with either gender justice or the fate of women overall must also direct us to issues of *redistribution*, alongside issues of identity and recognition.[52] It is a socialist imaginary, combined with feminism, that has always stressed the sufferings caused by the material exploitation, deprivation and social marginalization of women and other oppressed groups around the world. These cannot be either superseded or replaced by battles over discursive marginalization and invalidation. The two objectives, though relatively distinct, are also intricately interwoven: the one turning feminists *outwards* towards women in struggle; the other directing us *inwards* towards refiguring a hitherto abjected 'femininity'. Once we address both sets of issues, then some differences will matter more than others in generating political interventions.

However plural and irreducibly complex our characterization of the social, any politics seeking the most inclusive transformation of socio-economic and cultural marginalization must seek to challenge the major systems of domination. This means seeking to understand just what they are at this historical moment: uncovering why, and how, they persist, as well as their interaction with whatever specific location we occupy. Fearful of totalizing generalizations we may be, and cautious we must be, but the central global axes of economic exploitation and cultural oppression continue to construct and reconstruct themselves in the interrelated terms of 'gender' (tied in with sexual orientation), 'class' (tied in with nationality and ethnicity) and 'race' (tied in with nationality, ethnicity and religion), within what is currently the ever more totalizing control of a transnational capitalist market. The invocation of specific differences can only serve broadly based transformative ends as part of some wider political project seeking to dismantle these basic structures of domination.

The Anglo-American reception of poststructuralism, with its central place in 1990s' feminist theory, came to prominence at a political moment far removed from that which generated the confident hopes Women's Liberation took to the streets. (Ironically, some explications and critiques of 'postmodernism' present it as *responsible* for putting feminism on the political agenda, as in Eagleton's recent *The Illusions of Postmodernism*;[53] while others would see its influence as quite the reverse.) Distrustful, when not dismissive, of traditional forms of collective action and reformist political agendas, especially when class-based, feminism faces inhibiting dilemmas in describing how either attention to the discursive specificity of 'feminine' difference, or the proliferation of categorial heterogeneity and transgressive display, might ever again bring women together in any transformative feminist project.

We need to remember that the word 'feminist' has a history. Sometimes feminists have focused directly on issues of sexual difference; at other times feminism has been more a movement for the transformation of the whole of society. At the close of the nineteenth century, 'feminism' first appeared in English to describe the movement of women campaigning for the right to vote, but within a few decades the concept had expanded to include a variety of different types of moral, economic, social and political campaigns waged by women. The second wave of Western feminism has similarly drawn upon different meanings, at times stressing social transformation (especially in its early days), at others emphasizing gender-specific issues.[54] The difficulties of generalizing from women's experiences (or 'corporeal existence', through whatever mode of representation) are not hard to document. Nevertheless, it is premature to downplay the significance of gender in favour of a plurality of differences. The tenacity of men's power over women means that feminists must just as tenaciously seek to emphasize the diverse and multiple effects of gender hierarchy on the lives and experiences of women. But if feminism is to address the problems of the many women who need it most, it must see that the specificities of women's lives do not reduce to gender, which means working in alliance with other progressive forces combating class, racialized, ethnic and other entrenched social hierarchies.

Interestingly, one of the continuing threads between 1970s' and 1990s' feminisms (and there are many such threads, although we may not read about them in a significant number of 1990s' feminist texts) is the continuing growth and vision of the international human-rights movements, now often in the form of NGOs.[55] Even there, however, as Suzanne Gibson and Laura Flanders have described, it has proved far easier for women to get their demands taken seriously by the United Nations when they have addressed gender-specific, apparently fashionable, issues like rape and violence against women, than when they have addressed employment rights, illiteracy or poverty.[56] Back in Britain, there will be little significant change in the situation of the women who are worst off until public resources are shifted to provide far greater welfare provision, without the constraints of market considerations. Yet today's Foucauldian-informed feminists who write about the state reject earlier feminist analysis of its structures and functions, claiming, like Rosemary Pringle and Sophie Watson, that '[i]n poststructuralist accounts of the state, "discourse" and "subjectivity" rather than structures and interests become the key terms.'[57] But such re-theorizing only leads us further away from any analysis of the state itself, and the way in which it has been changing in recent years. The state now embraces market forces in most of the areas from which they were previously excluded, and precisely against the interests of, in particular, women, children and all dependent people.

Britain, like North America, has been moving as fast as it can in quite the opposite direction to that which might assist those women in greatest need of economic and social support. This is why I remain a socialist-feminist: still hoping for more dialogue than I find at present between different generations of feminism. Sometimes, as one of my colleagues writes, recalling his own formative moments in Northern Ireland, you need to have the 'courage of your anachronisms'.[58]

Notes

1. Sheila Rowbotham, 'Reclaim the Moon', in *Dreams and Dilemmas*, Virago, London, 1983, p. 348.
2. This is a revised version of a talk given at the Radical Philosophy Conference, 'Torn Halves: Theory and Politics in Contemporary Feminism', London, 9 November 1996.
3. Patricia Romney, unpublished notes prepared for roundtable discussion, 'Writing about a Visionary Movement in the "Get Real" World of the '90s: The History of Women's Liberation in the United States', at the 10th Berkshire Women's Conference, North Carolina, June 1996.
4. Margaret Strobel, at the 10th Berkshire Women's Conference, North Carolina, June 1996.
5. Michèle Barrett and Anne Phillips, eds, Introduction, *Destabilizing Theory: Contemporary Feminist Debates*, Polity Press, Cambridge, 1992, p. 2.
6. A few years earlier Michèle Barrett had expressed her reservations about her own 'seventies' thinking in *Women's Oppression Today* – in a new preface – indicating (accurately) that recent feminist debate has problematized the notion of 'women' and 'woman', while suggesting that the notion of oppression 'looks decidedly dated today'.
7. Judith Butler and Joan Scott, eds, *Feminists Theorize the Political*, Routledge, London, 1992.
8. Ibid., p. xiii.
9. Butler, 'Contingent Foundations', in ibid., p. 16.
10. Ibid.
11. See, for example, Linda Gordon, 'Review of *Gender and the Politics of History* by Joan Wallach Scott', *Signs* 15, Summer 1990.
12. Joan Wallach Scott, 'Response to Gordon', *Signs* 15, Summer 1990, p. 859. See also the measured and thoughtful account of the erasure of feminist theoretical heterogeneity in Susan Stanford Friedman, 'Making History', in Diane Elam and Robyn Weigman, eds, *Feminism Beside Itself*, Routledge, London, 1995.
13. Patricia Clough, *Feminist Thought*, Blackwell, Oxford, 1994.
14. Rowbotham, *Dreams and Dilemmas*, p. 354, emphasis added.
15. Ibid., pp. x, 351.
16. Ibid., p. 351.
17. Sally Alexander and Barbara Taylor, 'In Defence of Patriarchy', in Raphael Samuel, ed., *People's History and Socialist Theory*, Routledge & Kegan Paul, London, 1981.
18. Rowbotham, *Dreams and Dilemmas*, pp. 353, 2.
19. Sheila Rowbotham, *Woman's Consciousness, Man's World*, Penguin, Harmondsworth, 1973, pp. 66, 34.
20. Rowbotham, *Dreams and Dilemmas*, p. 83.
21. Ibid., pp. 59, 75.

22. Ibid., pp. 32–3.
23. Joan Scott, 'Experience', in Butler and Scott, eds, *Feminists Theorize the Political*.
24. Rowbotham, *Woman's Consciousness, Man's World*, p. 27.
25. Ibid., p. x. Rowbotham prefers, as she writes in 1972, the idea of 'consciousness moving' to 'consciousness raising', since 'your own perception is continually being shifted by how other women perceive what has happened to them ... The main difficulty, still, is that while the social composition of women's liberation remains narrow it isn't possible to move naturally beyond certain limitations in perspective' (Rowbotham, *Dreams and Dilemmas*, p. 59).
26. Ibid., *Dreams and Dilemmas*, pp. 74, 208, 218.
27. Ibid., p. 83.
28. Ibid., p. 82.
29. Elizabeth Wilson, *Women and the Welfare State*, Tavistock, London, 1977; Mary McIntosh, 'The State and the Oppression of Women', in Annette Kuhn and AnnMarie Wolpe, eds, *Feminism and Materialism: Women and Modes of Production*, Routledge & Kegan Paul, London, 1978. Some later commentators, though sympathetic to the accounts of the state provided in this writing, would suggest, I think correctly, that they diminished the intrinsically male-dominated structures, practices and discourses of the many differing sectors of the state (S. Franzway, D. Court and R.W. Connell, *Staking a Claim: Feminism, Bureacracy and the State*, Paladin, London, 1989).
30. Michèle Barrett and Mary McIntosh, *The Anti-Social Family*, Verso, London, 1982.
31. Sheila Rowbotham, *The Past Is Before Us: Feminism in Action since the 1960s*, Pandora, London, 1989.
32. Valerie Amos, Gail Lewis, Amina Mama and Pratibha Par-mar, Editorial of *Many Voices, One Chant: Black Feminist Perspectives, Feminist Review* 17, Autumn 1984.
33. Melissa Benn, 'Women and Democracy: Thoughts on the Last Ten Years', *Women: A Cultural Review*, vol. 4, no. 3, 1993, p. 237.
34. Lynne Segal, *Is the Future Female? Troubled Thoughts on Contemporary Feminism*, Virago, London, 1987.
35. Catharine MacKinnon, 'Pornography, Civil Rights and Speech', in Catherine Itzin, ed., *Pornography, Women, Violence, and Civil Liberties*, Oxford University Press, Oxford, 1992, p. 456.
36. Hélène Cixous, 'The Laugh of the Medusa', in E. Marks and I. de Courtivron, eds, *New French Feminisms*, Schocken Books, New York, 1981, p. 256.
37. Cixous,'The Laugh of the Medusa'; Luce Irigaray, *This Sex Which Is Not One*, Cornell University Press, Ithaca NY, 1985, p. 32.
38. See, for example, Laura Kipnis, 'Looks Good on Paper: Marxism and Feminism in a Postmodern Wold', in *Ecstasy Unlimited: On Sex, Capital, Gender, and Aesthetics*, University of Minnesota Press, Minneapolis, 1993.
39. Lynne Segal, 'Whose Left? Socialism, Feminism and the Future', *New Left Review* 185, January–February 1991.
40. For imaginative political appropriations of 'French feminism', see for example Drucilla Cornell, *Beyond Accommodation: Ethical Feminism, Deconstruction and the Law*, Routledge, London, 1991; Moira Gattens, *Imaginary Bodies: Ethics, Power and Corporeality*, Routledge, London, 1996.
41. Gayatri Chakravorty Spivak, 'French Feminism in an International Frame', in *In Other Worlds*, Routledge, London, 1988; Barbara Christian, 'The Race for Theory', in Linda Kaufman, ed., *Gender and Theory: Dialogues on Feminist Criticism*, Basil Blackwell, New York, 1989; Deborah McDowell, 'The "Practice" of "Theory"', in Elam and Weigman, eds, *Feminism Beside Itself*.
42. See, for example, Alice Jardine, 'Men in Feminism: Odor di Uomo Or Compagnons de Route?', in Alice Jardine and Paul Smith, eds, *Men in Feminism*, Methuen, London, 1987, p. 58.
43. Gayatri Chakravorty Spivak, *Outside in the Teaching Machine*, Routledge, London, 1993, p. 4.
44. See, for example, Denise Riley, *Am I That Name? Feminism and the Subject of 'Women' in History*, Macmillan, London, 1988.
45. Donna Haraway, 'A Manifesto for Cyborgs: Science, Technology, and Socialist Feminism in the 1980s', in L. Nicholson, ed., *Feminism/Postmodernism*, Routledge, London, 1990, pp. 197, 215.
46. Ibid., p. 215.
47. Gayatri Chakravorty Spivak, 'Remembering the Limits: Difference, Identity and Practice', in Peter Osborne, ed., *Socialism and the Limits of*

Liberalism, Verso, London, 1991, p. 229, emphasis in original.
48. Judith Butler, *Gender Trouble: Feminism and the Subversion of Identity*, Routledge, London, 1990, p. 33.
49. See Tania Modleski, *Feminism Without Women: Culture and Criticism in a 'Postfeminist' Age*, Routledge, London, 1991.
50. Judith Butler, *Bodies That Matter: On the Discursive Limits of 'Sex'*, London, Routledge, 1993, p. 231; see also Peter Osborne and Lynne Segal, 'Gender as Performance: An Interview with Judith Butler', *Radical Philosophy* 67, Summer 1994.
51. See, for example, Gregor McLennan, 'Feminism, Epistemology and Postmodernism: Reflections on Current Abivalence', *Sociology*, vol. 29, no. 3, August 1995, pp. 391–401.
52. See, for example, Nancy Fraser, 'From Redistribution to Recognition? Dilemmas of Justice in a "Post-Socialist" Age', *New Left Review* 212, July–August 1995.
53. Terry Eagleton, *The Illusions of Postmodernism*, Blackwell, Oxford, 1996, p. 22.
54. See Sheila Rowbotham, *Women in Movement: Feminism and Social Action*, Routledge, London, 1992, pp. 8–15.
55. See Julie Peters and Andrea Wolper, eds, *Women's Rights Human Rights: International Feminist Perspectives*, Routledge, London, 1995.
56. See Suzanne Gibson, 'On Sex, Horror and Human Rights', *Women: A Cultural Review*, vol. 4, no. 3, Winter 1993; Laura Flanders, 'Hard Cases and Human Rights: C. MacKinnon in the City of Freud', *The Nation*, 9–16 August 1993, pp. 174–7. For an important and stimulating commentary on the challenge of human-rights internationalism to the recent philosophical embrace of a 'politics of difference', see Bruce Robbins, 'Sad Stories in the International Public Sphere: Richard Rorty on Culture and Human Rights', *Public Culture*, vol. 9, no. 2, Winter 1997.
57. Rosemary Pringle and Sophie Watson, '"Women's Interests" and the Post-Structuralist State', in Barrett and Phillips, eds, *Destabilizing Theory*, p. 65.
58. Francis Mulhern (quoting Jonathan Rée) in Francis Mulhern, Introduction, *The Present Lasts a Long Time: Essays in Cultural Politics*, Cork University Press, Cork, 1998.

11 INTRODUCTION TO FRANÇOISE COLLIN

PENELOPE DEUTSCHER

In 1973 the philosopher Françoise Collin (1928–2012) founded, with Jacqueline Aubenas, the first French-language feminist journal, *Les Cahiers du Grif*. Collin was also a writer of fiction and *récits* (*Rose qui peut*, *Le jour fabuleux*, *331 W 20*, *Le Rendez-vous*), a poet (*Le jardin de Louise*, *On dirait une ville*), a public intellectual and an essayist (*Je partirai d'un mot*, *Le différend des sexes*). She introduced the work of Hannah Arendt into France (*L'homme est-il devenu superflu? Hannah Arendt*), and was the author of a watershed work, the first study of Maurice Blanchot (*Maurice Blanchot et la question de l'écriture*). She was a vigorous feminist activist, producing numerous anthologies, conferences, seminars, translations (Gertrude Stein; Woolf's *The Waves*), essays on contemporary gender politics, and on new women artists and writers.

She had specialized in phenomenology, training at Louvain, before her first publications – poetry and novels – appeared with Éditions du Seuil. Merleau-Ponty and particularly Levinas would continue to be critical (and criticized) points of reference, as would psychoanalytic theory. Her first work of philosophy was her book on Blanchot, whose writing of the disaster, and treatment of writing in its relationship to impossibility, were for Collin an 'absolute force'.[1]

It was characteristic of Collin to espouse thinkers whom she assiduously destabilized and challenged. Thus it was no accident that her gesture, as a Blanchot expert, was later to confront his work with that of Hannah Arendt, and with a different relationship to the disaster:

> One could see these as two bodies of work in relation with the disaster, the ontological and/or the historical disaster. ... They are the bodies of work of 'surviving' [*du 'survivant'*]. But the term is interpreted differently. Blanchot asks how to maintain the relation with the disaster. Arendt asks how to survive the disaster, how to live together [*vivre ensemble*] after the disaster.

She argued that Blanchot and Arendt offered truths which were conflicting, but which also supported and called to each other: 'Blanchot's truth stands in no need of correction. But it sustains, it even calls to, another truth: that of Arendt, that of the event.' Collin's aim was not to amend Blanchot – and certainly not, she said, with voluntarist optimism. Confrontation was not correction. Thus thinking of our relation to impossibility, death and the disaster did not invalidate (to the contrary, in Collin's sense it 'called to') a thinking of the relationship to birth as critical to life, as offering a constant relationship to the possible, the new and the beginning.[2]

Arendt also stimulated in Collin's theoretical work questions that would be important for her feminism: 'how to think plurality?' 'How to live together?' Her characteristic mode of challenge to the thinkers she most appreciated manifested again when both Arendt and Jean-François Lyotard provided Collin with the resources not only to ask how to think the *différend* but also how to think it from the perspective of sexual difference, as *Le différend des sexes* (1999). She argued that the *différend*, and a thinking of the historical and ontological disaster, could characterize crimes against women in genocidal contexts, hate crimes and violence targeting women. A register of catastrophe was also embedded in the historical pursuit of human rights as rights of 'Man', given the traditional exclusion of women and others by those rights.[3]

Collin was dismayed by the slow pace of integration of sexual difference as a 'philosopheme' within contemporary French university studies, particularly in disciplines such as philosophy and political theory. She considered it an obstinate delay, particularly when compared with the state of studies in many fields in Anglo-American scholarship. In addition to an edited volume devoted to feminist approaches to epistemology and philosophy of science (*Le sexe des sciences*, 1992) and a co-edited volume offering some of the first French translations of Anglo-American philosophers such as Carole Pateman, Martha Nussbaum, Nancy Fraser, Catharine MacKinnon and Judith Butler (*Repenser le politique: l'apport du féminisme*, 2005), Collin co-edited a voluminous critical anthology *Les Femmes de Platon à Derrida* (2000). Reconstructing a vast dossier on the preoccupation with the role and nature of women and sex in the canonical writings of philosophers and political theorists going back to Plato, Collin repudiated the view that these questions, and attention to them, should be seen as merely 'feminist' or marginal. Collin was a critic of the French education system's hostility to innovation, perhaps explained by its centralization and pretensions to universalism. But universalism, argued Collin, was really a form of 'double particularism'. It embodied the excluding habits of nationalism and the long and complex traditions through which the knowing subject had been tacitly sexed as masculine.[4]

Collin's repudiation of the posturings and hypocrisies of a false sex neutrality also inflected her sympathy with the more frankly sexed character of Lacan's writing on sexual difference. In her eyes, Lacan and Freud did not pretend that a speaking and writing subject was detached from its masculinity. They allowed complex, ambiguous, problematic but also problematizing ways of understanding that masculinity. It was typical of Collin to give her most engaged and curious attention to a number of figures she might have been expected to repudiate: characteristic to have engaged concertedly with Arendt *as* a Blanchot scholar, with feminism *as* an Arendt scholar, and similarly with Lacan *as* a feminist. Many in the feminist milieu with which she engaged were not keen readers of Lacan, and Collin did not assume that Beauvoir was a point of reference among psychoanalytic communities engaging with Lacan. She might have taken a degree of mischievous satisfaction in arguing – as she does in the 1999 essay translated here, 'Nom du père, On de la mère: De Beauvoir à Lacan' – that certain paths taken by Lacan were ones that had been opened by Beauvoir.

If Collin devoted herself to feminism, she also had a taste for deflating its passions, its pretensions, its ideologies, its risks, its security borders – to a degree equal to her vigorous and lifelong commitment to it. This, for Collin, was the form of active engagement par excellence. Hagiography was as foreign to her disposition as irony was dear. After the French philosopher Sarah Kofman's death, Collin organized an important memorial conference on her work and published the resulting collection of essays. Valuable essays on Kofman by Derrida and Nancy, and many others, were produced for this occasion and thanks to her efforts. Among them, Collin's own piece was brilliant and unique. She valued the malicious eye of Sarah Kofman, and took care to mention it, warmly and publicly. In the terms of a writing of the disaster she considered Kofman's autobiographical depiction of her childhood as a young Jewish girl, hidden during the French Occupation. She took care to present Kofman not as a maximally sympathetic figure, but as capable (particularly as a young girl, particularly as a victim) of scenes crueller, said Collin, than Sade's visions.[5] The keen eye brought to the subtle forms of Kofman's mercilessness was Collin's form of solidarity with her. Her memorial essay on Kofman was also the occasion for a simultaneously generous and uncompromised response to her work.

Collin directed her sharpest attention to sacred cows and treasured memories. In a wonderful essay on Beauvoir and pain,[6] she repudiated feminists of the 1970s who saw in *The Second Sex* a declaration that the personal was political. She did not primarily value in the work a preoccupation with injustice. Instead, she emphasized in Beauvoir's writing a recognition of the excess to human agency, of all which necessarily escapes our control. A politics which does not recognize this excess, and its role in linking together individuals and forms of community (sexed or otherwise), risks a new violence, a new form of inhumanity, an unanticipated kind of monstrosity. Interpreting Beauvoir, she wrote:

> We are united by dying as much as by living. To misrecognize this would convert feminism to the monstrous: to the community of victors [la communauté des gagnantes].

A feminism hoping to form *la communauté des gagnantes* would disavow its constitutive *impouvoir*. Not to minimize injustice, nor its importance in Beauvoir's work, Collin emphasized a generalized, ontological damage that exceeds justice. This is why, in addition to *The Second Sex*'s *on ne naît pas femme, on le devient*, Beauvoir's concurrent depiction of ageing, suffering and the experience of being cheated (Beauvoir's *j'ai été flouée*[7]) were so important to Collin. They were interpretable as fundamental, not contingent, to existence, and to every feminism.

Collin insisted that redress for imbalances of power could be sought, all the while affirming an ontological *impouvoir*: politically, poetically and, as she argued in 'Beauvoir et la douleur', philosophically. She spoke for a feminism invigorated, not debilitated, by the force of its irony.

Notes

Thanks to Sylvie Duverger for many details provided, including online resources for Collin's publications and interviews.

1. Françoise Collin, *Je partirais d'un mot: Le champ symbolique*, Fus Art, Paris, 1999, p. 142.
2. Ibid., pp. 143, 142.
3. Ibid., p. 11.
4. Françoise Collin, Evelyne Pisier and Eleni Varikas, eds, *Les Femmes de Platon à Derrida*, Plon, Paris, 2000, p. 9.
5. Françoise Collin, 'L'impossible diététique. Philosophie et récit', *Les Cahiers du Grif*, NS, 3, *Sarah Kofman*, 1997, pp. 11–28. She brings a similarly caustic – and extraordinary – eye to her own cruelty as a daughter, and to the depiction of her mother, in her *récit*, *Le Rendez-vous*.
6. www.sens-public.org/article.php3?id_article=731.
7. Ibid., pp. 7–8. To Our Lady of the Pillar in Zaragossa, perched on her column, 'But there is something more, a *jouissance* beyond the phallus.'

Name of the father, 'one' of the mother: From Beauvoir to Lacan

FRANÇOISE COLLIN

If I take a few aspects of the thought of Jacques Lacan, and investigate their relation to Simone de Beauvoir around one specific point, I have no intention of making him out – against received opinion – to be a feminist who didn't know it and even less of turning him into a disciple of the author of *The Second Sex*.[1] My aim is simply to indicate how the 'question of women' is introduced into his reflection on the basis of a chapter of Beauvoir's book. And by 'the question of women' I do not mean the question about women – psychoanalysis cannot shut up 'about' women – but the question that comes from women, whether they formulate it or not: women *as* question. Moreover, this question was explicitly put to Lacan by the psychoanalysts of the first wave of feminism who attended his seminars in the 1970s. But if he received it head-on at that point, it was because it had resonated with him much earlier. And everything leads one to think that he had already seen it emerge in *The Second Sex*. So it is a historical point as well as a point of doctrine that I will try to deal with briefly here.[*]

Born or made

When the question of women comes up in Lacan's discourse, it always seems to provoke a feeling of unease in him. He generally responds to this feeling with defensive sallies where he displays his position as a (masculine) man. These are like the symptoms of the displacement that his thought undergoes, of his development, for in fact Lacan allows himself to be interpellated by this upsetting question, even as he protects himself from it, and protects himself from it precisely to the extent that it interpellates him.

These sallies have a frankly misogynist quality. They generally consist of putting women in their place – which is not his – and in talking about them in the third person: 'In no way do I have a disrespectful judgement of *these beings*, let *those persons* be assured' (my emphasis) he says at one point, which illustrates the matter sufficiently. But this is just after having asserted that the 'unbelievable' manner in which woman is treated in discourse and more particularly in psychoanalytic discourse comes from the fact that she is most often only seen as the 'object of (masculine) desire'. As if it was necessary to compensate with a reductive movement for the audacity of what he had just put forward. So that he seems to incarnate just what he has announced if not denounced in others: 'The most famous things that have come down to us about women in history are literally what one can say that is infamous.' 'She is called woman and defamed.'[2]

Simone de Beauvoir and Jacques Lacan met each other through common friends (Georges Bataille – whose wife, Sylvie, Lacan later married – and Michel Leiris) towards the end of the war, or more precisely in 1944, according to Elisabeth Roudinesco.[3] They were present with others during the public reading by some of them (including Beauvoir) of a play by Picasso – *Desire Caught by the Tale* – in Leiris's apartment. Beauvoir seems already to have read Lacan's early texts and to have consulted him before the publication of *The Second Sex*. Lacan estimated that it would require at least five or six months of interviews to sort out the problem; Beauvoir abandoned the idea. She only devoted a short chapter of *The Second Sex* to 'The Psychoanalytic Point of View' and quotes Freud rather than Lacan.

But what Roudinesco's biography does not reveal is that Lacan almost certainly read *The Second Sex* on its publication, having been notified about its appearance; indeed the book was not likely to have escaped his legendary curiosity. And there are such correspondences between the references essential to his reformulation of the feminine and those – much earlier – of Simone de Beauvoir that he could only have borrowed them in order to follow his own path. Thus, at one point, he follows the steps of the author of *The Second Sex*: the moment when he analyses the figure of the mystic. The meeting goes no further but it merits reflection since it touches on a decisive point.

Before analysing the effects of this encounter, however, it is necessary to stress that Lacan never denied or ignored the socio-historical conditions of the sexual relations that were otherwise, if not exclusively, the object of Beauvoir's reflection. If he attempted to elucidate their structural relationship, he did not ignore their conjunctural variations. Whether in his early texts – on the family[4] – or in the later seminars, this parameter is present just beneath the surface. One can see this, for example, when he analyses courtly love at length – as he analyses Greek love, elsewhere. For if courtly love makes sense, for Lacan, beyond its historical moment, it is nevertheless well identified as belonging to it. As Lacan (reader of Lévi-Strauss) writes:

> The style of this story simply shows the effective position of woman *in feudal society*. She is strictly speaking what is indicated by the elementary structures of kinship, i.e., nothing more than a correlative of the function of social exchange, the support of a number of goods and of signs of power. She is essentially identified with a social function that leaves no room for her person or her own liberty, except with reference to her religious rights.[5]

Lacan confronts this instrumental and social function with the different but no less negative use that is made of 'her' in courtly poetry where 'the Lady is never characterized by any of her real, concrete virtues' because in this poetic field 'the feminine object is introduced by the very singular gate of privation, of inaccessibility' and 'emptied of all real substance' in favour of 'the pleasure of desiring, or more precisely the pleasure of experiencing unpleasure'[6] – the pleasure of desiring that belongs to men, not to women.

Nor does Lacan miss the opportunity to pick up and comment on Ernest Jones's reflections on whether women are 'born' or 'made'. He stresses that Jones 'does not seem to note, in this regard, that the Oedipal defile manufactures – if this is what is at issue – men no less'; the question is posed for both sexes, even if what 'made' means is different in each case.[7]

We might assume that we hear here, in Jones's English, the formula that so often identifies Beauvoir's thought, even without reading her books: 'on ne naît pas femme, on le devient'; 'one is not born a woman, but becomes one'. Woman is not 'born' but 'made'. Nevertheless one should not be too hasty to identify the two positions because what Jones or Lacan means by becoming a woman or man is, as the latter says, the work of the 'Oedipal defile' rather than a social operation. The articulation of the two nevertheless merits reflection, and the alternative of 'born' or 'made', as Lacan and Beauvoir each present it in their different terms, outlines a problematic dimension – both serious and persistent – of sexuation.

The figure of the mystic

Lacan makes a qualitative leap in his reflections with his approach to mysticism. In his seminar of 20 March 1960, 'Love of One's Neighbour', he already makes an opening – hesitant and still rather ironic – towards mysticism:

> No doubt the question of beyond the pleasure principle, of the place of the unnameable Thing and of what goes on there is raised in certain acts through which they provoke our judgement, as when someone [*on*] tells us, for example, of a certain Angela de Folignio who joyfully lapped up the water in which she had just washed the feet of lepers; I will spare you the details ... or when someone [*on*] recounts that – with quite as much spiritual reward – the blessed Marie Alacoque ate the excrement of a sick man.[8]

The female mystic is here characterized as one whose jouissance is nourished by the horror of the unnameable rather than leading towards pleasure. Her position is otherwise not elaborated; the beyond of pleasure is not yet 'beyond the phallus' as it will be formulated later.

But who is this 'someone' [on] who brings these acts to our attention, this 'someone' [on] whose proper name Lacan fails to supply? A rereading of the chapter on mysticism in the second volume of *The Second Sex* allows us to identify Simone de Beauvoir. In fact, she has recourse to precisely these two examples, and in the same terms: 'We know that Marie Alacoque cleaned up the vomit of a sick woman with her tongue' and 'Saint Angèle de Foligno tells that she joyfully drank the water with which she had just washed the hands and feet of a leper.'[9] She also evokes other names, such as that of Teresa de Avila, referring to 'the statue of Bernini which shows us the saint swooning in an excess of sudden delight', the statue that will inspire Lacan's later seminar, *Encore*, in 1973 – at the moment when the women's movement is at its height – leading his heirs and publishers to put the image of Bernini's famous work on the cover of their edition of the seminar. Thus the relation of Lacan's text to Beauvoir's is not merely general and accidental: it takes up from it its principal points.

It is nevertheless important to emphasize not just the interest that Beauvoir had in the dimension of mysticism and her erudition on this matter (as on many others) but also the location of the chapter devoted to its discussion: at the end of the third part of volume II, just before chapter 4, which, in conclusion, defines her political perspective under the title 'Towards Liberation'.[10] The figure of the mystic appears here as a form of affirmation of the feminine figure, or a mode of expression of her freedom, albeit a freedom not yet transcended by the moment of liberation, which can only be collectively accomplished, by its inscription in the social. Mysticism is perhaps a form of purely individual 'salvation' that 'has no purchase on the world', as Beauvoir writes. She nevertheless sees with great lucidity how through the mystical position a woman both annihilates and recovers, at the same time, her body and her jouissance, and finds a form of articulation that goes from 'contemplation to action', going as far even as its foundation. For her it is not a question of an extreme form of subjection that provokes a pure, ecstatic passivity: God is an alternative to the figure of the master and not another disguise for him. Beauvoir stresses that one can discern here a figure of 'transcendence'; 'the bodily mimicry can be enveloped in a surge of freedom', she writes. And about Teresa de Avila, at least, she specifies that it would be wrong to interpret her emotions as a 'simple sublimation of sexuality', a 'redemption of femininity' which seems nevertheless to characterize some of her 'lesser sisters'. She is, like Catherine of Sienna, of a 'quite virile type', Beauvoir says in a note – and we know that in her writing this characterization indicates a rupture with conventional femininity. For these major figures at least, the position of mysticism is a way of going beyond the relations of mastery and servitude which characterize sexual relations, but in a movement that is sufficient to itself and cannot be a common leaven for social transformation. To attach oneself to God is to escape submission. So there is action – and not just passion – in mysticism, but a *singular* action. And we understand that mysticism is not a political position in the sense defined in 'Towards Liberation': it has 'no purchase on the world'. The fact remains, however, that the texts of these mystics reached Beauvoir, and so challenged her that she wrote an important chapter of her book on 'the second sex' on them. This seems to indicate that their existence is not exhausted in pure singularity, that it has left a trace, that it broached – even overturned – the symbolic apparatus where women find themselves assigned to their place.

If in 1960 Lacan took up the examples of Marguerite Marie Alacoque and Angèle de Foligno with a certain amusement, slightly disgusted but nevertheless testifying to their having outlined a path for him, when he returned to them thirteen years later at the moment of feminism's apogee, it is in another state of mind. Teresa de Avila will now allow him to make a fundamental move, which he will express in terms of a jouissance 'beyond the Phallus'. It is then that he makes a real breach in the phallocentric, phallogocentric and totalizing thought that he had inherited from Freudian doctrine and enters resolutely and explicitly into a new conception of the difference between the sexes and, at the same time, of Truth – and this link is important. He stakes out this advance with the term 'not-all': woman is 'not-all', traversing the order of the all, the whole, but exceeding it. In this operation, God, as the (Big) Other,[11] is dissociated from the Father, at least to the extent that he is not the mouth-hole god of the theologians – another version of the Father – but the god-hole of mysticism, who is attested to in 'language' not in the 'service of goods'.[12] 'There is a hole there and that hole is called the Other. At least that is what I felt I could name it, the Other, qua locus in which speech being deposited founds Truth and with it the pact that makes up for the non-existence of the sexual relationship.'[13]

The Name of the Father

For a long time psychoanalysis has seemed to support the traditional hypothesis of a division between the sexes and the articulation of one sex – the 'second sex' – with the other. The centrality of the phallus, founded on the empirical reality of the penis to which women can only relate as something which they 'lack', has been the object of numerous critical engagements by women. This sexual distribution inscribed in dogmatic analysis has been questioned all the more as Freud himself finally admitted that he did not know what a woman was, not because, as Lacan would write 'The' woman (Woman) does not exist, but because she evades his investigations. It seems, then, from the founding texts, that it is a man – that is, a human being of the male sex – who thinks and speaks, first of all on the basis of his own self-analysis as man and son: what is said in the texts about women does not have the same status as what is said about men, even if this rests – in a second stage – on the analysis of numerous patients. One can read this admission in Freud and more explicitly in Lacan: 'when one is a man one sees in one's partner that which is one's own support, what supports one narcissistically', he writes in relation to Freud. Now, when founding concepts are what one might describe as 'blown off course', during their elaboration and articulation, the results are no doubt irreversible. At best one might proceed to their erasure, for example by accentuating the difference between the penis and the Phallus to which both sexuated individuals would relate. Psychoanalysis is founded by a male subject – a subject of desire – and from his position. And at no point does it claim that the sexuated position is indifferent, even if the 'feminine' and the 'masculine' can be appropriated by beings of either sex, by the sex other than the one to which the term has been first attributed. What is said of one sex can certainly be supposed of the other, but what is not a matter of indifference is the meaning of the attribution that is made in either case: women *also* are phallic; men *also* are hysterics.

This to-ing and fro-ing characterizes the whole of analytic thought and is undoubtedly unavoidable in the treatment of the question of sexual difference: there are thus two of them and there is one of them, at the same time. Sexual characteristics are at the same time interchangeable and specific. The advantage of Lacanian thought over so-called postmodern thought is precisely that it remains suspended in this fertile contradiction, when postmodernism generally makes an economy of two – that is man and woman – in the interest of the indifferent difference of the 'feminine'.

The originary dissymmetry of the conceptualization is problematic. When we read Lacan's text (or Freud's) we do not read a text detached from the person who is speaking and writing, but rather a text where the masculine character of the subject of discourse as well as the speaking subject (since the term of the subject is curiously conserved) is constantly betrayed or avowed. What Lacan can and does do is to return to this originary dissymmetry and 'retouch' it – touch it again – without being able to refound the doctrine. It resists, so much so that even if a female analyst takes it up, she can only do so through excess: she is introduced into it rather than modelling it, the subject of speech without being the subject of discourse in which this speech is inscribed and which she displaces. This characteristic is undoubtedly the case whenever women enter scientific or symbolic discourse, but it is even more paradoxical when it rests precisely on the irreducibility (*a minima*) of sexuated positions. And when Lacan, at various points, interpellates women psychoanalysts, summoning them to speak themselves, he seems to presuppose that speaking the difference between the sexes can only be a half-saying, if not a dialogue, and that this half-saying is still lacking in psychoanalysis.

'Being introduced into' rather than constituting has certainly become a feminine – even feminist – 'methodology', a 'cunning of the feminine' or hysterical position, but it is at the very least a singular cunning, where we do not know if it consists of women 'giving ground on their desire' – accepting loss in order to win, giving up their 'pound of flesh' – or, on the contrary, sustaining their desire.

Lacan is conscious that this chunk of the science of desire, if there is one, was a chunk that Freud skirted around. So he writes, in 1973:

> What I am working on this year is what Freud expressly left aside: *Was will das Weib?* 'What does woman want?' Freud claims there is only masculine libido. What does this mean if not that a field that is not negligible is ignored. That field is the one of all beings that take on the status of woman.

He quickly adds his usual catty afterthought to this remark: 'assuming that that being takes on anything whatsoever of her destiny'. The formulation is such that in designating actual women, it covers also every speaking being that is put or puts itself in that place (we have already emphasized the ambiguity that persistently holds sway over the designation of sexuated positions and allows their double meaning room to play). And it is to this dark continent that he will devote himself by elaborating the distinction between the Father and the Other, or between the Father, God and the Other. Because 'Woman has a relation to the signifier of the Other, insofar as, qua Other, it can but remain forever Other.'[14] That is to say, the Other does not enter into the regime of the totality of the One, where the law of opposites holds, does not belong to the register of phallic jouissance that Lacan suddenly qualifies as the 'jouissance of the idiot' to which the practice of masturbation attests. At various points he challenges the Freudian idea that woman's relation to castration is based on a privation (the lack of the penis) and he explicitly distinguishes these two terms: the relation to lack is not determined by a natural 'having or not having'.

If Lacan often declares himself to be the disciple of Freud, whom he designates as 'the father of all of us, the father of psychoanalysis', his protestations of fidelity have to be accepted, but must include the quite ferocious criticisms that at the same time (or later) he addresses to this 'father'. First, these focus – and with great vehemence – on the anthropological description (which he calls naturalized) of the murder of the father described as the 'father of the horde' in *Totem and Taboo*: 'As if there has ever been the slightest trace of him, the father of the horde. We have seen orangutans. But the father of the human horde? We've never seen the slightest trace of him.'[15] It is according to these terms a 'cock and bull story'. And he speaks no less ironically of the way this tale stages the prohibition of incest and the appropriation of all the women by the father:

> And then they all decide with one mind, that no one will touch the little mummies. Because there is more than one of them, to top it off. They could exchange since the old father had them all. They could sleep with their brother's mother, specifically, since they are only brothers through their father.

In some sense the 'murder of the father' in its Freudian version covers over the unacceptable: the death of the father, his mortality, and mortality as such, the impotence of power; 'he who enjoys all the women is inconceivable to imagine, whereas it is fairly normally observable that being enough for one is already quite a lot'.[16]

From the Father to the Other: the little hole

However, generally, Freud's concentration on the relation to the father leaves Lacan sceptical and seems tied to Freud's blindness and deafness concerning women. He psychoanalyses it rapidly: 'And it is just because he loved his father that it was necessary to grant him a stature, to the extent of granting him the size of the giant of the primal horde.' He brings together Freud's relation to the father and the 'uxoriousness' of his relations with women. Manifestly there is something over which Lacan stumbles and which he seeks to, if not transcend, then at least apprehend otherwise. He writes: 'someone could have got a little bit excited about this paternal metaphor and known how to make a little hole.'[17] And he adds: '*It is what I have always desired*' (my emphasis). He continues: 'that someone should make some progress, make a trace for me, begin to show a little path. Anyway, be that as it may, it has never happened and the question of Oedipus is still intact.'

But not altogether, however, because Lacan is really in the business of making this 'little hole' in the paternal metaphor and in the question of Oedipus, all the while pretending not to, just at the moment that he goes back to the question of 'feminine jouissance'. But we should not forget that it was already concerning this central point that he had worked on the Freudian corpus. In substituting the Name of the Father for the Father of the Horde, for the orangutan, he detaches the signifier from masculine reality in an important way, he detaches the Father from the *Name*, he detaches the Father from the signifier; he disarticulates them in the articulation of his formula. The 'Name of the Father' introduces the Name, jettisons the Father in favour of the Name.

In the context of *Encore*, Lacan makes further progress. It is not simply a question of denaturalizing the differences but of reformulating them by taking into account a splitting of the difference between the sexes. It is a farewell to the One, to which the emergence of the concept of the Other bears witness – the Other which is not an other nor the other of the One. This Other has a relation to what Lacan calls 'the other sex'; that is to say, that which is apparently not his at the moment when he speaks (but which he will claim nevertheless). And what is proper to this other sex is not to be, or not only to be, of the order of the All [*du Tout*], were this to be a lack of All, but rather 'not-all'; in her essence woman is not-all. In fact, in relation to phallic jouissance, she enjoys [*connaît*] a supplementary remainder and not – Lacan insists – a complementary one, which would take us back to the order of the all and of lack, of privation. In fact he specifies: 'It is not because she is not-all. She is not that at all. She is fully that. But there is something more ... a jouissance ... beyond the phallus' the peculiarity of which is that she experiences it but does not know it, because it is not, and cannot be, an object of knowledge. So Lacan makes this little hole in the Father, as he desires to: he calls it God, or the Other. Not the God mouth-hole of theology but the God Hole of Teresa of Avila.

Certain so-called women attest to this Hole, not only in their postures but also in their texts. And it is here that Lacan returns to the example of the mystics, and alights on the case of Teresa of Avila, who was at the heart of Simone de Beauvoir's chapter. Nevertheless, throughout his long development, he cannot avoid the sarcastic tone that he adopts when he touches on these matters in general and in particular on points concerning women. 'Woman knows nothing of this jouissance ... in all the time that people have been begging them, begging them on their hands and knees ... to try and tell us, not a word!' But 'there is nevertheless a little connection when you read certain serious persons, like women, as if by chance.'[18]

This supplementary jouissance to which the mystics attest is not in fact parallel to phallic jouissance: it is not part of the phallic economy and is not its alternative – it exceeds it. Woman, as the mystic evidences, takes in the phallic function: 'she is fully in it. But there is something more.'

The formulation is important, subversive even. Because the 'more than', the 'extra', passes through the phallic function in order to exceed it. That is to say, there is a modality of desire which goes beyond, exceeding the phallus, that makes a 'little hole' in the Father, a little hole of the Other, or of God (we do not distinguish here). Men and women are determined in relation to the phallus – the Freudian position is maintained in this regard – but there is more. The dimension of the Other comes to supplement the dimension of the Father.

So Lacan – going beyond Beauvoir, along the path that she had opened up but not then followed – somehow splits the register of desire. Splits without making it double, without distinguishing, without severing: 'one sees the "cross-sightedness"' he says. 'There you have it, the register of the Father and the register of God – that does not make two Gods but it doesn't make just one either.'

This, then, is the point where Lacan opens the road to a thought of what he will call 'the feminine', which is not foreign to the masculine but is not identical with it. What escapes the phallic even whilst referring to it is no longer thought in terms of lack (as in Freud), but in terms of exceeding. The One of the Freudian phallic law, where sexuation is marked in quantitative terms of positive and negative – of more and less, as in Aristotle – is surpassed.

The feminine position as a relation to the Other is first located in women. But Lacan recalls that, on the one hand, certain men are situated on the same side as them, and, on the other, that certain mystics can be situated on the side of the phallic function – like Angelus Silesius.

It is not necessary to be a mystic to occupy this position and Lacan himself claims it: 'And add the writings of Jacques Lacan because they are of the same order', he writes, placing his own œuvre in this register opened up by mysticism, the order (or disorder) of the 'more than'.

This remark is a good indication that what is said of 'jouissance' as more than phallic jouissance is not just swooning but is inscribed in the text, even supporting the weft of the text, in so far as Truth is not reducible to a knowledge of the object, to a thesis, in so far as it functions as what Lacan calls 'La langue' (and what in another way Derrida calls *différance* – with an *a*: the movement of differing, already enunciated by Blanchot): a fundamental experience of the writer. This jouissance in/of the text: also revealed, in its own way, by analysis, 'that is the objectivation of that which the speaking being spends its time speaking of in vain'. Writings, and Lacan's writings in particular, are woven, at one and the same time, by what refers to the phallic function and what refers to the more than: they are at the same time under the watch [*garde*] of the Father and the inattention [*mégarde*] of the Other. I would prefer to say that they are deployed within the ambiguity and indecision of the Father and the Other, between Father and Other. Speaking, writing are between knowledge and non-knowledge, between knowledge and Truth – for Truth is not science – both at the same time.

Thus Lacan – unlike some of his contemporaries – will not assert that writing is feminine, because the Father and the Other are neither complementary nor separable: writing is made up of both. What is held under the sole watch of the Father or abandoned to the pure inattention of the Other cannot be written. If he claims for himself here the feminine position of the more than, and if we can follow him along this path with the light irony that he himself practises, it is because the form and style of his work overflow the relation to knowledge – the constitution of a science – that is exercised there. In this work, nearly all of it spoken before being written down, there is a point of inspiration that escapes the phallic order to run, as literature runs, in its drift, something which is accorded to loss, and not to the cunning of loss where 'whoever loses wins' but to pure loss.

Because saying [*le dire*] has a relation with God [*dieu*] – Lacan invents the word *dieur*: saying, writing, has a relation with the Other, induces what he calls 'the God hypothesis'.

So, in Lacanian thought, the Father of the Horde first slips towards the 'Name of the Father' as signifier. But God, or the Other, is another signifier. Or rather the same one as the Name of the Father said otherwise – but this 'otherwise' matters.

La pas toute passe par tout
Simone de Beauvoir – who opened the way to this other order of assertion, which dissociates itself from, without abandoning, the phallic law to answer to the voice of the Other in swooning and action, in serenity and fury, in *jouissance* – will, in the end, recall that whatever the importance of this opening, it remains in the order of singularity and cannot be negotiated in the form of a common law.

The relation to the Other is not the principle of a new social organization, not of a new status for women. The gush of freedom is not the guarantee of liberation, and it is liberation that first and foremost concerns the author of *The Second Sex*. Without putting it in precisely these same terms, Beauvoir is occupied by the debate – or the vicious circle – that Hannah Arendt did make explicit: the debate between freedom and liberation. That is, one needs freedom in order to liberate oneself, but liberation is necessary for the exercise of freedom. One does not do without the phallic economy; the so-called feminine position does not dispense with it. When Beauvoir frames her last chapter and entitles it 'Towards Liberation' she recalls, in Lacanian language, that the not all [*pas tout*] – or woman as not all [*pas toute*] – is only such by traversing the all, on pain of otherwise being simply 'less than'. And there woman is not nothing at all; she is even fully within the phallic order, which is the order of liberation, where the claim of equality may appear and which we therefore cannot do without. But there is something more. Which is no doubt what prevents Beauvoir from succumbing to the fascination of access to the universal that would consist of women 'becoming man'. Not because she wants to inhabit the artifices of femininity but because she never ceases to say in the tacking of her text that 'the feminine' cannot be reduced to the effects of masculine domination.

Beauvoir's œuvre, without lingering on mysticism, is nevertheless occupied by the question that it inscribes. If she sometimes thinks the becoming of women as an assimilation to the order of men, to what she calls the universal appropriated by the masculine 'man', she always retains something that cannot be reduced to this over-ordered order, to this pseudo-universal. What she calls liberation is not access to the masculine position, but that of the not all that passes through the all in order to be not all. The not all that passes through the all [*La pas toute qui passe par tout*]: that is, Beauvoir's woman, between freedom and liberation.

It goes without saying that Lacan's thought cannot be reduced to that of Beauvoir; yet at one moment, at least, Jacques and Simone meet, or more exactly, Jacques, reading or rereading Simone, twelve years, then twenty-five years after the appearance of *The Second Sex*, finds within it a fertile point for his own thought, as well as a subtle opening on to the commandment of the One of the phallic law, which however does not replace the One by the Two. And drawing his thread from this reading, he gives back ('a hundredfold'?) what he has taken from it.

In this confrontation, one cannot forget that Beauvoir's articulation of her problematic took place immediately after the war – 1948 – and in the framework of dialectical thought, in the grip of the horizon of the All. Lacan's problematic articulation – in 1960 and especially in 1973 – was still in dialogue with the dialectic but belonged to a philosophical register which had succeeded it, which one calls post-structuralist or postmodern: along with Heidegger, at least, he had broken with the idea of the All. Moreover, between 1948 and 1973, in the course of twenty-five years, women had also shifted ground: it was with the women of 1973 that Lacan recalled Beauvoir 'the mother of us all' (Gertrude Stein). But without citing her, without even naming her.

For 'A huge crocodile in whose jaws you are – that's the mother' and 'One never knows what might suddenly come over her and make her shut her trap.'[19] The son, if he sneaks away, will not close *his* trap for a long time. Except when it comes to the Name of the crocodile, to his 'One'.

TRANSLATION BY PHILIP DERBYSHIRE

Notes

1. Lacan's 'anti-feminism' is emphasized in various critical analyses. Among others we could cite Marcelle Marini, *Lacan*, Éditions Belfond, Paris, 1986.
2. 'Ce qui de plus fameux dans l'histoire est resté des femmes, c'est à proprement parler ce qu'on peut en dire d'infamant. On la dit-femme. On la diffame.'
3. Elisabeth Roudinesco, *Jacques Lacan*, trans. Barbara Bray, Columbia University Press, New York, pp. 168–9.
4. Jacques Lacan, *Les complexes familiaux dans la formation de l'individu*, Éditions Navarin, Paris, 1984.
5. Jacques Lacan, *The Seminar*, Book VII: *The Ethics of Psychoanalysis*, ed. Jacques Alain Miller, trans. Dennis Porter, Tavistock/Routledge, London, 1992, p. 150.
6. Ibid., p. 152.
7. Jacques Lacan, *Le Séminaire*, Livre V: *Les formations de l'inconscient*, ed. Jacques Alain Miller, Éditions du Seuil, Paris, 1998, p. 279. [The words 'born' and 'made' are in English in Collin's text.]
8. Lacan, *The Ethics of Psychoanalysis*, p. 188.
9. Simone de Beauvoir, *The Second Sex*, trans. and ed. H.M. Parshley, Penguin Books, Harmondsworth and New York, 1972, p. 685.
10. Ibid., p. 689.
11. François Balmès has analysed the relationships between Lacanian concepts – the Father, the Other, God – in a seminar given at the Colloquium '"God is Dead": Today', which he organized in January 1998 under the auspices of the Collège International de Philosophie in Paris. It was in this same setting that I presented the elements of what I am developing here under the title 'Hole and mouth-hole'.
12. One might ask if, in another context, Levinas is not operating a similar distinction in the relation or non-relation of 'Totality' and 'Infinity' of the Jewish God and the God of the Theologians in *Totality and Infinity* (Duquesne University Press, Pittsburgh PA, 1969).
13. Jacques Lacan, *The Seminar*, Book XX: *Encore: On Feminine Sexuality*, ed. Jacques Alain Miller, trans. with notes by Bruce Fink, W.W. Norton, New York and London, 1992, p. 114.
14. Ibid., pp. 80–81.
15. Jacques Lacan, *The Seminar*, Book XVII: *The Other Side of Psychoanalysis*, ed. Jacques-Alain Miller, trans. with notes by Russell Grigg, W.W. Norton, New York and London, 2007, pp. 112–13.
16. Ibid., p. 124.
17. Ibid., p. 13.
18. Lacan, *Encore*, p. 76.
19. Lacan, *The Other Side of Psychoanalysis*, p. 112.

12 Black Socrates? Questioning the philosophical tradition

SIMON CRITCHLEY

> Inconsiderateness in the face of tradition is reverence for the past.
> Martin Heidegger, *Sophistes*
>
> Funk not only moves, it can remove.
> George Clinton, *P. Funk (Wants to Get Funked Up)*

Philosophy tells itself stories.[1] One might go further and claim that the life of philosophy, the memory that ensures its identity and its continued existence as something to be inherited, lived and passed on, consists in the novel repetition of certain basic narratives. And there is one story in particular that philosophy likes to tell, which allows philosophers to reanimate, theatrically and sometimes in front of their students, the passion that founds their profession and which, it seems, must be retold in order for philosophy to be capable of inheritance. It concerns, of course, Greece – or rather, as General de Gaulle might have said, a certain idea of Greece – and the passion of a dying Socrates.

Philosophy as detraditionalization

Socrates, the philosopher, dies. The significance of this story is that, with it, we can see how philosophy constitutes itself as a tradition, affects itself with narrative, memory and the chance of a future, by repeating a scene of radical *de-traditionalization*. For Hegel and Nietzsche, to choose two examples of philosophers who affect themselves with a tradition – although from seemingly opposed perspectives – the historical emergence of philosophy, the emergence of philosophy into history, that is to say, the decisive break with mythic, religious or aesthetic world-views, occurs with Socrates' death.[2]

Who is Socrates? So the story goes, he is an individual who claims that the source of moral integrity cannot be said to reside in the traditional customs, practices and forms of life of the community, what Hegel calls *Sittlichkeit*; nor, for Nietzsche, in the aesthetico-religious practices that legitimate the pre-philosophical Greek *polis* – that is to say, attic tragedy. Rather, Socrates is an individual who demands that the source of moral legitimacy must lie in the appeal to universality. It must have a universal form: what is justice? The philosopher does not ask 'What is justice for the Athenians?' or 'What is justice for the Spartans?', but rather focuses on justice in general, seeking its *eidos*. Socrates announces the vocation of the philosopher and establishes the lines of transmission that lead from individuality to universality, from the intellect to the forms – a route which bypasses the particular, the communal, the traditional, as well as conventional views of ethical and political life.

The vocation of the philosopher is *critique* – that is, an individual interrogation and questioning of the evidence of tradition through an appeal to a universal form. For Hegel and Nietzsche, Socrates' life announces the death of tragedy, and the death of the allegedly *sittlich* (ethical) community legitimated through the pre-philosophical aesthetico-religious practices. In Hegel's words, Socrates' death marks the moment when tragedy comes off the stage and enters real life, becoming the tragedy of Greece.[3] Socrates' tragic death announces both the beginning of philosophy and the beginning of the irreversible Greek decline that will, for Hegel and Nietzsche, take us all the way from the legalism of the Roman Republic to the eviscerated *Moralität* (abstract morality) of post-Kantian Germany. Of course, one's evaluation of Socrates' death will vary, depending on whether one is Hegel or Nietzsche. For the former (not without some elegiac regret for the lost Sophoclean *polis*) it is the first intimation of the principle of subjectivity; for the latter, Socrates' death ignites the motor that drives (Platonic-Christian) nihilism. But, despite these differences of evaluation, the narrative structure is common to Hegel and Nietzsche. The story remains the same even if the moral is different: Socrates' death marks the end of tragic Greece and the tragic end of Greece.

It is a beautiful story, and as I recount it I am once again seduced by its founding passion: the historical emergence of philosophy out of the dying Socrates is the condition of possibility for de-traditionalization. It announces the imperative that continues to drive philosophy, *critique*, which consists in the refusal to recognize the legitimacy of tradition without that tradition having first submitted itself to critical interrogation, to dialogue *viva voce*.

Philosophy as tradition

However, if on my view philosophy is de-traditionalization, that which calls into question the evidence of tradition, then what is philosophy's relation to its own tradition? What is the relation of philosophy to the stories it tells about itself?

With the admittedly limited examples given above, one might say that the philosophical tradition is a tradition of de-traditionalization, of stories where the authority of tradition is refused. As Descartes famously writes, 'I will devote myself sincerely and without reservations to the general demolition of my opinions.'[4] As we will see presently with reference to Husserl and Heidegger, the philosopher's appeal to tradition is not traditional; it is, in Derrida's words, 'an appeal to tradition which is in no way traditional'.[5] It is a call for a novel repetition or retrieval of the past for the purposes of a critique of the present, often – for example, in Husserl – with a view to the construction of an alternative ethical teleology. But, slightly getting ahead of myself, should we believe the stories that philosophy tells to itself? Should these stories themselves be exempt from philosophical critique? More particularly, what about the story of the dying Socrates? What more can I say about this story apart from feeling its beauty and pathos despite (or perhaps because of) its being so often recounted?

To ventriloquize a little: 'One might point out that the story of Socrates' death is a *Greek* story, a narrative that recounts and reinforces the Greek beginning of philosophy. Indeed, it is a story that can be employed to assert the exclusivity of the Greek beginning of philosophy: Philosophy speaks Greek and only Greek, which is to say that philosophy does not speak Egyptian or Babylonian, Indian or Chinese and therefore is not Asian or African. Philosophy can only have one beginning and that beginning has to be the Greek beginning. Why? *Because we are who we are.* We are Europeans and Europe has a beginning, a birthplace, which is both geographical and spiritual, and the name of that birthplace is Greece. What takes place in Greece, the event that gives birth to our theoretical-scientific culture, is *philosophy*. By listening to the story that philosophy tells to itself, we can retrieve our beginning, our Greek beginning, the Greek beginning or the European Spiritual adventure. Furthermore, by appropriating this beginning as our own we will be able to come into our own as authentic Europeans, to confront the crisis of Europe, its spiritual sickness, a malaise which consists in the fact that we have forgotten who we are; we have forgotten our origins and immersed ourselves unquestioningly in tradition. We must de-traditionalize the tradition that ails us and allows us to forget the crisis – be it the crisis of objectivism (Husserl), rationalization (Weber), commodification (Marx), nihilism (Nietzsche) or forgetfulness of Being (Heidegger). We must project another tradition that is truly our own. The only therapy is to face the crisis as a crisis, which means that we must tell ourselves the story of philosophy's Greek beginning, of philosophy's exclusively Greek beginning – again and again. If philosophy is not exclusively Greek, we risk losing ourselves as Europeans, since to philosophize is to learn how to live in the memory of Socrates' death.

This troubling ventriloquy is very loosely based on Husserl's 1935 Vienna Lecture, 'Philosophy and the Crisis of European

Humanity',[6] which in many ways perfectly exemplifies the concerns of this essay and the position I am seeking to question. We could also quote examples from Hegel, Nietzsche, Heidegger, Merleau-Ponty, Arendt, Gadamer, and an entire German and English romantic tradition. What such remarks testify to, I believe, is the importation of a certain model of ancient history, centred on the exclusivity of Greece, into philosophy as the foundation stone of its legitimating discourse. I would briefly like to explore and question the historical basis for this belief.

Philosophy as invented tradition

One of the most challenging consequences of reading Martin Bernal's *Black Athena*[7] – regardless of its many alleged scholarly infelicities, which I am simply not in a position to judge – is the way in which he traces the genealogy of the invented historical paradigm upon which Husserl bases his remarks; the 'Aryan Model' of ancient history, which (astonishingly) only dates from the early decades of the nineteenth century and was developed in England and Germany. Prior to this period, and indeed for most of Western history, what Bernal calls 'The Ancient Model' of classical civilization had been dominant. The latter model believed, among other things, that the Egyptians invented philosophy, that philosophy was essentially imported into Greece from Egypt, and that Egypt – and remember Plato visited there around 390 BCE – was the font of all philosophical wisdom. In addition to the Egyptian influence on Greek civilization, it was also widely assumed that Greece was subject to colonization and extensive cultural influence from Phoenician traders and mariners, and that, therefore, Greek civilization and the philosophy expressed by that civilization were largely a consequence of the influence of near-eastern cultures on the African and Asian continents. That is to say, Greek culture – like all culture – was a *hybrid ensemble*, a radically impure and mongrel assemblage, that was a result of a series of invasions, waves of immigration, cultural magpieism and ethnic and racial mixing and crossing.

Contesting this picture of the African and Asiatic roots of classical civilization given in the Ancient Model, a picture that Bernal wants to revise and defend, the Aryan Model claims that Greek civilization was purely Indo-European and a consequence of either the autonomous genius of the pre-Hellenes – resulting in what is sometimes called 'The Greek Miracle', the transition from *mythos* to *logos* – or of alleged invasions from the north by shadowy Indo-European peoples. Bernal's polemical thesis is that the displacement of the Ancient Model by the Aryan Model was not so much driven by a concern for truth as by a desire for cultural and national purity which, for chauvinistic, imperialist and ultimately racist reasons, wanted to deny the influence of African or Semitic culture upon classical Greece, and by implication upon nineteenth-century northern Europe.

The influence of this Aryan Model in philosophy can be seen in the way the canon of the history of philosophy was transformed at the beginning of the nineteenth century.[8] Up until the end of the eighteenth century, the history of philosophy was habitually traced back to multiple so-called 'wisdom traditions' in Egyptian, Hebraic, Babylonian, Mesopotamian and Sumerian cultures. However, from the early 1800s, these traditions were generally excluded from the canonical definition of 'philosophy' either because of their allegedly mythical or pre-rational status or because they were largely anonymous, whereas the Greeks, like Thales, had names. The individual thinker rather than a body of thought becomes the criterion for philosophy. The consequence of this transformation of the canon is the belief that philosophy begins exclusively among the Greeks; which is also to say that philosophy is indigenous to the territory of Europe and is a result of Europe's unique spiritual geography – setting aside the unfortunate geographical location of certain pre-Socratics on the Ionian coast, which is usually explained away by calling them Greek colonies, an explanation that conceals a slightly anachronistic projection of the modern meaning of colonialism back into the ancient world.

The hegemony of the Aryan model can also be seen in the development of the discipline of Classics in England in the nineteenth century based on the German model of *Altertumswissenschaft*. Both are premissed upon a vision of the Greeks as quasi-divine, pure and authentic. What Bernal shows is the way in which this vision was complicit with certain northern European nationalisms and imperialisms (particularly in England and Germany), where contemplation of the Greeks was felt to be beneficial to the education of the future administrators of empire. It is on this point of a possible link between culture and imperialism that one can perhaps link Bernal's analysis to the wider problematic of the invention of tradition in the nineteenth century, as diagnosed by Eric Hobsbawm and others.[9] Hobsbawm shows that traditions were invented with extraordinary rapidity in this period by various states (notably Britain, France, Germany and the USA) in order to reinforce political authority and to ensure the smooth expansion of electoral democracy – for males at least.

More specifically, the traditions invented in this period – which in Britain were as grand as the fabrication of a modern monarchy complete with its jubilees and public processions, or as small as the invention of the postage stamp complete with image of the monarch as symbol of the nation; or, more widely, the proliferation of public statuary in France and Germany, with the ubiquitous image of Marianne in the former and Bismarck or Kaiser Wilhelm in the latter, or the spread of national anthems and national flags – culminate, claims Hobsbawm, in the emergence of *nationalism*. It was nationalism that became the quasi-Rousseauesque civic religion of the nineteenth century, and that, crucially, ensured social cohesion and patterns of national identification for the newly hegemonic middle classes, providing a model which could then be extended to the working classes, as and when they were allowed to enter the political process. The power of invented tradition consists in its ability to inculcate certain values and norms by sheer ritualization and imposed repetition, and to encourage the belief that those traditions are rooted in remotest antiquity, in the case of English nationalism in the sentimental myth of 'a thousand years of unbroken history'.

My concern, as someone who teaches philosophy, is the extent to which the version of tradition that is operative and goes largely unquestioned in much philosophical pedagogy and post-prandial parley (the belief in the exclusivity of the Greek beginning of the philosophy and the centrality and linear continuity of the European philosophical tradition) remains tributary to an invented historical paradigm, barely two centuries old, in which we have come to believe by sheer force of inculcation and repetition. Is the vision of philosophy offered by those, like myself, working on the geographical and spiritual edges of the Continental tradition, tributary to the Aryan model of ancient history and thereby complicit with a Hellenomania that buttresses an implicit European chauvinism? Indeed – although this is not my direct concern here – might one not be suspicious of the nationalist motives that lead to the retrieval within an Anglo-American tradition suspicious of the high metaphysics of 'Continentalists' of a specifically 'British' empiricist tradition in the 1950s to justify either an Anglicized logical positivism or Oxford ordinary language philosophy?[10] Or the self-conscious retrieval of pragmatism or transcendentalism as distinctively and independently *American* traditions in the work of thinkers as diverse as Stanley Cavell, Richard Rorty and Cornel West?[11]

All of which brings me to some critical questions: must the Greco-European story of the philosophical tradition – from Ancient Greece to modern northern Europe, from Platonism to its inversion in Nietzsche – be accepted as a legitimating narrative by philosophers, even by those who call themselves philosophers only in remembrance? Must philosophy be haunted by a compulsion to repeat its Greek origin? And if so, what about the possibility of other traditions in philosophy, other beginnings, other spiritual adventures? Could philosophy, at least in its European moment, ever be in the position to repeat another origin, announce another beginning, invent another tradition, or tell another story?

More gravely, and with reference to Bernal and also to David Theo Goldberg's *Racist Culture*,[12] is there perhaps a racist logic intrinsic to European philosophy which is founded on a central *paradox*, hinted at above in the coincidence of the geographical and the spiritual or the particular and the universal in Husserl? That is, philosophy tells itself a story which affirms the link between individuality and universality by embodying that link either in the person of Socrates or by defining the (European) philosopher as 'the functionary of humanity',[13] but where at the same time universality is delimited or confined within one particular tradition, namely the Greco-European adventure? Philosophy demands universal validity, or is defined by this demand for universal validity, yet it can only begin here, in Europe. We are who we are, and our supranational cultural identity as Europeans is founded in the universality of our claims and the particularity of our tradition; a tradition that, for Husserl, includes 'the English dominions' – that is, the USA – but does not extend to the Gypsies, 'who constantly wander across Europe',[14] like some living memory trace of Egypt. No other culture could be like us, because we have exclusive rights to philosophy, to the scientific-theoretical attitude.

In the light of Edward Said's work, such philosophical sentiments do not seem far from the core belief of imperialism: namely, that it is the responsibility or *burden* of the metropolitan powers to bring our universal values to bear on native peoples; that is, to colonize and transform other cultures according to our own world-view and to conceal oppression under the cloak of a mission. As Said puts it, why are most professional humanists unable or unwilling to make the connection between, on the one hand, the prolonged cruelty of practices such as slavery, colonialism, imperial subjection and racial oppression, and, on the other hand, the poetry, fiction and philosophy of the societies that engage in such practices?[15]

However, if we provisionally admit that there is a racist or imperialist logic in philosophy – and this is as much an accusation against myself as against Husserl – then could it ever be otherwise? That is, would it be conceivable for philosophy, or at least for 'we European philosophers', to be in a position to repeat another origin? Wouldn't this be precisely the fantasy of believing oneself to speak from the standpoint of the excluded without being excluded, of wishing to speak from the margins whilst standing at the centre – that is to say, the fantasy of a romantic anti-Hellenism or Rousseauesque anti-ethnocentrism? If so, where does this leave us? How do we proceed? As a way of sharing my perplexity, rather than resolving it, I shall try to illuminate these questions by taking a slightly different tack.

Sedimentation, reactivation, deconstruction
Tradition can be said to have two senses: (1) as something inherited or handed down without questioning or critical interrogation; (2) as something made or produced through a critical engagement with the first sense of tradition, as a de-traditionalization of tradition or an appeal to tradition that is in no way traditional. Of course, this distinction is artificial in so far as it could be claimed that the consciousness of tradition *as such* only occurs in the process of its destruction; that is to say, with the emergence of a *modernity* as that which places in question the evidence of tradition.

However, it is this second sense of tradition, the philosophical sense, that is shared – not without some substantial differences – by Husserl and Heidegger. For the Husserl of the *Crisis of the European Sciences*, the two senses of tradition correspond to the distinction between a *sedimented* and a *reactivated* sense of tradition. Sedimentation, which in one passage of the *Crisis* Husserl compares to 'traditionalization',[16] and which it is helpful to think of in geological terms as a process of settling or consolidation, would consist in the forgetfulness of the origin of a state of affairs. If we take Husserl's celebrated example of geometry, a forgetfulness of the origin of geometry leads to the forgetfulness of the historicity of such a discipline, of the genesis of the theoretical attitude expressed by geometry, and the way in which the theoretical attitude belongs to a determinate *Lebenswelt*. What is required to counter the sedimentation of tradition is the *reactivation* of the origin in what Husserl calls 'a teleological-historical reflection upon the origins of our critical scientific and philosophical situation'.[17] Thus, philosophy in the proper sense of the word – that is, transcendental phenomenology – would be the product of critical-historical reflection upon the origin of tradition and the (re)active making of a new sense of tradition against the pernicious naiveties of objectivism and naturalism.

Matters are not so different with the early Heidegger's conception of *Destruktion*, the deconstruction of the history of ontology, which is precisely not a way of burying the past in nullity, but rather of seeking the positive tendencies of the tradition. *Destruktion* is the production of a tradition as something made and fashioned through a process of repetition or retrieval, what Heidegger calls *Wiederholung*. The latter is the assumption of the tradition as a genuine repetition, where the original meaning of a state of affairs (the temporal determination of the meaning of Being, to pick an example at random) is retrieved through a critical historical reflection. In the period of *Being and Time*, Heidegger articulates the difference between a received and destroyed tradition in terms of the distinction between tradition (*Tradition*) and heritage (*Uberlieferung*), where the possibilities of authentic existing are delivered over and disclosed.[18]

It is important to point out that the target of Husserl's and Heidegger's reflections on tradition – and this is equally true of Hegel's reflection on the history of Spirit and Nietzsche's conception of nihilism – is not the past as such, but the *present*, and precisely the *crisis* of the present. The true crisis of the European sciences (Husserl) or distress of the West (Heidegger) is felt in the absence of distress: 'crisis, what crisis?' At the present moment, when the Western techno-scientific-philosophical adventure is in the process of globalizing itself and reducing humanity to the status of happy consumers wearing Ronald McDonald Happy Hats, we are called upon to reactivate the origin of the tradition from which that adventure sprang, and to do this precisely in order to awaken a sense of crisis and distress. Thus, a reactivated sense of the tradition permits us a critical, perhaps even *tragic*, consciousness of the present. As Gerald Bruns points out in an essay on tradition,

> On this line of thinking a good example of the encounter with tradition would be the story of Oedipus and his discovery of the truth of what has been said about him by seers, drunks, and oracles, not to mention what his own awakened memory can tell him. I mean that from a hermeneutical standpoint the encounter with tradition is more likely to resemble satire than allegory, unmasking the past rather than translation of the past. Or, as I've tried to suggest, the hermeneutical experience of what comes down to us from the past is structurally *tragic* rather than comic. It is an event that exposes us to our own blindness or the limits of our historicality and extracts from us *an acknowledgement of our belongingness to something different,* reversing what we had thought. It's just the sort of event that might drive us to put out our eyes.[19]

The Husserlian-Heideggerian sense of reactivated tradition which destroys the past in order to enable us to confront the present achieves this by consigning us, as Derrida puts it,[20] to the security of the Greek element with a knowledge and confidence which are not comfortable, but which permit us to experience crisis, distress and tragedy.

But we must proceed carefully here: on the one hand, it seems that the Husserlian–Heideggerian demand for the reactivation of a sedimented tradition is a necessary and unavoidable move; it is the step into philosophy and critique – that is, into the realization of tradition as something made or fashioned (re)actively as a way of confronting the tragedy of the present. However, on the other hand, the problem here is that the tradition that is retrieved is uniquely and univocally Greek; it is only a Greek tragedy that will permit us to confront the distress of the present. The way in which globalized techno-scientific ideology is to be confronted is by learning to speak Greek. My problem with this conception of tradition, as pointed out above, is that it might be said to presuppose implicitly an imperialist, chauvinist or racist logic. One recalls the remark that Heidegger was reported to have made to Karl Löwith in 1936, where he asserted that his concept of historicity was at the basis of his political engagement with National Socialism.[21]

It is with this problem in mind that I want to make an excursion into Derrida's 1964 essay 'Violence and Metaphysics', which deals with the thought of Emmanuel Levinas in so far as that work might be said to offer an ethical challenge to the Heideggerian and Husserlian conceptions of tradition. I think it is justified to claim that Derrida's thinking of tradition, at least in the early work, is dominated by the problem of closure, that play of belonging and non-belonging to the Greco-European tradition, which asserts both the necessity and the impossibility of such a tradition. Broadly stated, the problem of closure describes the duplicitous or ambiguous historical moment – *now* – when our language, institutions, conceptuality and philosophy itself show themselves to belong to a metaphysical (or logocentric) tradition that is theoretically exhausted, while at the same time searching for the breakthrough from that tradition.[22] The problem of closure describes the liminal situation of late modernity out of which the deconstructive problematic arises, and which, I believe, Derrida inherits from Heidegger. Closure is the double refusal of both remaining within the limits of the tradition and transgressing that limit. Closure is the hinge that articulates the double movement between the philosophical tradition and its other(s).

In 'Violence and Metaphysics', Derrida's general claim is that Levinas's project cannot succeed except by posing the question of closure, and that because this problem is not posed by Levinas in *Totality and Infinity*[23] his dream of an ethical relation to the

Other, which is linguistic but which exceeds the totalizing language of the tradition, remains just that, a *dream*. Derrida calls it the dream of pure empiricism that evaporates when language awakens. Levinas's discourse – and Derrida repeats this strategy with regard to all discourses that claim to exceed the tradition, those of Foucault, Artaud, Bataille or whoever – is caught, unbeknownst to itself, in an economy of betrayal, in so far as it tries to speak philosophically about that which cannot be spoken of philosophically.

Now, one conservative way of understanding the problem of closure is to argue that Derrida demonstrates the irresistibility of the claims of the Greco-Roman tradition and the impossibility of claiming any coherent position outside of this tradition – 'Hegel, Husserl and Heidegger are always right!' Although this interpretation is to some extent justified, it is by no means the whole story. The logic of closure works within a double bind; that is, if there is no outside to the philosophical tradition from which one can speak in order to criticize its inside, then, by the same token, there is no inside to the tradition from which one can speak without contamination by an outside. This is why closure describes the *liminal* situation of late modernity, and why it is a *double* refusal of both remaining within the limits of the tradition and transgressing those limits. Thus, there is no pure Greek inside to the European tradition that can be claimed as an uncontaminated origin in confronting the crisis. This, I believe, explains Derrida's strategy when confronted with a unified conception of tradition, when he works to show how any such conception is premissed upon certain exclusions which cannot be excluded. One thinks, for example, of his unpicking of Heidegger's reading of Nietzsche or of Foucault's reading of Descartes, or again in *Glas*, where the focus is on that which refuses the dialectical-historical logic of *Aufhebung*, and in *La carte postale*, where Heideggerian unity of the Greek sending of Being (*envoi de l'être*) is undermined and multiplied into a plurality of sendings (*envois*).

Tradition as a changing same

Turning from the philosophical tradition to tradition as such, the deconstructive thinking of tradition leaves one in the situation of the double bind discussed by Derrida in relation to European cultural identity:

> It is necessary to make ourselves the guardians of an idea of Europe, of a difference of Europe, *but* of a Europe that consists precisely in not closing off in its own identity and in advancing itself in an exemplary way toward what it is not, toward the other heading or heading of the other, indeed – and this is perhaps something else altogether – toward the other of the heading, which would be the beyond of this modern tradition, another border structure, another shore.[24]

Although such statements are problematic, not the least because Derrida tends to assume too much unity to the 'European culture' that is being deconstructed, it is clear that, for him, being European means obeying the irreducibility of a double duty (and why only a double duty? Why not a triple, quadruple or multiple duty?): to retrieve what Europe is or was, whilst at the same time opening Europe to the non-European, welcoming the foreigner in their alterity.

On a deconstructive account, then, any attempt to interpret tradition and culture in terms of a desire for unity, univocity and purity must be rigorously undermined in order to show how this desire is always already contaminated by that which it attempts to resist and exclude. If deconstruction has a sociology, then it is a sociology of impurity, of contamination. Culture and tradition are hybrid ensembles; they are the products of radically impure mixing and mongrelism. For example, being British today means recognizing the way in which the dominant English culture has been challenged and interpellated by previously dominated cultures, be they Scottish, Welsh, Irish, Afro-Caribbean or Asian. As Edward Said persuasively suggests, the consequence (and inverted triumph) of imperialism is the radical hybridity of culture, where histories and geographies are intertwined and overlapping, troubling any appeal to cultural and national exclusivity. Cultural identity (or perhaps one should say cultural self-differentiation) is relationally negotiated from among competing claims that make conflicting and perhaps awkward demands upon us.

Of course, one response to this conflict is racism, or the essentialist identification of race, culture and nation that is shared by white supremacism, Tebbit-esque British nationalism and oppositional Black nationalism. Needless to say, I do not think the latter are the most felicitous responses to the hybridity of culture and tradition; but the cultural-political task facing the Left, as I see it, lies in hegemonizing hybridity. As Said intimates, this can only entail an internationalist politics, which would try to hegemonize those oppositional movements – Said speaks of the *intifada,* the women's movement, and various ecological and cultural movements – that resist the global political cynicism of 'hurrah capitalism'. The vocation of the intellectual (whatever that much-maligned word means at this point and whoever it includes and excludes) consists in trying to focus and exacerbate these internationalist energies by being the exilic consciousness of the present through the practice of what Said calls *contrapuntal criticism.* The latter would be a form of critical-historical, genealogical or deconstructive reflection that would bring us to the recognition of the hybridity of tradition, culture and identity. Contrapuntal criticism, the comparative analysis of the overlapping geographies and intertwined histories of present cultural assemblages, would reveal hybrid ensembles as hybrid ensembles and not as unities or essences.

A recent and stunning example of such a contrapuntal criticism is Paul Gilroy's *The Black Atlantic.*[25] The basic polemical point of this book is to oppose any easy (and fatal) identification of race or culture with nation, where notions of racial purity function as legitimating discourses for nationalistic politics, for example within Black nationalism. In opposition to the latter, the black Atlantic is a transnational and intercultural framework that exceeds the borders of existing or Utopian nation-states;

it is a 'rhizomorphic, fractal structure' that opposes 'the ethnic absolutism that currently dominates black political culture'.[26] What is most impressive about Gilroy's book is the way in which the frequently reified and reifying discourse on race and roots is transposed onto a discourse of routes: a historical tableau of traversals and criss-crossings signifying upon a vast oceanic surface; a diaspora, which Gilroy courageously compares to Jewish experience, but where the potentially Mosaic discourse of roots and the promised land is maintained as a mosaic of routes. Gilroy engages in what we might call a spatialization of history, where the potential essentialism of historical narrative is problematized through a recourse to geography.

But it is Gilroy's conception of tradition that, for me at least, forms the centre of the book and that speaks directly to the concerns of this essay. Gilroy's basic historical thesis is that it is not possible to view slavery as an epiphenomenon within modernity, or as some residue of premodern barbarism carried over into modernity. Rather, using Zygmunt Bauman's terminology, slavery and black Atlantic experience as a whole constitute a distinct *counterculture* within modernity that complicates and disrupts certain versions of modernity's emancipatory project. The question here is whether there is room for a memory of slavery within modernity; that is to say, for Gilroy, is there room for a personalized, sublime and perhaps pre-discursive moment of liberatory creativity within modern experience? This emphasis upon creativity and aesthetic experience takes us to Gilroy's main contention, which is that black expressive culture, particularly music, is the means for articulating this counter-culture and for activating this memory. For Gilroy, black music is 'a cipher for the ineffable, sublime, pre-discursive and anti-discursive elements in black expressive culture'.[27] Black music is, in Gilroy's words, a *changing same*. Taking the examples of dubbing, scratching, sampling, mixing, borrowing and alluding that one can find in hip hop, rap, reggae and more recent musical hybrids, Gilroy argues against the notion of an authentic racial art and the conception of black music as a fixed dialogue between a thinking racial self and a stable racial community. In this sense, black musical expression exemplifies the relation between identity and difference that is constitutive of cultural traditions and tradition as such. Thus, cultural traditions, like music, cannot be reduced to 'the transmission of a fixed essence through time', but are rather a series of 'breaks and interruptions'. In this sense tradition itself 'may be a distinct though covert response to the destabilizing flux of the post-contemporary world'.[28]

Tradition is a changing same – that is, by insisting on the place of the memory of slavery within modernity, Gilroy disputes the supposed opposition between tradition and modernity, where, for example, black nationalists might claim the purity and authenticity of an African tradition in order to oppose the oppression of European and American modernity. This can be seen vividly in George G.M. James's attempt to show how the Greco-European tradition that culminates in modernity and racism is, in fact, a stolen legacy from a prior Egyptian and African civilization.[29] In contradistinction to such attempts, Gilroy fascinatingly proposes a *black modernism*; that is to say, a self-consciously modernist relation to tradition, where the specificity of the modern lies precisely in the consciousness of the problematic relation between the past and the present, between tradition and the individual talent. For the modernist, and the resonances with Derrida's notion of closure here become apparent, tradition is that to which we simultaneously belong and do not belong, what Gilroy suggestively calls 'a *non-traditional tradition*, an irreducibly modern, ex-centric, unstable and asymmetrical cultural ensemble that cannot be apprehended through the manichean logic of binary coding'.[30] Tradition is that duplicitous experience of continuity and rupture or of belonging and non-belonging that we have tried to discuss already in relation to Derrida. In response to this conception of tradition, what is required, according to Gilroy, is a Du Boisian experience of double consciousness, or simultaneous attraction and repulsion, where one recognizes the doubleness of one's identity as being shaped by modernity without feeling fully part of it.[31] An experience of modernity as something which one is both unable to believe in and unable to leave. In Toni Morrison's words, tradition, like the supple and evasive rhythms of funk, 'slaps and it embraces, it slaps and it embraces'.[32] Tradition is the story of overlapping geographies and intertwined histories, perhaps an ultimately non-narratable narrative that thwarts the desire for cultural, racial or philosophical purity.

Contrapuntal philosophy?
Drawing together the threads of this discussion into a conclusion, in addition to the two senses of tradition we introduced above, we are now in a position to add a third.

1. *Sedimented tradition*: where tradition is inherited as forgetfulness of origins, as pre-critical inheritance or pre-philosophical *doxa*, as the moral world-view that is inculcated into us by family, schooling, and so on.
2. *Reactivated tradition*: the Socratic moment of a critical, philosophical engagement with the first sense and the retrieval of an 'authentic' Greco-European tradition (histories and genealogies of Spirit, of nihilism, of Being's oblivion, of the forgetfulness of origin). This is the *philosophical* articulation of sedimented tradition, which one might conceive as a defining characteristic of modernity.
3. *Deconstructed tradition*: where the unity, univocity and linearity of the reactivated traditions would be critically questioned, and where the founding presuppositions of such traditions would be shown to be premised upon certain exclusions that are non-excludable, leaving us in the double bind of closure, and encouraging us to face up to the doubleness (or more than doubleness) or hybridity of tradition, culture and identity. This would be the contrapuntal or double consciousness of tradition as a changing same.

So, deconstruction provides a third sense to the concept of tradition, where the reactivated philosophical-critical sense of tradition – a perpetual modernity – is not rejected or set aside, but rather where its power for getting us to face the crisis of the present is both incorporated and – crucially – *contested*, where the philosophical tradition is forced to acknowledge the limits of its jurisdiction and the failure of its demand for exclusivity.

As I see it, the position I have argued for has three important consequences for those concerned with philosophy and its history: (i) The acceptance of the necessity of the Greco-European tradition as the linguistic and conceptual resource with which what 'we Europeans' (leaving the limits of this 'we' deliberately vague) call thinking takes place. (ii) The necessary failure of any attempt to constitute an uncontaminated Greco-European tradition, a pure inside that would presuppose the European exclusivity of philosophy and the privileging of the European over the non-European. The identity of the European tradition is always impurely traced and contaminated by the non-European other that it tries unsuccessfully to exclude. (iii) The acceptance of the impossibility of a pure outside to the European tradition for 'we Europeans', the irretrievability of an other origin, the fantasy of a European anti-Eurocentrism, of anti-ethnocentrism, of romantic anti-Hellenism, of all post-Rousseauesque versions of what Derrida calls *nost-Algérie*.

Tradition, culture and identity are irreducibly hybrid ensembles. The purpose of critical-historical, genealogical or deconstructive reflection – contrapuntal criticism – is to bring us to a recognition of these ensembles *as* ensembles. On analogy with the latter, I wonder – and this is the tentative expression of a (Utopian) hope rather than the statement of a programme – whether it would be possible to study and practise philosophy contrapuntally. That is, to philosophize out of an experience of the utter contingency of historical being (and being as such in so far as the latter is constituted historically) and with reference to the intertwining and overlapping of those histories and geographies that make up something like a philosophical canon or tradition. As I see it, this would mean studying the history of philosophy not as a unified, universal, linear, narratable and geographically delimitable (i.e. European) procession stretching from the Athens of Socrates to Western late modernity, but rather as a series of constructed, contingent, invented and possible non-narratable contrapuntal ensembles that would disrupt the authority of the hegemonic tradition. Can one conceive of the philosophical tradition as a series of contrapuntal ensembles? I have two closing suggestions in this regard. First, might it be possible to conceive of the history of philosophy in terms of what Derrida calls with reference to Levinas *seriature*; that is, an interrupted series, or series of interruptions that would constitute less a teleologically destined succession of epochs or figures of spirit and more a multiplicity of sendings in the manner performed in *La carte postale*?[33] Second, might the history of philosophy be approached *geographically* as a series of plateaux in the manner of Deleuze and Guattari; that is, as a multiplicity of dated, stratified assemblages?[34] Might not such a contrapuntal consciousness of the philosophical tradition have the potential to transform philosophy into a practice of radical reflection rooted in the acceptance and affirmation of hybridity as the condition of possibility for philosophy's historical emergence and its future flourishing?

Notes

1. These thoughts were first assembled for a conference on the theme of de-traditionalization held at Lancaster University in July 1993. They were extensively reworked for a conference on the work of Edward Said held at Warwick University in March 1994. But their real source lies in conversations with Robert Bernasconi over the past few years and, more recently, with Homi Bhaba. I am particularly grateful for the careful comments of Jonathan Rée and Peter Osborne, although I don't think I have fully responded to either of their criticisms.
2. See G.W.F. Hegel, 'Tragedy and the Impiety of Socrates', in *Hegel on Tragedy*, ed. A. and H. Paolucci, Harper & Row, New York, 1975, pp. 345-66; F. Nietzsche, *The Birth of Tragedy*, trans. W. Kaufmann, Vintage, New York, 1967; and 'The Problem of Socrates', in *Twilight of the Idols*, trans. R.J. Hollingdale, Penguin, Harmondsworth, 1968, pp. 29-34.
3. Hegel, 'Tragedy and the Impiety of Socrates', p. 364.
4. René Descartes, 'Meditations on First Philosophy', in *The Philosophical Writings of Descartes*, vol. II, trans. J. Cottingham et al., Cambridge University Press, Cambridge, 1984, p. 12.
5. Jacques Derrida, 'Violence and Metaphysics', in *Writing and Difference*, trans. A. Bass, Routledge, London and New York, 1978, p. 81.
6. In Edmund Husserl, *The Crisis of the European Sciences and Transcendental Phenomenology: An Introduction to Phenomenological Philosophy*, trans. D. Carr, Northwestern University Press, Evanston IL, 1970, pp. 269-99.
7. Martin Bernal, *Black Athena: The Afroasiatic Roots of Classical Civilization*, Volume 1: *The Fabrication of Ancient Greece 1785-1985*, Vintage, London, 1991 [1987].
8. I rely here on Robert Bernasconi's article 'Heidegger and the Invention of the Western Philosophical Tradition', *Journal of the British Society for Phenomenology*, vol. 26, no. 3, 1995, pp. 240-54.
9. *The Invention of Tradition*, ed. E. Hobsbawm and T. Ranger, Cambridge University Press, Cambridge, 1983; see esp. pp. 1-14, 263-307.
10. See Jonathan Rée, 'English Philosophy in the Fifties', *Radical Philosophy* 65, Autumn 1993, p. 15.
11. In this regard, see especially Cornel West, *The American Evasion of Philosophy*, Macmillan, London, 1989.
12. David Theo Goldberg, *Racist Culture, Philosophy and the Politics of Meaning*, Blackwell, Oxford, 1993, p. 6. See also in this regard Harry M. Bracken, 'Philosophy and Racism', *Philosophia* 8, 1978, pp. 241-60. In an innovative and provocative discussion of racism and empiricism, it is argued that Lockean (and, to a lesser extent, Humean) empiricism facilitates 'the expression of racist ideology *and* that Locke was actively involved in formulating policies (compatible with those theories) and encouraging practices (e.g. the African slave trade and perpetual racial slavery) which were racist in character' (p. 255). In contrast to empiricism, and by way of a covert defence of the Cartesianism of Chomsky's linguistic theory, Bracken argues that Cartesianism contains 'a modest conceptual barrier to racism' (p. 254).
13. Husserl, *The Crisis of the European Sciences*, p. 17.
14. Ibid., p. 273.
15. Edward Said, *Culture and Imperialism*, Chatto & Windus, London, 1993, p. xiv.
16. Husserl, *The Crisis of the European Sciences*, p. 52.
17. Ibid., p. 3.
18. Martin Heidegger, *Being and Time*, trans. J. Macquarrie and E. Robinson, Blackwell, Oxford, 1962; German edn, p. 395; English edn, p. 447.
19. Gerald L. Bruns, *Hermeneutics Ancient and Modern*, Yale University Press, New Haven CT and London, 1992, p. 204 (my emphasis).
20. Derrida, 'Violence and Metaphysics', p. 82.
21. Karl Löwith, 'My Last Meeting with Heidegger in Rome, 1936', in R. Wolin, ed., *The Heidegger Controversy*, MIT Press, Cambridge MA and London, 1993, p. 142.
22. For a detailed discussion of the problem of closure in Derrida, see my *The Ethics of Deconstruction*, Blackwell, Oxford, 1992, pp. 59-106. For an illuminating discussion of tradition in Derrida in comparison with Walter Benjamin, see Alexander Garcia Düttmann, 'Tradition and Destruction', in A. Benjamin and P. Osborne, eds, *Walter Benjamin's*

Philosophy, Routledge, London and New York, 1993, pp. 33-58.
23. I argue that matters become much more complicated in Levinas's later work, *Otherwise than Being or Beyond Essence*; in this regard, see my 'Eine Vertiefung der ethischen Sprache und Methode', *Deutsche Zeitschrift für Philosophie*, vol. 42, no. 4, 1994, pp. 643-51.
24. Jacques Derrida, *The Other Heading*, trans. P.-A. Brault and M. Naas, Indiana University Press, Bloomington, 1992, p. 29.
25. Paul Gilroy, *The Black Atlantic: Modernity and Double Consciousness*, Verso, London, 1993.
26. Ibid., pp. 4-5.
27. Ibid., p. 120.
28. Ibid., p. 101.
29. George G.M. James, *Stolen Legacy: Greek Philosophy Is Stolen Egyptian Philosophy*, Africa World Press, Trenton NJ, 1992 [1954].
30. Gilroy, *The Black Atlantic*, p. 198 (my emphasis).
31. Incidentally, this is also how Cornel West defines the situation of the prophetic critic, in *Keeping Faith: Philosophy and Race in America*, Routledge, London and New York, 1993, p. xxi.
32. Ibid., p. 78.
33. See Jacques Derrida, 'At this very moment in this work here I am', trans. R. Berezdivin, in R. Bemasconi and S. Critchley, eds, *Re-Reading Levinas*, Indiana University Press, Bloomington, 1991; and J. Derrida, *The Post Card*, trans. A. Bass, University of Chicago Press, Chicago, 1987.
34. Gilles Deleuze and Félix Guattari, *A Thousand Plateaus: Capitalism and Schizophrenia*, trans. B. Massumi, (Athlone, London, 1988. Although, with regard to Deleuze and Guattari, it should be noted that they also insist upon the exclusivity of the Greek beginning to philosophy: 'If we really want to say that philosophy originates with the Greeks, it is because the city, unlike the empire or state, invents the agon as the rule of society of "friends", of the community of free men as rivals (citizens)' (*What is Philosophy?* trans. G. Burchell and H. Tomlinson [Verso, London, 1994], p. 9; and cf. pp. 43-4 and ch. 3, 'Geophilosophy', pp. 85-113). Although Deleuze and Guattari insist upon the contingency of the historical origin of philosophy in Greece, and emphasize the crucial role that migrants and foreigners played in the formation and articulation of Greek culture, their representation of philosophy and the ancient world is pervaded by the power of invented tradition as presented in this essay. For example, their representation of the space of the *polis* as the pre-philosophical plane of immanence and the condition of possibility for philosophical concept creation would seem, in a manner that is absolutely traditional, to link the historical emergence of philosophy to the political form of democracy in opposition to the alleged hierarchy and transcendence of all forms of imperial or theological space. But this is precisely to forget that the space of the Greek *polis* was, at once, powerfully imperial and theological. In this context, I would merely like to signal my intention here of continuing the work begun in this essay in a critical discussion of Deleuze and Guattari's notion of 'geophilosophy'.

CRITIQUE IN THE EXPANDED FIELD

13 Marx's Eurocentrism: Postcolonial studies and Marx scholarship

KOLJA LINDNER

> The English jackasses need an enormous amount of time to arrive at an even approximate understanding of the real conditions of ... conquered groups.
>
> Karl Marx, 1879

A great deal of ink has already been spilled on the question of Marx's Eurocentrism. The debate turns on his relationship to colonialism, the conception of Asian societies which informs it, and his theory of social formations and social progress. Special attention has been paid to Marx's 1853 article on British colonialism in India. In the field of Marxian studies per se, approaches to the subject have been either apologetic or strictly philological. A few exceptions aside, comprehensive treatments of the theme written from an anti-authoritarian (*herrschaftskritisch*)[1] standpoint are non-existent, and neither does there exist a systematic examination of Eurocentrism in Marx's work as a whole. The chief contribution of Marx scholarship here resides in the ongoing publication of the scholarly edition of his writings, which provides the basis for a balanced discussion of the subject.

The question has also been addressed in postcolonial studies. Here, critical voices dominate. Marx is said to have defended a 'Eurocentric model of political emancipation that consistently ignores the experiences of colonized subjects in non-Western societies' and to have 'failed to develop his studies of India and Africa into a fully elaborated analysis of imperialism'; his analyses neglect 'disenfranchised groups such as colonised subjects'.[2]

Edward Said, whose study of Orientalism has become a classic in the field, goes so far as to accuse Marx of a racist orientalization of the non-Western world.[3] There accordingly exists a powerful tendency in postcolonial studies to dismiss Marx as a Eurocentric or even Orientalist thinker, the author of a philosophy of history.

Against this backdrop, I attempt, in the pages that follow,[4] to contribute to a dialogue between these two strands of Marxian studies, on the one hand, and postcolonial studies, on the other. I begin by considering the postcolonial critique of Eurocentrism, concretizing it in an analysis of one of Marx's sources, François Bernier's Indian travelogue. My aim is to show, among other things, what Marxian studies can learn from postcolonial studies. I also trace Marx's treatment of 'non-Western' societies through his life's work, in so far as it is available to us. (In Marx, and therefore in the present essay as well, 'non-Western' is used as a synonym for 'precolonial' or 'precapitalist'.) It will appear that Marx's work evolves in this respect. In sum, he gradually comes to reject Eurocentric assumptions. Thus this article also constitutes an objection to the often hasty dismissal of Marx in postcolonial studies.

Marx's abiding theoretical preoccupation with various (non-European) forms of (pre-capitalist) land ownership plays a particularly important role in his progressive abandonment of Eurocentrism. Since Marx himself never journeyed to the regions of the non-Western world he wrote about, and never carried out systematic empirical research on them, his knowledge derives in part from massively Eurocentric sources, above all British, such as travel writing, parliamentary reports and theoretical treatises. On the view prevailing in this literature, there was no private land ownership in Asia.[5] This is a false, Orientalist notion that has since been thoroughly discredited by historians. Charting Marx's gradual turn from Eurocentrism therefore also involves determining the degree to which he freed himself from these notions, the stock-in-trade of 'the English jackasses'.

The concept of Eurocentrism

It makes sense, given our objectives here, to define Eurocentrism. It has four dimensions:

1. A form of ethnocentrism distinguished not only by the presumption that Western societies are superior, but also by the attempt to justify this presumption in rational, scientific terms. This world-view goes hand in hand with the aspiration to subject the whole world to such rationality.[6] The discourse in question treats Western Europe as the political, economic, theoretical and, sometimes, *racial* centre of the world.[7]
2. An 'Orientalist' way of looking at the non-Western world which has less to do with the real conditions prevailing there than with what Said calls the 'European Western Experience'. The world as a whole is imagined from a regional standpoint. The measure used in compiling impressions of the extra-European world conveyed by diverse genres of writing is furnished not by reality, but by a Western European conceptual system. There emerges, as an expression of economic, political, cultural and military domination, an institutionally sanctioned geopolitical discourse which creates these 'other' regions of the world in the first place ('the Orient' in Said's analysis; 'Asia' in Marx's) by means of homogenization, co-optation, and so forth. Their inhabitants are transformed into distorted mirror images of the European self-image.
3. A conception of development which by means of a 'false universalism ... uncritically makes the cultural and historical patterns of capitalist Western Europe the established standards for all human history and culture'.[8] With this in mind, it is sometimes taken for granted, or even demanded, that the whole world should develop, or be developed, on the Western European model.
4. Effacement of non-European history, or, more precisely, of its influence on European development. What is known as 'global history' seeks to counteract this by focusing on the interaction

between different regions of the world. It thus denies Europe an exclusive position, transforming or 'provincializing' its universalistic conceptions with the help of particularistic history. The premiss here is that 'ideological and political conflict had ... achieved a global scale, *before* economic uniformities were established across much of the world.'[9] Thus the suppression of the 'interweaving of the European with the extra-European world' – that is, of the 'history of [their] intertwining' – can be regarded as Eurocentric.[10]

A thin line separates the first two dimensions of Eurocentrism from racism. The border is crossed when the ethnocentric assumptions are articulated in a discourse about essential differences. The other two dimensions generally culminate in an authoritarian universalization of the particular.

Marx's 1853 essays on India

Marx produced his famous essays on India in the framework of a series of articles that he wrote in the early 1850s for the *New York Daily Tribune* (*NYDT*). One hallmark of these essays is Marx's perception of India's social structure as static. India's climatic conditions, on his analysis, necessitated an artificial irrigation system, which, as a result of the low level of social development and the sheer size of the country, could be created and maintained only by a central state authority. It was characterized by a unity between agriculture and manufactures (handicrafts) that limited the development of productivity. Such a system discouraged the emergence of urban centres. Marx regards the structure and isolation of India's village communities as 'the solid foundation of oriental despotism' and of the country's 'stagnatory life'.[11] Finally, he proceeds on the assumption that the state, in this 'Asiatic society', is 'the real landlord' thanks to complicated tax and property laws.[12]

Marx's condemnation of British colonialism is based on this conception of the structure of Indian society. It is ambivalent:

England, he says, 'has to fulfill a double mission in India: one destructive, the other regenerating the annihilation of old Asiatic society, and the laying of the material foundations of Western society in Asia'.[13] Manifestly, he sets out from the premiss that colonialism has promoted India's development. The consolidation of the Indian railway system,[14] on his analysis, could facilitate further development of the overtaxed irrigation system.[15]

He further assumes that the introduction of steam-driven machinery or scientific methods of production would induce the separation of agriculture and manufactures in the country.[16] Moreover, India's integration into the world market, Marx says, would rescue it from its isolation. Finally, British rule, in his estimation, has led to the emergence of a system based on private land ownership.[17] In short, the economic bases of the Indian village system are disintegrating, and colonial intervention has led to 'the only social revolution ever heard of in Asia'.[18]

To be sure, Marx's ambivalent picture of colonialism includes the idea that India can profit from technological transfer only on condition that it cast off the colonial yoke, or that 'in Great Britain itself the now ruling classes shall have been supplanted by the industrial proletariat'.[19] Furthermore, Marx by no means ignores the colonial power's selfish approach to the development of productive forces in India or the destructive aspects of colonialism. It remains the case, on his view, that 'whatever may have been the crimes of England she was the unconscious tool of history in bringing about that revolution';[20] in other words, in creating 'the material basis of the new world'.[21]

Marx's articles on India are Eurocentric in all of the senses defined above. In the first place, they one-sidedly treat Europe as a society with a superior technology, infrastructure, legal system, and so on. In this connection, Marx attaches special importance to private land ownership. His assumption is that European property relations make social progress possible in consequence of class divisions and, thus, the class conflicts that go hand in hand with them. The situation in India, by contrast, is marked, in his view, by despotism and stagnation. This description of Indian village communities is deceptive, in so far as it presents them as stagnant, self-enclosed entities which, isolated and lacking all communication with the outside world, stood over against a king who was sole owner of all land; it masks the fact that these communities were themselves traversed by class divisions. There was, moreover, unmistakable development of the productive forces as well as commodity production in precolonial India, whose social structure must therefore be regarded as conflictual and dynamic.[22]

In line with the third dimension of Eurocentrism, Marx elevates a particularistic development to the rank of the universal: the creation of a 'Western social order in Asia' is, he assumes, a necessary station on the path to the creation of a classless society, a path he conceives as human 'destiny'.[23] This is problematic not only because India's indigenous potential for development is not taken into account, but also because its social structure is perceived exclusively as a barrier to progress or, at any rate, as standing in need of radical transformation. Moreover, the overestimation of the development of Western Europe is predicated on the highly speculative assumption that European conditions could be transferred intact to India and would thus serve as the point of departure for a revolutionary movement there. Marx fails to see that, in international capitalism, the different regions of the world are integrated into the world market asymmetrically, or are confronted with different possibilities and perspectives for development.[24] It is less a question of 'an inevitable transformation' of pre-capitalist modes and their transformation by capitalist relations' than of 'an articulation between different modes of production, structured in some relation of dominance'.[25]

With respect to the fourth dimension of Eurocentrism, Marx's articles on India must be regarded as Eurocentric in the sense brought out by students of global history. While it is true that Marx emphasizes the interaction between different regions of the world, his analyses are confined to the economic sphere. Moreover, they are, with rare exceptions, one-sided, since, as a rule, he is interested only in the effects that integration into the world market has on non-European countries, not on the European countries themselves. Intertwined histories outside the economic sphere, as elaborated in the Indian case by, say, Chakrabarty, are quite simply nowhere to be found in Marx.[26]

Marx's Eurocentric sources: François Bernier

In what follows, I pay particular attention to the second dimension of Eurocentrism, 'Orientalizing the Oriental'.[27] Marx takes over the Eurocentrism of his sources without reflection. Critical examination of those sources is a task that Marx scholarship has, generally speaking, neglected, a deficiency particularly conspicuous when it comes to travel writing, about which Said says: 'From travelers' tales, and not only from great institutions like the various India companies, colonies were created and ethnocentric perspectives secured.'[28] Discussion of Marx's source material, even by writers concerned with his Eurocentrism, has hitherto focused on his use of classical political philosophy and political economy.[29] This is puzzling, not only because of the significance of travel writing for the development of the Western imagination, but also because Marx writes, in a 2 June 1853 letter to Engels (three weeks before the *NYDT* published the first of his articles on India), that 'on the subject of the growth of eastern cities one could hardly find anything more brilliant, comprehensive or striking than *Voyages contenant la description des états du Grand Mogol*, etc. by old François Bernier (for 9 years Aurangzeb's physician).'[30] It is, moreover, this source which Marx takes as justification for his conclusion that the non-existence of private property in Asia is 'the real *clef*, even to the eastern heaven'.[31] Finally, Engels, in his response to Marx four days later, himself cites Bernier in defence of the thesis that the non-existence of private ownership of land is due to the climate and to soil conditions,[32] a thesis that Marx adopts, in part verbatim, in his first article on India. I shall consider Bernier's travelogue in some detail, not only because it has so far been neglected by Marx scholars, but also because such analysis offers, in my view, an example of the way that Marxian studies could apply insights gleaned from postcolonial studies to a comprehensive study of Marx's Eurocentrism partially based on a critical examination of his sources.

François Bernier (1620–1688) was a French doctor and physicist who spent a total of twelve years in India. After returning to France in 1670, he wrote an influential travel narrative that was translated into several European languages and saw several editions.[33] It was one of the main sources of the widespread belief, shared by Western thinkers such as Montesquieu and Hegel, in the existence of something known as 'Oriental despotism'.[34] Bernier contended that, in India, only the monarchs owned the land, deriving the revenues they lived on from it.

> The king is sole proprietor of all the land in his kingdom. Whence, by a certain necessity, the fact that capital cities such as Delhi or Agra derive their income almost entirely from the militia and are accordingly obliged to follow the king when he leaves for the countryside for a certain period.[35]

This thesis is an Orientalist projection par excellence. It is rooted in a subjective impression of the superiority of the European social and legal order and has nothing to do with real conditions in India. The 'jackass', even if he is French rather than English in the case to hand, has not arrived at even an 'approximate' understanding of 'real conditions': numerous historical analyses have established that, in precolonial India, land ownership was not centralized and landed property could be alienated – that is, that private land ownership existed.[36] The denial of private land ownership is only one aspect of the Orientalist discourse that traverses Bernier's travel account from one end to the other. His description of superstition in India is another. Bernier depicts it as a determining feature of Indian society: Indians consult astrologers, he says, 'in all their undertakings'.[37] Stuurman argues that this is not a 'straightforward affirmation of European superiority', inasmuch as Bernier also rails against European superstition and makes fun of Western missionaries.[38] I would counter that Bernier's Orientalism makes itself felt nonetheless. In the passage just cited, for example, he does not attribute superstition to certain social circles alone, inevitably leaving European readers with the impression that Indian society in general is characterized by a mental darkness distinguishing it from its European counterpart. Marx's depiction of India as a stagnant country incapable of progress, whose modernity does not stem from internal factors, has one of its sources here.

Bernier's text displays other Orientalist features. I agree with Stuurman that, although *race* is not a structuring category in his travelogue, whiteness is an omnipresent subtext in it. Bernier's descriptions often spill over into manifest essentialization. Thus we read that Indian craftsmen are 'extremely lazy by nature',[39] that a majority of Indians are 'of a slow, indolent disposition',[40] and so on. Such essentialization goes hand in hand with typically Orientalist outbursts of enthusiasm about 'this little earthly paradise, the Indies'.[41] Bernier does not, however, merely acquit himself of these mandatory Orientalist exercises; he sets himself apart from the Orientalist crowd by announcing that he knows no Sanskrit.[42] The grounds for his broad generalizations about India thus remains rather obscure; they are not, in any case, based on native sources. In the context of the nascent European colonization of India, the objective of which was to bend the colonized regions to European interests, this is hardly surprising. We must here take into account the tendency, established by postcolonial studies, to treat classical autochthonous texts with suspicion as sources of knowledge, relying instead on one's own observations, on the assumption that 'the Orient' is incapable of speaking for itself.[43] It is an integral part of the comprehensive colonialist undertaking.

Another point in Bernier's narrative that has received some attention in postcolonial studies should be mentioned here:

Western discourses about the burning alive of widows in India. Without trying to justify this custom, Gayatri Spivak has shown how these discourses limit subaltern women's capacity to speak and act.[44] One can indeed see, in Bernier's travelogue, how his intervention in favour of a widow menaced with immolation is not only of a piece with the depiction of her as hysterical or pathological, thereby constricting subaltern female agency, but is also bound up with a denunciation of the 'barbaric customs' of this 'idolatrous people'.[45] Thus the rescue of an Indian widow becomes, for the Frenchman, a 'signifier for the establishment of a good society'[46] – a discourse which, in the final analysis, imposes still heavier ideological constraints on these women than the colonial situation itself already has.[47]

Thus Bernier's narrative can be summarily described as an 'imaginative examination of things Oriental'.[48] Like any other Orientalist discourse, his descriptions not only project a picture of the 'other', but also help construct the European self-image. Thus 'superstitious', 'stagnant' India stands over against the 'disenchanted' Western societies of the day, marked by dramatic social upheavals. The fantasy of Indian 'indolence' and the Indian 'paradise' transforms the country into a foil for early capitalist Western Europe, characterized by diligence, dynamism and self-denial. The ultimate effect is to contrast 'Asian despotism' with the 'enlightened Absolutism' of Europe and 'barbaric customs' with the 'good society'.[49]

In short, Marx would have done well to subject his source to a critical examination rather than distilling a central element of his own assessment of India's social structure from it. Despite this failing, however, his differences from Bernier leap to the eye. He never engages in essentialization. He does not cross the thin line between Orientalism and racism. While it is true that, as in his treatment of colonialism, he takes certain 'facts' from Orientalist or racist sources and incorporates them into a discourse on progress that is in many respects Eurocentric,[50] the fact remains that he does not reproduce the essentialization informing such sources. This problematic procedure, which is certainly quite naive, shows that Marx's discussion of colonialism and slavery by no means unfolds in a generally anti-authoritarian context; an approach of that sort would attribute a place of its own to the extremely complex question of racism, which can by no stretch of the imagination be reduced to the question of the division of labour.[51] Nevertheless, in the light of the foregoing, the affirmation that Marx himself is a racist[52] seems to me unwarranted.

At any event, there can be no doubt that the Marx of the early 1850s had at his disposition neither a discriminating, non-Eurocentric perspective on colonialism nor sources that might have helped him to develop an accurate understanding of precolonial societies (one capable of realistically focusing attention on the social upheavals precipitated by colonialism). In the 1860s and beyond, he produced a more finely shaded account of these societies. In what follows, I shall accordingly try to indicate how he went about elaborating a more carefully drawn picture of colonial expansion, especially in his journalism of the 1860s, thereby breaking with at least two dimensions of Eurocentrism. I shall then look briefly at certain Orientalist themes in the critique of political economy.

India versus Ireland: the beginnings of Marx's turn from Eurocentrism

There is disagreement as to whether Marx's study of British colonialism in India or, rather, Ireland first led him to take a more carefully balanced position on the question. Pranav Jani contends that Marx overcame his Eurocentrism in studying the 1857–59 Indian uprising. It is true that he acknowledges that the rebellion was partially justified[53] and mentions the difficulty of grasping Indian conditions using 'Western concepts'. There is, however, little basis for Jani's claim[54] that Marx's initial acceptance of British assumptions about the passivity of the colonized gradually gives way, in his articles on the revolt, to the insight that the subaltern Indians were capable of taking independent action, the more so as these 1857/1858 articles are, unlike those of 1853, primarily intended to convey information, and do not contain nearly as much theoretization, speculation and pointed political analysis. Marx's viewpoint in the late 1850s is basically military and strategic[55] – a perspective buttressed by the stereotypical portrayal of the Indian rebels and the evocation of a general Western superiority in Engels's texts on the subject. *Pace* Jani, the commentaries on the British colonial power's military logistics and battle plans are hardly marked by a critical attitude, let alone a shift in perspective towards anti-Eurocentrism. Reinhard Kößler has, moreover, rightly pointed out that, in Marx's estimation, the rebellion was made possible in the first place by Britain's creation of an indigenous army. Thus resistance to colonization is supposed to have become possible only as a result 'of innovations set in motion by the colonization process, not as a prolongation of class struggles in the colonized countries themselves or thanks to specific structures forged by traditional social conditions and the revolutionary effects of the penetration of capitalism'.[56]

It is difficult, in this light, to regard Marx's texts on the Indian uprising as steps on the way to his break with Eurocentrism. However, I share Bipan Chandra's view[57] that, by the 1860s at the latest, Marx (and Engels) had developed an awareness of the underdevelopment due to colonialism or the overall colonial context. They did so in connection with Ireland. Thus Marx depicts the suppression of industry in Ireland,[58] the systematic elimination of markets for Irish agriculture, the outbreak of famines and rebellions, and Irish emigration to North America and Australia.[59] The emphasis on the British use of violence, however, influenced his shift of perspective less decisively than did his new assessment of the prospects for development opened up by colonialism. In the case of India, Marx observes that destruction and progress go hand in hand; this explains his ambivalent appreciation of England's 'double mission'. The example of Ireland, in contrast, shows him that colonialism ultimately brings the colonies' asymmetrical integration into the world market, while actually throwing up barriers before the establishment of a capitalist mode of production, rather than promoting it. Ireland, says Marx, is the victim of murderous superexploitation – military, agricultural and demographic.[60] Essential to the accumulation process in the 'motherland' is Ireland's colonial status, not its socio-economic development.

Interestingly, Marx draws political consequences from this insight; he concludes that, in order 'to accelerate the social development in Europe', social struggle will have to be waged in Ireland.[61] He goes still further, positing that 'the decisive blow against the English ruling classes (and it will be decisive for the workers' movement all over the world) cannot be delivered in England, but *only in Ireland*.'[62] It is true that Marx's perspective here is still partially marked by teleological notions of progress. Nevertheless, in contrast to India, said to be capable of throwing off the colonial yoke only if 'in Great Britain itself the now ruling classes shall have been supplanted by the industrial proletariat', political upheaval is assigned, in the Irish case, decisive importance for revolutionary developments in the country of the colonizers itself. It is therefore no exaggeration, in my opinion, to speak of a 'revision' of Marx's positions on colonialism or national liberation by the latter half of the 1860s at the latest.[63] It is precisely this shift in Marx's position that leads to his first break with Eurocentrism.[64] He undoubtedly continues to regard England as a superior society, but he no longer credits English colonialism with initiating progressive developments in other regions of the world. Thus the universalization of the 'Western social order' which the example of India was supposed to illustrate begins to crumble. Finally, Marx now conceives of the interaction between various areas of the world differently: it is no longer thought of in strictly economic or linear terms.

Orientalist themes in Marx's *Critique of Political Economy*

Marx's critique of political economy is the most substantial and most fully elaborated part of his work. An examination of all four dimensions of Eurocentrism in the countless manuscripts and publications that make it up would constitute a research project in its own right. I shall here consider only the persistence of Orientalist themes in it.

Marx's relatively unsystematic reflections on precapitalist societies in *Grundrisse* (in the section on 'Forms which precede capitalist production',[65] are almost as well known as his 1853 articles on India. Central assumptions of the 'Asiatic conception' are to be found here, notably the idea that there is no private land ownership and that social stagnation is due to the 'unity of agriculture and manufactures'.[66] The latter factor is said to account for the fact that a transformation of property relations can be effected only 'by means of altogether external influences'[67] such as colonial rule. Furthermore, cities in Asia, 'where the monarch appears as the exclusive proprietor of the agricultural surplus product ... [, are] at bottom nothing more than wandering encampments' or 'royal camps'.[68] Not long after, in *A Contribution to the Critique of Political Economy*, Marx formulated this 'Asiatic conception' still more sharply. Although this 1859 text contains no comparably detailed remarks on precapitalist societies, the Introduction deploys the much discussed concept of the 'Asiatic mode of production', which is here presented in terms that are anything but clear. In the early 1860s as well, in *Theories of Surplus-Value* or, more precisely, his debate with Richard Jones, Marx assumes that land was owned exclusively by the state in Asia[69] and that there was 'unity of agriculture and industry' in the 'Asian communal system'. Here, too, he makes a positive allusion to 'Dr. Bernier, who compares the Indian towns to army camps'.[70] Finally, we find in *Capital* itself comments about the 'blending of agriculture and handicrafts',[71] on which Marx blames the stagnation of Indian rural communes. Similarly, we find a passage about the state whose power is based on 'the regulation of the water supply',[72] in whose hands land ownership is supposedly concentrated. It therefore falls to England, Marx says, 'to disrupt these small economic communities'[73] by expanding trade.

In *Capital*, one also comes across the very naive notion, also already defended by Marx in 1853, that the railway technology introduced by the English in India had acquired a dynamic of its own, was being appropriated by Indians, and had set in motion the construction of modern industry and disintegration of the caste system.

Despite the persistence of Orientalist themes in the critique of political economy, two mitigating factors, it seems to me, should be stressed. First, Marx's analysis of precapitalist societies within the framework of that economic critique is quite contradictory. He neither makes an unambiguous distinction between 'primitive communism' and the 'Asiatic mode of production', nor clearly defines the latter.[74] Furthermore, it is impossible to situate the social relations Marx describes historically or geographically. Second, it is anything but obvious what influence these Orientalist themes have on the categories that Marx mobilizes in his economic critique, categories supposed, after all, to depict 'the inner organization of the capitalist mode of production', 'its ideal average'.[75] No hasty conclusions should be drawn here – they would be just as inappropriate as the simplistic defence which has it that the critique of political economy evinces 'a significant shift in the perception of tradition village communities', 'from a negative assessment of their isolation and stagnation to a positive appreciation of their socially integrative power and endurance'.[76] We would be better advised to maintain, with Amady A. Dieng, that Marx by no means possessed 'sufficient knowledge about the colonies of Africa, Asia, Latin America, or the Pacific Islands'.[77] It must, however, be pointed out that the 'jackasses' whose 'wisdom' Marx worked like a beaver to assimilate bear much of the blame for his, at best, 'approximate understanding of the real conditions' of non-Western societies.

The accelerating turn from Eurocentrism in Marx's late work
Marx's late work represents a still largely unpublished and, in that sense, truncated corpus of writings. It has already been

noted on diverse occasions, quite rightly, that his revision of the first volume of *Capital* for the French translation, which appeared between 1872 and 1875, already contains important revisions of the idea that Western European history can serve as a model for international development. Of pivotal importance to the transformation of Marx's view of non-Western societies were, above all, his studies of questions of land ownership from the later 1870s on. They had a direct influence on his exchanges with the Russian Social Revolutionaries.

Marx devoted considerable attention to the book *Communal Ownership of Land* by the Russian legal historian Maxim M. Kovalevskii immediately following its 1879 publication. Of the North American, Algerian and Indian forms of property discussed in it, he took a special interest in the last-named. He excerpted Kovalevskii's book at length, commenting as he went, so that his excerpt as a whole 'essentially reflects Marx's own position'.[78] Marx noted the existence of 'archaic property forms' in precolonial Algeria, which the Western colonial powers refused to acknowledge because that was not in their interest: 'The French lust for loot makes obvious sense; if the government was and is the original proprietor of the entire country, then there is no need to acknowledge the claims of the Arab and Kabyl tribes to this or that concrete tract of land.'[79] We observe a similar shift in his position with respect to the Indian case. In his notes, Marx underscores 'the variety of forms of property relations'[80] and the fact that the disintegration of communal property forms was already well under way: '*arable* fields and, often, threshing floors are the private property of different members of the commune, and only the "appurtenances" (*ugoda*) remain their common property.'[81] About the Mongol Empire, Marx notes: '*Four centuries later*, the principle of private property was so solidly anchored in Indian society that the only remaining demand was that such sales [of real estate] take place publicly.'[82] This accurate understanding of the property relations governing land ownership, as Marx's excerpts from Kovalevskii show, stemmed in part from knowledge of sources that were, for linguistic reasons, a closed book to Bernier and others: 'In the annals of certain Indian communities, a source that was still essentially unavailable to historians ignorant of Sanskrit, we find evidence of the way private property suddenly sprang up, suddenly and *en masse*, as a result of measures taken by the Rajas and to the detriment of communal property.'[83] Marx not only takes his distance from his former positions, but, somewhat later in the same text, even lashes out at the 'miserable "Orientalists"' who had turned to the Koran for information on land ownership instead of analysing the historical realities of the situation.[84] It is true that Marx, in notes he assembled under the heading 'the English economy and its influence on India communal property', still lists, among his sources, the 'Letter to Colbert found as a supplement in *"Voyages de François Bernier"*. Amsterdam. 1699'. However, he immediately appends the following comment: 'Dupeyron (see Mill: *History of British India*, 1840 edition, vol. 1, p. 310 etc.) Dupeyron (*priloženie*) was the first to realize that, in India, the Grand Mogul was not the sole property owner.'[85] In the light of this new information and these new sources, Marx's own judgement of colonialism in India is more carefully balanced. Unmistakably, the English had occasionally acknowledged the existence of communal property forms.[86] Where they had striven to abolish them, they had done so 'in fact in order to promote European colonization'.[87] Even the 'modernizing' effect of the crumbling of communal property forms was, in every case, open to question. Although the English portrayed it 'as a mere result ... of *economic progress*', it was in fact actively promoted by the colonial authorities: 'The inhabitants (peasants) are so attached to the soil that they prefer to remain on their former farms as mere rural labourers rather than seeking higher wages in the city.'[88]

For present purposes, the chief interest of Marx's 1880–81 *Ethnological Notebooks* resides in that fact that he adopts Lewis H. Morgan's standpoint in them: property is a historically transitory form, which he contrasts with 'a higher stage of society'.

Marx cites Morgan to the effect that this higher stage should represent 'a resuscitation ... in a superior form, of freedom, equality, and fraternity of the old Gentes'[89] – that is, of communal property. According to a passage Marx excerpts from Henry S. Maine, 'the form of private ownership in Land' quite clearly enjoyed legal recognition – 'yet the rights of private owners are limited by the controlling rights of a brotherhood of kinsmen, and the control is in some respects even more stringent than that exercised over separate property by an Indian village community.'[90] According to another passage excerpted by Marx, 'property in its modern form [was] established' when a man's property was divided up by his direct descendants at his death, even if the family did not cease 'to influence successions'. Marx comments: '"property in its modern form" is in no way established thereby: see the Russian communes f.i.'[91] The excerpts from Maine, then, confront us with a kaleidoscopic mix, in which property forms and actual enjoyment of property can diverge. These confused conditions, according to Marx's critical commentary on Maine, cannot be grasped by way of the putative 'English equivalent': 'This blockhead identifies the Roman form of absolute land ownership with the "English form of ownership".'[92]

With regard to the different dimensions of the concept of Eurocentrism that we distinguished in setting out, the excerpts Marx made late in life are significant in three respects. First, he now no longer considers England a superior society that, by means of colonization, initiates social progress in India. In support of his new position, Marx even makes his source say more than it actually does: thus Haruki Wada has shown that Marx's hostility to colonial land policy is much more emphatic than Kovalevskii's.[93]

Second, in his finely shaded discussion of various forms of land ownership in the extra-European world, Marx breaks with Eurocentrism in a way consonant with Said's critique of Orientalism. We find, in his notes, such a broad range of distinctions in the approach to land ownership that these notes can hardly be mobilized in support of the view that he sticks to a monolithic 'Asiatic conception'. Moreover, he explicitly rejects approaches to non-Western regions of the world grounded on the European experience alone, and he expressly criticizes the assumption (bound up with the thesis of the non-existence of private property) that the state holds a monopoly on land – formerly an integral part of his 'Asiatic conception' – as a 'legal fiction'.[94] Finally, he points to the fact 'that even in the earliest Indian class societies, if only formally, by way of "donations" by the Raja, "private property" suddenly came into existence "en masse"'.[95] In short, Eurocentrism no longer authorizes a homogenizing approach; Marx now recognizes that the 'real conditions' are more complex than he had supposed.

Third, Marx breaks with the Eurocentric conception of development for which the patterns that led to the emergence of Western European societies are the measure of human history as such. Thus, although he points to the 'feudalization' of India under Muslim rule, he is careful to emphasize that this process differs from the one observable in Europe because of the absence of hereditary rights in Indian law. Furthermore, he upbraids Kovalevskii for basing what he says on a conception of 'feudalism in the Western European sense' while ignoring the absence of serfdom.[96] Similarly, the *Ethnological Notebooks* vehemently criticize the authors they discuss for the historical analogies in which they indulge. John Phear, for example, is a 'jackass' who calls 'the structure of the villages "feudal"'.[97] Thus the late Marx regards 'the application of the category of feudalism to the Oriental polity' as a 'form of ethnocentrism that presses world history into a European mould'.[98] He consequently opposes 'too stark a generalization of the concept of feudalism, and, more generally, the straightforward extrapolation of concepts of structure developed on Western European models to Indian or Asiatic conditions'.[99]

Thanks not least to the emergence of Russian revolutionary movements, for which, because of the agricultural structures that prevailed in Russia, the question of land ownership and the rural commune played a central role, Marx devoted particular attention to conditions there.[100] Late in 1869, he started learning Russian and took part in Russian debates about *Capital*, a Russian translation of which appeared in 1872. In what follows, I shall be using, above all, texts written in this context to show how, at the end of Marx's life, there materialized a break with the various dimensions of Eurocentrism that we began by sketching.

In connection with the Russian rural commune, Marx initially expresses what seem to be familiar ideas: 'the land in the hands of the Russian peasants has never been *their private property*.'[101] However, he also notes the existence of the kind of communes which, he says, 'descended from a more archaic type', 'in Germany' as well.[102] 'Go back to the origins of Western societies; and everywhere you will find communal ownership of the land.'[103] Marx regards this form of communal property, which he claims was widespread in Asia, as economically superior. There were, he affirms, different reasons for the dissolution of these archaic communes; in Western Europe, above all, it was 'an immense interval' that 'separated' it 'from the birth of capitalist production', that is seen 'embracing a whole series of successive economic revolutions and evolutions of which capitalistic production is merely the most recent'.[104] These characteristics of the rural commune provide the backdrop against which Marx projects a specific Russian form of development. Thus he affirms that his 'historical sketch of the genesis of capitalism in Western Europe', in the chapter on so-called primitive accumulation in *Capital*, Volume 1, must not be transformed into

> a historic-philosophical theory of general development, imposed by fate on all peoples, whatever the historical circumstances in which they are placed, in order to eventually attain this economic formation which, with a tremendous leap of the productive forces of social labour, assures the most integral development of every individual producer.[105]

It follows that the 'historical inevitability' of so-called primitive accumulation is *expressly* limited ... *to the countries of Western Europe*'.[106] Because Russian peasants do not own their land, the movement that led to the triumph of capitalist property relations in Western Europe cannot simply be projected onto the Russian case. There 'communist property' would be transformed into 'capitalist property'.[107] Moreover, Russian agriculture would 'try in vain' to get out of the '*cul-de-sac*' in which it found itself by means of 'capitalist farming on the English model', even judging matters 'from the economic point of view alone'. The only way to overcome the problems besetting Russian agriculture leads through development of the Russian rural commune.[108]

Thus Marx opposes hasty universalization of historical development, insisting that, when it comes to social transformations, what is decisive is the historical surroundings in which they unfold. In the Russian case, those surroundings facilitate transformation of the rural commune into an 'element of collective production on a nationwide scale'.[109] Without having to 'first pass through the same process of dissolution as constitutes the historical development of the West', the commune could 'pass directly to the higher form of communist common ownership'.[110] 'Thanks to its contemporaneity with capitalist production', the Russian rural commune 'is thus able to appropriate its fruits without subjecting itself to its *modus operandi*'.[111] Communal ownership land offers this rural commune 'the basis for collective appropriation':

> its historical surroundings, its contemporaneity with capitalist production, lend it all the material conditions of communal labour on a vast scale. It is thus in a position to incorporate all the positive acquisitions devised by the capitalist system without passing through its Caudine Forks. It can gradually replace parcel farming with large-scale agriculture assisted by machines, which the physical lie of the land in Russia invites. It can thus become *the direct point of departure* for the economic system towards which modern society tends, and turn over a new leaf without beginning by committing suicide.[112]

In sum, the Russian agricultural commune can, according to Marx, appropriate the fruits 'of Western capitalist production' 'without subjecting itself to its modus operandi'.[113] If it does, it will become the 'fulcrum of social regeneration in Russia'[114] or, rather, the 'starting point for communist development'.[115]

Given the various questions that Marx's view of non-Western societies in the 1850s and 1860s raises, three points in his exchanges with revolutionary movements in Russia should be emphasized. First, we should note the shift in Marx's position on colonialism in India, which begins to materialize in the Kovalevskii excerpt. When Marx has occasion to discuss the Indian case in the 1880s, he observes that the English have managed only 'to ruin native agriculture and double the number and severity of the famines'.[116] He also notes 'the suppression of communal landownership out there was nothing but an act of English vandalism, pushing the native people not forwards but backwards.'[117] It can therefore hardly be asserted that Marx maintained, overall, his 1853 'assumption that social conditions would be homogenized throughout the world' as a result of the expansion of the Western–capitalist mode of production, while making an exception for Russia. By the end of the 1860s, at the latest, Marx possessed an adequate understanding of colonialism; it helped shape, thereafter, his perception of the non-Western world.

Second, it is noteworthy that Marx now sees the need to criticize his sources. Only 'Sir H[enry] Maine and others of his ilk',[118] he remarks, remain blind to this 'English vandalism'.

> When reading the histories of primitive communities written by bourgeois writers it is necessary to be on one's guard. They do not even shrink from falsehoods. Sir Henry Maine, for example, who was a keen collaborator of the British Government in carrying out the violent destruction of the Indian communes, hypocritically assures us that all the government's noble efforts to support the communes were thwarted by the spontaneous forces of economic laws![119]

Marx emphasizes that 'it is in the interest of the landed proprietors to set up the more or less well-off peasants as an intermediate agrarian class, and to turn the poor peasants – that is to say the majority – into simple wage earners.'[120] There exists, in other words, in Russia as well,[121] an interest in the dissolution of the rural communes that hold property in common. This interest is comparable to that of the Western colonial powers in Asia and North Africa.

Third, it must be admitted that, even in the Marx of the 1880s, we find features reminiscent of his 'Asiatic conception'. Thus he considers the isolation of the Russian rural communes an obstacle to development, since it favours a 'central despotism'. However, he adds that this obstacle could itself be overcome if the *volosts* (government bodies) were replaced by a peasant assembly.[122]

> The isolation of rural communes, the lack of connexion between the life of one and the life of another, this localised microcosm is not encountered everywhere as an immanent characteristic of the last of the primitive types, but everywhere it is found, it always gives rise to a central despotism. ... It seems to me an easy matter to do away with the primitive isolation imposed by the vast extent of the territory as soon as the government shackles have been cast off.[123]

These continuities notwithstanding,[124] the texts that grew out of Marx's exchanges with Russian revolutionary movements bear witness to a politically reinforced version of his break with dimensions of Eurocentrism. First, Marx no longer premisses the one-sided superiority of Western societies, but, rather, confirms 'the economic superiority of communal property'.[125] Second, his preoccupation with Russia cannot be dismissed as 'imaginary investigation' of a non-Western region of the world which only serves to buttress a European self-image. For behind Marx's efforts here lies a long, careful examination of the issue of property relations in the extra-European world, as well as an endeavour to articulate capitalist penetration and local social conflict. On this basis, Marx's appreciation of English colonialism in India undergoes sharp modification: what he once called the 'double mission' of destruction and renewal becomes, unambiguously, 'vandalism'. Third, Marx no longer conceives of modernization as 'Westernization', which is to say that he no longer regards European development as the sole valid historical measure. Rather, it would appear that Russia is in many respects treated as a model of development for the West. Thus Marx affirms that the crisis of the Western–capitalist world will only be overcome with the 'elimination' of capitalism and 'the return of modern societies' to a superior form of 'an "archaic" type of collective property'.[126] As we have seen, Marx's critical reception of authors such as Morgan, 'one of the few people of his time to have conceived of progress along a number of different lines',[127] stands behind these developments. Even if recent research has shown that Marx's 'analysis of the Russian rural commune [is based] on altogether erroneous premises', it does not follow that his 'conceptual approach to them' has lost all relevance: 'At bottom, it is a question of the construction of human history. Here, Marx's sketch of several different paths of development for human societies stands in sharp contrast to unilinear, evolutionistic notions.'[128] Fourth, Marx meets the standards of global history. With his positive political attitude towards the Russian rural commune, he charts an explicitly non-Eurocentric orientation for a classless society: in communist perspective, Europe is reduced to a mere province. Marx does more than merely sketch a conception of communism that draws on many different experiences. He also conceives of an interaction between diverse areas of the world, one situated in the realm of the political: a revolution in Russia could become the 'signal for a proletarian revolution in the West', 'so that both complement each other'.[129]

Marx studies and postcolonialism – shaken, not stirred

We began by pointing to the existence of two problems. In Marxian studies, one finds no systematic critical study of Marx's Eurocentrism. In postcolonial studies, one finds a fully elaborated critique of Marx's Eurocentrism that largely ignores the changes in his thinking that occurred after he wrote his articles on India in 1853, changes that have been brought to light by Marx scholarship, thanks notably to the project to publish a comprehensive edition of his writings. This situation can be overcome only if each of these fields of knowledge is willing to learn something from the other. Only if we take Marx's entire œuvre into account can we make a valid judgement of his Eurocentrism; only if we have a carefully worked out idea of just what Eurocentrism is can we say exactly what constitutes Marx's Eurocentrism.

Bart Moore-Gilbert has rightly pleaded for cooperation between Marxian studies and postcolonial studies. Militating in favour of it, he argues, is the fact that both fields often have the same object of research, have been relegated to the margins of academia, and boast theoreticians such as C.L.R. James or Frantz Fanon, whose work cannot be confined to either of the two fields. Marx scholarship could learn something about 'the historical differences and cultural specificities of the non-Western world'.[130] On the other hand, Marxian studies could mark out the limits of various postcolonial projects, with analyses, for example, of the international division of labour. If such cooperation is to become a reality, however, both sides must abandon polemics, and must undertake 'more finely calibrated, attentive readings'.[131]

What has so far prevented postcolonial studies from embarking on such a project, it seems to me, is the fact that Marx's study of Russia and the conclusions he drew from it have gone largely unknown. Thus a majority of those who have entered the debate see Marx as an optimistic believer in progress or a teleologically minded Eurocentric. It is to be hoped that further publication of his work in the second *MEGA* – for example, release of the Marx manuscript known as the *Chronological Excerpts* (excerpts from world history) – together with studies of this less familiar material, will help to bring postcolonial studies, as well, to a more balanced assessment of his Eurocentrism. Further work on Marx's sources, of the kind exemplified by my discussion of Bernier's travel account, is also indispensable if old prejudices are to be shed.

Marxian studies needs to cooperate with postcolonial studies for three reasons. First, because they need to deepen their analysis of the contradictions and complexity of capitalism by adopting a global perspective. This should make it clear that capitalism's totalizing claims have been only partially realized: certain social spaces remain beyond its reach.[132] Capitalism would then appear not as 'a self-identical system that emanates from the West and expands to the periphery, but as a changing ensemble of worldwide relations that assumes different forms in specific regional and national contexts.'[133] This would also make it possible to lay the foundations for an adequate understanding of colonialism, which was precisely not some 'local or marginal subplot in some larger history (for example, the transition from feudalism to capitalism in western Europe, the latter developing organically in the womb of the former)', but, rather, takes on, viewed from this standpoint, 'the place and the significance of a major, extended and ruptural world-historical event'.[134] Marxist discussion of international relations of domination, especially Marxist study of imperialism, has apparently not yet set out to acquire this kind of carefully differentiated understanding.[135]

Second, Marxian studies has to acquire a new understanding of historical progress. Here, it seems to me, the potential of world-systems theory has yet to be fully realized. Thus Immanuel Wallerstein has pointed out that the traditional evolutionist conception of the emergence of capitalism as the replacement of a ruling feudal group is highly dubious:

> Instead, the correct basic image is that historical capitalism was brought into existence by a landed aristocracy which transformed itself into a bourgeoisie because the old system was disintegrating. Rather than let the disintegration continue to uncertain ends, they engaged in radical structural surgery themselves in order to

maintain *and significantly expand* their ability to exploit the direct producers.[136]

Jettisoning evolutionist notions of progress would call into question the idea that 'capitalism as a historical system has represented progress over the various previous historical systems that it destroyed or transformed',[137] or would, at any rate, raise the crucial problem of the standard to be applied to measure progress. I think that the decisive criterion should be freedom from domination, not a specific concept of the form in which the productive forces are developed. The late Marx expressed this by raising the perspective of 'free equality' during his study of the Russian rural communes; it is a perspective which seeks to establish connections with already existing historical forms, without forcing them into the mould of one or another scheme of development. This perspective also implies, however, that progress is no inevitability, but must be achieved through struggle. This insight, too, is contained in the late Marx's outline of a conception of communism rooted in a global history.

Third, Marxian studies must make theoretical room for contingency. Hauck, for example, has pointed out that 'historical contingency' was of decisive importance to the historical emergence of capitalism in Europe:

> Commodity production, private property, and wage-labour, juridical freedom, and exploitation of labour-power based on economic constraint (lack of the means of production), legal security, and relative non-interference of the state in the economy (responsible, in large measure, for the separation of the economic from the political specific to capitalism), the existence of intermediary instances and the separation of religious and political power, the plundering of peripheral regions, and phases in which science and technology expand – all these are phenomena which, in defiance of all positions based on Eurocentric theories of modernization, most modern societies have at some point experienced. In seventeenth and eighteenth century England, they operated in conjunction, making possible the historically unique emergence of capitalism.[138]

The project of a non-teleological reading of Marx developed by Althusser's school also zeroes in on this problem. It might provide a springboard for dialogue between Marxian studies and postcolonial studies. As early as *Reading Capital*, Balibar pointed out that 'the history of society can be reduced to a discontinuous succession of modes of production'.[139] Althusser, in his late work, insists that we must conceive of the irruption of capitalism as a contingent 'encounter' of independent elements, the results of which endured only in Europe, that were by no means predestined to come together: money capital, labour-power, technological development, and a nascent domestic market.[140]

Even if it took Marx 'an enormous amount of time' to arrive at 'an understanding of the real conditions' of extra-European development, he freed himself, at the end of his life, from the influence of the European 'jackasses' – which is what his twenty-first-century readers would make of themselves if they failed to take up the challenge of bringing Marxian studies and postcolonial studies into dialogue. The goal is not only to pave the way for the return of Marx, declared a dead dog in the wake of the events of 1989–90. It is, no less, to produce a comprehensive anti-authoritarian analysis of society, which has as much to learn from Marx as from postcolonialism.

TRANSLATED BY G.M. GOSHGARIAN

Notes

A longer version of this text, in German, is to be found in Werner Bonefeld and Michael Heinrich, eds, *Kapital und Kritik. Nach der neuen Marx-Lektüre*, VSA, Hamburg, 2010.

1. *Herrschaftskritisch*: a concept popularized by the Frankfurt School which means, literally, critical of all forms of domination, based on class, race, gender, etc. [*Trans.*]
2. María do Mar Castro Varela and Nikita Dhawan, *Postkoloniale Theorie. Eine kritische Einführung*, Transcript, Bielefeld, 2005, p. 64.
3. Edward Said, *Orientalism*, Vintage, New York, 1978, p. 155.
4. I thank Lotte Arndt and Urs Lindner, among others, for helpful suggestions and comments.
5. In the present context (contrast the market for real estate in advanced capitalism), the decisive criterion for private ownership of land is its alienability. Crucial here is the economic aspect of ownership (disposability/ appropriation), not the juridical elaboration of it.
6. See Gerhard Hauck, *Die Gesellschaftstheorie und ihr Anderes. Wider den Eurozentrismus der Sozialwissenschaften*, Westfälisches Dampfboot, Münster, 2003, p. 14.

7. See Jani Pranav, 'Marx, Eurocentrism, and the 1857 Revolt in British India', in Crystal Bartolovich and Neil Lazarus, eds, *Marxism, Modernity, and Postcolonial Studies*, Cambridge University Press, Cambridge, 2002, pp. 81–97, here p. 94.
8. Gunter Willing, 'Eurozentrismus', in Wolfgang F. Haug, ed., *Historisch-kritisches Wörterbuch des Marxismus*, vol. 3, Argument, Hamburg and Berlin, 1997, pp. 1023–32, here p. 1023.
9. Christopher Bayly, *The Birth of the Modern World 1780–1914: Global Connections and Comparisons*, Blackwell, Oxford, 2004, p. 7.
10. Sebastian Conrad and Shalini Randeria, 'Einleitung. Geteilte Geschichten – Europa in einer postkolonialen Welt', in Sebastian Conrad and Shalini Randeria, eds, *Jenseits des Eurozentrismus. Postkoloniale Perspektiven in den Geschichts- und Kulturwissenschaften*, Campus Verlag, Frankfurt am Main, pp. 9–49, here p. 42.
11. Karl Marx, 'The British Rule in India', *NYDT*, 25 June 1853, *MECW*, vol. 12, p. 132.
12. Karl Marx, 'The War Question', *NYDT*, 19 July 1853, *MECW*, vol. 12, p. 215.
13. Ibid., p. 217.
14. See Karl Marx, 'The Western Powers and Turkey', *NYDT*, 4 October 1853, *MECW*, vol. 12, p. 316.
15. See Karl Marx, 'The Future Results of British Rule in India', *NYDT*, 8 August 1853, *MECW*, vol. 12, p. 217.
16. See Marx, 'The British Rule in India'.
17. See Marx, 'The Future Results of British Rule in India'.
18. Marx, 'The British Rule in India', p. 132.
19. Marx, 'The Future Results of British Rule in India', p. 221.
20. Marx, 'The British Rule in India', p. 132.
21. Marx, 'The Future Results of British Rule in India', p. 222.
22. See Hassan Gardezi, 'South Asia and the Asiatic Mode of Production: Some Conceptual and Empirical Problems', *Bulletin of Concerned Asian Scholars*, vol. 11, no. 4, 1979, pp. 40–44, here pp. 40ff.; and Brendan O'Leary, *The Asiatic Mode of Production: Oriental Despotism, Historical Materialism and Indian History*, Blackwell, Oxford, 1989, pp. 299ff.
23. Marx, 'The British Rule in India', p. 132.
24. See Aijaz Ahmad, *In Theory: Classes, Nations, Literatures*, Verso, London and New York, 1994, pp. 226, 241. See also Bipan Chandra, 'Marx, His Theories of Asian Societies and Colonial Rule', in *Sociological Theories: Race and Colonialism*, UNESCO, Paris, 1980, pp. 383–451, here pp. 399ff., pp. 428ff.
25. Stuart Hall, 'Race, Articulation, and Societies Structured in Dominance' (1980), in Houston Backer, Manthia A. Diawara and Ruth H. Lindeborg, eds, *Black British Cultural Studies: A Reader*, University of Chicago Press, Chicago and London, 1996, pp. 16–60, here p. 33.
26. See " Chakrabarty, *Provincializing Europe: Postcolonial Thought and Historical Difference*, Princeton University Press, Princeton NJ, 2008, pp. 180ff.
27. Said, *Orientalism*, p. 49.
28. Ibid., p. 117.
29. See Amady A. Dieng, *Le marxisme et l'Afrique noire. Bilan d'un débat sur l'universalité du marxisme*, Nubia, Paris, 1985; O'Leary, *The Asiatic Mode of Production*, pp. 47–81.
30. Marx to Engels, 2 June 1853, *MECW*, vol. 39, p. 332.
31. Ibid., pp. 332, 334.
32. See Engels to Marx, 6 June 1853, *MECW*, vol. 39, p. 341.
33. See Lucette Valensi, 'Bernier François', in François Pouillon, ed., *Dictionnaire des orientalistes de langue française*, Karthala, Paris, 2008, pp. 98–9.
34. See Perry Anderson, *Lineages of the Absolutist State*, Verso, London, 1979, pp. 464ff.; O'Leary, *The Asiatic Mode of Production*, pp. 43–73.
35. François Bernier, *Voyages dans les États du Grand Mogol* (1724), Fayard, Paris, 1981, p. 73. Marx cites this passage in his June 1853 letter to Engels, underscoring the words 'sole proprietor of the land' and 'capital city'.
36. See Anderson, *Lineages of the Absolutist State*, pp. 487ff., 496ff.; Chandra, 'Marx, His Theories of Asian Societies and Colonial Rule', pp. 419ff.; O'Leary, *The Asiatic Mode of Production*, pp. 290ff.
37. Bernier, *Voyages dans les États du Grand Mogol*, p. 120.
38. Siep Stuurman, 'François Bernier and the Invention of Racial Classification', *History Workshop Journal* 50, 2000, pp. 1–21, here p. 7.
39. Bernier, *Voyages dans les États du Grand Mogol*, p. 145.
40. Ibid., p. 254.
41. Bernier, *Voyages. Contenant la Description des États du Grand Mogol, De L'Hindoustan, du Royaume de Kachemire, &c.*, 2 vols, Paul Marret, Amsterdam, 1699, vol. 1, p. 250.

14 Who needs postcoloniality? A reply to Lindner

HARRY HAROOTUNIAN

In Marx's articles for the *New York Tribune* on British colonialism in India and the events leading to the Second Anglo-Chinese War (Opium War), critics have caught sight of a double mission attributed by him to British imperialism and colonialism to tear down the structure of archaic societies and lay the foundations for a new social order that would eventually reflect the capitalist model. A much later variation of this double mission was promoted by modernization and convergence theory during the early days of the Cold War (before the USA discovered the technique of proxy wars against the Soviets), whereby colonialism, which this theory of development often ignored or overlooked, was credited with putting into place the proper infrastructure for the later, successful postcolonial modernization of states like India, and, especially, Taiwan and South Korea, both of which were said to have benefited from the Japanese imperial intervention. While the modernizing mission of colonialism can be found in Marx's early articles, it was replaced by modernization theory dedicated to 'endowing' a world-historical narrative (Hegel) 'with a civilizational grammer and direction', as well the task of overseeing 'a transnational experience' by administering capitalism as 'it ideologically captures historical time and deploys it as means'. During the Cold War, modernization theory and its knowledges aimed to 'manage 'life' in the so-called 'Third World' through the imperial instrumentality of a developmentalist policy, which was 'perceived as a form of neocolonialism.'[1] But the accusations of Eurocentrism and Orientalism were particularly important for a postcolonial theory, which 'dematerialized' Said's version of colonial discourse in the name of radicalizing it, and its campaign to 'provincialize Europe' and 'unthink Eurocentrism'.[2]

Kolja Lindner's recent essay 'Marx's Eurocentrism: Postcolonial Studies and Marxian Scholarship' (*RP* 161)[3] is a recent reminder of both the persistence of this question and its capacity to fuel discussion. In these discussions, what is interesting is the fascination, bordering on desire, that postcolonial discourse, especially, has continued to exert for Marxism, and the possibility of establishing some sort of rapprochement that might end the academic division of labour between two antagonistic intellectual strategies and put to rest the apparently embarrassing charges of Eurocentrism. It should be stated that this peacemaking mission began several years ago, with attempts to imagine a Marxian postcolonial approach that might open the path to a more productive partnership. In her introduction to *Marxism, Modernization and Postcolonial Studies* (2002), Crystal Bartolovich observed the near-absence of 'direct' and 'serious' dialogue between Marxism and proponents of postcoloniality.[4] Noting that too often postcolonial theory's indebtedness to post-structural philosophy encouraged dismissal of Marxism or ignored it out of 'neglect' and even ignorance, Marxism, for its part, fell into discounting postcolonial studies frequently for overlooking the material dimensions of imperialism and colonial life, especially the intervening mediations posed by capitalism and colonial enterprise. Any reading of the novel *The Singapore Grip* by J.G. Farrell (a writer who was not a Marxist), with its narrative of how British businessmen were planning to sell their rubber to the Japanese, whose troops were already within the city, will reaffirm Bartolovich's judgement. In this dispute, she correctly proposed that the existence of a large fund of misunderstanding linking the two discourses in mutual antagonism was often accompanied by caricature and misrecognition.

If Marxism was vulnerable to charges of an inaugural Eurocentrism, postcoloniality was answerable for its collaboration with imperialism in its most contemporary manifestation of globalization. This apparent complicity with forms of neocolonialism stemmed from its prior relationship with the Cold War and, in the aftermath, its affiliation with modernization theory. Despite competing claims, Bartolovich was convinced that 'Marxism is the theoretical perspective suited to accomplishing' the necessary critique of both the colonial violence of contemporary neocolonial residues, what the writer Kiran Desai (*The Inheritance of Loss*, 2006) described as the 'shabbiest modernity', and the more distant colonial past.[5] Regardless of the distance separating these discourses, she is persuaded that they do have something to say to each other, if for no other reason than such an engagement would provide the opportunity to air their respective differences. But postcolonial discourse would hardly cede its own claim to theoretical privilege.

A few years later Neil Lazarus remarked that silence on class in postcolonial studies, especially beginning with the class location of the postcolonial theorist 'relative to that of whom he or she is theorizing', is precisely the problem – 'the gap' – that needs to be examined since it undoubtedly has played a principal role shaping the particular field of inquiry.[6] Lazarus has also pointed to the preponderant culturalist bias informing postcolonial studies, its inordinate concerns with subaltern address and enunciative capability, the formation of subjectivity drawn from psychoanalytic theory yoked to unstated claims of cultural authenticity (and reductionism), and coupled, I would add, with declarations of neo-nativism, ironically echoing an understanding of the world outside of Euro-America founded on the assumption that Foucault was less Eurocentric than Marx.[7]

Whatever the complex reasons prompting this Marxian attention to postcolonial studies, it has, I believe, much to do with the successful institutionalization of postcolonial studies and cultural studies in colleges and universities of the USA and UK, first in departments of English and then in semi-autonomous programmes of instruction and graduate training. For its part, Marxism, at least in US colleges and universities, has always been marginalized and never occupied a position to play the role commanded by postcolonial studies. In a way this was acknowledged by Fredric Jameson, when he proposed that cultural studies constituted a 'desire',[8] which, among its many ambitions, was the yearning to succeed Marxism and replace it, a challenge that persisted at the heart of the Marxian effort to win recognition by establishing a dialogue with postcolonial studies, by situating itself in such a way as to refigure its critique in order to gain entry into the academic procession. Beyond this institutional detour there was also the politics of a reigning textualism in the literary fields and the insinuations of history and political economy into disciplines traditionally unreceptive to what they had to offer. It is often overlooked, in this connection, that a symmetrical relationship was forged between English literary studies and a postcoloniality preoccupied with England's largest former colony, India – and especially the province of Bengal. (Ireland seems like a natural candidate, with a history of 500 years of continual occupation but the British always had a problem with seeing it as a colony.[9]) Specifically, I am calling attention to the way English studies, armed with new textual strategies (Saidian colonial discourse and poststructural philosophy) turned towards colonies that had been intimately implicated in the metropolitan country once the discipline had exhausted the productivity of received practices. Inadvertently, the development of postcolonial studies made India (Bengal) the condensed substitute of choice – what Lindner describes as 'projecting false universalism' – for reshaping the colonial world according to the protocols of a local experience in such a way as to imply a commonality everywhere. In the vast literature on postcoloniality, it's hard to find much emphasis on the French, Dutch, Portuguese, American and Japanese colonial possessions, and even less consideration of their significant experiential differences. The alliance between postcolonial studies and post-structural theory resulted in the emphasizing of subject formation (and thus culture) and thus led to a dematerializing of the subject by substituting subaltern agency – finding a voice – (itself a form of cultural identity) where identity is transferred to ethnicity. Marx considered ethnicity a 'historical value', as opposed to the roles played (and personified) by worker and capitalist, the subjects of 'value-in-process' – that is, 'capital in every moment.'[10] It is, I believe, this legacy that loosely accepted the Cold War caricature of Marxism as 'Eurocentric', which led to the subsequent postcolonial accusation that capitalism formed simply another Western narrative and that history was another name for Europe. In this vocation to distance itself from an imperial self by foregrounding the suppressed other, a dyad recently put into question by a number of thinkers, postcoloniality has run the risk of sliding into an unstated valorization of cultural authenticity and, perhaps, signalling the end of its productivity.

None of these considerations appears in Lindner's informed essay, which often echoes the Cold War caricature. But it also gives a glimpse of the kind of cultural and political lag between the world of German scholarship and its preoccupation and those of the USA and the UK. On the one hand, Lindner aims to show through a reading of the *New York Tribune* articles how Marx moved from a perspective that viewed England's colonization of India as accruing eventual benefits that would lead to the necessary transformation of the subcontinent (the conceit of the 'English jackasses'), and put it on the road to socialism to the abandonment of this expression of Eurocentrism and cultural superiority. On the other hand, this tack is accompanied by the recognition that Marx's substantive and theoretical writings relating to the critique of political economy, capitalism and the world market revealed, despite Orientalist hangovers, the existence of pre-capitalist communal organization throughout the ancient world and its importance for later history. Further, the expansion of capital would result in establishing conditions leading to changes in the received order according to differing circumstances in time and place. But the trouble with this twin positionality is that it is unnecessary in its desire to have it both ways: to show that Marx pulled back from an earlier Eurocentrism. For a show of sympathy for societies outside Euro-America might satisfy a postcolonial demand to be free from racism but it is outweighed by Marx's coextensive account of political economy and how it transforms every society it manages to touch. Recognition of this could not have been acceptable to postcolonialism's proponents since it would have required subordinning its own theoretical aspirations to those of Marxism. It should be recalled that in some versions of postcolonial theory, Asia (i.e. India) was designated as the site of an 'alternative modernity'. With this dedication to an 'alternative modernity' (and all its names), we have already entered the precinct of the cultural dominant – the colonizing space of culture – which demands a parallel move, away from considerations of time and its relationship to space, to spatial primacy, whereby the possibility of temporal conjuncture loses its momentary and historical status to become a fixed and unmoving countenance. The Marxian critique of political economy was historical, always referred to the world at large, and joined colonial expropriation to the expansion of capitalism as it became the lever in forming the world market. Postcolonial studies has been less worldly and more local and reflects the moment when decolonization resulted in disappointment with what came after. In Lindner's reckoning, the disclosure of Marx's later ethnological notebooks concerning societies of Euro-America clinches the argument against charges of Eurocentrism, even though much of this material was published in Lawrence Krader's Introduction to Karl Marx's *Ethnological Notebooks* (1974) and found its way into the under-used *The Asiatic Mode of Production* (1975) and was amplified recently in Kevin Anderson's important *Marx at the Margins* (2010).[11] What therefore seems evident is that the more theoretical texts provide ways to circumvent the instances of Eurocentric sentiment that occasionally crept into the newspaper articles, and supplied a prefiguration for the heterogeneous history Marx was demonstrating in his letters to Vera Zasulich and Russian progressives and in his ethnological notebooks.

Rather than pursue this narrative demonstrating Marx's ethnological consciousness in later life, detailed by both Lindner and Anderson, I'd like merely to follow through on some of the possibilities offered by Marx's conception of history (articulated in the *Grundrisse*) and the analysis of capital's logic and pre-capitalist formations, which both the *Grundrisse* and *Capital* provide. Such an accounting requires envisaging *Capital* not as an 'x-ray of national capitalism' transformed into an ideal type, but instead as the 'abstraction of a constitutive historical process'. It is less about a configuration of national economies which will establish relations between sovereign states than a network of international exchange and the crystallization of national markets. 'Genealogically, commercial and finance capital were constituted on the periphery of social formations', in the widening fulcrum of international exchanges. 'But the capitalist mode of production, properly called, implies the submission of production itself to the law of capital.'[12] In other words, capital presumes the exchange of commodities in their function as value and is thus not preoccupied with the pre-capitalist exchange and production of goods. Hence, the historic genesis of capitalism, the existence of the world market, appears only in the 'tearing' of a coherent synchronic system, with other categories (representing practices) – like primitive accumulation, the incidence of the tendency of the falling rate of profit, and the formation of finance and commercial capital – following successively throughout the volumes of *Capital*.[13] There is no place in Marx's analysis for a separate accounting of the world market that will demand a degree of unification more advanced than what this market has already attained. It is not accidental, Daniel Bensaid has remarked, that the literature inspiring Marxist narratives on modern imperialism originated in the stage of colonial expansion and the formation of finance capital dating from the late nineteenth and early twentieth centuries.[14]

In fact, it was the contemporaneity of this synchronic system, a system in which the expansion of capital will result in value independently valorizing itself, that commanded Marx's analytic attention. This would explain why he appeared less concerned with the history of pre-capitalist formations, and somewhat ambiguous toward the possibility of knowing them, even though their putative historicity is considered in the *Grundrisse*. Yet it is also in this same text that he envisioned a new understanding of history departing from his reflections in the *German Ideology* precisely at the moment he was driven to construct a critique of the world of contemporary bourgeois political economy. It is because bourgeois economy is the 'most developed historic organization of production' that a new understanding of history is required, especially in view of the convention of political economy to posit the natural development of capitalism and 'smudge over all differences' to 'see bourgeois relations in all forms of societies'.[15] Here, too, Marx introduced the observation of unevenness, when he noted that bourgeois society is itself a panoply of contradictory forms of development 'derived from earlier forms' found within it only in 'stunted form, or even travestied'.[16] The upshot is thus a mode of 'historical presentation of development ... founded ... on the fact that the latest form regards the previous ones as steps leading up to itself.' This rejection of the 'retrospective illusion' led to imagining a 'real history of the relations of production' based on 'observing and deducing its laws, as having themselves become in history ... like the empirical numbers ... in natural science – which point towards a past behind this system'. Such indications, he continued, accompanied by a correct grasp of the present, offers the key to understanding the past.[17] Moreover, the suspension of the 'present form of production relations' will supply the signification of its 'becoming – foreshadowings of the future'. In these passages and elsewhere, Marx clearly outlined what Bensaid has called a 'new temporality of knowledge.' The societies of the past are never historical in their immediacy but only acquire this status through the present. There is no horizontal trajectory here, as supposed by a linear, chronological historical trajectory – the before and after – but rather verticality, the necessity of excavating the depths of the present, where the traces and residues of pasts coexist with and within it, often remaining hidden or unrecognized, like the purloined letter or appearing in 'stunted', and 'caricatured form ... but always with an essential difference'.[18]

What Marx showed in the *Grundrisse* was the historic shape of pre-capitalist formations as communal and clan-based typifications that might have existed before the separation from land that marked the momentous beginnings of primitive accumulation and the installation of wage labour. Reflecting an uncertainty relating to the accessibility of knowledge on ancient societies, Marx, in one of his letters to the Russian Vera Zasulich, he confesses how little is known of these archaic communities and that what is known from available sources represents the formation in its *'final term'*.[19] Implied in this new account was a division between history, which referred to the order that concepts and categories appeared historically, and capital logic, which arranged their relationships to each other differently according to a more formal principle.[20] But in both cases we have instances of the workings of contingency, not teleological destiny. Marx's historic perspective was concerned with presuppositions, what he named 'suspended presuppositions', the 'merely historical', 'past and gone', that were no longer visible or evident but clearly important to later development but 'in no way to its *contemporary* history, that is, not to the real system of the mode of production'.[21] With *Capital*, moreover, Marx outlined capital's immense conceptualization of the organization of time and with the establishment of the working day the successive permeation of value throughout everyday life. In this respect, the world of pre-capitalist social formations would always remain hostage to the capitalist present, always mediated by the unstated force of its temporal accountancy.

Since so much of the *Grundrisse* was concerned with showing how wage labour developed from the separation of free workers from the land and their fall into a state of dependence based solely on the only thing they owned, the sale of their labour power, it is not surprising that Marx's description of the prior moment would reflect the opposite of what had previously existed, namely the absence of working to create value.[22] Here, the presupposition of capital was the free worker before being released from the land as his 'natural workshop', which meant the 'dissolution of small, free landed property' under clan-based communal ownership 'resting on the oriental commune'.[23] These communal organizations functioned like chronotopic variations of an earlier pre-capitalist mode of production, whereby a specific conception of space dissolved time. What seemed to characterize the 'Asiatic' forms (Marx earlier called them 'Oriental despotism') was the 'commonality of labour' and the extraction of surplus product.[24] Anderson has proposed that Marx took a 'more even handed position' towards these communities from the views expressed in the 1853 articles on India.[25] But it is important that in the *Grundrisse*, Marx includes areas outside of Asia, emphasizing the centrality of the 'commonality of labour' throughout diverse regions of the archaic world, implying a universal disposition, which stands in contrast to what replaced it after the great 'separation' from conditions of living labour and the means of existence.[26] More importantly, Marx additionally saw the incidence of 'free day labourers' in all places where either the Oriental community (*Gemeinwesen*) or the western commune (*Gemeinde*) 'dissolved into individual element' through the loss of conditions of self-sustaining labour.[27] Here, Marx asserted that a 'presupposition of wage labour' historically is 'free labour'.[28] The result of this inversion was the disappearance of free workers as proprietors – 'members of the community' 'who at the same time work'.[29] Here, it seems, Marx resorted to the tactic of inverting

CRITIQUE IN THE EXPANDED FIELD   333

the inversion (recalling the negation of the negation), whereby the naturalness attributed to capitalism by political economy already constituted an inversion of the historical real, which he now tried to restore with a second inversion. Communal land owners, in any case, worked not to create value, but to maintain the individual proprietor and his family, not to forget the 'total community' itself.[30] While Marx emphasized this form's relationship to the 'property of the community', whereby each individual constitutes a link as a member and proprietor, he was convinced that the form could be realized in very different ways – in the Asiatic, Slavonic and Romanian communes, if not the Russian *mir*. The various forms present variations of a primary historic presupposition, not evolving in progressive sequences and stages in a unilinear chronology but rather moving according to different and uneven temporalities contingent on their historically different circumstances. The commune, wherever encountered, appeared as a 'coming-together' (*Vereinigun*g) – a 'unification made up of independent subjects, landed proprietors, not as a unity'.[31] Their aim was survival through reproduction,[32] and the collapse of these archaic communities followed a rhythm determined by their different circumstances. The Asiatic, Marx observed, held out longest, owing to its presuppositions that the individual does not become independent vis-à-vis the community – that is, their difference from a universalist norm of 'communal labour' and 'naturally arisen, spontaneous communal property'.[33]

The temporal unevenness accompanying the dissolution of the ancient form was at the heart of Marx's new view of history. By the same measure *Capital* makes clear that his 'sketch' derives from the English example, which represents the 'classic form'. But the history of the expropriation of agricultural producers 'assumes different aspects in different countries, and runs throughout various phases in different orders of succession, and different epochs'.[34] To be sure, primitive accumulation referred only to countries already embarked on the capitalist route, but there is no reason to exclude those colonized regions like

India and China in the late nineteenth century, where forms of wage labour were already established in certain enterprises devoted to the production of tea, if not opium. This suggests that differential temporal rates, if not histories, marked each society's development along a capitalist itinerary that reflected the 'uneven development of material production relative to, for example, artistic development'[35] and indeed between different spheres of social activity and among a diversity of societies. It is interesting to note that Japanese philosophers before World War II who were not Marxists had already recognized the different temporalities and histories lived by different societies and had identified the false universalism represented by the 'European' model.[36] The new historical temporality did away with the image of a universal history and its 'abstract notion of progress', which was invariably based on the presumption of a linear and homogeneous history, 'wherein the flow of time and meaning coincide'.[37] In fact, logical order took precedence over genetic order, which, accordingly, was 'confused with empirical history'.[38] But this was precisely the conception of historical time promoted by the nation-state. When both nation form and the representation of history were designated as the political form for entry into the world market and the placeholder for capital, the necessity to extinguish spectral reminders of unevenness and untimeliness became even more compelling. At this juncture the time-lag appeared and was exported to regions outside of Euro-America as the sign of their collective underdevelopment, even though it functioned to conceal both its instance within 'advanced' capitalist societies and capitalism's own unscheduled cycles, waves, irregular rhythms – the world of *zeitwidrig*, non-contemporaneity, discordance.[39] By contrast, the temporality of time lag in postcolonial theory – primarily an economic category – was transmuted into the moment of subaltern address, just as the spectre of unevenness was reinscribed as hybridity and diasporic cosmopolitanism! Each present, then, supplies a multiplicity of possible lines of development, as Marx proposed in his letters to Zasulich when he envisioned the possibility of the Russian commune freeing itself gradually from the fetters of primitiveness to promote production on a national scale. Yet, 'precisely because it is contemporaneous with capitalist production, the rural community may appropriate all its positive achievements without ... frightful vicissitudes.'[40] (Such trajectories do not possess the same 'index of normality', on which only the second and third internationals insisted.[41])

We can infer from all this that Marx had moved towards envisaging the multiple possibilities for radical transformation among the world's societies that no longer depended upon their capacity to replicate the European model supplied by colonial experience and that, as his views on Russia showed, could utilize the residues of prior modes of production to create either a new register of formal subsumption or bypass capitalism altogether. Lindner reminds us that in the early 'British Rule in India' (1853) Marx already raised the question of whether mankind could fulfil its destiny without a fundamental revolution in the social state of Asia. If not, he replied, whatever may have been the crimes the British committed, the nation was the unwitting and unconscious tool of history in bringing about that revolution. But only if Asia fails to do so on its own and from its resources. In this regard, the *Grundrisse* was more hopeful when Marx remarked that 'when the limited bourgeois form is stripped away, what is wealth other than the universality of individual needs, capacities, pleasures, productive forces etc. created through universal exchange? ... The absolute working out of ... creative potentialities, with no presupposition other than the previous historical development', whereby mankind 'strives not to remain something ... [it] has become, but in the absolute movement of becoming'?[42] With this view, the question we must ask is, who needs postcoloniality? For Lindner, it is important for Marxism to enter into a cooperative discussion between a Marx stripped of charges of Eurocentrism and cultural superiority and postcolonial studies that will 'deepen their analysis of contradictions by adopting a global perspective'. Yet what else was Marx's critique and Marxism but an analysis devoted to dissembling capital's contradictions on a global scale? Postcolonial studies provides a new perspective for understanding historical progress. But in the heterological history made possible by uneven flows and the prospect of untimeliness, 'progress' would, as I have suggested, have to be released from its unilinear mooring and rethought as a relative progress that considers missed opportunities and vanished, defeated possibilities.[43] Marxism must be open to the prospect of contingency. Here, Lindner quotes approvingly from Louis Althusser, who, at the last count, was a Marxist of long standing, and points to his reflections on the 'materialist philosophy of the encounter'. But Althusser, following Marx and Lenin, saw this 'encounter' as identical with the idea of 'conjuncture', the optic through which to think the historical reality of those moments when a diversity of circumstances from different sectors confront each other to present 'a world, torn between powers in collusion and the "crises" which unites them in a circle'.[44] This historical reality referred to the conviction that while historical periods have their laws, 'they can also change at the drop of a hat revealing the aleatory basis that sustains, ... without reason ... without intelligible end'.[45] This is the history of capitalism, a series of contingent historical encounters producing practices, which subsequently were reordered as categories into a logic of relationships to become the mature form of capitalism. Well before Althusser, I should add, the Japanese economist Uno Kozo had already worked out this Marxian conception of contingency and recognized how it necessarily separated history from logic. Where the cleft remains between Marxism and postcoloniality, in the final analysis, is in the dematerialization of the latter as a condition of its own discursive possibility and opposition to the former. For its part, what Marxism needs to learn is how to shed its parochial 'Western' identity (in what has been named 'Western Marxism'), since it has contributed to reinforcing the idea of a unified West. This modest task might hopefully be begun by ending the practice of referring to regions outside Euro-America in the negativity of 'non-Western'. It might also learn to acquire a sensitivity towards postcolonialism's concerns for memory and a melancholy provoked by the irretrievable loss inflicted by capitalism's immeasurable destruction of what Fanon described as received 'cultures of reference'.[46]

Notes

Thanks, again, to Kristin Ross for critical commentary and editorial suggestions.

1. John Kraniauskas, 'Difference Against Development: Spiritual Accumulation and the Politics of Freedom', in H. Harootunian and H.O. Park, eds, *Problems of Comparability/Possibilities for Comparative Studies*, special edition of *boundary 2*, vol. 2, no. 2, Summer 2006, p. 68.
2. Neil Lazarus, 'The Fetish of the West in Postcolonial Theory', in Crystal Bartolovich and Neil Lazarus, eds, *Marxism, Modernity and Postcoloniality*, Cambridge University Press, Cambridge, 2002, p. 6.
3. Kolya Lindner, 'Marx's Eurocentrism: Postcolonial Studies and Marxian Scholarship', *RP* 161, May/June 2010, pp. 27–41; Chapter 13, above, in this volume.
4. Bartolovich and Lazarus, *Marxism, Modernity and Postcoloniality*, p. 1.
5. Ibid., p. 3.
6. Neil Lazarus, ed., *Cambridge Companion to Postcolonial Literary Studies*, Cambridge University Press, Cambridge, 2004, p. 6.
7. Ibid., p. 9.
8. Fredric Jameson, 'On Cultural Studies', in *The Ideologies of Theory*, Verso, London and New York, 2008, pp. 598–635.
9. See J.G. Farrell, *Troubles*, Review Books Classics, New York, 2002, on the last days of the British imperial presence in Ireland, centred on the irreparable hotel of this fading glory, the Majestic, a sure inspiration for the later *Fawlty Towers*.
10. Karl Marx, *Grundrisse, Introduction to the Critique of Political Economy*, trans. Martin Nicolaus, Penguin, London, 1973, p. 536. In *Capital*, Volume 1, Marx was equally clear when he wrote 'In truth … value is here the subject of a process' that 'valorizes itself independently', an 'automatic subject' (trans. Ben Fowkes, Penguin, London, 1976, p. 255).
11. Lawrence Krader, Introduction to Karl Marx, *Ethnological Notebooks*, Van Gorcum, Assen, 1974; *The Asiatic Mode of Production: Sources, Development and Critique in the Writings of Karl Marx*, Van Gorcum, Assen, 1975; Kevin Anderson, *Marx at the Margins: On Nationalism, Ethnicity and Non-Western Societies*, University of Chicago Press, Chicago, 2010.
12. Daniel Bensaid, *La Discordance du temps*, Éditions de la Passion, Paris, 1995, p. 18.
13. Ibid., p. 19.
14. Ibid.
15. *Grundrisse*, pp. 105, 460.
16. Ibid., pp. 105–6.
17. Ibid., pp. 460–61.
18. Bensaid, *Marx for Our Times*, p. 27; *Grundrisse*, p. 106.
19. Teodor Shanin, ed., *Late Marx and the Russian Road*, Monthly Review Press, New York, 1983, p. 106.
20. Stavros Tombazos, *Les catégories du temps dan l'analyse économique*, Cahiers des Saisons, Paris, 1994. This proposition was advanced much earlier in the writings of the Japanese economist Uno Kozo.
21. *Grundrisse*, p. 459.
22. Ibid., p. 471; Anderson, *Marx at the Margins*, p. 156.
23. Ibid., p. 471.
24. *Grundrisse*, p. 473; Anderson, *Marx at the Margins*, p. 157.
25. Anderson, *Marx at the Margins*, p. 157.
26. *Grundrisse*, p. 463.
27. Ibid., p. 465.
28. Ibid., p. 471.
29. Ibid.
30. Ibid., p. 472.

31. Ibid., p. 483.
32. Ibid., p. 493.
33. Anderson, *Marx at the Margins*, p. 161; *Grundrisse*, p. 472.
34. *Capital*, Volume 1, p. 876.
35. *Grundrisse*, p. 109.
36. See Koyama Iwao, *Sekaishi no tetsugaku* (The Philosophy of World History), Tokyo, pp. 446ff. This text was actually written in 1941, by one of the leading philosophers of the Kyoto School, and represents the most thorough nationalist critique of European models of modernity.
37. Bensaid, *Marx for Our Times*, p. 21.
38. Ibid., p. 26.
39. Ibid., p. 23.
40. Shanin, *Late Marx*, p. 106.
41. See Bensaid, *Marx for Our Times*, p. 32.
42. *Grundrisse*, p. 488.
43. Bensaid, *Marx for Our Times*, p. 32.
44. Louis Althusser, *Philosophy of the Encounter*, ed. François Matheron and Olivier Corpet, trans. G.M. Goshgarian, Verso, London, 2006, p. 188.
45. Ibid., p. 196.
46. Leela Gandhi, *Postcolonial Theory*, Columbia University Press, New York, 1998, pp. 5–17.

15 Race, real estate and real abstraction

BRENNA BHANDAR & ALBERTO TOSCANO

The crises and mutations of contemporary capitalism have rendered palpable Marx's observation according to which in bourgeois modernity human beings are 'ruled by abstractions'.[1] The processes of financialization animating the dynamics of the 2007–8 crisis involved the violent irruption into the everyday lives of millions of a panoply of ominous acronyms (ABSs, CDOs, SIVs, HFT, and so on), indices of highly mathematized strategies of profit extraction whose mechanics were often opaque to their own beneficiaries. At the same time, this process of financialization was articulated to the most seemingly 'concrete', 'tangible' and thus desirable use and exchange value available to the citizens of so-called advanced liberal democracies: the home. This is a site, a social relation, that as Ferreira da Silva and Chakravartty have noted encompasses the 'juridical, political and economic', thus serving as a lived material synthesis of the three main axes of modern thought.[2]

In the United States it was quickly revealed – indeed, it had been pointed out before the crisis by some critical geographers[3] – that the devastating socialization of the costs of accumulation via the housing market took deeply racialized (and gendered) forms, grafting, through a host of complex mediations, the forbiddingly impersonal realities of derivative contracts onto the deep and ongoing racial history of property markets and urban geographies. In this article, we want to think through this articulation of race, property and capitalist abstraction, exploring how attention to the forms of property may permit novel and politically urgent insights into the relationship between capitalism and race, addressing a critical area of social contestation in which processes of racialization are intensely present, but in which they are also frequently 'disappeared'.[4] We revisit the place of property in Marxist theories of abstraction, to consider whether it can provide us with some of the instruments to think the present conjuncture, but also to explore the ways in which a consideration of the racial logics of property may require us to recalibrate our understanding of the violence of abstraction.

Separation, dissolution, abstraction
If we take Marx to have been engaged in the practical, emancipatory critique of capitalism, not just as a class system of exploitation but as a social form of abstract domination, then we can understand that under the misleadingly simple slogan 'the abolition of private property' lies the formidable problem of transcending a social relation, 'bourgeois property', which serves as the crucial nexus between the state (the object of Marx's earliest critique) and the economy. In what sense is the question of private property a question of abstraction? Above all, perhaps, in the sense that private property (understood not as personal possession but as the legally sanctioned power to dispose of the means of production, and thus to dispose of labour-power: property as synonymous with capital) depends on a social process of *separation* – abstraction in the etymological sense of pulling out, extracting. In one of Marx's most important mature treatments of the question of property, the section on pre-capitalist formations in the notebooks later collected as the *Grundrisse*, this separation is discussed in terms of a *dissolution*.

In passages that foreshadow his treatment of so-called primitive accumulation in the first volume of *Capital,* Marx depicts capitalism as the first system in which political or communal relations are no longer presupposed by property but are 'posed' by it. Far from being conditioned by a pre-existing community, property qua capital becomes the only real community, the one dominated by abstraction, by money. As he writes, 'the relation of labour to capital ... presupposes a process of history which dissolves the various forms in which the worker is a proprietor, or in which the proprietor works.' He is alluding to the dissolution of the relation to the earth, in which there is 'direct common property';[5] the dissolution of proprietorship of the instrument (in craft production); the dissolution of the means of subsistence; and the dissolution of serfdom and slavery. These are the 'historic presuppositions' 'needed before the worker can be found as a free worker, as objectless, purely subjective labour capacity confronting the objective conditions of production as his *not-property*, as *alien property*, as *value* for-itself, as capital'.[6] This process, which Marx strikingly terms that of 'dissolution into capital', is one in which 'The objective conditions of labour now confront these unbound, propertyless individuals only in the form of values, self-sufficient values.'[7] 'Private property' is thus understood as a double movement of abstraction, one which is conditioned by historical processes of separation but which in its real subsumption of social life continues to serve as a potent agent of dissolution.

This theme of dissolution was already present in Marx's thinking about the political and economic functions of *landed* property back in the *Economic and Philosophical Manuscripts*, where he wrote: 'It is necessary that this appearance be abolished – that landed property, the root of private property, be dragged completely into the movement of private property and that it become a commodity; that the rule of the proprietor appear as the undisguised rule of private property, of capital, freed of all political tincture.'[8] For the purposes of our argument, we should be sensitive to the different accents given in Marx's early and later work to this theme of property as the dissolution (which is to say the abstraction) of social bonds. Roughly, property is presented in the early Marx's work as an agent of abstraction whose real subsumption of social life (and destruction of concrete community) serves as a kind of tragic but necessary prelude to emancipation, to the emergence of a universality antagonistic to that of capital. In the *Grundrisse* we can instead discern a way of thinking both the rupture represented by the emergence of capitalist property and the persistence (albeit overdetermined by capitalist forms) of so-called pre-capitalist relations. This is what the Hegelian formulation – property now posing its own presuppositions – entails. (It is also, as we shall discuss below, what Stuart Hall was trying to capture in his deployment of the Althusserian notion of *articulation*.)

In his *Intellectual and Manual Labour*, elaborating on Marx's insights into the commodity form, the German philosopher Alfred Sohn-Rethel argued that the origins of the abstract concepts of ancient philosophy were to be located in what he called 'the exchange-abstraction', the activity of generalized commodity-exchange and monetization that served as the unconscious practical 'social synthesis' of Ancient Greek society. It was the existence of a *really abstract social practice* which stood as the presupposition of mental or intellectual abstraction. It was because the Ancient Greeks acted abstractly, so to speak, that they could think abstractly. Marx's uniqueness for Sohn-Rethel lay in being able to provide the means for fully historical, practical explanations of the emergence of seemingly ahistorical forms. Applying Marx's understanding of the commodity to the study of the social unconscious of philosophy allowed one to see how the practice of exchange served as the concrete spatio-temporal basis for a thinking that could powerfully abstract from both space and time. To paraphrase Sohn-Rethel: abstraction is therefore the effect of the action of men, and not of their thought. In reality, it takes place 'behind their backs', at the blind spot, so to speak, of human consciousness.[9] That is where the thinking and efforts of men are absorbed by their acts of exchange.

Now, in what sense can we treat property (more accurately: the legal forms of private property) as a 'real abstraction'? However we may frame or interpret it, there is a prima facie force to the notion that the imposition and generalization of private property did (and continue to) play a formidable role in dissolving social and communal relations, or at the very least in 'positing' them as internal to a property logic. Private property's role as an agent of separation from means of production and subsistence is also not in doubt, and lies at the centre of a vibrant contemporary debate on the 'commons' and 'common goods'.[10] Yet a key feature of the account of real abstraction in Sohn-Rethel, arguably present in certain formulations of Marx also, is troubled by greater attention to the *legal* forms of property. That feature is the *unconscious* character ascribed to commodity-exchange as a form of practical abstraction. Any account of the pre-capitalist presuppositions of capitalist abstract domination cannot rest content, as Sohn-Rethel seems to, with investigating the exchange-abstraction in ancient forms of commodity-based socialization. It also requires thinking of the specificity of legal abstractions as deliberate devices of social organization which were in turn necessary but not sufficient presuppositions for the emergence of capitalism.

The legal historian Yan Thomas, writing on Roman law, suggests we should think of abstraction as constitutive of the operations of the law. This is true of the 'formal *dispositif* that isolates in each of us, abstracting from what is irreducibly singular in us, a juridical personality, in which almost nothing appears of our physical, psychic and social reality, because it is reduced to a single function: our capacity to hold and exercise rights'.[11] Here we can see how modern law is conceived in terms of a twofold process 'of incarnation and naturalization, on the one hand, and of separation and abstraction, on the other, of the juridical person'.[12] It is also at work, importantly, in what Thomas presents as the 'juridical constitution of things in general',[13] where the *res* stands both for appropriable things of property and commerce, on the one hand, and sacred or public inappropriable things, *res nullius in bonis*, on the other.[14] Thomas presents his 'proceduralist' approach as one that can reveal how

Roman law 'already had a formalist and abstract idea of the economy' (by contrast with what has been argued by the historical anthropology of the ancient world); for him, 'the history of law partakes of a history of the techniques and instruments through which the putting into abstract form of our societies has taken place.' If that is not properly grasped, he warns, 'the singularity of that history and the specificity of its object' will be totally missed. Thomas shows how the reduction of a thing (*res*) to its price (*pretium*) – the identity of being and value, in other words – was itself a product of juridical procedure, or legal judgment, in which the *res* was 'abstracted and reduced to its value', permitting a 'representation of a purely countable substance of goods',[15] in its turn made possible by the circumscription of a sacred or public sphere of unappropriable goods. In Michele Spanò's gloss, 'law – the most efficacious speech – has a power of transformation without equals: it is a machine for abstraction which, through the medium of language, translates the real and produces it otherwise.'[16]

In light of the Marxist debate surveyed here, the question arises: what is the relation between the social practices of abstraction (grounded in abstract labour and the commodity form) that Marx and Marxists have posited as somehow 'beneath' or 'before' the juridical, though articulated with it, and even requiring it as an 'indispensable moment', and what Thomas calls 'the political construction of the commodity'[17] by law, which would appear to present the operation of abstraction as a deliberate juridical procedure, conditioning economic valorization and accumulation, rather than the other way around? Answering such questions might also require at least posing the problem of the extent to which private property as a moment of capital and private property in property law are superimposable without remainder.

Property between law and capital

In 1865 Marx wrote this about Proudhon:

Thus history itself had expressed its criticism upon past *property relations*. What Proudhon was actually dealing with was *modern bourgeois property* as it exists today. The question of what this is could have only been answered by a critical analysis of '*political economy*', embracing the totality of these *property relations*, considering not their *legal* aspect as *relations of volition* but their real form, that is, as *relations of production*.[18]

In this passage is encapsulated what would become, especially in the 1960s and 1970s, a vexed question within Marxist debates about law, debates which were in many ways motivated by the now largely forgotten debates about the forms of property and the transition to socialism, but which were perhaps most memorably encapsulated in E.P. Thompson's much-quoted acerbic retort to Althusser that in the history of English capitalism law was to be found 'at every bloody level'. Without trying to summarize these debates we can note that Marx himself stayed true to his observation, made as early as 1847 in 'Moralizing Criticism and Critical Morality', that 'private property is not an abstract concept or a simple relation but the totality of bourgeois relations of production'[19] and thus that treating private property as synonymous with its purely legal form or that form's conceptual and ahistorical hypostasis was insufficient.

Whence the various attempts to distinguish, in ways which at times seem to re-propose the old distinction between (real) possession and (legal) property, between property as legally inscribed and property as a social relation that may exceed its legal form.[20] Thus Nicos Poulantzas would write of how he and Charles Bettelheim had 'noted that it is necessary to distinguish, in the term "property" used by Marx, formal legal property, which may not belong to the 'individual' capitalist, and economic property or real appropriation, which is the only genuine economic power'.[21] In *Reading Capital*, Étienne Balibar notes that for Marx juridical forms are supremely ambivalent, as they 'express' and 'codify' at the same time as they mask economic reality. More importantly for our purposes, though he recognizes the need to keep the space between law, politics and economy open, he also observes how in the specific case of property this is rendered terminologically and conceptually arduous:

> Hence a difficult *terminological* problem as well, since the concepts in which the relations of production are expressed are precisely concepts in which the economic and the legal are indistinct, starting with the concept of *property*. What is 'property' insofar as it forms a system within the relatively autonomous structure of production, and logically precedes the law of property peculiar to the society considered? Such is the problem which must be initiated for capitalism *too*.[22]

Every element in the mode of production under capitalism is said by Balibar, then, to receive a 'juridical qualification'; it is inscribed in a legal system marked by its abstract universality, a universality which is a reflection of the commodity system – such that the commodity would serve as the cell-form for social abstraction under capitalism.[23] Criticizing Bettelheim's notion of 'economic property' in a later text, Balibar would go further and note that the risk in such a notion (aside from introducing the law of property into a concept whose purpose was to keep it at a distance) was that while rightly not wishing to confuse relations of production and juridical forms of property, it neglected the practical historical role of juridical forms of property, the fact that juridical form was an indispensable moment in capital accumulation; that the accumulation and concentration of capital 'cannot take place without a systematic use of the resources of property law'.[24]

This bears some relation to the critique rendered by Paul Hirst of the place of property in the Marxist legal theories of Evgeny Pashukanis and Karl Renner. Hirst criticizes Marxist theories of the law that reduce legal subjectivity down to the archetypical capitalist, the subject of property right, who engages in economic calculation.[25] The joint-stock company and the shareholder, Hirst argued, represents a type of ownership that is not confined by the 'triple coincidence of property, possession and calculation [in exchange]' that lies at the heart of Marxist considerations of property law. Moreover, the problem of what 'capital' is cannot be separated from questions of the legal definition of its form of organization. As the emergence of the joint-stock company illustrates, 'there is no given form of this organization'.[26] In other words, inventiveness, and a certain amount of flexibility in legal forms, enabling the emergence of new configurations of ownership and market relations, may be as central to our understanding of property as a juridical, economic and social relation as are laws which are taken to directly express the commodity form in its fundamental coordinates.

Articulating race and property
In light of the aforementioned discussions, we can say that to understand the *abstractive powers* of property law – and their articulation with and use of racial difference in processes of propertization and profit – we cannot simply treat property forms as reflections or adjuncts of commodity forms, which is also to say that we cannot treat the question of the practical reality of abstraction as one which is simply adjudicated at the (very abstract) level of the formal analysis of capital. What we would seem to require is a way of thinking the *articulation* between distinct and sometimes independent modalities of abstraction. We would need to be able to think the articulation between *events* and *processes* of abstraction/dissolution (the moments of primitive accumulation or accumulation by dispossession); the 'unconscious' abstracting social *practices* (as grasped, for instance, in Sohn-Rethel's account of the exchange-abstraction); the high-level *logic* of abstraction intrinsic to value as a social form of capitalism; and the relatively autonomous and deliberate *practices* and *devices* of abstraction (scientific, mathematical, linguistic, but also political and *juridical*) that are either articulated with real abstraction or posed by it as its 'presuppositions'. The problem of the creation and use of racial difference within practices of accumulation and dispossession, and its link to financialized abstraction and property law, in the case under

consideration, would thus require not a reduction or integration, but an articulation of different modalities of abstraction, including race itself as an abstraction. 'Racism', writes Ruth Wilson Gilmore, 'is a practice of abstraction, a death-dealing displacement of difference into hierarchies that organize relations within and between the planet's sovereign political territories.' Processes of abstraction, Gilmore notes, figure humans in relation to inhuman persons in a hierarchy that produces the totalizing category of the 'human being'.[27]

We take this notion of articulation from the work of Stuart Hall in the late 1970s and early 1980s, in particular from his theoretical and political interventions into contemporary debates about Marxist method, interventions which centred on the question of race. Besides testaments to Hall's capacious scope and the generous engagement with a welter of different positions, these texts are unique in taking the different formations of race within capitalism as the impetus to rethink Marx's method of abstraction, and vice versa. In this regard, they can be said not only to address the varieties of racialized capitalism, in a way which can hopefully elucidate the place of property within them; they also offer vital perspectives through which to revisit those problems of abstraction and concreteness most memorably outlined in Marx's '1857 Introduction', a text to which Hall returned time and again.[28]

Though it is not possible to do much justice to Hall's insights here, we can note that his return to Marx's dialectic of the abstract and the concrete via Althusser's theory of overdetermination was aimed at generating a Marxist theory capable of truly thinking difference. Against an ultra-Hegelian reading of Marx that would view his mature work through the lens of the self-movement of capital's categories, Hall stressed that Marx's were concepts 'which *differentiate* in the very moment that they reveal hidden connections'; though capitalism 'tends to reproduce itself in expanded form *as if* it were a self-equilibrating and self-sustaining system',[29] it constantly relies on precarious social and political mediations, including racisms themselves, none of which are guaranteed by an ineluctable logic. Though Hall, unlike many of his peers, does not jettison the notion of totality, he repeatedly asserts that capitalist social formations are complexly structured differentiated totalities, unities that require differentiation, in which, to use Neil Smith's formulation, the production of sameness or equivalence is always accompanied by a production of difference. From the Althusser of *For Marx* (which Hall plays off against what he perceived as the overly rigid structuralism of *Reading Capital*), he draws 'the recognition that there are different social contradictions with different origins; that the contradictions which drive the historical process forward do not always appear in the same place, and will not always have the same historical effects'.[30] Hall's counter-intuitive avowal that Althusser 'enabled me to live in and with *difference*'[31] is brought home by his autobiographical analysis of the contrasting overdeterminations of class by race in the UK and Jamaica, and of the ways in which these different structurations-in-dominance – one in which the immigrant 'black' was starkly opposed to the native 'white', the other in which 'black' sat at one end of a spectrum in which 'white' was the absent apex – shaped everyday life and discourse.[32] Hall's insistence that in certain societies race can be the way 'the modality in which class is "lived", the medium through which class relations are experienced, the form in which it is appropriated and "fought through"',[33] is here compounded by the account, bolstered by a Marxism of difference, of how the abstract categories or systems of representations attached to race are experienced. The abstractions of race are in this regard not just real, but lived. This is among the reasons why 'there is nothing simple about the dynamics of racism'.[34]

Applied to the problem of race in capitalism, Althusser's concepts of articulation, overdetermination, and of societies structured-in-dominance, permitted Hall, by his own account, to undermine the teleological reductivism and economism of a certain Marxism – which would see race inevitably dissolved by class contradiction – as well as culturalist or ethnocentric accounts which treated race and racism as purely autonomous variables.[35] Both of these positions elide the historical specificity, which is also to say the political cognizability, of social formations in which race plays a structuring role. They helped Hall to think, especially in the collaborative project *Policing the Crisis*, how

> the structures through which black labour is reproduced ... are not simply 'coloured' by race: they work through race. The relations of capitalism can be thought of as articulating classes in distinct ways at each of the levels of instances of the social formation – economic, political, ideological. These levels are the 'effects' of the structures of modern capitalist production, with the necessary displacement of relative autonomy operating between them.[36]

We would like to propose that contemporary debates on race and property could also be thought according to this model, to detail the ways in which property law also *works through race*,[37] and to investigate how, to use Hall's terms, the absence of any necessary correspondence between race and class, or race and property, by no means entails 'necessarily no correspondence' between them.[38]

At stake in thinking about legal forms as both *articulated with* and an *articulation of* economic and social relations, is continuing the excavation of how capitalist property relations preserve and rely upon 'other relations that are not ascribable within the "social relations of production". These include distinctions at the level of culture and values' – maintained by institutional structures, particular forms of political power, and of course, histories of colonization and slavery. For example, in commenting on the work of sociologists such as John Rex writing in the 1970s about South Africa, Hall notes that specifically colonial modes of labour were foundational to the establishment of a capitalist market economy:

> The 'origin' of the capitalist mode in conditions of conquest, coupled with the 'peculiar institutions' of unfree labour thus preserve, at the

economic level, and secure its continuing racially ascriptive features. This is a capitalism of a very specific and distinctive kind: 'there are a number of different relationships to the means of production *more subtle than can be comprehended in terms of distinction between owners and non-owners*' each of which 'gives rise to specific class situations ... a whole range of class situations'.³⁹

Both before and after Hall's writing, the articulation of different strategies of accumulation, embedded in colonial modes of land appropriation, feudal social relations, and free and unfree labour, conceived of as constituting the mode through which legal forms of property and relations of ownership take root, has been undertaken by many scholars writing in the black radical tradition and indigenous studies. It is to them that we now turn.

Race, dispossession and the subject of property

At the turn of the twentieth century, Peruvian socialist Jose Mariátegui wrote incisively of the dispossession of Indian communities in Peru as the ground upon which the *latifundistas* built an agrarian economy that largely failed, in his view, to escape feudal social relations. Nonetheless, this was a feudalism that contained within it an 'incipient capitalism'.⁴⁰ Mariátegui posited the 'Indian land question' as one that was inherently economic, while also identifying those social and cultural aspects of 'indigenous communism' that were so severely diminished by the gradual imposition of colonial capitalist land ownership. Roxanne Dunbar-Ortiz has also identified the dispossession of indigenous lands as the central motor force of primitive accumulation in the United States.⁴¹

Dunbar-Ortiz maps the conquest of New Mexico through an exploration of three different but interlocking modes of ongoing capitalist expropriation: primitive accumulation based on the appropriation of native land, the appropriation of key resources, namely water, and the exploitation of native labour on the large estates, which was facilitated by successive imposition of non-native property law and land tenure and military occupation.

Dunbar-Ortiz reveals how, contrary to orthodox Marxist understandings of the development of capitalism, the 'expropriation of the land, the means of production, and the resources' of the indigenous population, including their labour, are each coterminous with the development of agrarian capitalism in the USA, and continue into the present. We could also mention here the work of Silvia Federici,[42] Glen Coulthard[43] and Ruth Wilson Gilmore, as demonstrating how contemporary capitalist accumulation relies on an amalgam of older and newer inventive mechanisms that preserve racial and gendered logics established during colonial settlement and slavery. In her landmark book, *The Golden Gulag*, Ruth Wilson Gilmore explores the many different economies involved in the intensification of incarceration in California. She examines how chronic unemployment and deindustrialization, planning laws, the use of financial instruments by public authorities to generate revenue, and of course a racial moral panic about crime, provided the fertile ground for prison expansion in California. Crucially, Wilson Gilmore illuminates the human cost of the forms of expropriation detailed in the book, emphasizing that entire ways of life are unmoored by capital flight.[44]

Employing the framework of articulation as a way of understanding contemporary forms of dispossession also offers one way of addressing the very salient question of legal subjectivity. As noted above, Hall endorses John Rex's observation that the distinction between owner and non-owner is no longer adequate, if it ever was, fully to understand racialized capitalist social formations, and, we could say by extension, contemporary forms of property and relations of ownership. This is not only because legal forms of property have proliferated so intensely in late modernity, rendering the function of ownership somewhat ambiguous in relation to key functions traditionally ascribed by Marxist theorists to ownership, namely exclusive control over the means of production. Hall seconds this observation because when we examine the specificities of how historically embedded forms of racism and patriarchy overlapped with particular economic structures, the attributes normally ascribed to the 'owner' are much more complex. For instance, the individual self-interest of black property owners and their involvement in race-based land expropriation in the 1960s and 1970s can only be explained, as N.D.B. Connolly does in his book *A World More Concrete: Real Estate and the Remaking of Jim Crow South Florida*, because of the long history of slavery and legalized racism that made property ownership the most prized path to full citizenship. In other words, merely seeing black property-owners as driven by the same profit motive as white landlords, or employing an economically reductive analytical framework, truly fails to grasp what the meaning of ownership is for black landlords, given the social relations and histories of race and racism that have shaped the US real-estate market.

Connolly argues that immigrants, black land- and property-owners, and even indigenous people 'made tremendous investments in racial apartheid, largely in an effort to govern growing cities and to unleash the value of land as real estate'.[45] Exploitative landlord and tenant relations between black landlords and black tenants were triangulated through that 'white apex' we have already encountered in Hall, embodied concretely in the real property that signified full citizenship and political power. The ideology of ownership embraced by these particular groups of people and individual landowners was mediated through histories of dispossession and displacement. The concept of the self-possessive individual that is variously assumed and critiqued by Marxist scholars also requires a deconstruction that takes into account the persistence of racism configured through relations of ownership. Scholars such as Saidiya Hartman have foregrounded C.B. Macpherson's failure to account for the history of slavery and, subsequent to that, Jim Crow laws that formed the conditions in which the ideal-typical possessive individual came into being. Hartman has argued that freedom from slavery, which granted former slaves entry into the framework of possessive individualism as free subjects, entailed a cruel contradiction. Self-possession was characterized, for instance, by the taking of a surname, often that of the ex-master, that 'conferred ... the paradox of emancipation and the dispossession that acquires the status of a legacy'.[46] Moving from the status of an object to that of a labouring subject was marked by debt peonage and labour conditions so brutal that they could hardly be said to reflect the alienation of one's labour through free choice.[47] As Hartman writes, '[t]he propertied person remained vulnerable to the dispossession exacted by violation, domination, and exploitation' that existed during slavery.[48] This is the recent history that informs present ideologies of ownership and the cultural and social significance of ownership for people of colour in the USA, and particularly within black and indigenous communities.

The notion of 'articulation' also opens up the figure of the self-possessive individual to considering the colonially inscribed concepts of race in the fashioning of the modern legal subject. Balibar's *Identity and Difference* has begun to bridge the long-standing gap between Locke's theory of consciousness in the *Essay on Human Understanding* and his theory of property elaborated in the *Two Treatises of Government*.

How might Balibar's reflections on Locke assist us in accounting for the place of race and patriarchy in the identity–property nexus, or the contact point between propriety and property? In drawing out and emphasizing the temporal dimension of Locke's concept of self-consciousness, the concept of the self in the *Essay* not only moves closer to the political philosophy of property in the *Two Treatises of Government*, but bears traits or qualities that mirror Lockean concepts of property and ownership. Balibar argues here that the connection between identity and property ownership is relational, encompassing both an interiority of the self and the exteriority of the world (and social relations) outside of it. This relational aspect of the self in Locke's thought mirrors the relational nature of property itself, an ideational concept that travels between an ontological plane and the exterior world of relations of ownership.

In this expansive reading of Locke, Balibar outlines a theory of *constituent* property; an 'originary property' that is not 'measured' by pre-existing institutions because it is 'individuality itself'. With constituent property, 'property as such is the exercise of liberty' in the sense that 'every free man must always be considered *somehow a proprietor, or an "owner" of something*' which is individuality itself. Individuality, as noted above, is constituted through the self-recognition of one's memory of past and present thoughts. The idea that every man has property in himself brings propriety back into contact with property; or, to put it another way, Balibar presents a theory of a relation between constituted property and constituent property. The proper subject is not only he who actually owns property, or is able to 'freely' alienate his labour, but is, fundamentally, he who has the capacity to engage in the conscious reflection that marks out or defines the internal stage, 'an indefinitely open field in which [self-consciousness] is both actor and spectator'.[49]

Here we can attempt to identify the ways in which a racial anthropology of the human is smuggled into the ontological grounding of the possessive individual. The primary place of interiority in the conceptualization of this subject – one version of Spivak's 'transparent "I"' – sets the scene for an analytic of raciality that emerges in the nineteenth century. By locating the sovereign source of the self in Reason, Ferreira da Silva finds 'the negation, the declaration of the onto-epistemological inexistence of, exterior things, that is, the affirmation that, as objects of knowledge, phenomena, they constitute but effects of the interior tools of "pure reason".'[50] Racial subjects – the black slave, the Native, the savage – are located in an exterior realm of Nature by scientific and philosophical discourses that give primacy to the subject of interiority. Ferreira da Silva intervenes in our understanding of how the relationship between interiority and exteriority – as a defining characteristic of the modern subject – is mapped onto the globe and world history, so as to render most inhabitants of the non-European world as mere effects of the powers of Reason, which lie in the sole custody of their European superiors.

Taking the self-possessive individual back to the somewhat more specific scene of American real estate, it becomes evident that this articulation of specific histories of race and modes of possession – or, to be more specific, the social relations of race and class that are reflected in practices of redlining and the changes in lending practices – can quite easily become disarticulated from the crisis caused by the financialization of mortgage-backed securities, making the confluence of race and financialization seem more coincidental than a structurally integrated form of articulation, one critical to the reproduction of the US capitalist social order. For instance, in Gary Dymski's article 'Racial Exclusion and the Political Economy of the Subprime Crisis', the author analyses how redlining practices led to the 'creation of a multi-racial community-based movement' that advocated for an increase in mortgage financing for low-income 'minority' households.[51] This would allow for wealth accumulation through home ownership. Dymski poses the question, from a 'capital-accumulation perspective … why would profit-seeking firms not set aside racial bias and make profitable loans' to minority households? He then states the following:

> Two responses suggest plausible explanations of this paradox. First, while lenders seek profits, most lending institutions and lending officers are non-minority, and thus susceptible to perceptual racial bias (despite their commitment to profit-maximization). Second, the perceived risks associated with lending in minority-areas and to minorities are sufficiently great to deter lending.[52]

We want to suggest that these 'plausible explanations' actually disarticulate the racial foundations of property ownership in the US real-estate market. Long histories of racial-economic dispossession are sidelined, and instead racial prejudice as a generalized, almost transhistorical, phenomenon is offered as an explanation for race-based lending practices, alongside the 'rational discrimination' argument. Similarly, the explanation for why racial exclusion was then replaced in part by extortionary racial inclusion in the form of subprime loans is reduced down to a matter of economics. And while greed certainly does explain a lot, it does not adequately account for how these lending practices exploited the social and cultural significance of ownership for communities who had not only been denied the credit facility, but for whom full juridical subjectivity and political inclusion had been denied on the basis of a certain ideal figure of the possessive individual, and, practically and historically speaking, had been defined in opposition to the black slave as object of ownership. In other words, how predatory lending targeted communities in which race is lived through property (along with class and gender), and vice versa.

This brings us to the greatest challenge for thinking race and class formations in relation to ownership through Marxian categories of analysis. Ownership, for black people in the USA, for indigenous people throughout North America, and for working-class immigrants, has always been refracted through the value of life itself, not reducible down to the category or reality of labour, be it free or unfree. If freedom was and remains bound to a debt that can never, it seems, be fully paid off, it seems that justice might require a disarticulation of the fetishes produced by racial and propertied abstractions, a *de-propertization* of the thinking of racial difference and of the legal form itself.

Notes

This article is a revised version of a paper given at the 'Powers and Limits of Property' workshop, organised by the Centre for Philosophy and Critical Thought, Goldsmiths, University of London, 11 June 2015.

1. Karl Marx, *Grundrisse*, trans. Martin Nicolaus, Penguin, Harmondsworth, 1973, p. 164.
2. Paula Chakravartty and Denise Ferreira da Silva, 'Accumulation, Dispossession, and Debt: The Racial Logic of Global Capitalism – An Introduction', *American Quarterly*, vol. 64, no. 3, September 2012, p. 362.
3. See, for example, Elvin K. Wyly, Mona Atia, Holly Foxcroft, Daniel J. Hamme and Kelly Phillips-Watts, 'American Home: Predatory Mortgage Capital and Neighbourhood Spaces of Race and Class Exploitation in the United States', *Geografiska Annaler: Series B, Human Geography*, vol. 88, no. 1, March 2006, pp. 105–32.
4. Elvin K. Wyly and Steven R. Holloway, 'Invisible Cities: Geography and the Disappearance of "Race" from Mortgage-Lending Data in the USA', *Social and Cultural Geography*, vol. 3, no. 3, 2002, pp. 247–82.
5. Marx, *Grundrisse*, p. 497.
6. Ibid., p. 498.
7. Ibid., p. 502.
8. Karl Marx, 'Economic and Philosophical Manuscripts', in *Marx and Engels Collected Works*, Lawrence & Wishart, London, 1986, p. 267.
9. Alfred Sohn-Rethel, *Intellectual and Manual Labour: A Critique of Epistemology*, Macmillan, London, 1978, p. 33.
10. See, among others, Peter Linebaugh, *Stop, Thief!: The Commons, Enclosure, and Resistance*, PM Press, Oakland CA, 2014; Michael Hardt and Antonio Negri, *Commonwealth*, Harvard University Press, Cambridge MA, 2011; Pierre Dardot and Christian Laval, *Commun. Essai sur la révolution au XXIe siècle*, La Découverte, Paris, 2015; Ugo Mattei, *Il benecomunismo e i suoi nemici*, Einaudi, Turin, 2015; Stefano Rodotà, *Il terribile diritto. Studi sulla proprietà privata e i beni comuni*, il Mulino, Milan, 2013.
11. Olivier Cayla and Yan Thomas, *Du droit de ne pas naître. À propos de l'affaire Perruche*, Gallimard, Paris, 2002, quoted by Giorgio Agamben in 'Tra il diritto e la vita', preface to Yan Thomas, *Il valore delle cose*, ed. Michele Spanò, Quodlibet, Macerata, 2015, p. 11. This Italian volume is built around the translation of Yan Thomas, 'La valeur des choses. Le droit romain hors la religion', *Annales HSS*, November–December 2002, pp. 1431–62.
12. Thomas, cited by Agamben, 'Tra il diritto e la vita', p. 13.
13. Thomas, *Il valore delle cose*, p. 24.
14. The latter are to be distinguished in turn from *res nullius*, 'awaiting' appropriation.
15. Thomas, *Il valore delle cose*, pp. 66, 79.
16. Michele Spanò, afterword to Thomas, *Il valore delle cose*, p. 89.
17. Thomas, *Il valore delle cose*, p. 56.
18. Karl Marx, 'On Proudhon' [Letter to J.B. Schweitzer], in *Marx and Engels Collected Works*, vol. 20, Lawrence & Wishart, London, 1985, pp. 27–8.
19. Karl Marx, 'Moralising Criticism and Critical Morality', in *Marx and Engels Collected Works*, vol. 6, Lawrence & Wishart, London, 1976, p. 337.
20. This lag between 'real' property, or property as a power, and legal property, was thought crucial to think the problems of transition, whether from feudalism to capitalism, or capitalism to socialism.
21. Nicos Poulantzas, 'The Problem of the Capitalist State', in *The Poulantzas Reader*, ed. James Martin, Verso, London, 2008, p. 177.
22. Étienne Balibar, 'The Basic Concepts of Historical Materialism', in Louis Althusser and Étienne Balibar, *Reading Capital* (1968), trans. Ben Brewster, Verso, London, 1979, p. 230.
23. Here the Balibar of *Reading Capital* also seems to be leaning towards a view of law as real abstraction not miles away from Pashukanis's *General Theory of Law and Marxism*.
24. Étienne Balibar, 'Plus-value et classes sociales: Contribution à la critique de l'économie politique', in *Cinq études de materialisme historique*, François Maspéro, Paris, 1974, p. 163 n65.
25. Paul Hirst, 'The Law of Property and Marxism', in *On Law and Ideology*, Macmillan, London, 1979, p. 98.
26. Ibid., p. 137.
27. Ruth Wilson Gilmore, 'Fatal Couplings of Power and Difference: Notes on Racism and Geography', *The Professional Geographer*, vol. 54, no. 1, 2002, pp. 15–24; p. 16.

28. See especially Stuart Hall, 'Marx's Notes on Method: A "Reading" of the "1857 Introduction"', *Cultural Studies*, vol. 17, no. 2, 2003, pp. 113–49. This text was originally published in 1974 in *Working Papers in Cultural Studies*, the journal of the Centre for Contemporary Cultural Studies in Birmingham.
29. Ibid., pp. 118, 125.
30. Stuart Hall, 'Signification, Representation, Ideology: Althusser and the Post-Structuralist Debates', *Critical Studies in Mass Communication*, vol. 2, no. 2, June 1985, p. 92.
31. Ibid.
32. In 'Signification, Representation, Ideology', Hall employs this Althusserian framework to shed light on two painful family stories, two 'interpellations' of sorts, the first having to do with his Jamaican mother's exclamation 'I hope they don't mistake you over there [in Britain] for one of those immigrants', the second with the family tale that his sister had looked into his crib and asked 'Where did you get this Coolie baby from?' Hall writes: 'From that moment onwards, my place within this system of reference has been problematic. It may help to explain why and how I eventually became what I was first nominated: the "Coolie" of the family, the one who did not fit, the outsider, the one who hung around the street with all the wrong people, and grew up with all those funny ideas. The Other one.' (p. 110). John Akomfrah's film *The Stuart Hall Project* (2013) also touches on these experiences.
33. Stuart Hall, 'Race, Articulation and Societies Structured in Dominance', in *Sociological Theories: Race and Colonialism*, UNESCO, Paris, 1980, p. 341. Earlier, Hall had observed that 'racial oppression was the specific mediation through which this class experienced its material and cultural conditions of life, and hence race formed the central mode through which the self-consciousness of the class stratum could be constructed.' Stuart Hall, Chas Critcher, Tony Jefferson, John Clarke and Brian Roberts, *Policing the Crisis: Mugging, The State and Law and Order*, Macmillan, London, 1978, p. 387.
34. Stuart Hall, 'Race, Culture, and Communications: Looking Backward and Forward at Cultural Studies', *Rethinking Marxism*, vol. 5, no. 1, 1992, p. 15.
35. '[O]ne cannot explain racism in abstraction from other social relations – even if, alternatively, one cannot explain it by reducing it to those relations'. Hall, 'Race, Articulation and Societies Structured in Dominance', p. 337.
36. Ibid., p. 340.
37. Though Hall does not elaborate upon the property-race relationship, he does comment on 'juridical racism' and on the 'ideological work' required for plantation slavery to persist as a kind of enclave in societies predicated on other legal and property forms. Hall, 'Race, Articulation and Societies Structured in Dominance', p. 338.
38. Hall defines articulation as 'a connection or link which is not necessarily given in all cases, as a law or fact of life, but which requires particular conditions of existence to appear at all, which has to be positively sustained by specific processes, which is not "eternal" but has constantly to be renewed, which can under some circumstances disappear or be overthrown, leading to the old linkages being dissolved and new connections – re-articulations – being forged. It is also important that an articulation between different practices does not mean that they become identical or that the one is dissolved into the other. Each retains its distinct determinations and conditions of existence, the two practices can function together, not as an "immediate identity" (in the language of Marx's "1857 Introduction") but as "distinctions within a unity"' (pp. 113–14). See also 'Race, Articulation and Societies Structured in Dominance', pp. 326–30.
39. Hall, 'Race, Articulation and Societies Structured in Dominance', p. 311; our emphasis.
40. José Carlos Mariátegui, 'The Land Problem' (1928), in *An Anthology*, ed. Harry E. Vanden and Marc Becker, Monthly Review Press, New York, 2011, p. 72.
41. Roxanne Dunbar-Ortiz, *An Indigenous Peoples' History of the United States*, Beacon Press, Boston MA, 2015; see also her *Roots of Resistance: A History of Land Tenure in Mexico*, University of Oklahoma Press, Norman, 2007.
42. Silvia Federici, *Caliban and the Witch: Women, the Body and Primitive Accumulation*, Autonomedia, New York, 2004; see also 'Women, Land Struggles, and Globalization: An International Perspectve', in *Revolution at Point Zero:*

Housework, Reproduction, and Feminist Struggle, PM Press, Oakland CA, 2012.
43. Glen Coulthard, *Red Skin, White Masks: Rejecting the Colonial Politics of Recognition*, University of Minnesota Press, Minneapolis, 2014.
44. Ruth Wilson Gilmore, *Golden Gulag: Prisons, Surplus, Crisis, and Opposition in Globalizing California*, University of California Press, Berkeley CA, 2007, p. 179.
45. N.D.B. Connolly, *A World More Concrete: Real Estate and the Remaking of Jim Crow South Florida*, University of Chicago Press, Chicago, 2014, p. 3.
46. Saidiya Hartman, *Scenes of Subjection: Terror, Slavery, and Self-Making in Nineteenth-Century America*, Oxford University Press, Oxford, 1997, p. 155.
47. Ibid., p. 135.
48. Ibid., p. 134.
49. Étienne Balibar, *Identity and Difference: John Locke and the Invention of Consciousness*, Verso, London, 2013, pp. 14–15.
50. Denise Ferreira da Silva, *Toward a Global Idea of Race*, University of Minnesota Press, Minneapolis, 2007, pp. 60–61.
51. Gary Dymski, 'Racial Exclusion and the Political Economy of the Subprime Crisis', *Historical Materialism*, vol. 17, no. 2, 2009, p. 153.
52. Ibid., p. 154.

16 Anti-castism and misplaced nativism: Mapping caste as an aspect of race

MEENA DHANDA

From September 2013 to February 2014 I led a project on 'Caste in Britain' for the UK Equality and Human Rights Commission (EHRC).* It culminated in two research reports.[1] The remit of the project was, first, to review existing socio-legal research on British equality law and caste, and, second, to conduct two supporting events with the aim of bringing together interdisciplinary expertise and a range of stakeholder views on caste, and discrimination on the basis of caste, in the UK. In April 2013, MPs and peers had voted in both Houses of Parliament to enact the Enterprise and Regulatory Reform Bill, Section 97 of which requires government to introduce a statutory prohibition of caste discrimination into British equality law by making caste an aspect of the protected characteristic of race in the Equality Act 2010 (EA 2010).[2] Following direction by the government, the EHRC contracted a team of academics from different universities, led by me, to carry out an independent study on caste in Britain. We set out to identify concerns and common ground in relation to the implementation of the statuary prohibition on caste discrimination in advance of and in anticipation of the required secondary legislation that will make caste 'an aspect of race' in the EA 2010.

The research for the project, particularly in fulfilment of its second aim of garnering stakeholder views, was quite challenging due to the range of opinions and heightened sensitivities of both the pro-legislation and the anti-legislation organizations whom we brought face to face in a day-long workshop. It took all my skills as a philosopher (listening, arguing, clarifying, mediating, tracking truth and ensuring fairness) to generate an environment for a sustained exchange of views between divergent opinions – from the extreme right wing to the extreme left wing – interspersed with perspectives of a medley of some very seasoned and other rather new campaigners, not versed in any definite political tendency, but pragmatically open to any party that supported their particular pro- or anti-legislation stance.[3] The political multi-logue enacted on the day was fed by many conversational streams and continues in various ways in different forums. Among the academic experts we invited the range of opinions was narrower than at the stakeholders' workshop; nonetheless, it included a comparable variety of positions of support for legislation on the one extreme and scepticism about the use of law on the other, inflected with varying degrees of political self-consciousness.

The manner of inclusion of caste as an aspect of race in equality law is not yet settled; the outcome of continuing conversations between stakeholders is as yet unpredictable. In this article I will highlight some extralegal difficulties in mapping caste as an aspect of race and point out the pernicious role played by the ethos of multiculturalism in exacerbating these difficulties. Multiculturalism occludes the processes of becoming 'different', by naturalizing difference as pregiven. In the context of the experience of what I will call 'casteism' the effect of multiculturalism is to layer denial upon denial. To track truth in such circumstances requires attending to the exchanges between multiple 'other' voices

One such voice was an academic lawyer of Gujarati Indian background, teaching in a prestigious university in the UK, who, by the time we invited him, had recorded, through his blogs, an opposition to the inclusion of caste in the EA 2010.

He uses the framework of legal pluralism. The blogger writes:

> When discussing caste and, more seriously, when legislating on it, a series of confusions occurs about what we are talking of and what we are aiming to do. The emotions stirred by the issue of caste, and a measure of self-righteousness, have a role to play in shaping the level of the discussion but, more critically, there is confusion as between Indian senses of caste and Western understandings of it.... When discussing caste, many Indians too speak as if they operate from within the Western framework.

Here is the charge of Orientalism against us. First, that we are imposing a Western frame on an Indian reality, which cannot be captured within it. Second, that caste is not what it appears to us, and we are mistaken in making it the object of legislation. And third, that we are 'emotional' rather than 'critical' about it. These charges are further built upon in subsequent posts four months after the publication of our reports in a long response signed by a number of Hindu organizations, including the Alliance of Hindu Organizations, Anti-Caste Legislation Committee, British Hindu Voice, City Hindus Network, Coalition for Dialogue, Hindu Lawyers Association, Hindu Swayamsevak Sangh (UK), National Council of Hindu Temples (UK), National Hindu Students Forum (UK), Vishwa Hindu Parishad (UK), and Nitin Mehta.[4] A snippet reads thus:

> The idea that Indian society is composed of a caste system is based on Christian representations of Indian society and culture, which were taken up by Orientalists and contemporary social scientists who assumed their truth. The idea of a caste system was created because of the frustration of Christian missionaries who decided that Brahmins, who they typified as the 'priests' of the Hindu religion, were responsible for the failure of their efforts to convert Indians to Christianity. The idea of the caste system is therefore directly linked to Christian conversion efforts in India.[5]

Here a further accusation is added: that our alleged Orientalism is not only an epistemic drawback but is also suspicious for serving an imagined political purpose – that of furthering Christian conversion efforts in India.

In October 2014, as the chair of Coalition for Dialogue, the same academic raises a scare about the implication of the proposed legislation for business. Repeating the argument about the Orientalist construction of caste, he concludes:

> Our assessment is that judges will be all too ready on the basis of alleged facts to assume that caste discrimination is made out. ... Europeans invariably bring up the caste system when they are conversing with Indians. Judges, who are also educated within the same cultural milieu, will not be immune to such stereotyping. This effectively lowers the applicable balance-of-probabilities standard of proof, and the burden of proof will be upon the South Asian employer, business, professional, other service provider or senior employee to defend themselves against what will effectively be a [sic] that caste discrimination has occurred. This exposes South Asians and their businesses to further discrimination in the operation of the law and ... disadvantages them in being able to insure against caste-based claims.[6]

In the last blog entry, the fear of racism emerges with full force. Judges too, it is feared, will be unable to escape an Orientalist mindset that sees a problem in a benign social identity. In sum, as report writers, we are being accused of exposing South Asian businesses to a new possibility for racist stereotyping, should the government follow our recommendation in the manner of instituting the statutory secondary legislation to make caste an aspect of race in the EA 2010.

Is this charge of Orientalism defensible? The first part of this article will address this question through a brief historical exploration of the caste system and of opposition to it. It is followed, in the second part, by the examination of a connected question: if caste is an indeterminate concept, does it follow that legislation against caste discrimination is not defensible?

The bugbear of Orientalism and precolonial caste

The problem I want to raise here is not about the general state of philosophy and how we have unquestionably failed to bring colour to our curriculum. It is rather about the dangers of misunderstanding that we, the excluded people of colour, face when we raise our critical voices. We point out the ways in which our 'communities' are divided by differences that ought to be removed, but we end up bringing those differences into sharper relief, and introduce greater fissures than existed before. Mainstream curricula can be enlarged by adding mainstream 'others' or by adding 'others' among those 'others'. Perhaps this tension is how it should be. There can be no cosmetic solution to the inclusion of cultures with deep-rooted divisions within them, not least because of the slipperiness of the 'cultures' within which differences get manifested: 'Culture alive is always on the run, always changeful', as Spivak writes. Cosmetic solutions of the multiculturalist variety, accommodating differences through so-called 'dialogue', are also complicated when deeper interests are served by keeping some differences in place. As students of 'cultural politics' we can join Spivak in asking: 'In what interest are differences defined?'[7] Such a question should take us to another level, beyond individual intentional behaviour correctible through personal appeals.

Attempting to unmask the many faces of prejudice using the available resources within our discipline finds the vocabulary insufficient, the concepts missing. Even so, I will try to answer the first question that the blogger's attack generates. Put in a different way: am I being an Orientalist in using the vocabulary of 'caste' to name the experiences of humiliation, prejudice and discrimination that many of my Dalit respondents report?

There are competing intellectual histories of the idea of 'caste', which has been compared to 'race' in different ways. I will briefly outline these histories and consider a conceptual comparison of 'caste' and 'caste identity' with 'race' and 'race identity'. I shall leave aside the legal elements of the comparison, and instead focus on the phenomenology of caste developed through my ethnographic research over the last eight years, and offer further suggestions towards the conceptual understanding of caste identity that I haltingly began in 1993.[8] In this undertaking I find a fellow traveller in the person of Uma Narayan, professor of philosophy in the USA, whose refusal to take the 'emissary position' in Western contexts is both astute and brave. She knows full well that her feminist writings critical of Indian social practices can 'be represented as anti-nationalist or anticommunity betrayals that collude with negative "Western views" about Third-World contexts'.[9] Yet, fully armed with her critical insights, she fights the uncritical nationalist's reprimands on the one hand and the Western feminist's 'condescending form of moral paternalism' on the other. Western feminists, sensitized to the erasure of 'Otherness', in their sisterly concern warn her that she might 'reinforce Western stereotypes about Indian culture' in her manner of revealing uncomfortable truths about the undeniable presence of misogynistic social practices within Indian culture. The western feminists' advocacy of caution doubly excludes the excluded – first by placing the excluded as 'different', then by restricting the excluded from opening up differences within 'difference'.

The central pursuits of the discipline of philosophy are largely dictated by the concerns of the privileged insiders. Our subject neglects taking up uncomfortable questions from the vantage point of the excluded. Philosophy as such is predominantly an upper-class (upper-caste) male discipline and the Western philosophical canon is white. Even as lip service is paid to the impression Eastern philosophies may have made on some European thinkers (for example, Schopenhauer), what is taught in academic departments is a selection of texts by white Western philosophers. The learning and teaching of the subject is done without critical reflection on how our ways of thinking may have suffered as a result of such a restricted diet. As Charles Mills puts it: 'Most Western philosophers have been white and have taken their racial standing for granted, not seeing how it enters into their identity and affects their relationship with the universe.'[10] We could slightly modify this statement to say that 'Most Indian philosophers have been upper-caste and have taken their caste standing for granted, not seeing how it enters into their identity and affects their relationship with the universe.' And this would not be an effect of Orientalism, but of Brahmanism, which Dr Bhimrao Ramji Ambedkar (1891–1956) made it his life's mission to dismantle. Ambedkar was uncompromising and scathing in his criticisms, with no superficial attempt to keep peace with those he criticized.

With a surname (Dhanda) found among Dalits and non-Dalits, my situation is one of complicated positionality – of complicity (through 'upper-caste' family privilege) and resistance (as anti-caste feminist) inextricably coupled together. I assume that there is no 'pure' opposition possible to any system of oppression or marginalization. Orientalism is a real enemy, but the blogger misidentifies its location within anti-castism espoused by academics trained within 'western frameworks' of thought. And by making caste identity appear a benign phenomenon 'misunderstood' by Orientalists his own stance is one of a misplaced 'nativism' that de facto reinforces the hierarchical status quo.

The blogger's nativism, the clinging to an 'Indian' sense of caste occluded by a 'Western' sense, emerges from a sharp division between the West and the 'rest'. Chetan Bhatt, in a different vein from Spivak, provides an intellectual historiography of the bifurcation between East and West initiated by Voltaire, taken forward by Herder through Hegel to Schopenhauer.[11] The blogger has adopted the East/West bifurcation but ignores the praise Western philosophers, accused of Orientalism, reserved for the 'immortalizing' philosophies of the East.[12] That these philosophies are subject to thoroughgoing ethico-legal criticism by insiders, such as in the criticism made of the philosophy of Hinduism by Ambedkar, is also conveniently ignored.

A Dalit by birth, a scholarship student of John Dewey at Columbia, Ambedkar read Nietzsche and juxtaposed him to Manu, the lawgiver. He writes in *Philosophy of Hinduism*:

> *Thus Spake Zarathustra* is a new addition of *Manu Smriti*. If there is any difference between Manu and Nietzsche it lies in this. Nietzsche was genuinely interested in creating a new race of men which will be supermen as compared with the existing race of men. Manu on

the other hand was interested in maintaining the privileges of a class who had come to arrogate to itself the claim of being supermen ... Nietzsche's supermen were supermen by reason of their worth, Manu's supermen were supermen by reason of their birth.... Manu's is a degraded and degenerate philosophy of superman as compared with that of Nietzsche and therefore far more odious and loathsome than the philosophy of Nietzsche.[13]

Much can be cited from the *Manusmriti* that shows contempt towards labourers (the Shudra). But some Hindus, particularly followers of the Arya Samaj, a reformist sect from Northern India, would want to differ with Ambedkar on the centrality of this text in the lived experience of Hindus. The Indian philosopher and statesman S. Radhakrishnan chose the *Upaniṣads* as the definitive texts containing the essence of Hinduism, with clear acceptance of the supremacy of the Brahmin (*Brāhmaṇa*), but allowing some questioning about who counts as a Brahmin. *Vajrasūcika Upaniṣad*, included in his compilation *The Principal Upaniṣads*, directly addresses the question thus:

> The Brāhmaṇa, the Kṣatriya, the Vaiśya and the Śūdra are the four classes (castes). That the Brāhmaṇa is the chief among these classes is in accord with the Vedic texts and is affirmed by the Smrtis. In this connection there is a point worthy of investigation. Who is verily, the Brāhmaṇa? Is he the individual soul [*kiṁ jivaḥ*]? Is he the body [*kiṁ dehaḥ*]? Is he the class based on birth [*kiṁ jātiḥ*]? Is he the knowledge? Is he the deeds (previous, present or prospective)? Is he the performer of the rites?[14]

The remainder of the *Vajrasūcika Upaniṣad* gives reasons to answer each of the questions about the identity of the Brāhmaṇa in the negative – he is not the soul, not the body, not the birth-ascribed class, not holder of knowledge, not the performer of rites – and concludes that the Brāhmaṇa is only identifiable by his qualities. He must be

> rid of the faults of desire, attachment, etc., and endowed with the qualities of tranquillity, etc., rid of the states of being, spite, greed, expectation, bewilderment, etc., with his mind unaffected by ostentation, self-sense and the like, he lives. He alone who is possessed of these qualities is the Brāhmaṇa. This is the view

of the Vedic texts and tradition, ancient lore and history. The accomplishment of the state of the Brāhmaṇa is otherwise impossible.[15]

Taking this idealized definition of a Brāhmaṇa, no one could be a Brāhmaṇa by birth, and most would fail the accomplishment test, which is supposedly open to anyone to aspire to. It is this interpretation that the deniers of the caste hierarchy in the Hindu tradition have in mind. Indeed Radhakrishnan comments at the end of the text that 'It is valuable to recall the teaching of this Upaniṣad which repudiates the system that consecrates inequalities and hardens contingent differences into inviolable divisions'.[16] For Radhakrishnan the inequality between a Brāhmaṇa and a Śūdra as particular individuals is merely contingent, which a 'system' converts into rigid divisions. This leaves open the intellectual possibility of imagining away the systematic differences between the two, an appealing option for the deniers.

The first problem with this approach is that it does not place the Brāhmaṇa as a member of a group, with identifiable and exclusive symbols of group membership, including privileged access to the language of ritual, place of residence, occupation and even codes of dress. If, as the anthropologist G.D. Berreman notes, 'where group affiliation is relevant, individual attributes are irrelevant',[17] then the exit option provided by the Upaniṣhads of denying ritual status to a Brāhmaṇa who lacks the requisite accomplishments of a true Brāhmaṇa is a chimera. The status ascription, tied as it is to group membership not to individual attributes, cannot be shaken by merely pointing out individual failings. However, if and when Brāhmaṇas were to decline in importance as a group, due to other reasons, then pointing out individual failings may work to dislodge the superior status accorded to an individual Brāhmaṇa by participants in the system.

The second problem with the intellectualizing approach is that it is does not answer why ordinary people, Hindus and non-Hindus alike, are not impressed by the idealized definition of a Brāhmaṇa and continue to take the four Varnas as birth-ascribed? The answer perhaps lies in the influence of other texts – *Manusmriti* (the Law Book of Manu) and *Bhagwat Gita*, a text that forms an undeniably central part in the daily incantations of many Hindus.

Ambedkar shows that the *Bhagwat Gita* incorporates *Manusmriti*'s division of society into four *Varna* (sections) underpinned by inequality: '*Gita* is Manu in a nutshell'. The Hindu deity Lord Krishna says in the *Gita*: 'I myself have created the arrangement known as Chaturvarna (i.e. the fourfold division of society into four castes Brahmans, Kshatriyas, Vaishyaa and Shudras) assigning them different occupations in accordance with the native capacities ... *Gita*. IV. 13'; 'There is bliss in following the occupation of one's own varna, even if death were to result in performing it ... *Gita*. III. 35.'[18] Further, as Ambedkar argues, the *Gita* gave a new lease of life to *Varna*, which 'would have otherwise petered away', precisely by providing 'a philosophical foundation to the *Varna* system by arguing that the *Varna* was based on the innate qualities of man'.[19]

M.K. Gandhi (1869–1948) spoke in favour of *Varna*, and thus entered into a bitter dispute with Ambedkar. For Gandhi, 'hereditary occupation' is 'the soul of the caste system. ... To change it is to create disorder.' He wrote in his Gujrati journal: 'The caste system is a natural order of society ... I am opposed to all those who are out to destroy the caste system.'[20] In his *Varnavyavastha* Gandhi defends hereditary occupations thus: 'The object of the *Varna* system is to prevent competition and class struggle and class war. I believe in the *Varna* system because it fixes the duties and occupations of persons'; '*Varna* means the determination of a man's occupation before he is born'[21] and also that 'everyone shall follow as a matter of dharma – duty – the hereditary calling of his forefathers, in so far as it is not inconsistent with fundamental ethics.'[22]

Outside the *Chaturvarna*, there is a fifth category, the *avarna*, referred to by various terms – *caṇḍālā* ('outcastes' in the

Upaniṣads), *Harijan* ('children of God' by M.K. Gandhi), Schedule Castes and Schedule Tribes (in the Indian Constitution) and *dalit* (in contemporary political discourse). The word 'Dalit' emerged as a political term of self-identification in the 1970s but may be regarded as offensive by some to whom it is applied because of the painful histories of subordination and humiliation that it recalls. 'To call oneself Dalit, meaning "ground down", "broken to pieces", "crushed" is to convert a negative description into a confrontational identity.'[23]

From Ambedkar's critique of the *Philosophy of Hinduism*, we can identify one startling respect in which the impact of the *Manusmriti* is in evidence today in everyday 'lived experience'. This is in the practice of naming a Hindu child. Ambedkar explains that Manu gives directions as to what the first and second parts of the temporal name of a Hindu should denote:

> The second part of a Brahman's name shall be a word implying happiness, of a Kshatriya's a word implying protection; of a Vaishya's a term expressive of prosperity and of a Shudra's an expression denoting service. Accordingly the Brahmans have *Sharma* (happiness) or *Deva* (god), the Kshtrayas have *Raja* (authority) or *Verma* (armour), the Vaishayas have *Gupta* (gifts) or *Datta* (giver) and the Shudras have *Das* (service) for the second part of their names. As to the first part of their names ... in the case of a Shudra, Manu says the first part of his name should denote something contemptible!![24]

Attention to the names of South Asians can give one a fairly good idea of the 'caste' of the person.[25] However, given several other complicating factors in acquiring names – place of birth to feudal associations – there is of course no foolproof method of deducing the caste of a person from their name. Ambedkar's point in drawing attention to the *Manusmriti*'s recommendation is to show how deeply ingrained its teachings are. The deniers of caste hierarchy may want to pull out a little-known Upaniṣad (cited above) for support, but we simply have to look at our naming practices to accept the veracity of Ambedkar's claim that the *Manusmriti* has been influential in directing our lives.[26]

Returning to the charge that the British imposed a Western model for understanding the supposedly benign phenomena of caste affiliation, which was essentially fluid, we need to look at pre-colonial times. It is undeniable that some consolidation of "traditional" India took place under British rule, but, as the historian Nicholas Dirks succinctly states, 'The assumption that the colonial state could manipulate and invent Indian tradition at will, creating a new form of caste and reconstituting the social, and that a study of its own writings and discourse is sufficient to argue such a case, is clearly inadequate and largely wrong.'[27] The suggestion that caste was not invidious because in pre-colonial India it was in a sense eclectic is to betray one's distance from the writings of indigenous reformers of medieval India, who forcefully enlighten us about the blight of caste.[28] Indeed there are many historical examples of pre-colonial protests against caste. In the Introduction to a new edition of Ambedkar's key text, *Annihilation of Caste*,[29] Arundhati Roy lists some of these: 'In the mid-twelfth century, the Veerashaivas led by Basave challenged caste in South India, and were crushed. From the fourteenth century onwards, the beloved Bhakti poet saints – Cokhamela, Ravidas, Kabir, Tukaram, Mira, Janabai – became and still remain the poets of the anticaste tradition.'[30] She does not add the Sikh Gurus to this list. There are numerous lines in *Shri Guru Granth Sahib* (*SGGS*), the sacred text of the Sikhs, with clear challenges to caste hierarchy, and caste-induced pride/honour, *jāt-pat*.[31]

The limitation, though, is that these challenges do not grapple with the socio-political disabilities that stem from caste, but offer spiritual equality as an antidote to caste prejudice. This limitation of equality to the sacred realm renders the Sikh response to caste prejudice limited in its effect to this day. Within the sacred space of the Gurudwara, equality is preached but outside this space inequality returns with a vengeance. Our point in listing these medieval protests to caste, limited though they may be, is to establish that well before the British set foot in India caste divisions were challenged by revolutionary poets, saints and seers. Caste or *Jati* was never benign. It was felt as a burden to be overthrown. A precursor of Ambedkar, Jotiba Phule (1826–1890), decried the caste system as 'the code of crude and inhuman laws to which we can find no parallel among other nations'.[32]

This part of our pre-colonial history also shows that ideas of equality stirred the minds of Indians well before the colonial encounter and did not spring for the first time from Christian missionary activities. The blogger is mistaken in thinking otherwise. Indeed one could argue that these pre-existing ideas of equality, coupled with their incongruent socio-economic realization, made the victims of castism receptive to the colonizers' offer of legal equality in the latter period of colonization. The blogger's nativism is misplaced for the further reason that he underestimates the cultural resources of the Indic civilization – whilst spawning inequality it also produced elements of an antidote.

Caste continues to be seen as a birth-ascribed status, and, even though historical ties to occupations have loosened for those who accept the religious hierarchical order, caste is still connected to ritual purity/pollution. It combines elements of social class, hierarchy and privilege sustained by endogamy (marrying restricted within a group). There is undoubtedly a fluidity in the way people follow caste-based prescriptions; some even give them up altogether, sometimes with grave personal costs. I have gathered some evidence of rebellious anti-caste liaisons in my recent work on runaway marriages in the Punjab.[33] Further, in the Indian context caste stratifications maybe regionally variable. Nonetheless, caste invariably denotes constraints, and in the case of those in the lower sections it spells deprivation, atrocities, violence and discrimination. Caste divisions are tied to unequal access to valued resources. Humiliation of certain groups considered socially inferior is routine; even as rebellion grows against such treatment, it is often met with a violent response. Gopal Guru's moving studies *Humiliation* and *The Cracked Mirror* argues forcefully that reflection on experience, rather than ungrounded abstraction, ought to be the basis of social scientific theorizing.[34]

Caste as a confrontational identity, symbolized in the self-ascription of the term 'Dalit', is quite different from non-Dalit caste identifications, supposedly from a non-confrontational and non-hierarchical perspective. This perspective on caste, viewing it as a harmless identity, has been recently suggested as a theoretical alternative[35] to Louise Dumont's structuralist understanding of caste as fundamentally about *hierarchy*. This new understanding has been criticized as the 'culturalization of caste', a phrase coined by Balmurli Natarajan, who perspicuously describes it as a 'counter-revolution' whereby the project of annihilation of caste is derailed, and caste identity is accommodated within a multicultural celebration of 'difference'. The hidden politics of this counter- revolution is the normalization of the 'pretension that caste is not about antagonistic, exploitative or oppressive relations'[36] which require politico-legal interventions. Ambedkar's message that caste must be annihilated, by using legal means if necessary, has neither been heard nor heeded by these new defenders of caste identity in its purportedly non-confrontational, celebratory mode.

Conceptual indeterminacy and the phenomenology of caste

We can now ask our second question: if caste is an indeterminate concept, does it follow that legislation against caste discrimination is not defensible? The view we took in our research report was that we must pay attention to the manifestation of caste. Its 'meaning' must be gleaned from how people experience caste. The point may now be developed as follows. Even if the meaning of caste is indeterminate – that is, even if it means one thing to one group and something else to another, if it is considered hurt-inducing by some and joy-inducing by others – the concern of the law is with the behaviour that emerges from the beliefs about caste. If there are identifiable patterns of behaviour that spring from the belief 'as if' caste has the fixed meaning of superiority of some when compared to others, then it makes sense to address such casteist behaviour as a systematic expression of caste prejudice. Thus, even though caste is an indeterminate concept, legislation on the basis of caste is defensible.

Focusing on the experience of caste, in a pilot study on the conversion of Dalits to Buddhism and Christianity in Wolverhampton, I found that caste is felt as a permanent, deeply embedded cultural tradition and that conversion does not leave caste behind. Bitter, visceral and emotive language is used to describe caste: it is 'a monster', 'a disease'; 'It sticks'. Among the converts, there is powerlessness in relation to caste: it is something 'done to you' that you are 'lumbered with'.[37] Dalits choose to convert, attempting to escape caste by adopting religious traditions doctrinally opposed to casteism, but in the eyes of the 'upper-caste' these converts remain 'lower-caste'. Caste manifests in the education sector in Britain, in bullying and name-calling;[38] it surfaces in religious practice in Gurdwaras, for example in the reluctance to allow Valmikis – a Dalit caste grouping who have collectively dropped their caste name to adopt a religious label as followers of sage Valmiki – 'to distribute karah prashard'.[39] It manifests in the workplace with the example of those from the 'higher caste' refusing to take orders from 'lower caste' managers.[40] Recent reported incidents of caste discrimination in the UK that emerged at the seminars I organized as a part of the Caste in Britain project included caste stereotyping used to undercut business, sexual harassment in the workplace, and the refusal of taxi service on finding out the caste status of passengers. Many of these examples[41] suggest patterns of behaviour that would become actionable under discrimination law, when caste is made an aspect of race. Research on recent Nepali migrants to Oxfordshire shows evidence of 'active revival of caste' manifest in 'residential patterns' bordering on Untouchability.[42] Through marriage, education and networking, this cycle of new migrants continues to reproduce the pattern of 'diasporal elites utilizing and profiting from an immigrant underclass', suggesting 'a need to consider the range of experiences mediated by caste and gender as well as the potential for exploitation'.[43]

If legislation against caste discrimination is thus defensible, what can we learn from a comparative perspective on race and caste? In a seminar in London in 1966 on Caste and Race: Comparative Approaches, it was noted that the caste system comprised 'groups', 'discrete, bounded, ranked entities' and 'a system of institutionalized inequality';[44] interestingly, the French structuralist Louise Dumont urged that the point of the comparative approach was to 'rediscover hierarchy' in order to throw light on 'the dark corners of our own society'.[45] For G.D. Berreman, caste systems are 'always in disequilibrium, like pots of water on fire, always threatening to boil over. They are characterized not by consensus but by conformity. They are maintained not by agreement but by sanctions.'[46] This reiterates Ambedkar's observation that 'No one who knows anything about the Manu Smriti can say that the caste system is a natural system. What does Manu Smriti show? It shows that the caste system is a legal system maintained at the point of a bayonet.'[47]

Berreman criticizes the tendency among those who study and analyse caste systems to idealize or intellectualize caste. 'Caste is people ... interacting in characteristic ways ... a caste system is a pattern of human relationships and it is a state of mind.'[48] Most importantly, it was noted in a way that is still relevant today that even though there may be disequilibrium, the system persists through change. Regardless of the inconclusive theoretical debates on its meaning, caste continues to be vividly present in the experiential realm, sometimes just below the surface. This suggests that it is through a phenomenology of caste that we may be able to grasp its meaning. This chimes with the observations of the philosopher Sally Haslanger, a white mother of two adopted black children. In *Resisting Reality*, Haslanger writes of racism:

> it is a mistake to suggest that the ultimate source of the problem is 'in our heads' (in our conceptual scheme, our language, or our cultural ideals), or alternatively that it is in the unjust structure of our social arrangements, as if it must be one or the other; 'culture' and 'social/institutional structure' are deeply intertwined, so much so, that they are sometimes inextricable.[49]

And so it is with caste. As with racial identity, caste identity is also 'largely habitual' and 'often ritualized', but, unlike racial identity, caste identity is not 'regularly unconscious'; it is rather quite overt. The difference, I think, emerges from what Ambedkar describes as a system of 'graded inequalities'. With respect to each group there is someone lower and someone higher. In this situation, caste identity may not manifest itself in the presence of those with whom there is no direct competition, and in these cases it may remain 'unconscious'; but in cases where the competition for resources is sharp, caste identity becomes overt. I agree with Haslanger that, because of our socialization as embodied subjects, 'not just rational, cognitive agents', caste identity – like race identity – is 'training the body to feel, to see, to touch, to fear, to love' in particular ways. Focus on 'the intentional is to miss the many ways that we unintentionally and unconsciously participate in racism and sexism'[50] – and, I would add, 'in casteism'.

However, any possible definition of 'caste' will be in one important respect different from Haslanger's and other definitions of 'race', to the extent that the latter focus on visible marks of skin colour. The visibility of caste is not the visibility of skin colour but of the clothed body, the body in the space of action, meaning and vulnerability – where 'being clothed' includes wearing expressions as well as being dressed, projecting a voice, carrying the smell of clothes, body odours, being armed with the tools of the trade, marked or unmarked by scars, wrinkles and other signs of toil, age, exposure to the elements, displaying or hiding one's possessions. In our clothed encounters, other bodies are first marked not by skin colour but by these identity markers that run ahead of us, as we approach each other. Our bodies reside within social spaces – it is the acting body that we see, or hear first of all, not a coloured, white, brown or black face.

Our relationship to clothes – what they mean to us – is marked by caste, class and race. It is in this sense that caste is 'visible', when it is certainly not visible in terms of skin colour. We use social maps to orient ourselves in this saturated space, drawing inferences about people's caste on the basis of our tacit knowledge. In urban settings, people may not directly ask what someone's caste is, but they ask searching questions about the inhabited space – Where do you live? What temple/gurdwara/church do you worship in? What do your parents do? Caste is deduced from the answers to these questions.

This way of looking at caste identity has some similarity with Charles Mills's account of race when he writes:

> Race [Caste] is not 'metaphysical' in the deep sense of being eternal, unchanging, necessary, part of the basic furniture of the universe. But race [caste] is a *contingently* deep reality that structures our particular social universe, having a social objectivity and causal significance that arises out of *our* particular history.... Because people come to think of themselves *as* 'raced', as black and white [as Brahmin and non-Brahmin], for example, these categories, which correspond to no natural kinds, attain a social reality. Intersubjectivity creates a certain kind of objectivity.[51]

Armed with the parallel between how race and caste are experienced, we can now turn to the remark of Lord Bhikhu Parekh on 22 April 2013 in the House of Lords, opposing the amendment to include caste as an aspect of race in the EA 2010:

> Talking about abolishing the caste system is extremely problematic because it could mean getting rid of the category, getting rid of the hierarchy among the categories or getting rid of the principle of heredity which determines the caste. Where do you start? I suggest that caste as a category of discrimination is therefore not in the same league as race, religion or any of the other protected categories.[52]

In one sense it is not surprising that Parekh should highlight the particularity of the category of 'caste', wanting to hold on to the identity-conferring role of caste, but denying that it could work in law as an identifiable basis of discrimination. At one level this is a continuation of the Gandhian project of saving in name an element of the Hindu tradition. For Gandhi it was *Varna*, for Parekh it is caste. For proponents of multiculturalism, misunderstanding a culture and its traditions is ironically the worst thing that can befall members of minority communities, worse even than allowing the continuation of discriminatory practices stemming from notions of superiority/inferiority intrinsically linked to caste identifications.

Parekh lists four 'major difficulties'[53] that stand in the way of attempts to make caste an aspect of race for the purposes of anti-discrimination legislation, but we have a reply to each of them. First, Parekh claims that 'there will be frivolous complaints based on caste … Since every Indian who is Hindu carries the caste mark with him, every action that he does with respect to another can be subsumed under one or another form of caste discrimination.' But carrying the 'caste mark' as a confrontational identity in the face of denigration is different from carrying it as uncritical mark of pride. The facts of the case would determine whether or not a claimant of the charge of discrimination could establish a pattern of behaviour that can be seen to manifest caste prejudice and discrimination. To imagine an eruption of frivolous complaints is merely scaremongering, not least because the cost of litigation is so high and the chances of success so low.

Second, Parekh claims that 'once you take away the untouchability bit, there is no evidence of any kind to show that caste discrimination takes place.' But, on the contrary, there is sufficient evidence of discrimination to warrant the inclusion of caste in the EA 2010, as the research that I have cited shows.

Third, Parekh asks 'How do you define caste?', implying, correctly, that this is no easy undertaking. But it is not necessary to have a definition of caste as such for the purposes of legislation, just as 'race' is left undefined in the EA 2010.

Finally, Parekh claims that 'A category as indeterminate as that [of caste] does not deserve to be enshrined in domestic legislation.' But all we need to identify caste *discrimination* is the ability to identify patterns of behaviour that would reasonably be seen as discrimination on the basis of caste by the victims of discrimination. What matters in not the meaning of the term 'caste' but the identification of the pattern of behaviour that can be identified as casteist.

Parekh's misgivings about the inclusion of caste in the EA 2010 mirror the 'nativist' concerns. These concerns were anticipated by the chairperson of CasteWatch UK, Satpal Muman, in 2000 whilst actively lobbying for legislation against caste discrimination. He said:

> One concern that I have is this: Asians are already victims of racism in Britain. There may be a curious affect caused whereby the indigenous community may use the Caste divisions amongst the Asians as a weapon of further oppression. The Asians could be accused of in-fighting and those Asians who are fighting against Racism itself may see their work being undermined by our outcry against Caste. Some thought ought to be given to this as to how best we can achieve our goals notwithstanding the fact there will certainly be a backlash at least from the conservative elements of the Indian community for placing Caste System in the public domain. The Right wing Fascists could also use this to further their aims.[54]

Muman was right to anticipate opposition from 'the conservative elements in the Indian community'. Just prior to the May 2015 general election, the National Council of Hindu Temples UK, the Hindu Forum of Britain and the British Sikh Consultative Forum each issued a letter, urging voters to use their vote to defeat parties supporting the legislation on caste in the UK.[55] (The NCHTUK is now accused of flouting Charity Commission guidelines in issuing electoral support for the Conservative Party.[56]) But the 'backlash' Muman feared has also materialized in a more disturbing form than he might have imagined. The most recent statement of the deniers of caste reads:

> For the avoidance of doubt, we re-iterate that the fluid and equitable, Dharmic non-hereditary, non-endogamous social structures which are repeatedly detailed in Hindu, Sikh and Jain scriptures, in no way match the Caste system which was created by the despotic medieval Popes in Europe, then exported by colonial missionaries to the Empire.[57]

As the muddled spectre of Orientalism thus rises again it is worth reminding ourselves of Edward Said's claim that the 'disadvantaged postcolonial states and their loyalist intellectuals' have drawn the wrong conclusion if they 'attempt to improve, enhance, and ameliorate the images currently in circulation without doing anything to change the political situation from which they emanate'.[58] The legislation on caste discrimination is precisely an attempt to 'do something' to change the situation which generates the unflattering 'image' feared by the deniers, following Said's recommendation that a reflective and critical 'decentred consciousness' should generate 'political and practical' activities that are 'marginal, and oppositional with reference to the mainstream'.[59]

If we want to move away from the 'treacly pieties' of multiculturalism[60] and its mindless celebration of branded 'difference' we will need to reinvigorate the 'critical spirit' appropriate to philosophical engagement with disturbing questions that seek to name, to understand and to find ways of eliminating the experience of unjustified discrimination.

Notes

1. Meena Dhanda et al., *Caste in Britain: Socio-Legal Review*, Research Report 91, Equality and Human Rights Commission, UK, Manchester, 2014. First published online 28 February 2014, www.equalityhumanrights.com/publication/research-report-91-caste-britain-socio-legal-review. Meena Dhanda et al., *Caste in Britain: Experts' Seminar and Stakeholders' Workshop*, Research Report 92, Equality and Human Rights Commission, UK, Manchester, 2014. First published online 28 February 2014, www.equalityhumanrights.com/publication/research-report-92-caste-britain-experts-seminar-and-stakeholders-workshop.
2. For a detailed background of the inclusion of caste in the Equality Act 2010, see Annapurna Waughray, 'Capturing Caste in Law: Caste Discrimination and the Equality Act 2010', *Human Rights Law Review*, vol. 14, no. 2, 2014, pp. 359–79; first published online 13 May 2014. See also Waughray, 'Caste Discrimination: A Twenty-First Century Challenge for UK Discrimination Law?', *Modern Law Review*, vol. 72, no. 2, 2009, pp. 182–219, the first article to discuss the legal recognition of caste as a ground for discrimination in UK law.
3. Of the 60 organizations invited, 43 sent representatives to the stakeholders' workshop in London on 9 November 2013. For details of the participating organizations, see Dhanda et al., EHRC Research Report 92.
4. Several of these organizations were invited and participated in our EHRC project workshop for stakeholders.
5. 'Response to Two Reports on Caste published by the Equality and Human Rights Commission', posted on 25 June 2014, https://aryalegal.wordpress.com/2014/06/25/response-to-two-reports-on-caste-by-the-equality-and-human-rights-commission; accessed 26 March 2015.
6. 'UK Caste Discrimination Legislation: Implications for Business and Employers', posted on 9 October 2014, para 17, https://aryalegal.wordpress.com/2014/10/09/uk-caste-discrimination-legislation-implications-for-business-and-employers; accessed 26 March 2015.
7. See Gayatri Chakravorty Spivak, *A Critique of Postcolonial Reason: Toward a History of the Vanishing Present*, Harvard University Press, Cambridge MA, 1999, p. 357.
8. In 1993, I noted the limitations of the application of Kant's notion of respect to people negotiating with the powerful within a hierarchical setting of graded inequalities underpinned by caste identities. At the time when the first translations of ancient Indian scriptures were being undertaken, Kant wrote: 'Preferential tributes of respect in words and manners even to those who have no civil authority – reverences, obeisances (compliments), and courtly phrases marking with utmost precision every distinction in rank, ... a pedantry in which the Germans seem to outdo any other people in the world (except possibly the Indian castes): Does not all this prove that there is a wide spread propensity to servility in men? ... But one who makes himself a worm cannot complain afterwards if people step on him.' See Immanuel Kant *The Metaphysics of Morals*, intro., trans. and notes by Mary Gregor, Cambridge University Press, Cambridge, 1991, p. 232. Kant's harshness towards those constrained to perform utterances marking respect for rank is striking when applied to Dalits. See Meena Dhanda, 'L'éveil des intouchables en Inde', trans. Isabelle di Natale, in Catherine Audard, ed., *Le respect: De l'estime à la déférence: une question de limite*, Éditions Autrement, Paris, Série Morales No. 10, February 1993, pp. 130–45.
9. Uma Narayan, *Dislocating Cultures: Identities, Traditions and Third World Feminism*, Routledge, New York and London, 1997, p. 136.
10. Charles Mills, *Blackness Visible: Essays on Philosophy and Race*, Cornell University Press, Ithaca NY and London, 1998, p. 66.
11. Chetan Bhatt, 'Primordial Being: Enlightenment and the Indian Subject of Postcolonial Theory', in Peter Osborne and Stella Sandford, eds, *Philosophies of Race and Ethnicity*, Continuum, London and New York, 2002, pp. 40–62.
12. Kojin Karatani observes: 'Looking down on the other as an object of scientific analysis and looking up to the other as an aesthetic idol are less contradictory

than complicit.' 'Uses of Aesthetics: After Orientalism', *boundary 2*, vol. 25, no. 2, 1998, p. 147. I am grateful to Alexei Penzin for drawing my attention to Karatani.

13. B.R. Ambedkar, *Philosophy of Hinduism*, Critical Quest, New Delhi, 2010, pp. 32–3.
14. S. Radhkrishnan *The Principal Upaniṣads*, HarperCollins India, Noida, 2014 (1953), p. 935. I have added the square brackets to insert the transliterated Sanskrit text from the paragraph preceding the translation cited from p. 935.
15. Ibid., pp. 937–8.
16. Ibid., p. 938.
17. Gerald D. Berreman, 'Stratification, Pluralism and Interaction: A Comparative Analysis of Caste', in Anthony de Reuck and Julie Knight, eds, *Caste and Race: Comparative Approaches*, J. & A. Churchill, London, 1967, p. 48.
18. Ambedkar, *Philosophy of Hinduism*, pp. 70, 69–70.
19. Ambedkar, 'Gandhism', in Valerian Rodrigues, ed., *The Essential Writings of B.R. Ambedkar*, Oxford University Press, New Delhi, 2002, p. 164.
20. Gandhi, *Nava-Jivan*, 1921–2, cited in Ambedkar, *The Essential Writings of B.R. Ambedkar*, pp, 151, 151–2.
21. Gandhi, cited in ibid., p. 153.
22. See Gandhi's 'Introduction to *Varnavyavastha*', *Harijanbandhu*, 23 September 1934, in *The Moral and Political Writings of Mahatama Gandhi*, Vol. 3, ed. R. Iyer, Clarendon Press, Oxford, 1987, pp. 559–65. I have discussed Gandhi's views on *Varna* in Dhanda, 'L'éveil des intouchables en Inde', and in *The Negotiation of Personal Identity*, VDM Verlag Dr Müller, Saarbrücken, 2008.
23. Anupama Rao, *The Caste Question: Dalits and the Politics of Modern India*, University of California Press, Berkeley, 2009, p. 1.
24. Ambedkar, *Philosophy of Hinduism*, pp. 32–3.
25. I recall attending a philosophy conference some thirty years ago in India in which a Bengali professor asked me my family name and that of a female colleague accompanying me. He was puzzled by my name, but it took him just a few minutes to determine that my colleague was one of the twelve highest castes of Brahmins, and in even less time he switched attention to her to compare notes about their Brahmin lineage.
26. Anticipating objections to his making the *Manusmriti* rather than the *Upaniṣads* into the key text that defines the philosophy of Hindus, and enlisting the support of the revolutionary and rationalist Lala Hardyal – 'The treatises are full of absurd conceits, quaint fancies, and chaotic speculations' (Cited in Ambedkar, *Philosophy of Hinduism*, p. 74) – to downplay the relevance of the *Upaniṣads* for the lived experience of Hindus, Ambedkar concludes that the *Upaniṣad* philosophy 'turned out to be most ineffective and inconsequential piece of speculation with no effect on the moral and social order of the Hindus.' (*Philosophy of Hinduism*, p. 74).
27. See ibid.,., p. 74. Nicholas B. Dirks,. 'Castes of Mind', in *Representations* 37, Special Issue: Imperial Fantasies and Postcolonial Histories, Winter 1992, pp. 56–78.
28. Dhanda, 'L'éveil des intouchables en Inde'.
29. B.R. Ambedkar, *Annihilation of Caste*, in *The Essential Writings of B.R. Ambedkar*, ed. Valerian Rodrigues, Oxford University Press, New Delhi, 2010 (1936), pp. 263–305.
30. Arundhati Roy, 'The Doctor and the Saint', Introduction to B.R. Ambedkar, *Annihilation of Caste*, Verso, London, 2014, p. 37.
31. Guru Amar Das (SGGS 994) writes:

ਨਾਮੈ ਜਾਤ ਨ ਪਤਿ ਹ ਨਾਮੈ ਥੇਹੁ ਨ ਥਾਉ ॥
Nā mai jāt na pat hai nā mai thehu na thão.
I have no social status or honor; I have no place or home.

ਸਬਦਿ ਭੇਦਿ ਭਰਮੁ ਕਟਿਆ ਗੁਰਿ ਨਾਮੁ ਦੀਆ ਸਮਝਾਇ ॥੨॥
Sabad bhed bharam katiā gur nām dīā samjhāe. ||2||
Pierced through by the Word [of the Shabad], my doubts have been cut away. The Guru has inspired me to understand the Naam, the Name of the Lord. ||2||

Mahla 3, Guru Amar Das, www.srigranth.org.
To understand the rebellion against the degeneration of 'original anti-casteism of Sikh culture into merely a received glory', see Pritam Singh and Meena Dhanda, 'Sikh Culture and *Punjābiyat*', in *Oxford Handbook of Sikh Studies*, ed. Pashaura Singh and Louis E. Fenech,

Oxford University Press, New York, pp. 482–92.
32. Jotiba Phule, cited by Gail Omvedt, *Dalit Visions*, Orient Longman, New Delhi, 2006, pp. 17–18.
33. Meena Dhanda, 'Runaway Marriages: A Silent Revolution?', *Economic and Political Weekly*, vol. XLVII, no. 43, 27 October 2012, pp. 100–108.
34. Gopal Guru, ed., *Humiliation*, Oxford University Press, New Delhi, 2012. See also Gopal Guru and Sundar Sarukkai, *The Cracked Mirror: An Indian Debate on Experience and Theory*, Oxford University Press, New Delhi, 2012.
35. Chiefly the alternative is offered by Dipankar Gupta: 'castes are, first and foremost, discreet entities with deep pockets of ideological heritage. As they are discreet phenomena [sic], it is both logically and empirically true that there should be multiple hierarchies as each caste always overvalues itself', and 'no caste really thinks of itself to be inherently inferior to any other caste'. In 'Caste and Politics: Identity over System', *Annual Review of Anthropology* 34, 2005, pp. 409–27; 412, 419. This conclusion celebrating caste identity seems to emerge from disproportionate attention to the politics of upwardly mobile castes, and does not account for the continuing deprivation and relegation of most Dalits to the bottommost layers of society.
36. Balmurli Natarajan, *The Culturalization of Caste in India: Identity and Inequality in a Multicultural Age*, Routledge, Abingdon and New York, 2012, p. 9.
37. Meena Dhanda, 'Eastern Punjabi Dalits: A Case Study of Wolverhampton', paper presented jointly with Steve Taylor and Dave Morland, British Association of South Asian Studies annual conference, Edinburgh, 30 March–1 April 2009.
38. See Paul Ghuman, *British Untouchable: A Study of Dalit identity and Education*, Ashgate, Farnham, 2011; Meena Dhanda, 'Punjabi *Dalit* Youth: Social Dynamics of Transitions in Identity', *Contemporary South Asia*, vol. 17, no. 1, March, 2009, pp. 47–63.
39. See Eleanor Nesbitt, 'Valmikis in Coventry: The Revival and Reconstruction of a Community', in Roger Ballard, ed., *Desh Pardesh: The South Asian Presence in Britain*, C. Hurst London, 1994, pp. 117–41; 128.
40. Meena Dhanda, 'Certain Allegiances, Uncertain Identities: The Fraught Struggles of Dalits in Britain', in Om Prakash Dwivedi, ed., *Tracing the New Indian Diaspora*, Editions Rodopi, New York, 2014, pp. 99–119.
41. For more examples, see the government commissioned study, H. Metcalf and H. Rolfe, *Caste Discrimination and Harassment in Great Britain*, National Institute of Economic and Social Research, London, 2010.
42. Mitra Pariyar, 'Cast(e) in Bone: The Perpetuation of Social Hierarchy among Nepalis in Britain', Working Paper No. 85, University of Oxford, 2011.
43. Kaveri Qureshi et al., 'Migration, Transnationalism and Ambivalence: The Punjab–United Kingdom Linkage', in Pirkko Pitkänen, Ahmet Açduygu and Deniz Sert, eds, *Migration and Transformation: Multi-level Analysis of Migrant Transnationalism*, International Perspectives on Migration, Dordrecht and London, 2012, p. 56.
44. Berreman, 'Stratification, Pluralism and Interaction', p. 49.
45. See Louise Dumont, 'Caste: A Phenomenon of Social Structure or an aspect of Indian Culture?', in de Reuck and Knight, eds, *Caste and Race*, p. 37.
46. Berreman, 'Stratification, Pluralism and Interaction', p. 67.
47. Ambedkar, *The Essential Writings*, p. 164.
48. Berreman, 'Stratification, Pluralism and Interaction', p. 58.
49. Sally Haslanger, *Resisting Reality: Social Construction and Social Critique*, Oxford University Press, New York, 2012, p. 277.
50. Ibid., p. 285.
51. Mills, *Blackness Visible*, p. 48, my parentheses.
52. Lord Bhikhu Parekh, House of Lords Debates, *Daily Hansard*, 22 April 2013, column 1305, www.publications.parliament.uk/pa/ld201213/ldhansrd/text/130422-0003.htm
53. The four difficulties are listed in Parekh, ibid., Column 1305-1306. Parekh concludes that 'For these and other reasons I would be opposed to the amendment, while making it absolutely clear – so that I am understood outside this House – that untouchability exists. It is an abominable practice; people are sometimes discriminated against and the noble and right reverend Lord, Lord Harries, at a meeting he organised, produced people who were able to give evidence. Take for instance a bus driver who happens to be a Brahmin or whatever, and there is a person who works on the buses who he would not

want to team up with because the guy is supposed to have a surname that indicates he may be an untouchable. It exists in small pockets in those places where people are recognisable. It is not a pervasive phenomenon, but even if it is not pervasive, it is still not acceptable. The point is that it is only one extreme form of caste. By introducing caste as a general category in this way one is trying to catch too much and will end up catching too little.'

54. Satpal Muman 'Caste in Britain', in Dalit Human Rights, Report of the proceedings of an International Conference, London 16–17 September 2000, organized by Voice of Dalit International (VODI) and Dalit Solidarity Network, published by VODI, on 10 October 2000, pp. 71–79, p. 73, www.ambedkar.org/Worldwide_Dalits/caste_in_britain.htm. See also the Human Rights Watch 2001 report, *Caste Discrimination: A Global Concern*, www.hrw.org/reports/2001/globalcaste/caste0801.pdf.

55. In his letter, Satish K. Sharma, the general secretary of the NCHT (UK) wrote: 'the Conservative Party is the only party which has consistently listened to us and voted against the legislation and whose members are committed to repealing the Caste amendment if re-elected.' www.nchtuk.org; accessed 4 May 2015. The letter was removed from the website following announcement of a Charity Commission investigation.

56. See Siraj Datoo, 'Hindu Charity Investigated over Open Letter Endorsing the Conservatives', 5[t] May 2015. See www.buzzfeed.com/sirajdatoo/hindu-charity-investigated-over-open-letter-endorsing-the-co; accessed 15 May 2015.

57. Sharma letter; see n55.

58. See Edward Said, 'Orientalism Reconsidered', *Cultural Critique* 1, Autumn 1985, pp. 89–107; 100.

59. Ibid., pp. 105–6.

60. Gopal Balakrishnan, *Antagonistics: Capitalism and Power in an Age of War*, Verso, London and New York, 2009, p. 250. The phrase is from a review of Bhikhu Parekh's book *Rethinking Multiculturalism*, and where he, Parekh, is described as an 'eminently establishment figure' (p. 246) who has offered 'the de-Westernization of liberalism – a stealth liberalism' (p. 248).

Sources

The essays in this volume first appeared in the following issues of the journal *Radical Philosophy*:

CHAPTER 1   *Radical Philosophy* 179 (2013)
CHAPTER 2   *Radical Philosophy* 32 (1982)
CHAPTER 3   *Radical Philosophy* 113 (2002)
CHAPTER 4   *Radical Philosophy* 63 (1993)
CHAPTER 5   *Radical Philosophy* 117 (2003)
CHAPTER 6   *Radical Philosophy* 119 (2003)
CHAPTER 7   *Radical Philosophy* 140 (2006)
CHAPTER 8   *Radical Philosophy* 11 (1975)
CHAPTER 9   *Radical Philosophy* 118 (2003)
CHAPTER 10   *Radical Philosophy* 83 (1997)
CHAPTER 11   *Radical Philosophy* 178 (2013)
CHAPTER 12   *Radical Philosophy* 69 (1995)
CHAPTER 13   *Radical Philosophy* 161 (2010)
CHAPTER 14   *Radical Philosophy* 164 (2010)
CHAPTER 15   *Radical Philosophy* 194 (2015)
CHAPTER 16   *Radical Philosophy* 192 (2015)

Image credits

p. viii Gyula Varnai, *5 Perc*, installation, Hungarian Pavilion, Giardini, Venice Biennial 2017. Photograph © Peter Osborne.
p. 16 *Kantian Ripples*, 2019. Photograph © Peter Osborne.
p. 100 Red and black chess board construction, installation, *Red: Art and Utopia in the Land of the Soviets*, Grand Palais, Paris, 2019. Photograph © Peter Osborne.
p. 190 *Radical Philosophy* 11 (1975), p. 30.
p. 196 Recycle Group, *Blocked Content* (detail), installation, Russian Pavilion, Giardini, Venice Biennial 2017. Photograph © Peter Osborne.
p. 292 Kahlil Joseph, *BLKNWS*, 2018 (details), installation, Central Pavilion, Giardini, Venice Biennial 2019. Photographs © Peter Osborne.

Index

Althusser, Louis 321, 337, 343, 346, 349, 350
Ambedkar, Bhimrao Ramji 368–9, 371–4, 377–8–30
Arendt, Hannah 6, 247, 248–9, 273
Aristotle 203–6, 209, 264
Arnell, Barbara 136
Artaud, Antonin 282
Astell, Mary 114–16, 119

Balibar, Étienne 321, 346–7, 355–6
Barrett, Michèle 225
Bartolovich, Crystal 325–6
Bataille, Georges 204, 210, 253, 282
Battersby, Christine 37
Bauman, Zygmunt 123, 285
Baxandall, Rosalyn 224
Beauvoir, Simone de 103, 250–68
Beiser, Frederick 34
Benjamin, Walter 172, 214
Benn, Melissa 235
Bensaid, Daniel 330, 332
Bernal, Martin 163, 273–7
Bernasconi, Robert 10, 151–5, 180, 184–5
Bernier, François 296, 301–4, 308, 311
Berreman, G.D. 370, 377
Bettelheim, Charles 346–7
Bhandar, Brenna 7
Bhatt, Chetan 368
Blanchot, Maurice 247–9
Blumenbach, Hans 25, 31, 33, 133
Blyton, Enid 193

Boxill, Bernard 137, 139, 147
Bruns, Gerald 280
Butler, Judith 226, 240, 249

Cassirer, Ernst 110, 111
Cavell, Stanley 276
Caygill, Howard 173, 182
Chakrabarty, Dispeh 301
Chakravartty, Paula 340
Chandra, Bipan 306
Cixous, Hélène 237
Clinton, George 269
Clough, Patricia 227
Cohen, Hermann 169, 172, 182
Collin, Françoise 247–50
Condorcet, Nicolas de 119, 123
Connolly, N.D.B. 354
Coulthard, Glen 353
Critchley, Simon 12, 177

Deleuze, Gilles 71–95, 289
Derrida, Jacques 205, 229, 237, 265, 281–9
Descartes, René 135, 271, 282
Diderot, Denis 112, 210
Dieng, Amady A. 309
Dilthey, Wilhelm 11
Du Bois, W.E.B. 286
Dumont, Louise 375, 377
Dunbar-Ortiz, Roxanne 352–3
Dworkin, Andrea 235–6
Dymski, Gary 357
d'Alembert, Jean le Rond 110

Eagleton, Terry 242
Engels, Frederick 301
Eze, Emmanuel 132

Fanon, Frantz 319, 338
Farr, James 136–7
Farrell, J.G. 325
Federici, Silvia 353
Ferreira da Silva, Denise 340, 356
Feuerbach, Ludwig 216
Fichte, Johann Gottlieb 46, 52, 59, 64, 83, 84
Flax, Jane 108
Foucault, Michel 140, 237, 282
Fox-Genovese, Elizabeth 114
Frege, Gottlob 130
Freud, Sigmund 8, 201–5, 215–20, 249, 259, 262

Gadamer, Hans-Georg 273
Gandhi, M.K. 371, 372, 380
Gay, Peter 110
Gide 214
Gilroy, Paul 145, 284–6
Girard, René 219
Goldberg, David Theo 277
Gordon, Linda 224
Guattari, Félix 289
Guru, Gopal 375

Habermas, Jürgen 47, 50, 123
Hall, Stuart 343, 349–53
Hamann, Johann Georg 4–6, 36, 40
Haraway, Donna 239
Harding, Sandra 104
Hardt, Michael 71–3, 82
Hartman, Saidiya 354, 355
Haslanger, Sally 377–8
Hauck, Gerhard 321
Hegel, Georg Wilhelm Friedrich 5–6, 45–70, 72–4, 77, 82, 91, 93–4, 138, 151–63, 207, 211–13, 269–73, 302, 368
Heidegger, Martin 11, 130–31, 200, 216, 220–21, 269, 272–3, 278–82
Heilbrun, Carolyn 224
Hekman, Susan 107–8

Henrich, Dieter 83
Herder, Johann Gottfried 4–5, 28, 36, 143, 368
Hill, Thomas 137, 139, 147
Hirst, Paul 347, 348
Hobsbawm, Eric 275
Husserl, Edmund 171, 177, 179, 272–3, 277–81
Hyppolite, Jean 73–6
Hölderlin, Friedrich 138, 207, 210, 213

Irigaray, Luce 237

Jacobus, Mary 113
James, C.L.R. 319
Jameson, Fredric 327
Jani, Pranav 305
Jardine, Lisa 107–8
Jones, Ernest 255
Jünger, Ernst 199, 216

Kant, Immanuel 3–4, 8–10, 19–44, 45–70, 71–99, 106, 124, 125, 129–50, 151–9, 160, 203, 208
Klein, Melanie 9–10
Knox, Robert 164
Kofman, Sarah 250
Kortian, Garbis 5, 47–51
Kosofsky Sedgwick, Eve 9–11
Kößler, Reinhard 306
Kovalevskii, Maxim M. 310, 316
Kozo, Uno 337
Krader, Lawrence 329
Kristeva, Julia 228–9

Lacan, Jacques 92, 237, 249, 252–8
Lazarus, Neil 326
Leibniz, Gottfried Wilhelm 207
Lenin, Vladimir 337
Levinas, Emmanuel 10, 166–86, 247, 281–2, 289
Lindner, Kolja 7, 324–9, 330, 336–7
Locke, John 22, 129–3, 146, 159–60, 355–6
Louden, Robert 141–2
Lovibond, Sabina 105
Luhmann, Niklas 112, 116

Lukács, Georg 52
Lyotard, Jean-François 248
Lévi-Strauss, Claude 178, 219, 254
Lévy-Bruhl, Lucien 170
Löwith, Karl 281

MacKinnon, Catharine 236, 249
Macpherson, C.B. 354
Maine, Henry S. 312
Malebranche, Nicolas 24
Mariátegui, Jose 352
Markus, György 111, 122–3
Marx, Karl 3, 4, 7, 8, 45, 216, 272, 295–322, 324, 329–37, 341, 342, 345
McCarney, Joseph 159–64
McGettigan, Andrew 10
McIntosh, Mary 232
Merleau-Ponty, Maurice 168, 178–9, 247, 273
Mills, Charles 145, 367, 379
Montesquieu (Charles-Louis de Secondat) 302
Moore-Gilbert, Bart 319
Morgan, Robin 235
Morrison, Toni 287
Mosès, Stéphane 176
Moten, Fred 10
Musil, Robert 215

Narayan, Uma 366
Natarajan, Balmurli 375
Negri, Antonio 71–3, 82
Nietzsche, Friedrich 8, 201, 215–21, 269–73, 282
Nussbaum, Martha 249

Osborne, Peter 5

Paglia, Camille 236
Parekh, Bhikhu 379–81
Pashukanis, Evgeny 347
Pateman, Carole 249
Phillips, Anne 225
Phule, Jotiba 374
Plato 207, 249, 273
Potter, Beatrix 193–5
Poulantzas, Nicos 346

Proudhon, Pierre-Joseph 345

Radhakrishnan, Sarvepalli 369–70
Rendall, Jane 123
Renner, Karl 347
Rex, John 351, 353
Ricœur, Paul 8–9
Rorty, Richard 276
Rose, Gillian 5, 45–67
Rosenzweig, Franz 168, 171, 182–3, 214
Roudinesco, Elisabeth 253
Rowbotham, Sheila 223, 229–35
Roy, Arundhati 373
Ruge, Arnold 3
Ryle, Gilbert 130

Said, Edward 7, 283–4, 296–7, 382, 312, 327
Sandford, Stella 5, 8, 173
Sartre, Jean–Paul 103, 104, 174
Schelling, Friedrich 138, 207, 208, 210
Schlegel, Friedrich 207
Schopenhauer, Arthur 368
Scott, Joan 226–7
Segal, Lynne 13
Sloan, Phillip 24, 27, 28, 32
Sloterdijk, Peter 11
Smith, Neil 350
Socrates 203, 212, 269, 270–72, 277
Sohn-Rethel, Alfred 343–4, 348
Sophocles 204, 214
Spinoza, Baruch 72, 77–9, 82, 84, 207–8
Spivak, Gayatri Chakravorty 238–9, 304, 356, 366, 368
Strobel, Margaret 224
Stuurman, Siep 302–3

Thales 274
Thomas, Yan 344–5
Thompson, E.P. 346
Toscano, Alberto 7

Voltaire (François-Marie Arouet) 368

Wallerstein, Immanuel 320
Weber, Max 272
West, Cornel 276
Williams, Bernard 135
Wilson, Elizabeth 232
Wilson Gilmore, Ruth 349, 353

Wollstonecraft, Mary 105, 114–21

Zammito, John 28, 32
Zasulich, Vera 330, 332, 336
Zöller, Günter 32